iPOD & iTUNES GARAGE

The Garage Series

Street-smart books about technology

Each author **presents** a unique take on solving problems, using a fomat designed to replicate the **experience** of Web searching.

Technology presented and **organized** by useful topic—not in a linear tutorial style.

Books that cover **whatever** needs to be covered to get the project done. Period.

Eben Hewitt, *Java Garage.* ISBN: 0321246233.
Tara Calishain, *Web Search Garage.* ISBN: 0131471481.
Kirk McElhearn, *iPod & iTunes Garage.* ISBN: 0131486454.
Marc Campbell, *Web Design Garage.* ISBN: 0131481991.
Don Jones, *PHP-Nuke Garage.* ISBN: 0131855166.
Dan Livingston, *ActionScript 2.0 Garage.* ISBN: 0131484753.

```
                        <a garage is where you work.
        in a garage, you do your  work, not somebody else's.
        it's where you experiment and listen to the old ball
                                game. make music.
                                    get away.
                                      tinker.
        it's where you do projects for passion, make your own
                                      rules, and
                            plot like an evil genius./>
```

(Irreverent. **Culturally rooted.**)

Edgy and fun. Lively writing. (The impersonal voice of an omniscient narrator is not allowed!)

[**Eben Hewitt, series editor**]

Check out the series at www.phptr.com/garageseries

iPod & iTunes Garage

Kirk McElhearn

PRENTICE HALL
PTR

Prentice Hall Professional Technical Reference

Upper Saddle River, NJ • Boston • Indianapolis
San Francisco • New York • Toronto • Montreal
London • Munich • Paris • Madrid • Capetown
Sydney • Tokyo • Singapore • Mexico City

Many of the designations used by manufacturers and sellers to distinguish their products are claimed as trademarks. Where those designations appear in this book, and the publisher was aware of a trademark claim, the designations have been printed with initial capital letters or in all capitals.

The author and publisher have taken care in the preparation of this book, but make no expressed or implied warranty of any kind and assume no responsibility for errors or omissions. No liability is assumed for incidental or consequential damages in connection with or arising out of the use of the information or programs contained herein.

The publisher offers excellent discounts on this book when ordered in quantity for bulk purchases or special sales, which may include electronic versions and/or custom covers and content particular to your business, training goals, marketing focus, and branding interests. For more information, please contact:

U. S. Corporate and Government Sales
(800) 382-3419
corpsales@pearsontechgroup.com

For sales outside the U. S., please contact:

International Sales
international@pearsoned.com

Visit us on the Web: www.phptr.com

Library of Congress Cataloging-in-Publication Data:

McElhearn, Kirk.
  iPod & iTunes garage / Kirk McElhearn.
    p. cm.
  Includes bibliographical references and index.
  ISBN 0-13-148645-4 (pbk. : alk. paper)
  1. iTunes. 2. iPod (Digital music player) I. Title.

  ML74.4.I49M44 2005
  006.5—dc22   2004019675

ISBN 0-13-148645-4

Text printed in the United States on recycled paper at Edwards Brothers in Ann Arbor Michigan
First printing, December 2004

Contents

Preface: iPod Madness
Warn Your Children!

The book you are about to read may startle you. It would not have been possible, otherwise, to sufficiently emphasize the frightful toll of the new menace that is destroying the youth of America in alarmingly increasing numbers. In depicting its soul-destroying effects, no attempt has been made to equivocate.

The scenes and incidents depicted in this book are all based on actual research into the results of this menace. If their stark reality will make you think, will make you aware that something must be done to wipe out this ghastly menace, then the book will not have failed in its purpose.

Because the dreaded iPod may be reaching forth next for your son or daughter...or even you!

A disturbing scene has been witnessed across America in recent years and is spreading throughout the world at an alarming pace. People who look normal from the outside—young and old, rich and poor—have joined a new cult. They may be your neighbors, your doctor, your children's teachers, your stockbroker, your local mechanic or mailman, or even one of your children, but they are really part of a new cult that is slowly and quietly spreading its influence and capturing new members.

This cult sprang from nothing in 2001 to now count more than 6 million members, and its ranks are growing daily. There seems to be little the authorities can do to slow its progression, and if the current trend continues, the majority of Americans will be affected in just 12 years.

Update This Book!

Apple is likely to update the iPod and iTunes, or even release a new iPod, between the time this book goes to press and the time you purchase this book—or even later. For this reason, I'll be adding content at my blog, Kirkville (www.mcelhearn.com), about new iPods, new features in iTunes, and more. Check my blog regularly to keep up to date on the latest iPod and iTunes information.

You can spot the members of this cult by the glassy look in their eyes and the distinctive white wires that run from their pockets to their ears. Few people realize what these wires are for, but you see them on people everywhere: on campus; in buses, trains, and airplanes; even on people walking down the street. These odd people all exhibit strange, rhythmic body movements as they walk; some have been observed moving in similar ways when seated as well.

"They're everywhere," said Rob Griffiths, a webmaster from Portland, Oregon. "I counted at least ten people with those white wires the last time I took a plane trip. Even the guy sitting next to me had them!"

Is this an invasion by creatures from another planet? How have these people been taken over by these strange white wires? What purpose do they serve?

This book is the fruit of three years of research. From Maine to California, from the United States to France, I have investigated this odd new cult: the cult of the iPod.

Why do so many people wear these strange white wires, and what do these wires do to their brains? What are the tiny white devices, with cryptic symbols on their faces and a screen that displays text that looks like gibberish? In an attempt to answer these questions and many more, I went undercover, interviewed dozens of members of this cult, and even donned the accoutrements of one myself, all to provide you with this unparalleled exposé of truth.

This book contains five parts.

Part I: After a great deal of research and investigation, doors were opened to me, and I was able to examine the iTunes program, which is said to be the gateway for members of this cult to pass information onto their tiny electronic devices called iPods. I explain how it works, how cult members use it to manage "playlists," and how it serves as a conduit for the iPod itself.

Part II: After obtaining several iPods, at great risk and peril, I have plumbed their depths and attempted to understand how they function. I present to you, dear reader, the most harrowing details, the most surprising information about this tiny device. You will discover what the secret controls operate, how to decipher the text on their screens, and how to use them for their nefarious, mind-numbing effects.

Part III: Many people are worried about the influence of this cult, and none more so than musicians, who see it as a way to take total control of their music. I interviewed many representatives of this trade in search of their feelings on this new cult. While some cult members say they are "infatuated" or "obsessed," the musicians I spoke with shrink in horror at the potential ramifications of this device.

Part IV: In spite of warnings by authorities and public health officials, computer programmers around the world have created tools to further the influence of this cult and allow its members to manipulate information in ways unimagined when the cult first appeared. I scoured the lower depths of the Internet in search of the most powerful programs that cult members use, and present, here, an unabashed discussion of what these programs can do.

Part V: Perhaps the most worrying element of this phenomenon is the many vendors of trinkets and baubles designed for members of this cult so they can protect their iPods and use them for other evil tasks. To write this final section, I traveled across the seven seas to find out which of these products were the most popular and why members of the iPod cult would want to use them.

You will surely understand, dear reader, that I put my life in peril to investigate this cult. While the incidents presented herein are all factual, I have had to change some of the names to protect the obviously guilty.

This peril is real, dear reader, and it is coming for you. Only through education, such as what this book offers, can this scourge be wiped out. If you are not aware of the forms it takes and the ways it hides, *you may be its next victim.*

Acknowledgments

This is the part of the book where I get to thank all the wonderful people who contributed, in one way or another, to getting this book from my mind to your hands. A book is a complicated thing to make, and many, many people are involved.

It all started in late 2003, when my agent, Neil Salkind, told me about this cool new series called *Garage* that was in the works. I liked the idea right away and got in touch with John Neidhart, the editor for the series, to talk about a book on the iPod. Thanks first to Neil for his continued help and support, and thanks to John for being so supportive throughout the entire process of preparing and writing the book. Eben Hewitt came up with the original idea for this series, so thanks to Eben for priming the pump.

Then came the actual writing. I depended on myself for most of that, but Curt Frye wrote some of the Windows sections—I didn't want to have to reformat my iPod over and over, switching from Mac to Windows, so Curt gave me a hand. In addition, I must thank a few people who shared their thoughts, discussed key points with me, and helped in other ways. Rob Griffiths (who runs the Mac OS X Hints Web site, www.macosxhints.com) is a regular iChat buddy, even though he's nine time zones away. Rob was a lot of help as I tried to resolve problems or come up with good ideas; he gave me the idea for the preface, in fact. Mark Willan, who is much closer, is also an iChat buddy, as well as a phone friend. Mark helped by telling me about the way he uses the iPod, and by reviewing the manuscript and suggesting changes. Mark also told me about some of his favorite music; it's hard to believe that he grew up in Manchester, UK, and never saw The Durutti Column live. Dan Frakes, who is a headphone collector (and who is also nine hours away), told me about some of his favorite cans and helped with a few other technical questions. And Jean-Paul Florencio shared his enthusiasm for the iPod and gave additional help above and beyond the call of duty. Finally, James Bucanek, who was the book's technical editor, picked nits and spotted tiny technical errors. I've had the pleasure of working with James on three books already, and each time his help has been invaluable. Naturally, any errors that remain are all my responsibility.

Many thanks to all the musicians, authors, and others who contributed to this book, either by writing about their favorite music, or by allowing me to interview them about what they like best. I would especially like to thank Janis Ian, for her permission to reproduce an article she wrote about the music business, and Steve Wozniak, for contributing his thoughts on the iPod mini.

So then the book went into production, which means an army of people took my manuscript and sliced and diced it to get it into book form. Kim Arney Mulcahy not only managed the project when the book went into production (that's after I've written everything on Post-its and napkins), but shared her musical interests with me; it turned out that we had a lot of favorite music in common. I was graced with a top-notch copy editor, Debby English—with a name like that, you can tell she's in her element. (I bet she hears that all the time.) In addition, Debby's husband surprised her with a new iPod while we were working on the book; it's good to know that my book served a purpose, even before it was finished. Thanks again to Kim for twisting the words and graphics into this cool layout, Monica Groth Farrar for her careful eye during proofreading, and Jack Lewis for creating the book's index.

Back at Prentice Hall, Raquel Kaplan handled the laborious task of requesting permissions for all the things the lawyers were uncomfortable about, and did a great job managing other tiny details. I was fortunate in having Heather Fox and Robin O'Brien to handle marketing and promotion for the book, making sure that the word got out that this is the best iPod book around.

And on the home front, Marie-France helped by keeping things going, in spite of my frequent phone calls at dinnertime (all those people in different time zones), and Perceval shared his enthusiasm for the iPod mini (which I can no longer pry from his hands) and music in general.

Finally, to all the others who have made this book possible in many ways: to the trees who gave their lives so these pages could be printed, to the book-sellers who put the book in your hands, and everyone in between who makes it a pleasure to write books.

Last but not least, to use the time-worn cliché, the real heroes are all the musicians who write, compose, jam, and play the music that keeps music lovers happy. I was fortunate to be able to listen to a lot of music as I was writing this book, and to discover all kinds of new groups, singers, songwriters, and composers as I researched the iPod and iTunes.

If you want to know more about me or my other books, stop by my Web site: http://www.mcelhearn.com. And if you have any questions or comments, spot any mistakes, or want to share your feelings about the iPod, send me an e-mail at kirk@mcelhearn.com. Please include "iPod Garage" in the subject of your message so my spam filter doesn't nix it.

Enjoy this book, and, above all, enjoy your music!

PART I

iTunes

iTunes: The Digital Jack-of-all-Trades

Music has been one of the most popular forms of entertainment ever since the Neanderthals first banged a bone on a rock. Everyone listens to music: Some people are fanatics, and buy lots of CDs, go to concerts, and follow their favorite bands, and others hear music in elevators, supermarkets, and shopping malls. But no matter how you slice it, music is all around us.

One of the biggest revolutions wrought by computers is the way they empower us to listen to music in different ways. CD players started the revolution, allowing you to program the way you listen to a disc or turn on the shuffle function and listen to its songs at random, but software like iTunes goes much further, allowing you to create your own playlists. No longer do you have to depend on the whims (and kickbacks) of others to hear music; you choose the songs you want to hear and the order you want them to be played in.

Music has come a long way from scratchy discs played on windup Victrolas to high-quality music that you can listen to on pocket-sized digital music players. But to get music from your CDs to your computer, and then to a portable music player such as the iPod, you need software. Software like iTunes, to convert the music to digital files, to manage your music library, and to move these files to your iPod.

DO OR DIE:

> > Welcome to iTunes

> > What iTunes can do for you

> > Install iTunes on a Windows computer

BEWARE OF COPY-CONTROLLED CDS

Yeah, lots of record labels use copy-controlled CDs now. These discs are not "compact discs," because they don't meet the "red-book" standard, which guarantees that the discs will play in all

UNDER THE HOOD

iTunes 4 runs on the Mac or Windows. You'll need the following to use iTunes.

Macintosh requirements:
- Mac OS X v10.1.5 or later (Mac OS X v10.2.4 or later is required, to share music and burn DVDs).
- A 400MHz G3 processor or better.
- QuickTime 6.2 is required, to encode AAC.
- At least 128MB RAM, though 256MB RAM is recommended.
- A supported CD-R drive to burn CDs.
- A broadband (ADSL, cable, or LAN-based) Internet connection is recommended for buying music from the iTunes Music Store.

Windows requirements:
- Windows XP or 2000.
- A 500MHz Pentium processor or better.
- QuickTime 6.5 (included with the iTunes installer).
- At least 128MB RAM, though 256MB RAM is recommended.
- A supported CD-R drive to burn CDs.
- A broadband (ADSL, cable, or LAN-based) Internet connection is recommended for buying music from the iTunes Music Store.

Apple's iTunes is a jack-of-all-trades for working with digital music. Much more than a simple jukebox program, iTunes is your nerve center for working with digital music files. It does the following:

- Encodes (or rips) your CDs in any of five formats—MP3, AAC, Apple Lossless, AIFF, or WAV—and converts music files from these formats and from WMA files (Windows only)
- Downloads track information from the Gracenote CD database when you insert a music CD in your drive
- Manages your music library
- Lets you create playlists and smart playlists
- Provides a powerful search feature to find any song in your music library
- Plays music on your Mac or PC
- Provides eye candy as you listen to music, with its visual effects
- Provides an interface to the iTunes Music Store, where you can purchase music online
- Plays streaming audio from Internet radio stations
- Plays audiobooks from Audible.com, as well as other audiobooks in MP3 format
- Shares music across your network to other computers running iTunes
- Burns CDs from your playlists or library to a single CD or DVD, or to multiple discs if necessary
- Syncs music to your iPod

iTunes is incredibly simple to use, since most of its functions are accessible from its window; you don't need to dig into its menus to do the majority of tasks. iTunes has just one window (other than its Preferences), and you can do most everything by clicking its buttons or dragging files.

You can get iTunes easily. If you have Mac OS X, you've already got iTunes; it comes with the operating system, and it is installed by default. If you run Windows, you can download an iTunes installer from http://www.apple.com/itunes/download/. If you're a Windows user, you may be famil-

compact disc players. So, if you buy a copy-controlled disc, you won't be able to rip it and listen on your iPod.

Some copy-controlled discs let you listen at a pathetic bit rate on your computer, usually only on Windows computers. The music sounds as if

iar with other music software: Your PC probably has Windows Media Player, and you may also have Real Player or other programs. Since you'll be using iTunes to manage music for your iPod, you should check out all the functions of iTunes: With the exception of not playing WMA files, which iTunes can convert to other formats, iTunes does everything—and in many cases does it better—that other Windows music programs do. In addition, it does it all for free.

Installing iTunes on a Windows Computer

After you download the iTunes installer from the URL mentioned earlier, double-click its icon (Figure 1-1) to start installing the software.

While most of the installation options are self-explanatory, I'll briefly discuss some of the options the installer offers.

The screen in Figure 1-2 gives you three options.

- **Install desktop shortcuts:** This adds shortcuts to your Windows Desktop for iTunes and for the QuickTime Player. The iTunes installer also installs QuickTime, which is required to play back certain music files with iTunes.
- **Use iTunes as the default player for audio files:** This sets your system to open iTunes whenever you double-click compatible audio files. Don't check this if you want to use other music programs to play back your files. (You can always change this later in iTunes' preferences.)
- **Use QuickTime as the default player for media files:** As noted earlier, this sets QuickTime Player as the default player for the media files it can handle. Again, don't check this if you want to continue using other programs.

After you finish installing iTunes, you'll need to restart your Windows computer.

Figure 1–1

The iTunesSetup icon. Double-click this to start installing iTunes for Windows.

iTunesSetup

FAQ

Mac or Windows Screenshots?

When discussing iTunes, I'll alternate Mac and Windows screenshots throughout this book. When talking about a specific feature of iTunes that only one platform offers, or additional software to enhance iTunes or to work with your iPod, I'll show the appropriate screenshots (Mac or Windows). But I'm primarily a Mac user, so don't hold it against me if you're not, and if you notice that there are more Mac screenshots than Windows.

you're listening over the telephone or via a low-bandwidth stream from the Internet.

Be careful if you're using a Mac: There have been cases of copy-controlled CDs getting stuck in CD-ROM drives. You're better off checking and not even

6

trying to put them in your Mac. (If you do, by accident, straighten out a paper clip, and look for a tiny hole somewhere near the place you inserted the CD. Press the paper clip in this hole to eject it.)

Starting Up iTunes for the First Time

When you're ready to take control of your music, and open iTunes for the first time, whether on a Mac or on a Windows computer, the program greets you with its Setup Assistant. You get to choose from a number of options, telling iTunes how to work with your music files. None of the choices you make with this assistant are permanent, though. If you have a change of heart, you can undo them later in iTunes' preferences.

The first screen welcomes you and tells you that the assistant will configure iTunes. Click Next

If you are using a Mac, the Internet Audio screen (Figure 1-3) asks you how iTunes should use the Internet.

The Find Music Files screen (Figure 1-4) offers to browse your home folder (Mac) or your My Music folder (Windows) for existing MP3 and AAC files. If you use Windows, this dialog will also offer to find your WMA files.

Checking Yes may seem like the best way to go, and for many users this is the case. However, if you check Yes here, iTunes will snoop around and add all your music files to its library. You might not want to add everything, at least not right away. If not, check No.

Next, the Windows installer offers you the option of organizing your iTunes Music folder. If you check Yes, this stores all your files in folders with the artist's

Copy-controlled CDs should not have the "compact disc digital audio" logo; the ones that bear this logo are in violation of certain trademarks and copyrights. In fact, I've got one here that is copy-controlled and has the "compact

Figure 1-3

Choose from two options: If you want iTunes to be the default player for any Internet audio it can handle, check Yes for the first option. If you want iTunes to connect to the Internet without asking you, when it fetches CD information or connects to streaming audio servers, check Yes for the second option. If you check No, iTunes will ask you each time. Generally, if you have a permanent connection (cable, DSL, etc.), you should check Yes.

iTunes Setup Assistant

Internet Audio

Would you like to use iTunes to handle audio content from the Internet? The system settings will be changed to set iTunes as the helper application for audio you access with your Web browser.

- ⦿ Yes, use iTunes for Internet audio content
- ○ No, do not modify my Internet settings

On occasion, iTunes needs to access the Internet for information about audio CDs and streaming broadcasts. Do you want iTunes to automatically connect when it's necessary?

- ⦿ Yes, automatically connect to the Internet
- ○ No, ask me before connecting

(Cancel)   (Previous)   (Next)

ESSENTIAL MUSIC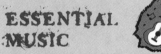

On Essential Music

You'll see, sprinkled throughout this book, sidebars of varying lengths talking about "Essential Music." Hubris aside, the point of these sidebars is to talk about music that has been remembered for musical or emotional reasons and will be remembered for some time to come. I've given musicians and authors a chance to talk about music that's special to them for some reason, and I've waxed nostalgic or poetic myself.

The first thing you'll notice is that all the music discussed in these sidebars is from the previous millennium. That's not surprising, since it takes a while for music to become essential. Sure, the latest hit by your favorite band may be essential now, as you sit with your boyfriend or girlfriend watching the sunset through the windshield of your car, or as you drive away from a previous girlfriend or boyfriend, ending a relationship. But the true test is time, and only time will tell what remains essential.

You'll also notice that the music discussed in these sidebars covers only a handful of genres. I've written a bunch of them myself (the ones with no name and byline at the end) and asked musicians of all types, as well as writers who I know are interested in music to share their thoughts, but my choices obviously reflect my own tastes. (But, hey, if you are a musician in any genre, or an author, an actor, or a director, or a former President of the United States who plays saxophone, and want to contribute to a future edition of this book, drop me an e-mail.)

Don't take these sidebars as gospel; they're only comments and thoughts by people who want to share with others the music that's important to them. But if you've never heard the music they're talking about, take the time to check it out; you might discover something you like or something that changes your mind about the types of music you generally ignore.

disc digital audio" logo. I put it in my Mac to try to rip it so I could add it to my iPod, but no dice. And it wasn't easy to eject, either. (Thanks, Red Hot Chili Peppers; I won't buy any more of your CDs.)

Figure 1-4

Choose whether you want iTunes to scour your computer and add your music files to its library.

name, and whenever you change the name or other information about a song, iTunes will automatically move it, if necessary. If you don't want to be hassled, this is a good thing to choose. However, if you want to be able to easily find your music on your hard disk, you may find this confusing at best. It's like someone rearranging your books without asking you. It's probably best to check No. (For the Mac version of iTunes, this choice is made in the Advanced preferences.) I'll tell you more about this in All about Your iTunes Music Library.

Finally, iTunes asks if you want to go to your music bookshelves or to the iTunes Music Store. Make your choice, then click Done. iTunes opens to your choice.

As you can see in Figure 1-5, iTunes looks the same whether on Mac or Windows. The only differences are the menu bars and window control widgets. (That's a technical word for the buttons and icons you click on windows.)

So, you're ready to roll. None of the choices you made in the Setup Assistant are undoable; you can change them all in the iTunes preferences. I'll look at them later, as I discuss the program's many functions. It's time to start using iTunes for its main purpose: to listen to music.

Should You Add All Your Music Files to Your Library?

In my opinion, the option that tells iTunes to scour your computer for music files is good for people who aren't organized and who don't put all their stuff in one place. If you're like that, check Yes in the assistant screen shown in Figure 1-4.

But if you're an experienced computer user, and you know how you organize your files, check No. Not only does this prevent iTunes from adding everything on your computer—you might not want all your music files added—but it lets you be in control of what music gets added and when.

What can I say? While I'm strongly against music piracy, and piracy of any kind of copyrighted content, I think copy-controlled CDs suck. Why shouldn't I be allowed to listen to my music—that I've purchased legally—on my iPod?

Figure 1-5

*iTunes for Mac (top) and Windows (bottom).
Apple made the Windows version of this program a carbon copy of the original Mac version.*

I'll look at the question of piracy more closely in Copyright, File Sharing,
and Piracy.

ESSENTIAL MUSIC

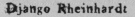

Django Rheinhardt

Django Rheinhardt. With the iPod, I've got his entire catalog, and it doesn't even make a dent in its hard disk. I cannot live without the man. Life is a lesson, and I'm a guitar player. When I'm not learning how to live life, I'm obviously learning as much as I can about the guitar, and until the day I die, I'll still be learning from that man.

He only had two fingers that were completely functional, and he used his thumb the way we're not supposed to use it, wrapped around the neck.

There's not much music; there are only about six or seven albums' worth of music, but it's quality, not quantity, that counts.

➤ Peter Frampton (http://www.frampton.com) is one of rock and roll's greatest guitarists.

Listening to Music
with iTunes

he best way to check out iTunes and discover its functions is to listen to a CD. Just slip a disc into your drive, and wait a few seconds. If you've set iTunes to connect to the Internet without asking, it will look up the CD's track information on the Gracenote CD database. It then displays the disc with its correct name, artist, tracks, time information, and more.

Sometimes, you'll see a dialog telling you that "multiple matches were found" for the CD. If this happens, select the one that looks closest, then click OK.

Figure 1-6 shows iTunes after it has downloaded track information for a CD.

You can control just about all of iTunes' functions by clicking the buttons on its interface. At the top left, you see a Play button, and a Fast Forward and Rewind button on either side of it. Click the Play button to listen to your CD. Sit back for a second, and, if you have good speakers, appreciate the sound that comes out of your computer. (If you don't have good speakers, you might want to check some out; if you're going to use iTunes to listen to CDs on your computer, you owe it to yourself to get the best sound you can afford.)

You'll notice, as you listen to your CD, that the Play button changes to a Pause button. Click Pause to stop. Click and hold the Fast Forward or Rewind

A NOTE ABOUT COMPRESSED MUSIC FILES
I opined that "MP3 files can sound nearly as good as the original CDs," but I need to toss a caveat into the ring. When you listen to MP3 files on an iPod, while walking down a city street, riding the

UNDER THE HOOD

[iTunes window screenshot]

	Song Name	Time	Artist	Album	Genre
1	☑ Cassidy	3:42	Bob Weir	Weir Here [Disc 1 – Studio]	Rock
2	☑ Mexicali Blues	3:27	Bob Weir	Weir Here [Disc 1 – Studio]	Rock
3	☑ Looks Like Rain	6:11	Bob Weir	Weir Here [Disc 1 – Studio]	Rock
4	☑ Playing In The Band	7:38	Bob Weir	Weir Here [Disc 1 – Studio]	Rock
5	☑ One More Saturday Night	4:31	Bob Weir	Weir Here [Disc 1 – Studio]	Rock
6	☑ Lazy Lightnin'	3:02	Bob Weir	Weir Here [Disc 1 – Studio]	Rock
7	☑ Supplication	2:56	Bob Weir	Weir Here [Disc 1 – Studio]	Rock
8	☑ Feel Like A Stranger	5:08	Bob Weir	Weir Here [Disc 1 – Studio]	Rock
9	☑ Easy To Slip	3:06	Bob Weir	Weir Here [Disc 1 – Studio]	Rock
10	☑ Wrong Way Feelin'	5:12	Bob Weir	Weir Here [Disc 1 – Studio]	Rock
11	☑ Shade Of Grey	4:30	Bob Weir	Weir Here [Disc 1 – Studio]	Rock
12	☑ I Want To (Fly Away)	4:00	Bob Weir	Weir Here [Disc 1 – Studio]	Rock
13	☑ Easy Answers	6:01	Bob Weir	Weir Here [Disc 1 – Studio]	Rock
14	☑ Two Djinn	9:05	Bob Weir	Weir Here [Disc 1 – Studio]	Rock
15	☑ Ashes And Glass	5:56	Bob Weir	Weir Here [Disc 1 – Studio]	Rock
16	☑ Wabash Cannonball	3:41	Bob Weir	Weir Here [Disc 1 – Studio]	Rock

16 songs, 1.3 hours, 789.4 MB

Figure 1-6

iTunes displays the track information for your CD if it's listed in the Gracenote CD database.

buttons to move ahead or back in a track; click these buttons to move to the next or previous track. That's all you need to know to listen to CDs with iTunes.

The display at the top of the window (Figure 1-7) tells you which song is playing and, by default, how much time has elapsed since the beginning.

You can get more information from the display. Click Elapsed Time to change the display to show Remaining Time; click again to show Total Time. Drag the diamond in the progress bar to move forward or backward in a song. And if you click the triangle at the left of the display, you can see a relatively useless frequency level indicator.

TOOL KIT

Shortcut: Play and Pause from the Keyboard

If iTunes is the active application, you can play and pause music by pressing the spacebar on the keyboard. If you look in the Controls menu, you'll see all the controls you can use, and you'll also see the keyboard shortcuts that let you take charge of iTunes from the keyboard.

subway, or jogging, you won't notice the loss in quality that the compression engenders. Since the ambient noise muffles what you hear, you won't miss the lost subtleties and dynamic range.

The rest of the iTunes controls are at the bottom of the window (Figure 1-8). These controls turn on and off certain functions (shuffle, repeat), give access to other features (visualizer, equalizer), or let you eject a CD.

From left to right, here's what you can do.

Playing In The Band
Elapsed Time: 2:27

Figure 1-7

The iTunes display shows what's playing and for how long.

- **New Playlist:** Click this button to add a new playlist; on the Mac, click while holding down the Option key to create a new smart playlist.

- **Shuffle:** Click to turn shuffle on or off. When you turn shuffle on, it applies to the currently selected playlist: If you are viewing the Library, it applies to the entire Library, but only when you click the Play button to play *all* your music. When you click the shuffle button for a playlist, it only affects that playlist; other playlists don't get shuffled.

- **Repeat:** Click this to repeat the playlist, or click it again to repeat the current song. Another click turns off repeat.

- **Show or hide artwork:** This displays or hides album or song art if you have any. (See Album Art for Your Tracks.)

- **Equalizer:** This displays the equalizer window. See Using the iTunes Equalizer for more on using the equalizer.

- **Visualizer:** This turns on visual effects. See Spacing Out with the iTunes Visualizer for more on this.

- **Eject:** Click this to eject a CD or, if you have an iPod connected, to eject or unmount your iPod.

In addition to the preceding buttons, the display at the bottom of the iTunes window (Figure 1-8) shows information about your selection. Here, with just one album selected, it shows the number of songs, the time, and the amount of disk space used. If you select your library or iPod in the Source list, you'll see

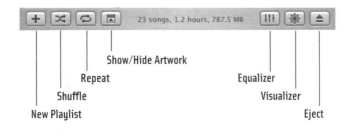

23 songs, 1.2 hours, 787.5 MB

Show/Hide Artwork

Repeat

Shuffle

New Playlist

Equalizer

Visualizer

Eject

Figure 1-8

The bottom of the iTunes window has two groups of buttons to control playback or access other features.

But if you listen to compressed music on your home stereo, without the dog barking or the kids screaming, you have a good chance of noticing the difference. Also, if you have really good headphones (see Headphones

Figure 1-9

The mini-mized iTunes control window

the same stats about your selection. Click this text to toggle between precise timings (days:hours:min-utes:seconds) and rounded timings to one decimal place (15.3 days; 12.9 hours).

Another way to control iTunes is to use the incredible shrinking iTunes window (Figure 1-9). This window only gives you access to the basic controls, but when it's the frontmost application, you can access other controls from its menus.

If you're using iTunes on a Mac, you can shrink the window by clicking the green Zoom button. On Windows, you can display a Mini Player by selecting Advanced > Switch to Mini Player or pressing Ctrl+M. You can then resize this window by dragging the handle on the bottom right corner. Drag it to the left to remove the display and have the tiniest possible window, or drag it to the right to increase the size of the display. To return to the full-size window, click the Zoom button again.

TOOL KIT

Controlling iTunes from the Mac OS X Dock or the Windows System Tray

iTunes lets you control many of its functions from the Mac OS X Dock icon, or from the Windows System Tray icon. Click the Dock icon and hold down your mouse button, or right-click the System Tray icon, and a menu displays showing the functions available.

You can Play and Pause, you can go to the Next Song or Previous Song, and you can turn on the shuffle or repeat functions from this icon. When a song is playing, the menu that displays shows the name of the current song and also lets you set a rating for it.

This is good for controlling iTunes without switching applications. No matter which application is visible, you can access the basic iTunes controls this way.

for Your iPod for more on headphones), you'll probably notice the difference.

Compression with most formats is a trade-off. You get smaller files, but you lose some quality. You can get around this by using higher bit

Ripping Music

Tunes without music is like a Corvette without gas—it looks nice, but it can't go anywhere. Sure, you can listen to CDs with iTunes, as I explained earlier, but you can do that on your stereo too. That's kind of the digital equivalent of leaning against your Corvette and watching people walk by in the street. iTunes becomes more useful when you build up your own music library from your CDs by ripping them and adding the digital music files to your hard disk.

The first thing you need to do, then, is get music into your iTunes music library. I'll look at manually adding music to your library later (All about Your iTunes Music Library), but let's start by ripping a few CDs.

Nothing could be easier: Just stick a CD in your drive, and, on a Mac, if iTunes isn't open or doesn't open automatically, launch the application.

If you're using Windows, you'll see a dialog asking you what you want Windows to do. You can choose Import Songs, Play Audio CD, or Show Songs. If you choose Show Songs, iTunes will try to find track information from the Gracenote CD database (CDDB), then display the album name and track info. You can rip the CD directly by choosing Import Songs, but you won't be able to check that the CDDB information is correct.

If you want to rip an entire disc, just click the Import button. iTunes displays an animated orange icon next to the track number and shows the progress of the import in the display at the top of the window (Figure 1-10).

rates than usual, and if you use a very high bit rate (320kbps), only audiophiles with excellent speakers or headphones will be able to notice the difference.

TOOL KIT

Setting Default Actions For Audio CDs

You may want to tell your computer to always do a certain action when you insert an audio CD in your drive.

If you're using a Mac, you can set a default action in the CDs & DVDs preference pane of the System Preferences application. Here, you can tell your Mac to open iTunes automatically when you insert an audio CD. Next, go to iTunes' preferences and click the General tab. From the On CD Insert popup menu, choose Show Songs, Begin Playing, Import Songs, or Import Songs and Eject.

You've got the same options in the Windows version of iTunes. The first dialog you see is a Windows XP dialog, asking you if you want to Import Songs, Play Audio CD, or Show Songs. If you want to set one of these as the default, check Always Do the Selected Action. But then iTunes kicks in. You can choose from the same four options as with the Mac version.

In most cases, you'll just want to choose Show Songs; this opens iTunes and displays the songs on the disc. But if you're having an all-night ripping marathon, because you just got an iPod and want to get lots of music on it right away, the Import Songs and Eject option is good to turn on temporarily. You'll be able to insert and remove CDs until you get to the bottom of your pile (or until you run out of hard disk space). The downside to this is that you can't edit the tags before ripping the CDs, but I'll tell you later (in Tags and Track Info) how you can edit them manually.

Figure 1-10

As iTunes imports a disc, it shows the current track, the time remaining, and the speed in the display at the top of its window.

#	Song Name	Time	Artist	Album	Genre
1	☑ Cassidy	3:42	Bob Weir	Weir Here [Disc 1 - Studio]	Rock
2	☑ Mexicali Blues	3:27	Bob Weir	Weir Here [Disc 1 - Studio]	Rock
3	☑ Looks Like Rain	6:11	Bob Weir	Weir Here [Disc 1 - Studio]	Rock
4	☑ Playing In The Band	7:38	Bob Weir	Weir Here [Disc 1 - Studio]	Rock
5	☑ One More Saturday Night	4:31	Bob Weir	Weir Here [Disc 1 - Studio]	Rock
6	☑ Lazy Lightnin'	3:02	Bob Weir	Weir Here [Disc 1 - Studio]	Rock
7	☑ Supplication	2:56	Bob Weir	Weir Here [Disc 1 - Studio]	Rock
8	☑ Feel Like A Stranger	5:08	Bob Weir	Weir Here [Disc 1 - Studio]	Rock
9	☑ Easy To Slip	3:06	Bob Weir	Weir Here [Disc 1 - Studio]	Rock
10	☑ Wrong Way Feelin'	5:12	Bob Weir	Weir Here [Disc 1 - Studio]	Rock
11	☑ Shade Of Grey	4:30	Bob Weir	Weir Here [Disc 1 - Studio]	Rock
12	☑ I Want To (Fly Away)	4:00	Bob Weir	Weir Here [Disc 1 - Studio]	Rock
13	☑ Easy Answers	6:01	Bob Weir	Weir Here [Disc 1 - Studio]	Rock
14	☑ Two Djinn	9:05	Bob Weir	Weir Here [Disc 1 - Studio]	Rock
15	☑ Ashes And Glass	5:56	Bob Weir	Weir Here [Disc 1 - Studio]	Rock
16	☑ Wabash Cannonball	3:41	Bob Weir	Weir Here [Disc 1 - Studio]	Rock

iTunes

Importing "Cassidy"
Time remaining: 0:31 (5.7x)

Search   Import

Source
- Library
- Party Shuffle
- Radio
- Music Store
- Weir Here [Disc 1...
- 60's Music
- My Top Rated
- Recently Played
- Top 25 Most Played

16 songs, 1.3 hours, 789.4 MB

But if you are an audiophile and have disk space to spare, Apple Lossless compression offers exactly the same quality as your CDs in half the space or less. So you can have the best of both worlds, sort of.

iTunes rips the music in the format set in its preferences (see the next section, Compression Formats) and places the music files in your iTunes Music folder. At the same time, the imported files are added to your iTunes library.

There are a few settings you should consider changing. By default, iTunes plays songs while importing them. You can change this by selecting iTunes Preferences (select Edit > Preferences in Windows, or iTunes > Preferences in Mac OS X), then clicking the Importing tab. Uncheck this option if you don't want iTunes to play your songs while it imports them. (iTunes won't play your CDs while importing if you are already listening to music with the program.)

Another option on this tab is Create Filenames with Track Number. This is on by default and is a good thing to leave as is. It ensures that all your digital music files begin with track numbers, making it easier to organize them manually on your hard disk, and this also helps sort tracks in album order within iTunes. If, however, iTunes doesn't find your CD in the CDDB, you'll need to manually enter the artist, album, and track info before ripping the CD. See Tags and Track Info for more on entering and editing tags.

FAQ

What Are Those Pesky Little Arrows?

You can see in Figure 1-10 that there are some little arrows next to the song, artist, and album names of music in iTunes. These arrows are the yellow-brick road that leads to the iTunes Music Store. Click one of them to find similar music. I'll talk about them more in Buying Music from the iTunes Music Store.

But they can do something else: Hold down the Option key (Mac) or the Shift key (Windows) to go into Browse mode and view more music by the same artist or view the contents of the album.

FRIDGE

Having a CD Ripping Party

You just got an iPod, and you want to start ripping your CDs so you can transfer them? Or maybe you don't have an iPod yet, but want to discover the flexibility of iTunes and its playlists? Why not have a ripping party?

Invite some friends, get some drinks and snacks, and pile your CDs up next to your computer. Set iTunes to import your music and eject the CDs when finished, and take turns, with your friends, in choosing which CD to put in next. You can set iTunes to play back the songs while importing, but when it's finished importing a CD, it'll spit it out, even in the middle of a song. So select a playlist in iTunes and click the Play button, if you want to listen to music while you're ripping, or use your stereo.

If you have lots of CDs, you'll be able to have an all-night or even an all-weekend party. Just make sure you've got enough to drink and eat...

Aside from choosing the right compression format and bit rate, ripping CDs with iTunes is a no-brainer. If you have lots of CDs to rip—if you've just gotten an iPod, for example, and want to digitize your entire CD library—go to the General preference tab, and click the On CD Insert popup menu. From here, you can select Import Songs and Eject, which tells iTunes to automatically import any CD you put in your drive, then eject it. All you need to do is hang around and put more CDs in as they get ripped and spit out of your computer. After you've finished importing all your CDs, change this setting back to Show Songs or Begin Playing, unless you're planning another marathon ripping session the next day.

Advanced Importing Features

While you can rip most CDs easily, as described earlier, iTunes has advanced features that come in handy in certain situations. For some classical or jazz recordings, or rock albums like Pink Floyd's *Dark Side of the Moon* or the Who's *Quadrophenia*, as well as live recordings, you might need to join tracks to avoid having silence between tracks that doesn't belong there. (You can set iTunes to play back your tracks with no gaps, but the iPod always pauses for a second between tracks.) To do this, insert a disc, click one of the tracks in the track list, then press Command+A (on Mac) or Ctrl+A (on Windows). This selects all the tracks.

Go to the Advanced menu and select Join Tracks. This tells iTunes to import all the selected tracks as one long track, in one big file. Some people may even prefer ripping their CDs as single tracks. If you want to only listen to entire albums, this can save you the headache of organizing lots of individual songs. But once you've ripped a disc like this, you can't split the tracks; you'll need to rip it again if you want individual tracks. (But, hey, if you've got enough hard disk space, you can do both.)

You won't always want to select all the tracks on a disc; in some cases, you need to join only a few tracks to overcome any transition problems. See the section, Ripping Classical and Jazz CDs for more on joining tracks.

Converting Music Files to Another Format

I've told you how to import music from CDs, and you'll see later (in Compression Formats—MP3, AAC, Lossless, and the Rest) how to choose which format and bit rate to use. But after you rip your CDs, you may want to convert your music files to another format. There are several reasons to do this.

- If you choose to rip your CDs as WAV, AIFF, or Apple Lossless files, which take up a lot of space, you may later want to change these to AAC or MP3 files.

- If you've ripped music in AAC format, you may want to convert it to MP3 to use on a music player or with software that doesn't support AAC files.

- If you have MP3 files that you ripped with other software, you may want to convert them to AAC files.

- Or you may simply want to change the bit rates of your files; one reason to do this would be to reduce the size of audiobook files that you may have imported at a bit rate which is normal for music but unneeded for the spoken word.

To do this, just select the new format and bit rate you want to use in the iTunes Importing preferences. (See the next topic for more on this selection.) Select the tracks you want to convert in your iTunes music library, or in a playlist, then select Advanced > Convert Selection to [format], where format is what you've selected in the preferences. You can convert files to different formats or simply to different bit rates; whatever settings you choose in the Importing preferences are used here.

When iTunes has finished converting the selected file(s), you'll find new files in your library, but not in any playlists. If you want to delete the old files, you'll have to find them in your library and remove them, then add the new ones to your existing playlists.

Note that you won't get better sound if you convert existing files to higher bit rates, and converting them to other formats may lead to a loss in quality.

ESSENTIAL MUSIC

Eat a Peach, by the Allman Brothers Band

The Allmans are my favorite band because of the diversity of their music and the different ways it can move me. More than any other album, *Eat a Peach* contains all the elements I love about them: great, acoustic or piano-driven songs ("Melissa," "Ain't Wasting Time No More"); revved up but true blues ("One Way Out," "Trouble No More"); and wide-open exploratory jamming ("Mountain Jam"). To top it off, it closes with two of my favorite songs, "Blue Sky" and "Little Martha," both of which are gentle and reflective yet muscular and grounded. Veritable musical perfection. After 20 years of listening, I still discover new things about the songs on *Eat a Peach* and find new reasons to love them.

➤ Alan Paul is associate editor of *Guitar World* magazine (http://www.guitarworld.com).

Compression Formats—MP3, AAC, Lossless, and the Rest

Compression is a seemingly magical function that reduces the size of digital files. You've seen it around a lot: You've probably used .zip, .sit, or .gz files (the first is the most common form of compression for Windows, the second for Mac, and the third for Unix and Linux), which allow you to shrink your data and store it in smaller files, or to transfer data over a network or the Internet more quickly. Compression software looks for similarities in bits of data, especially repeated characters or series of characters, and replaces them with shorter strings. You can compress text files to about half or one-third of their original size, and some graphic files can be compressed to less than 10% of their full size.

But when you compress some kinds of files you use on a computer, such as text files or applications, you need to use *lossless* compression—this means that after you decompress the files, you have exactly the same data you started with. Most compression schemes used for music are *lossy* compression, which saves space by removing certain data that is deemed unessential. For this reason, compressed music contains less data and is never as good as the original music on your CDs. But this is a trade-off; in most cases, you won't notice the difference. That's why MP3 compression became so popular. At standard rates of

DO OR DIE:

>> Get a master's degree in file compression

>> Learn about MP3 and AAC compression

>> Check out other compression formats with weird names

>> Choose the best compression format and bit rate for your music

GLOSSARY
MP3 is one of those arcane abbreviations that occasionally get adopted by the general public and become common terms. It stands for Moving Picture Experts Group 2 Audio Layer 3. MPEG,

UNDER THE HOOD

compression, MP3 files can sound nearly as good as the original CDs, at one-tenth the size of the original music files. (Well, to some ears...)

MP3 Files

If you listen to music, and if you've ever downloaded songs from the Internet, you've probably heard of MP3 files. In fact, if you read the papers, you've certainly heard of them, because they are a bone of contention for the RIAA (Recording Industry Association of America), which gets hives every time they hear about them. MP3 files are *compressed* music files, shrunken digital equivalents of the sound you hear on a CD.

MP3 compression is the most ubiquitous form of music compression, and just about every digital music device (including the iPod) and software (like iTunes) can play back MP3 files. You can choose different types of MP3 encoders with some software, and, especially, you can choose a bit rate and other settings, such as variable bit rate, or VBR, to refine the quality and size of your files. (See Choosing Compression Settings in iTunes for more on this.) With MP3 files, you can be sure that any digital music player will be able to spin your tunes. (Though some can't understand VBR files.)

AAC

Apple's choice of AAC (Advanced Audio Coding) for its iTunes Music Store was a bold choice and may be seen as similar to its choice of USB, back in the days when there were few USB peripherals, or its killing off of the floppy disk with the first iMac. This compression standard, which is part of the MPEG-4 audio and video standard, has been selected as the audio coder for 3G (third-generation) mobile phones, the Digital Radio Mondiale system, and will be used for the DVD-ROM zone of DVD-Audio discs. Developed by a consortium of companies covering many spectra of content usage, AAC (also known as MP4) will possibly, even probably, replace MP3 as the dominant form of music compression.

Like MP3, AAC is a lossy compression standard. But it offers much higher quality at the same bit rate, and even at lower bit rates, allowing you to cram more music onto your iPod or your hard disk. In addition, iTunes imports music as AAC files faster than it does MP3 files, so you'll save time ripping your music collection. But there's a downside to this: Not all digital music devices or software can play AAC files. While iTunes and the iPod can, most other portable

which is the abbreviation for this standards organization, is also the generic term for a certain type of digital video files. Audio Layer 3 is part of the MPEG standard, which defines the way music is encoded. You can find some

devices, and CD/DVD players, won't know what to do with your AAC files. But as AAC becomes more popular, we'll certainly see more devices that support this standard.

So, the choice of whether to use MP3 or AAC with iTunes and your iPod depends on several factors.

- **If you are only going to listen to music with iTunes or your iPod:** AAC gives you better quality at the same bit rate. Some third-party software, such as Real Player, also supports AAC.

- **If you want to be able to listen to music with other software or hardware:** Choose MP3 for now, until AAC becomes more common. You can always rip your music again if you really want to use AAC later.

- **If you only need MP3 files occasionally:** You can use AAC in iTunes, then convert your files to MP3 when you need to. This is easy to do (see Converting Music Files to Another Format for more on converting music files in iTunes), but it may take a while if you want to convert a lot of music.

You can use a combination of AAC and MP3 files on your iPod or with iTunes. If you already have a lot of MP3 files, you don't need to convert them to AAC files. The only real issue is whether you want to be able to use AAC files on other devices.

Apple Lossless Compression

When Apple introduced iTunes 4.5 in April 2004, they added a new compression format: Apple Lossless compression. This format reduces the size of music files without removing any data. While these files are much larger than MP3 files, they don't lose any sound quality. That's right, no quality loss at all!

The downside to this is that files compressed with this format take up from one-third to half the space of the original CD. So, for a CD that's about 650MB (an hour's worth of music), Apple Lossless takes up about 325MB or less. The actual size depends on the type of music you rip.

Now this is good news for audiophiles: No longer do they have to suffer the ravages of outrageous compression and the loss of quality (that they claim they can hear) when using AAC or MP3 files. But did I say this takes up a lot more disk space? If you're listening to music on your computer only, disk space is not much of a problem; you can always buy a bigger hard disk. But with your iPod, this gets a bit sticky. Perhaps this will motivate you to buy a bigger iPod to hold

heavy-duty technical information on the MP3 compression standard here: http://www.iis.fraunhofer.de/amm/techinf/layer3/index.html.

more music in perfect quality... Perhaps that's exactly what Apple wants you to do? In any case, Apple Lossless is perfect. Period.

Other Compression Formats

MP3, AAC, and Apple Lossless aren't the only forms of compression you can use for your music. These formats are not open, and manufacturers of hardware and software must pay royalties to use them. There is a free, open-source compression format that offers quality similar to AAC files: Ogg Vorbis (www.vorbis.com). This format is very popular with Linux users, since it is distributed with a GNU General Public License, which means that developers don't need to pay any consortium for the right to use it. But as with AAC, not many hardware devices can play back these files. There is, however, a lot of software that can play Ogg Vorbis files, and you can install a QuickTime plugin so iTunes can play these files.

Shorten (.shn) is a lossless compression format that is the format of choice for people who trade music by jam bands, such as the Grateful Dead, Phish, Pearl Jam, and other "trade-friendly" bands. See http://www.etree.org/shn-com.html for more on this format, as well as software to play back and convert .shn files.

TOOL KIT.

Get Your Ogg Vorbis Here

Download Ogg Vorbis encoders for Windows and Linux here:

> http://www.vorbis.com/download.psp.

You can find a Mac decoder for Ogg Vorbis here:

> http://www.illadvised.com/~jordy/.

And an encoder here:

> http://www.nouturn.com/oggdrop/index.html.

FLAC (Free Lossless Audio Codec) is another open-source project that provides a lossless compression format. It is not as popular as .shn, but offers some advantages. See http://flac.sourceforge.net for more.

There are also proprietary formats, such as Windows Media and RealAudio, but these formats only work with the corresponding software (though iTunes 4.5 or later for Windows can convert files from WMA format to any of iTunes' formats). While Microsoft is pushing to get hardware manufacturers to adopt the

UNDER THE HOOD

WHAT'S SAMPLE RATE?
The sample rate is the number of times an analog signal is measured, or "sampled," per second. This is expressed in kilohertz (kHz), and higher sample rates mean better sound. CDs are sampled at

Windows Media format, the quality is lower, and there's really no point using a format that is not part of a more common standard, such as MP3 or AAC.

Finally, you can use iTunes to create AIFF or WAV files of your music. Both AIFF and WAV files take raw sound data from a music CD and encapsulate it in file headers so this data can be used on computers. AIFF is a format created by Apple which does not compress the original music. If you have a few terabytes of hard disk space, AIFF is the best way to listen to your music, but you won't get much of it on your iPod. (AIFF files are only supported on the Mac version of iTunes.) WAV is a sound format created by Microsoft and IBM which, like AIFF, does not compress sound files. You can use this format to create system sound files, or to play back music on a Windows computer that doesn't have an MP3 player.

Compressing Music Files

After you've chosen which compression format you want to use, you'll need to think about how much compression you want to apply, or how much you want to shrink your files. (Though this doesn't apply to Apple Lossless compression; all settings are automatic.) This depends on the *bit rate* you select in the iTunes preferences. Bit rates tell the encoder how much data to use per second. For example, if you choose 128kbps, that means that every second of music will use 128,000 bits. If you encode your music in stereo (mono is only useful for spoken word recordings), this gets doubled. Multiply that again by the sample rate, and you get about 1MB per minute for MP3 files at 128kbps.

There's another option for encoding, though, which can change the size of your files. In iTunes, and in most other encoding software, you can choose from joint stereo or normal (or stereo). Joint stereo is a neat trick that uses mono recording for the lowest frequencies, similar to the way a three-speaker sound system uses two tweeters and a single subwoofer. You don't notice the difference between stereo and mono at low frequencies, because these waves are so long that human ears can't tell which direction they come from.

Bit rate affects the quality of the compressed music. You might not hear the difference in all conditions, especially if you're in your car, in a train, or walking on a noisy street, but higher bit rates make crisper, richer, more realistic sounding music. You may be satisfied with 128kbps for the music you listen to, and you might never notice the difference, but discerning listeners and audiophiles will use higher bit rates. For MP3 files, 192kbps is a good compromise between size and quality, though many jazz and classical music fans opt for 320kbps,

44.100kHz, but there's no point in using a higher sample rate when compressing your CDs; this just takes up more space for nothing.

which is often the maximum bit rate available. (For comparison, audio CDs are encoded at 1,411.2kbps.)

Another way to get better quality is to use *variable bit rate*. This encodes music at different rates according to the sound at every given moment. If the sound is complex, the bit rate used is higher, but lower bit rates are used whenever possible for simpler, easier-to-compress sound. You choose a minimum bit rate when using VBR encoding, and the encoder determines the actual bit rate on the fly, adjusting it according to the music. The downside to this is that many hardware devices, and even many software music players, don't support VBR encoding.

With AAC compression, you'll get higher quality than MP3 at any given bit rate. This compression is more efficient, so you'll find that a 128kbps AAC file will sound better than the equivalent MP3 file, but they'll both be the same size. You have two choices with AAC: Either use a lower bit rate to store more music on your player (96kbps AAC is said to be the same quality as 128kbps MP3), or use the same bit rate and get better sound. Or you can use a higher bit rate, up to 320kbps, for the best quality available for compressed files using iTunes. In any case, I wouldn't recommend that you use less than 128kbps, except for spoken word files.

Choosing Compression Settings in iTunes

You've seen in the previous pages that compression is an important issue, and if you understand all that, you could probably get a Ph.D. in music compression. But is it really that important? If you're like most people, and just want to listen to your music without any hassles, you could probably avoid this entire question. Apple has set 128kbps AAC encoding as the default for iTunes, so whenever you rip CDs, this is what you'll get, unless you change the settings. In addition, if you buy music from the iTunes Music Store, your music files will be compressed in the same way.

But we all know there are people out there who want to go the extra yard and make their music sound just a little bit better. (I confess; I'm one of them, but within limits.) For this reason, you have a great deal of latitude in the type of compression you choose for CDs you rip with iTunes.

As I said earlier, you won't notice much difference if you listen to your music in a noisy environment, but as you get more into digital music, you may just end up

FAQ

How Do You Choose the Right Bit Rate for Your Music Files?

Choose your bit rate according to the quality you want your compressed music files to retain and the space you have on your iPod. If you have an iPod mini, you'll want to use smaller file sizes, but if you have a 40GB iPod, you've got much more latitude and can use better-quality files. Table 1-1 shows a comparison of different compression formats and the resulting file sizes.

Table 1-1 **Comparison of Compression Formats***				
A FOUR-MINUTE SONG RIPPED AS:		HOURS OF MUSIC ON A:		
BIT RATE AND ENCODING	FILE SIZE	4GB IPOD MINI	20GB IPOD	40GB IPOD
96kbps AAC/MP3**	2.8MB	86	429	857
128kbps Ogg Vorbis	3.0MB	80	400	800
128kbps AAC/MP3	3.6MB	67	333	667
128kbps VBR MP3***	3.8MB	63	316	632
160kbps ACC/MP3	4.6MB	51	255	511
192kbps AAC/MP3	5.6MB	43	214	429
256kbps AAC/MP3	7.5MB	32	160	320
320kbps AAC/MP3	9.3MB	26	129	258
Apple Lossless****	≈ 20MB	12	60	120
AIFF or WAV	41.1MB	6	29	58

* These figures are not absolute, because other settings available when encoding music may make the files slightly smaller or larger. Also, figures for minutes on different devices are estimates and don't take into account any additional data (contacts, calendars, etc.) you may store on your iPod. I've assumed a 10% loss in disk space for formatting, since this produces figures that correspond to Apple's estimates of 1,000 songs on the iPod mini, 5,000 songs on the 20GB, and 10,000 songs on the 40GB. Apple bases these figures on four-minute songs encoded at 128kbps AAC.

** AAC and MP3 files are roughly the same size at an equivalent bit rate.

*** VBR files vary in size according to the type of music they contain. I used the same song for all examples in this table, but your mileage will vary.

**** The actual size of files compressed with Apple Lossless compression varies according to the type of music. They can range from half to as little as one-third the original size of the music files.

using your computer or iPod for *all* your music listening, and toss your CDs in a box in your basement. If this is the case, you'll want to use higher-quality compression; if you use your computer or iPod to pipe music through a stereo, and you have "discerning" ears, you'll be happier.

To change iTunes compression settings, go to the iTunes preferences and click the Importing tab. You'll see two popup menus. The first, Import Using, lets you choose a type of compression: AAC, AIFF, MP3, or WAV. The second menu, Setting, lets you adjust the bit rate, sample rate, and channels. For AAC, there are only two choices: High Quality (128kbps) or Custom. For MP3, there are three choices: Good Quality (128kbps), High Quality (160kbps) and Higher

Quality (192kbps). (If you want to encode AIFF or WAV, you'll probably just want to leave all the settings at Automatic.)

Beyond these basic settings, you can choose your own bit rate, sample rate, and channels. To change these for AAC, click the popup menu and select Custom. This opens a dialog for the selected encoder. You'll see that the Stereo Bit Rate menu lets you choose from 16kbps (that sounds like a telephone underwater) to 320kbps (crystal clear). The Sample Rate menu offers Auto, 44.100kHz, or 48.000kHz; choose Auto in most cases. And the Channels menu lets you choose Auto, Mono, or Stereo. Unless you really want to convert stereo sources into Mono, or vice versa, leave this set to Auto.

And if you want to go whole hog and have the best possible sound, choose Apple Lossless compression. 'Nuff said.

MP3 encoding offers additional settings. You choose the Bit Rate, Sample Rate, and Channels as mentioned earlier for AAC files, and you can also opt for Variable Bit Rate Encoding. I explained VBR earlier, so if you want to use this type of encoding, check the box and select a Quality from Lowest to Highest. Higher quality means that the maximum bit rate is higher.

You can also choose a Stereo Mode: Normal or Joint Stereo. This determines whether low frequencies are encoded as mono (Normal) or stereo (Joint Stereo). Bass-heavy music deserves Joint Stereo, and your files will be a bit larger.

The final two settings are Smart Encoding Adjustments, which tell iTunes to analyze your music and encoding settings to try to optimize the quality of the compressed files, and Filter Frequencies Below 10 Hz, which helps make smaller files by ignoring any frequencies that are too low to hear.

Kirk's Recommendation

So, it's recommendation time. After careful study and examination of the question at hand, here are my thoughts on the best encoding settings (whether you choose AAC or MP3).

- **You listen to music outdoors or on the go, have a small-capacity iPod, or just don't care much about the quality of your music:** Use 128kbps files. You'll be happy in most situations. You'll also fit a lot more music on your iPod and your hard disk.

- **You listen to music indoors, using your computer or iPod connected to a stereo:** Use 160kbps AAC or 192kbps MP3 encoding. You'll get richer sound, and the music will sound better in a quiet, indoor environment.

- **You're an audiophile or a musician and have discerning ears:** Go for the highest bit rate your hard disk or iPod will hold, if you want to use AAC or MP3 compression, or go all the way and use Apple Lossless. See Table 1-1 for the amount of music you can put on your iPod at higher bit rates. If you've got lots of hard disk space, go all the way. If you've got top-of-the-line speakers or headphones, you'll appreciate the difference. But you won't be able to put as much music on your iPod, so it's a trade-off. Of course, you could always buy a second iPod...

Whatever settings you choose, remember that you can always rip your CDs again at higher- or lower-quality settings if you change your mind. But it's a good idea to test different settings and decide which compression settings you want to use before you rip your entire CD collection.

Ripping Classical and Jazz CDs

While Apple is aggressively marketing its iPod to the younger generation, the iPod is also a great device for listening to classical music and jazz. However, to get the most out of this type of music, you need to reconsider the way you rip your CDs.

I've got eclectic musical tastes. My iPod contains music by the Grateful Dead, The Clash, Brian Eno, moe., and The Durutti Column; Miles Davis, John Coltrane, and Bill Evans; and Bach, Haydn, Handel, Schubert, and Charles Ives. I've long explored all types of music, and the capacity of my iPod lets me carry a diverse selection of tunes with me.

For rock and pop music, iTunes (and the iPod, by extension; all my explanations here apply to both) is easy to use: Insert a CD in your computer, rip the music, then create a playlist (or just listen to your songs in random order). But for classical music, and to a lesser extent jazz and live recordings, you need a different approach. There are constraints in most classical music that should make you consider ripping your CDs differently.

In operas, for example, there are often no pauses between recitatives and arias, or between orchestral movements and arias. If you rip your music as individual tracks, you'll get pauses. While you can eliminate these pauses in iTunes (go to the Effects preferences and set Crossfade Playback to 0 seconds), the iPod can't play tracks without an audible pause. Ideally, when ripping operas, you should convert each disc into a single track. To do this, insert

DO OR DIE:

>> Keep classical tracks in order

>> Listen to long works without pauses

>> Learn tried-and-true techniques for tagging your music

Ripping Classical and Jazz CDs

While Apple is aggressively marketing its iPod to the younger generation, the iPod is also a great device for listening to classical music and jazz. However, to get the most out of this type of music, you need to reconsider the way you rip your CDs.

I've got eclectic musical tastes. My iPod contains music by the Grateful Dead, The Clash, Brian Eno, moe., and The Durutti Column; Miles Davis, John Coltrane, and Bill Evans; and Bach, Haydn, Handel, Schubert, and Charles Ives. I've long explored all types of music, and the capacity of my iPod lets me carry a diverse selection of tunes with me.

For rock and pop music, iTunes (and the iPod, by extension; all my explanations here apply to both) is easy to use: Insert a CD in your computer, rip the music, then create a playlist (or just listen to your songs in random order). But for classical music, and to a lesser extent jazz and live recordings, you need a different approach. There are constraints in most classical music that should make you consider ripping your CDs differently.

In operas, for example, there are often no pauses between recitatives and arias, or between orchestral movements and arias. If you rip your music as individual tracks, you'll get pauses. While you can eliminate these pauses in iTunes (go to the Effects preferences and set Crossfade Playback to 0 seconds), the iPod can't play tracks without an audible pause. Ideally, when ripping operas, you should convert each disc into a single track. To do this, insert a CD into your computer, then select all the tracks on that CD and select Advanced > Join CD Tracks. This gives you a single track of the entire disc, and you won't have any inopportune pauses. (Note that this only works if you display the disc in ascending track order; this is the way it displays when you insert a CD. You can also only join tracks when you rip a CD; you can't do it later, so think ahead.)

When you do this, you won't be able to see the names of individual tracks in your operas. It's a trade-off, but if you listen to music on the go, you probably won't be bothered. (You can, however, always check the elapsed time of the track to know where you are.) There is another advantage to this approach: Your operas will only be three or four tracks, instead of hundreds, making it easier to browse music and organize your tunes. But if you want to make a playlist with your favorite arias or overtures, you're stuck. You'll have to rip them as individual tracks or selectively rip your favorites as single tracks.

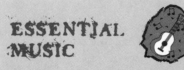

ESSENTIAL MUSIC

Bach Lute Suites, Performed by John Williams

Not long after I entered college, I discovered a recently released recording of the Bach Lute Suites by the classical guitarist John Williams. He isn't the same as the composer John Williams, but rather an Australian who learned guitar from his father and was already a prodigy at the age of 12. When he made his professional debut at 18, Segovia said about him, "God has laid a finger on his brow." Over the course of nearly 30 years now, I have listened to dozens of different recordings of these beautiful pieces, and Williams' extraordinary playing has remained the one I admire most. I've never tired of them. If I had to pick a single favorite among the tracks, it would probably be the Prelude to the Fourth Lute Suite—or the E-major Suite, as it is also known. I'm too poor a classical guitarist to play the piece myself, but perhaps at some point in my life I'll take a year off from my writing just to learn it.

If the recording appeals to you, you'll also enjoy Hopkinson Smith's two-disc set of the Lute Suites played on a lute rather than a guitar. In general the pace on a lute is much slower than a guitar, and while Williams is known for his brisk playing of Bach, the Hopkinson Smith recording is more languid and contemplative. Both are exceptionally beautiful.

➤ Arthur Golden is the author of the best-selling novel *Memoirs of a Geisha*. He owns two iPods and has a Mac dedicated to providing music to his home stereo using iTunes. He's currently listening to lots of music while working on his second novel, to be published in the fall of 2005.

When you rip classical music, you're confronted with another problem: that of correctly identifying the composer, artist, and album. iTunes uses the Gracenote CDDB (CD database), which records track and album information for hundreds of thousands of CDs. A lot of classical discs are included in this database, but I've found many that are either missing or incorrect. In addition, when you rip music with iTunes, it organizes your music by artist; in the case of classical music, this is usually the performer. I've seen some operas where a different artist is listed for each disc: This is usually just a variant of the actual orchestra and conductor, but it makes organizing the resulting music on your hard disk a bit of a hassle.

The solution to this is to change the information before ripping your disks. Again, select all the tracks, press Command+I on Mac or Ctrl+I on a PC, and fill in the fields. You should fill in the Composer field, since this is generally blank. Set whatever name you want for the album (again, the CDDB information is often incorrect here), then do the same for the artist. You'll find it easier to browse for music when the information you'll want to look for is already attached to your music.

Tags and Track Info

When you rip CDs, you import not only the music, but, ideally, the names of the tracks, the album name, artist info, and more. If you don't have this info, you'll get lots of tracks named Track01, Track02, and so on. Not very cool when you want to browse your music library.

Ripping music, like most of what you do with iTunes, is a snap. As I explained earlier, you just insert your CD and click the Import button. When iTunes reads your CD, it attempts to get information about your CD from the Gracenote CD database. If you've got an active Internet connection, iTunes sends some magic numbers from your CD to the Gracenote CDDB, which returns information on the disc and its individual tracks.

The Gracenote CDDB has an extensive database of albums and songs. In April 2004, Gracenote claimed to have more than 2.7 million albums and 34 million songs listed in its database. That's a lot of music!

Getting CD info from the CDDB is fast and easy—either iTunes does it automatically, or if you have unchecked Connect to Internet when Needed in the iTunes preferences (or when setting up iTunes), you can select Advanced > Get CD Track Names to get these tags.

The Gracenote CDDB can provide a great deal of information, but iTunes only records the data fields listed in Table 1-2.

DO OR DIE:

>> Tagging your music

>> Getting the tags right

>> Editing and converting tag info

THE GOOD, THE BAD, AND THE UGLY ABOUT INFO TAGS
The Gracenote CDDB saves you lots of time when you rip a CD. If not for this, you'd have to enter all that information manually. You

UNDER
THE
HOOD

Table 1-2 Gracenote CDDB Data Fields That iTunes Records	
ALBUM DATA FIELDS	
Album Title	The album title, including sort information so "The Wall" can be sorted under "W".
Artist	The recording artist, including sort information so "The Orb" can be sorted under "Orb".
Year	The year the CD was recorded or published.
Genre	The musical genre of the CD—every album can have both a primary and a secondary genre.
Composer	The composer(s) of the album. This can be entered for an entire album or set for individual tracks.
Compilation	A flag set for compilations, soundtracks with multiple artists, and so on. Unfortunately, this flag is often set for CDs that are not compilations.
Disc Number	This identifies a CD as a part of a box set, such as Disc 1 of 3.
TRACK DATA FIELDS	
Track Name	The track title, including sort information so "The Weight" can be sorted at "W".
Artist	The artist for the specific track, essential for compilations and multi-artist soundtracks.
Year	This may be different for each track of a compilation, soundtrack, or "Best Of" album.
Beats Per Minute	The number of BPM of the track. Used for DJ syncing.
Composer	The composer(s) of the track. This can be entered for an entire album, or set for individual tracks.
Genres	This can be entered for entire album or applied to individual tracks. There are 24 genres available in iTunes.

In most cases, artist, album, and song title information is all you need. You might want track timing information as well, but iTunes figures that out on its own; that doesn't come from the CDDB.

iTunes adds its own information to your music files when you rip CDs. In addition to the info that the Gracenote CDDB provides (not all tracks and

probably don't need most of it; as I mentioned earlier, artist, album, and song title are generally sufficient.

But if you want more info, you need to be aware that all is not perfect in the world of the CDDB. Much of the information you get, at least for older

If you select multiple tracks and then display the Info window, it is different from the window shown in Figure 1-13. The Multiple Song Information window lets you change common elements for the selected songs: the artist, album, genre, and so on. This is a good way to change tag info for many songs at once, but is only useful if all the selected songs share the same info.

Finally, you can change some information about your tracks only from a contextual menu. Right-click a track (in Windows, or in Mac OS X with a multi-button mouse) or hold down the Control key and click a track (in Mac OS X) to display this contextual menu. You can see in Figure 1-14 that this contextual menu gives you access to certain functions as well as letting you change some information.

What you can do from this menu is reset the play count (if you want to reset it to zero) and set a rating for the song. You can add it to the Party Shuffle playlist

FAQ

Is There a Trick for Tagging Classical Music?

A lot of classical music is pieces with multiple movements, such as sonatas, symphonies, and operas. In Ripping Classical and Jazz CDs, I mentioned that you can rip these works in single files by joining their tracks. But this only works if you do it when you import the music from your CDs, and only for works that are on a single disc. If you want to import Mahler's 3rd Symphony, for example, which is always on two discs, you'll end up with two files.

Well, there's a trick you can use to make classical works easier to find when browsing your music in iTunes or on your iPod.

There is no rule that says you need to keep the name of the album as it shows in iTunes after the program downloads its information from the CDDB. You can change this name, as you can change any of the other tags.

So, with Mahler's 3rd Symphony, why not select all six movements and change their album tag to 3rd Symphony? So what if it's on two separate CDs; your music is digital, and there are no time limits. This way, when you browse in iTunes, or on your iPod, you'll be able to select the entire symphony, and only that symphony. You can do the same for other multi-movement works, and, while this is especially useful for works that cover more than one CD, it's also practical for any piece of music that you want to be able to find more easily, even if the work is only part of a CD.

Gracenote CDDB (see the same section). If you find mistakes, try to help us all out by doing so.

Figure 1-14

The contextual menu for a track. You can change some track information here, as well as perform other tasks.

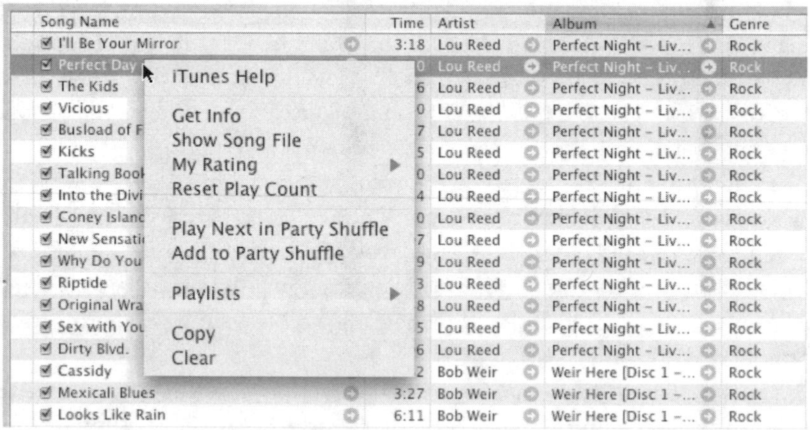

Song Name		Time	Artist		Album		Genre
☑ I'll Be Your Mirror	○	3:18	Lou Reed	○	Perfect Night – Liv...	○	Rock
☑ Perfect Day		0	Lou Reed	○	Perfect Night – Liv...	○	Rock
☑ The Kids		6	Lou Reed	○	Perfect Night – Liv...		Rock
☑ Vicious		0	Lou Reed	○	Perfect Night – Liv...		Rock
☑ Busload of F		7	Lou Reed	○	Perfect Night – Liv...		Rock
☑ Kicks		5	Lou Reed	○	Perfect Night – Liv...		Rock
☑ Talking Boo		0	Lou Reed	○	Perfect Night – Liv...		Rock
☑ Into the Divi		4	Lou Reed	○	Perfect Night – Liv...		Rock
☑ Coney Islanc		0	Lou Reed	○	Perfect Night – Liv...		Rock
☑ New Sensati		7	Lou Reed	○	Perfect Night – Liv...		Rock
☑ Why Do You		9	Lou Reed	○	Perfect Night – Liv...		Rock
☑ Riptide		3	Lou Reed	○	Perfect Night – Liv...		Rock
☑ Original Wra		8	Lou Reed	○	Perfect Night – Liv...		Rock
☑ Sex with Yo		5	Lou Reed	○	Perfect Night – Liv...		Rock
☑ Dirty Blvd.		6	Lou Reed	○	Perfect Night – Liv...		Rock
☑ Cassidy		2	Bob Weir	○	Weir Here [Disc 1 –...	○	Rock
☑ Mexicali Blues	○	3:27	Bob Weir	○	Weir Here [Disc 1 –...	○	Rock
☑ Looks Like Rain	○	6:11	Bob Weir	○	Weir Here [Disc 1 –...	○	Rock

Menu:
iTunes Help
Get Info
Show Song File
My Rating ▶
Reset Play Count
Play Next in Party Shuffle
Add to Party Shuffle
Playlists ▶
Copy
Clear

or cue it up to be played next in this special playlist. You can also find out which playlists the track is in (or which *other* playlists, if you've clicked a track in a playlist rather than in your library). And if you want to see the actual location file for the track, click Show Song File; a window opens showing the track.

Album Art for Your Tracks

DO OR DIE:

- >> Display album cover graphics
- >> Find album art on the Internet

It's cool to be able to download music or to rip your CDs, but there's something missing. If you grew up in the LP era, like me, you remember how great it was to look at some of the more imaginative album covers. When CDs came along, the available space shrank from 12" × 12" to 5" × 5", making the more detailed artwork on albums impossible to reproduce.

With digital music, you don't get covers at all, nor do you get liner notes. But when you buy songs from the iTunes Music Store, you get *art* with your tracks. The files you download include a low-resolution graphic of the album cover corresponding to the track you purchase.

You can display these graphics by selecting a track and clicking the Show/Hide Artwork button (Figure 1-15).

Clicking the Show/Hide Artwork button displays the artwork at the bottom of the Source column, as in Figure 1-16.

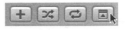

Figure 1-15

Click this button to show or hide artwork for the selected track.

If you've ripped your own CDs, your tracks won't have this album art, but you can add graphics to them yourself. Unfortunately, you need to do this for each track, one at a time. Select a track, then select File > Get Info (or do the right mouse button or Control-click thing, depending on whether you're using Windows or Mac, and select

UNDER THE HOOD

WHERE IS ALBUM ART STORED?

In your digital music files. You'll find that your music files get a little bigger if you add album art to them. If you really need to save

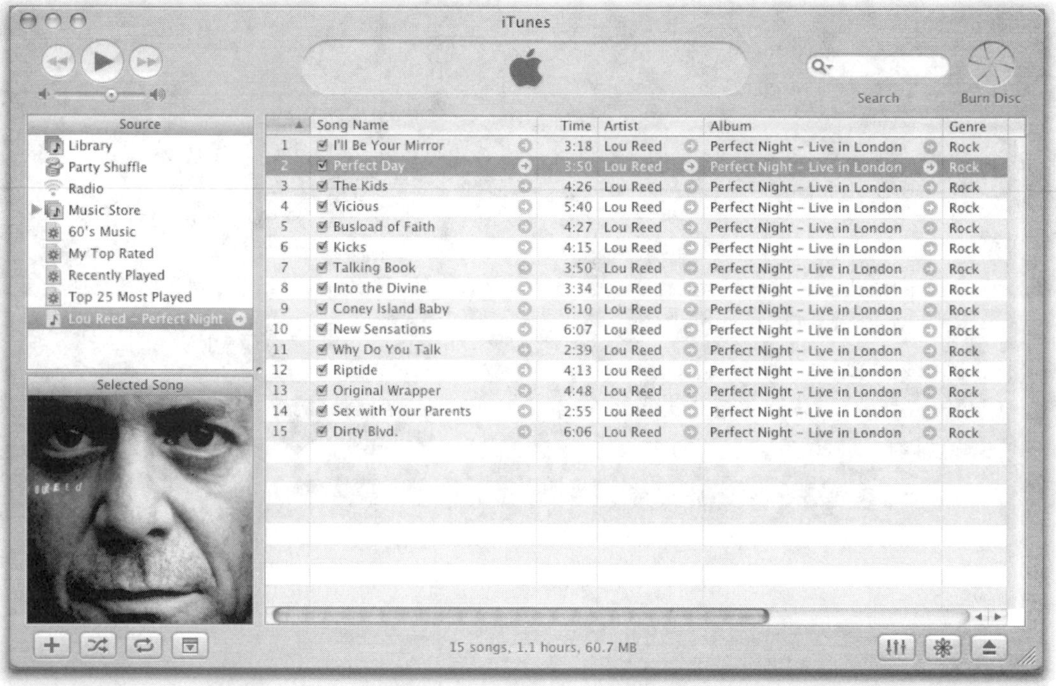

Figure 1-16

You can see the album cover corresponding to the selected song at the bottom of the Source list. Here, Lou Reed is watching me.

Get Info from the contextual menu), then click Artwork. This tab shows you the graphic for the track. If there is none, click Add... and find the graphic you want to add. You can scan your album covers, or you can get them from the Internet.

If you want to add art to all the tracks of an album, go to its playlist, or display all its tracks in your library by searching for its name. Then, after display-

How about Digital Liner Notes?

One thing that hard-core music fans miss when downloading music is liner notes. When you purchase an album from the iTunes Music Store or from another music service, you get the tunes and maybe a picture of the album cover, but you don't get anything else: no lyrics, no information on the musicians, and no ramblings by the artists.

It would be cool if you could get these liner notes, either in text or PDF format, at least when purchasing an entire album online. I'm sure iTunes could have a new feature to store these notes in its library and display them when you want. You could probably even download them to your iPod, at least their text, and view them there.

Apple, are you listening?

space, you can strip the album art by going to the Artwork tab of the Get Info window, clicking the graphic to select it, then clicking Delete.

ing the Info window, add the graphic to the first track, then click it to select it and copy it (Command+C on Mac or Control+C on Windows). Click Next to go to the info for the next track, paste the file (Command+V or Control+V), and continue until you reach the last track.

Actually, you don't need a special program to get this art, but it sure makes things faster. You can simply go to Amazon, the iTunes Music Store, or another online music store and copy album covers, then add them to your tracks. Or go to official sites for your favorite bands, or to other music sites that display album covers.

TOOL KIT

Getting Album Art from the Internet

There are lots of freeware and shareware programs that can download album art from the Internet, at least for Mac users. A lot of them merely check on Amazon.com to see if there is a graphic for the album that your tracks are from. Here are two programs you can use to add art to your tracks.

Macintosh:

Fetch Art for iTunes (http://staff.washington.edu/yoel/fetchart/) is a free AppleScript that checks Amazon.com for the appropriate graphics for selected tracks. After you install the script, select one or more tracks, then select Fetch Art from the AppleScript menu (see Tools for Doing More with iTunes for more on using AppleScripts in iTunes for Mac). The script scans Amazon, then displays a dialog showing the tracks and any art it's found. If you like the art, click Copy to iTunes, and Fetch Art for iTunes copies the graphic to your track file, so you can now see it in iTunes as explained earlier.

Another cool program for Mac is Clutter (http://www.sprote.com/clutter/ index.html), a freeware program that puts album art on your Desktop, allowing you to double-click an album to play it. Clutter also has an option to add album art to iTunes for your tracks. And it's got a neat browser window that gives you quick access to all your playlists; you might find Clutter an easier way to play music through iTunes.

Windows:

There are no Windows programs that do the same thing, but there are other alternatives. See next.

Platform agnostic:

Go to http://www.art4itunes.com, where you can upload a file containing your song list (File > Export Song List, and select to save the file as Plain Text, or Text) and have the site provide you with the art. You can then save the graphic files to your computer and add them to iTunes.

In all cases, you can add the art you save or download into the Info window. Display the Info window, then click the Artwork tab. To add artwork, click Add, and navigate to the image and click Choose, or drag an image into the artwork field.

Working with Playlists

P rofound pronouncement time:

DO OR DIE:

>> Zen and the art of playlists

>> Regular and smart playlists

>> The many ways to create playlists

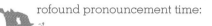

THE KEY TO iTUNES AND THE iPOD IS UNDERSTANDING PLAYLISTS

This may sound Zen-like, but it's true. If you don't grok playlists, you'll have nothing but a long list of songs in your iTunes library or on your iPod. Sure, you can listen to all that music at random, or just browse by artist or album and select an album, and if that's all you want to do, then just skip this section.

Playlists are the basic units within iTunes and on the iPod. If songs are atoms, then playlists are molecules. When atoms are correctly combined, they make useful molecules.

What's a playlist? Well, it's a list of songs that you play together, one after the other, with a first song and a last song. Kind of like a CD. Pretty basic, right? But playlists are more than that. A playlist is a self-contained unit, one that you can play in order or using the shuffle function; a group of songs that you can burn to a CD; and a bunch of tracks you can repeat in the same order again, after iTunes or your iPod gets to the end of the playlist.

A playlist can contain any number of tracks and can be the equivalent of an album, a longer work (such as a double-album set), a live concert, an opera, a compilation of your favorite songs by different groups, or a selection of music for a special occasion. A playlist could even be *all* your songs, if you want.

Let's distinguish between two types of playlists: "regular" playlists and "smart" playlists. Regular playlists are groups of songs that you set up manually, either by creating a playlist and dragging songs to it or by creating a playlist from a selection. The key word here is "manually": as you'll see later in this section, smart playlists are automatically created from conditions you select, but regular playlists require human intervention. Here's how you create playlists.

- **To create a "blank" playlist:** Click the + button at the bottom of the iTunes window, or select File > New Playlist. (Shortcut: Command+N on Mac, Control+N on Windows.)

- **To create a playlist from a selection:** Select a group of tracks in your library, then select File > Create Playlist from Selection. (Shortcut: Command+ Shift+N on Mac, Control+Shift+N on Windows.)

- **To create a smart playlist:** Select File > New Smart Playlist. (Shortcut: Command+Option+N on Mac, Control+Alt+N on Windows. You can also create a new smart playlist on Mac by holding down the Option key and clicking the + button, or on Windows by holding down the Alt+Shift keys and clicking the + button.)

Let's look at each of these ways of creating playlists, and what they offer you.

Blank Playlists

When you want to create a new playlist to add songs to, start by creating a new "blank" playlist as described earlier. Then, as you browse your library or search for tracks, you can drag tracks to the playlist. Once you've got several tracks in your playlist, you can reorder them by dragging them up or down in the play order. (You can only change the songs' order if the playlist is sorted by song number; click the first column header to enable this.) You can also sort the columns by clicking any of the column headers (for more on sorting, see All about Your iTunes Music Library), which sets the order of your playlist to follow the sort: by song title, artist name, album name, and so on.

When you create a playlist, it takes on the original name of "Untitled Playlist"; if you already have one with that name, it adds a number at the end. Whenever you want to, you can name your playlist. If you don't name it right after you create it, you can click its name in the Source list, then press Enter and type the name you want to give it.

What can you do with playlists like this? Well, you can search for songs in your iTunes music library, then add the ones you want to the playlist. You can browse by artist, genre, or album and add songs. Or you can just scroll up and down in your library and choose songs you want to add individually.

When you've got a playlist, you can, well, play it. See Listening to Music with iTunes for more on playing music in iTunes. You can use the Repeat and Shuffle buttons to play your playlist over and over until you're tired of it or to play the songs in a random order. You can also burn the playlist to a CD, and, depending on how you manage your iPod's music, the playlist will be copied to your iPod so you can listen to it there.

FAQ

Can I Add Songs to My Library While Creating Playlists?

If you create a blank playlist, you can also drag song files from any folder anywhere on your computer into the playlist window. This adds the songs not only to your playlist, but also to your iTunes music library, killing two birds with one drag.

Creating Playlists from a Selection

When you select a group of songs, you can create a playlist from this selection (as described earlier), which saves you the time of dragging individual songs. In addition, if all the songs are from the same album, the playlist automatically gets the name of the artist and album they belong to. This is the fastest way to create album-based playlists after your rip your CDs.

You can also use this feature to select a group of songs in your library and quickly create a playlist. This is a good way to make a playlist of your favorite songs, if you've given them ratings; sort your library by rating, then make a new playlist from all the five star songs, for example.

You can even create a playlist from a selection that is within another playlist. Say you only want half an album or part of a playlist you've already created. Select the songs you want, then create a playlist from the selection. However, if all the songs are from the same album, this playlist is named with the artist and album name, even if the playlist doesn't contain all the songs on the album, so you'll need to rename it to make sure you know what it contains.

Here's a quick way to create a playlist from a selection: Just press Command+Shift+N (on Mac) or Control+Shift+N (on Windows) after selecting some tracks.

Creating Playlists from a Folder

If you manage your iTunes music library manually (see All about Your iTunes Music Library), storing your folders as you want, rather than the way iTunes

TOOL KIT

Selecting Multiple Tracks in iTunes

Just in case you don't know the many options available, here are some ways to select songs in your library or in a playlist.

To select everything in your library (such as after you've searched for a specific artist or album) or in a given playlist, press Command+A (Mac) or Control+A (Windows); this selects everything that is currently displayed in the song section of the iTunes window.

To select a group of tracks that are next to each other, click the first track, then hold down the Shift key and select the last track. All the tracks between these two will be selected.

To select noncontiguous tracks, click one track, then hold down the Command key (Mac) or the Control key (Windows) and click another track. As long as you continue holding down the Command or Control key, you can keep clicking other tracks that are not next to the first ones and add them to the selection. If you've clicked one track and added it to the selection, and then decide you don't want it in the selection, just click it again while holding down the Command or Control key to deselect it.

wants, you may find that the easiest way to create a playlist from a folder is to just drag the folder to the Source column in iTunes. This creates a new playlist with the contents of the folder and names the playlist according to the name of the folder. If the folder contains several subfolders, the contents of these subfolders are added to the playlist.

This is most practical if you are copying music you've ripped or purchased on another computer, and don't want to put it in your library first and then search for the songs. Or if you download live concerts, legally shared over the Internet, you can add the concerts to your library and make playlists of them.

TOOL KIT

Creating Playlists from Recently Added Items

When I explained how to create playlists from a folder, I pointed out that this can be a bit of a hassle if your Source list is full. Here's another way to create playlists from folders.

Put the folder in the desired location on your hard disk, then click Library in iTunes' Source list. Drag the folder into the Library; this adds all the songs in the folder to your iTunes music library.

Next, make sure you can see the Date Added column in the iTunes window. If you don't, select Edit > View Options, and click Date Added, then click OK. Sort your library by date added; click the header of this column to sort by this criterion. If the sort arrow points up, click the column again so the sort arrow points down, which means that the most recently added items are at the top of the list.

You'll now see the files from the folder you just added to your library at the top of the list. Select them and create a new playlist from the selection.

The only problem with this approach occurs when your Source column is full. If you drag a folder onto a playlist, it gets added to the playlist. If you want to create a new playlist from the folder, drag it over the Source column, then toward the bottom of the column. When you see an outline around the Source column, release your mouse button. You may have to try this a few times to get the hang of it; there's not much margin for error.

Smart Playlists

If playlists are Zen-like, then smart playlists are like Zen koans. Filled with mystery and wonder, they automatically add songs to themselves, as if they sprout from your inner desires. Smart playlists give you the ultimate power over your music, but also hold their share of surprises. You may never want to use smart playlists, because you only listen to your albums in their original order, or you might want to use nothing but smart playlists, because music, like the universe, should obey other laws than linearity.

Here's the principle behind smart playlists: They act like a multicriteria search of your iTunes music library, adding songs that meet the criteria you select. Apple includes a few smart playlists by default so you can have an idea of what they can do (Figure 1-17).

Let's look at one of these smart playlists to see how it works. You can edit any smart playlist by selecting File > Edit Smart Playlist, or by right-clicking (Windows) or Control-clicking (Mac) a smart playlist and selecting Edit Smart Playlist. (On Mac, you can also Option-click a smart playlist to edit it.)

Figure 1-18 shows the Recently Played smart playlist.

As you can see in Figure 1-18, this playlist looks for songs that were Last Played in the last two weeks. Live Updating is checked, meaning that the playlist updates as you listen to songs.

Figure 1-17

The default smart playlists give you an idea of what you can use smart playlists for.

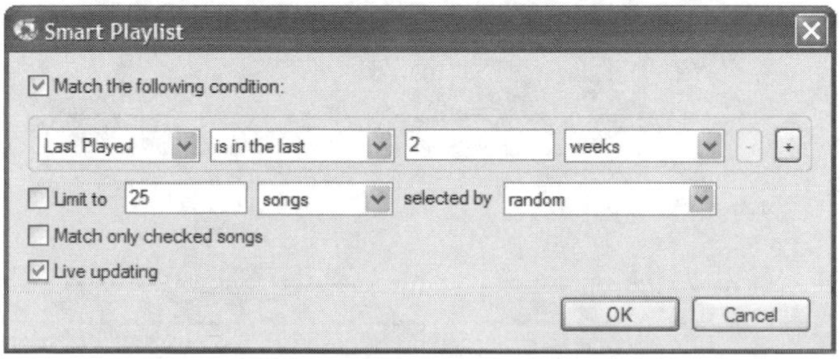

Figure 1-18

Recently Played, one of the default smart playlists

When a song is played, its Last Played date and time are updated, and it is added to the playlist behind the scenes.

There are other options. You can limit the playlist to a number of songs, minutes, hours, megabytes, or gigabytes and have them selected by any of a dozen criteria (random, album, rating, recently played, etc.). You can also choose to match only checked songs, meaning that songs that are not checked in your library won't get added to the playlist.

This, like the other default smart playlists (60's Music, My Top Rated, and Top 25 Most Played) is simple; they use only a single condition. But what if you want to use more complex criteria?

Try creating a new smart playlist as described earlier. Initially, the Smart Playlist window shows you a single condition: Artist Contains. You can enter all or part of an artist's name in this field, or you can click the first popup menu and select from about 20 options (Artist, Album, Genre, Last Played, etc.). The second menu changes according to what you select in the first menu. For names, such as Album, Artist, and so on, it lets you choose Contains, Is, Is Not, and other possibilities. For dates, it lets you choose Before, After, and so on.

Once you've selected a first condition, you can add others by clicking the + button at the right of the Smart Playlist window. A second line is added, offering the same choices. But here you can add a different condition than on the first line. For example, if the first line is Artist, the second could be Last Played. Figure 1-19 shows a smart playlist with two conditions.

When you have more than one condition, the top line of the Smart Playlist window changes, allowing you to decide whether the playlist should match any or all conditions you set. If you choose all, each condition narrows down the search; if you choose any, each one broadens the search.

The only limits to a smart playlist are the number of conditions you want to use. (Or the number that actually result in songs appearing in the playlist.) You can use as many conditions as you want, though you'll generally find that three or four is about the most you need. Figure 1-20 shows an example of a multicondition smart playlist.

Figure 1-19

This smart playlist has two conditions: an artist name and a song name.

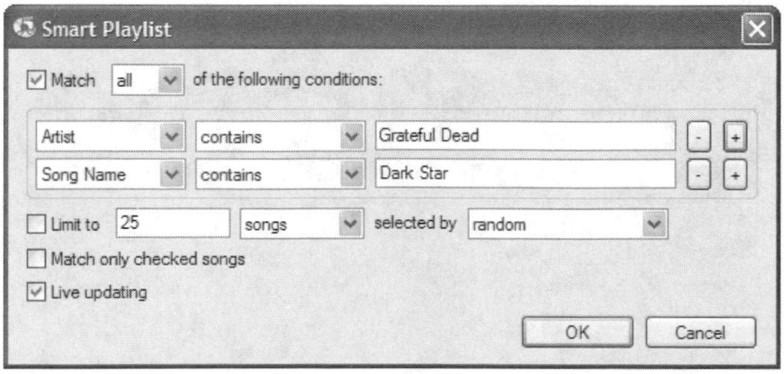

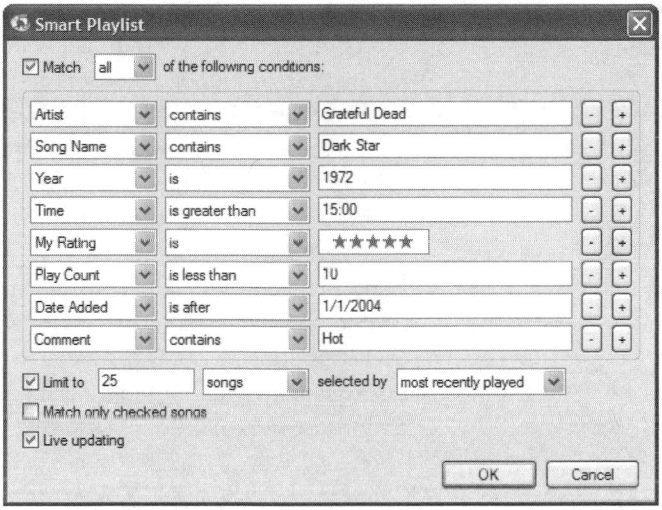

Figure 1-20

This smart playlist uses many conditions to narrow down a huge number of possibilities.

In Figure 1-20, you can see that I've included an artist name, a song name, and a year. Since I've chosen that the playlist should match all conditions, it therefore only works for music files whose tags contain this info. (See Tags and Track Info for more on using tags.) I then narrow down the selection further: versions of Dark Star that are over 15 minutes long, that I've rated five stars, that I've listened to fewer than ten times, that I've added to my library after January 1, 2004, and that I've added the comment "Hot" to. And to top it off, it's limited to 25 songs, selected by the most recently played.

You can do the same, using an erudite selection of conditions, to make magical smart playlists fill with music. Trial and error will show you what works; when you find nothing in your playlist, you'll have added one condition that narrows down the search too much.

Deleting Playlists

Welcome to the shortest section in the book. When you want to delete a playlist, select it and press Delete. If your playlist isn't empty, you'll see an alert asking if you're sure you want to delete the playlist. You can click Cancel if you've made a mistake, or click Yes to remove it.

If you're a fan of right-clicking or Control-clicking, just do that on the playlist you want to remove, and select Clear from the contextual menu.

Sorting Playlists

The Source list in iTunes shows all the music sources available (see Figure 1-21): first your Library, then Radio, the Music Store, then shared music if any (see

Figure 1-21

The Source list in iTunes, showing the different types of sources available

Source
Library
Party Shuffle
Radio
Music Store
Kirk's Music
60's Music
My Top Rated
Recently Played
Top 25 Most Played
Bill Evans – Live at the Village Van
Bob Weir – Weir Here
Brian Eno – Discreet Music
Lou Reed – Perfect Night
Lully – Persée
The Return Of Durutti Column

Sharing Music on Your Local Network for more on sharing your music), then smart playlists, in alphabetical order, and finally all your regular playlists, also in alphabetical order. You'll also see your iPod in this list if it's connected to your computer.

You have no control over the way this list is sorted. The first few sources are fixed—Library, Party Shuffle, Radio, Music Store—then comes shared music and playlists. Smart playlists are at the top, and the only way you can change their order is by changing their names. This is also the case for normal playlists.

Spotting Smart Playlists on your iPod

Using nonalphabetic characters can reorder your playlists and help you get to your favorites more quickly, but there's another reason to do so. While your smart playlists have different icons in iTunes, there are no icons on the iPod. There's no way of telling a smart playlist from a normal playlist when looking at your iPod's screen. I use asterisks in front of all my smart playlists so I can spot them at a glance on my iPod. You could use any character that stands out, as long as it comes before alphabetic characters in the sort order: how about a &, or a @, or even a !.

However, you can use a few tricks to help sort them more easily, adding some of your favorite playlists to the top of the list. Since the sort order is alphabetical, the easiest way to have a playlist appear at the beginning of the list is to start its name with a character that's higher up in the sort order. Other than letters (starting playlists with "a", "b", etc.), you can use characters like a hyphen (-), an asterisk (*), a slash (/), or a plus sign (+).

Exporting Playlists and Library Information

While you certainly back up your files (you do, don't you?) in case of data loss or corruption, you might want to back up your playlists as well. If your iTunes library files get corrupted, you may lose those playlists that took so long to create.

To do this, click a playlist to select it, then select File > Export Song List. Select XML from the Format popup menu, and save the file where you want. (If you just want to save a list of songs, to send to a friend or to use to print a CD label, select Plain Text from the popup menu.) If your playlist gets messed up, or if you lose it somehow, you can reimport it, and as long as you have the same songs in your library, iTunes acts as if it were never gone.

Not only does this make it easier to access your favorite playlists when using iTunes, but it helps you with your iPod as well: You won't need to scroll as much to get to any playlists named with these characters.

The Party Shuffle Playlist

Introduced in iTunes 4.5, the Party Shuffle playlist is like a random playlist on Viagra. It automatically selects songs from your library, according to the number you choose, and you can limit this choice to certain playlists. You can also add songs to this playlist or delete songs in its queue at any time.

This playlist only works with iTunes; it doesn't sync to your iPod. So it's really designed, as it suggests, for parties, when you'll want to use your computer, connected to speakers or a stereo, to provide music for your revelry. Though as one fervent user of the Party Shuffle pointed out on a mailing list, "Some parties only require two people and some Barry White tunes."

Take a look at Figure 1-22, which shows a Party Shuffle playlist. You can see a selection of music from my iTunes music library.

Figure 1-22

A Party Shuffle playlist selects tunes from among your recently played songs and some others at random.

At the bottom of the window in Figure 1-22, you can see how you control the Party Shuffle's selections. First, you can select a source. By default, this is your Library, but you can select a single playlist as well. You could, for example, create one playlist with all the music you'd like for your party, then select that as a source; this would avoid, for example, your Alvin and the Chipmunks songs coming up in the queue.

Next, you can choose to Play Higher Rated Songs More Often. If you rate your songs, this is a good idea; if not, this won't have any effect on the Party Shuffle playlist.

By default, the Party Shuffle displays five "recently played" songs; it would be more correct to call these "just played," since it shows the previous songs in case you want to find out what they are. It also displays 15 "upcoming" songs, or songs in the queue. You can change either of these numbers from the popup menus at the bottom of the window. If you don't want to see any songs you've already heard, set that to 0. If you want to see more upcoming songs, you can raise that number to as many as 100. Think of this as a jukebox, where you can see the songs that other people have selected when they put their quarters in the slot.

So, let's say you get a selection like the one in Figure 1-22. If you look at the songs, you'll see that there's one, near the middle, that's kind of long; it's the first act of Persée, an opera by Lully. Great tunes, but maybe not for parties. So if you don't want that one in the list, just select it and press Delete. This doesn't delete the track from your library, but removes it from the Party Shuffle playlist. When you do this, another song pops in to take its place. If you don't want to hear the current song, click the Next button, and it goes away, with the next song in the queue popping in to take its place.

If you want to change the order of your songs, just select one or more of them and drag them up or down in the list. The song that's covered by the blue 3-D highlighting is the current song. If you delete that one, the playlist stops.

There's another way to change the overall playlist. See the Refresh button at the top of the window in Figure 1-22? Just click that to change all the songs, with the exception of the current song, if it's being played; songs you've already heard, if any are displayed; and songs you've added manually to the Party Shuffle playlist. Don't like the selection? Click Refresh again. Let the randomness of the Party Shuffle playlist choose your music, and enjoy the serendipity of some of the relations among songs.

Upcoming songs are selected at random; however, if you want to add songs to the Party Shuffle playlist, just browse through your library or your other playlists and drag the songs you want to add. You can also right-click (Windows, or Mac with multibutton mouse) or Control-click (Mac) a song and select Play Next in Party Shuffle, to cue the song up to follow the current song, or Add to Party Shuffle, to add it to the end of the list.

The Party Shuffle playlist is not only for parties; it's a good way to turn your computer into a personal radio station, with no talk and no commercials. You've got plenty of time to see what's coming up, to nix the songs you don't want to hear, and to add the ones you feel like listening to. You may even find that this is your favorite way of listening to music with iTunes.

TOOL KIT

Creating a Smart Playlist as Your Party Shuffle Source

If you've got eclectic musical tastes, you may have lots of tunes in your iTunes music library that cover many genres. In addition, if you listen to audiobooks, you'll have spoken word tracks as well. If you use the Party Shuffle playlist, you can create some smart playlists that result in better selections than the purely random ones made by default from your library.

For example, say you want to listen to only your jazz and blues tunes; make a smart playlist with all the songs from these genres. Or say you want a playlist with no classical music or audiobooks; make a smart playlist with all songs that are not in these genres.

But you can only choose one source—either your library or one playlist—for the Party Shuffle playlist, so use your imagination. Try out some smart playlists that limit your selections to genres or other conditions, and you'll find that you can change your personal virtual radio station by merely selecting a new source for your Party Shuffle playlist.

The Selection Playlist

Some people have 80GB of music and a 20GB iPod. This is a problem. If you've got more music in your iTunes music library than your iPod can hold, the first time you sync your iPod, iTunes can create a special "selection" playlist. While many users of white iPods won't have this problem, those with an iPod mini will be confronted with it. Also, if you have a white iPod and purchase a mini, you'll run up against this as well.

When you connect your iPod for the first time, you'll see a message saying the following:

> The iPod "<your iPod's name>" does not have enough space to hold all of the songs in your music library. For your convenience, iTunes has created a new playlist named "<your iPod's name> Selection" which contains a selection of songs from your music library that will fit on this iPod. You may change the songs in this playlist at any time. Your iPod will be automatically updated with this playlist every time it is connected.

If you click OK, iTunes goes ahead and selects songs among the most-played and highest-rated songs and fills up your iPod. You can manually change this selection at any time, but the downside is that all the music is in a single playlist, and iTunes only copies individual songs, not playlists, to your iPod. It does, however, copy entire albums as much as possible, so you'll be able to browse by artist and album and choose your music that way. For better control, use manual management of your iPod; see All about Your iTunes Music Library for more on manually managing your playlists. Or buy another iPod...

BLOG: Playlists 101

he following is a transcript of an actual event. The names have been changed to protect the obviously dumb.

Teacher: Okay, class, listen up. Sshhh, quiet down. It's time to talk about your homework. Last week I asked you all to think about how you use playlists with iTunes, and make some notes to present to the class. I'm sure you all did your homework as usual.

(Snickers from the class.)

Teacher: Except you, Waldo. I know; your piranha ate it.

(More laughter.)

Teacher: So, who wants to start and tell me how you use your playlists?

(Silence, for about 30 seconds.)

Teacher: Come on, boys and girls, I know you all use iTunes and you all have iPods, so let's talk about your playlists. This is more than just homework; you can help your classmates use playlists better. There, Fred, I see you're raising your hand timidly in the back. Enlighten us.

Fred: Um, well, all my playlists are albums that I've ripped from my CD collection.

Teacher: Very good, Fred, that's the simplest way to create playlists. Jeannie, what about you?

Jeannie: Well, Mr. Whipple, I have some album playlists, like Fred, but I also have a lot of live concerts, so I've got lots of playlists that are shows by my favorite bands.

Teacher: Good point, Jeannie. Now, does anyone use smart playlists? Ah, Jonathan; you're finally going to grace us with your contribution.

Jonathan: Well, Teach, I've got one playlist.

Teacher: Just one?

Jonathan: Yep. It's smart.

Voice from the back of the class: Smarter than you.

(Laughter.)

Jonathan: Yeah, right. Anyway, I've got one playlist, and it plays all my songs.

Teacher: All of them?

Jonathan: Yeah, it just plays songs I haven't listened to in a week, and plays them at random.

Teacher: And you have no other playlists?

Jonathan: No. Why, should I?

(Much laughter.)

Teacher: No, Jonathan, that's fine. So, anyone else? How about you, Myrtle?

Myrtle: Well, sir, since I listen to a lot of classical music, it wouldn't make much sense to have playlists by album. I have lots of playlists by composer, and since I join my tracks when I rip CDs, I have each work in a single track. So, a Beethoven string quartet, even if it's four movements, is just one track.

Teacher: That's a good idea, Myrtle. So, what about your playlists?

Myrtle: Well, a lot of them are smart playlists that pick symphonies or concertos at random, but all by the same composer.

Teacher: Excellent idea, Myrtle. So, who else wants to contribute? How about you, Tom?

Tom: Well, I have all kinds of smart playlists based on my favorite tunes by genre. I have one for each genre I like—rock, ambient, techno, and so on—and each one has all my five-star rated songs.

Teacher: That's a good idea too. Anything else?

Tom: Yeah, I also have one called "New Songs." It just contains songs I've added in the past week. Since I add a lot of songs, especially ones I buy online, it lets me check out the new tunes and rate them as I listen.

Teacher: Thanks, Tom. Well, well, is that Waldo raising his hand?

(Laughter.)

Teacher: Go ahead, Waldo, you have something to add to this discussion?

Waldo: Yeah, man. I mean, like, sure. I've, like, researched the whole deal about playlists, man, and I've, like, got this down.

(More laughter.)

Waldo: Yeah, yeah, go ahead and laugh. Anyway, here's what I do. I've got a bunch of playlists by album, but I've also got a Favorites playlist, which is only five-star songs; an Oldies playlist, which is only songs I haven't listened to in at least six months; and a Random playlist, which plays anything at random. All these playlists are limited to one hour, because I don't usually listen to music longer than that. But then I've got smart playlists by genre, for all the genres I have (well, hard rock, industrial, and techno), and they're limited to two hours, for when I'm partying.

Class: Yeah! Party!

Teacher: Students, calm down. Thank you, Waldo, that was very enlightening.

Waldo: Like, yeah. Sure.

Teacher: Anyone else, before we move on to other things?

Alice: Yeah, I've got some ideas.

Teacher: Go ahead, Alice.

Alice: Well, I've got an iPod mini, and it's too small to hold all my music. So I manage my library manually, and I have a half-dozen playlists (each limited to five hundred megabytes)—one for my favorites, another for new songs, one for mellow music, and a few others. They all select music at random from my iTunes library, which is about sixty gigabytes. Since that takes up three gigabytes, I still have some room for a few of my favorite albums, but I change them every few days.

Teacher: Thank you, Alice. Well, class, it looks like you all understand playlists very well. I'm very happy to see that you've been doing your homework.

(Bell rings.)

Teacher: Have a nice weekend, everybody.

Smart Playlists and Classical Music

DO OR DIE:

>> Use smart playlists to leverage your classical music collection

've got a confession to make: I like classical music. And I like rock, jazz, ambient, blues, and lots of other types of music. Unlike most forms of music, however, classical music doesn't fit well into the iTunes song model. But after thinking out of the box, I discover that iTunes and the iPod can make classical music listening more interesting. The key is setting up smart playlists that play back music in random order.

At first glance, this may seem to be a heresy—after all, classical music isn't meant to be listened to with the Shuffle button pressed on your CD player. But there is a way of leveraging this function to enhance your listening.

Let me give you a couple of concrete examples. I have lots of box sets of classical music, some of which contain dozens of discs. There are two in particular that I ripped with iTunes to listen to on my iPod: The first is Dietrich Fischer-Dieskau's memorable recordings of Schubert lieder; the second is a set of Haydn symphonies by Adam Fischer and his Austro-Hungarian Haydn Orchestra. The Schubert set is 21 CDs (though I only use 18 of them in a random playlist, since the other three contain song cycles meant to be listened to in order), and the Haydn set is 33 CDs. (For information, the Schubert takes up about 1.5GB and the Haydn 2.4GB, ripped at 160bps AAC.)

For the Schubert, setting up a smart playlist was simple: I have it set to play 50 random songs that I haven't listened to in the last three months, guaranteeing that whenever I want to listen to some of these lieder, I'll get a playlist of two hours or more of songs I haven't heard recently. I don't listen to this music every day, and it takes a few months to get through the more than 400 songs, or over

ESSENTIAL MUSIC

Marin Marais' "Le Badinage"

I've always found the task of finding "the best one" a difficult exercise. This is certainly compounded when it comes to music. There are so many different styles, and music is a subject that has accompanied human beings since the dawn of time.

As a professional musician who has eclectic tastes, I find this undertaking even more arduous. I play baroque music on the viola da gamba but listen to jazz. However, if I reflect about it, there is one piece of music that has accompanied me for almost 30 years, faultlessly.

"Le Badinage," by Marin Marais. I first heard this piece more or less by happenstance in my second year as a viola da gamba student at Boston's New England Conservatory. One of my teachers brought in a recording by a Spaniard—Jordi Savall, who was accompanied by a theorbo, an early ancestor of the guitar. I had never heard such sonorities, such diversified nuances, such music.

Afterward my private teacher gave me one of Savall's recordings, and I proceeded to the listening library. I was so moved by Savall's playing of Marais that I raced through the crowded corridors of this monumental building and pounced on the first familiar face. "You *must* come and hear this." Immediately afterward, I purchased every existing Jordi Savall recording and would play the "Badinage" on my hi-fi every night before going to sleep.

The day of my wedding in Paris on the 27th December, 1985, I sat there with my viol, going over and over the theme to "Le Badinage" until my to-be wife and sister-in-law begged me to stop and proceed to the city hall.

Twenty years later, this same piece has become part of my standard repertoire. I never tire of it, and as the years pass, it reveals more of its special secrets. It is truly a masterpiece, music of the spheres, and belongs on the Mount Olympus of musical works.

➤ Jonathan Dunford (http://www.a2violes.com) plays viola da gamba, and performs, records, publishes, teaches, and lectures around the world. An American, he has lived in Paris, France, since 1985.

21 hours of music. With this smart playlist, I don't always hear the same songs, which I might if I were to listen to the CDs themselves, and I hear them in random order, increasing the variety of the music.

For the Haydn symphonies, it took a bit more work. I joined the tracks of each symphony (selecting the tracks and selecting Join CD Tracks for each symphony before ripping the CDs), and my smart playlist is set to play four symphonies among the least recently played. I won't hear the same symphony for a while, unless I listen to this playlist over and over for more than 36 hours. As with operas, you can't select individual movements, but if the CDDB information is correct, you'll see the names of the movements in the joined track name.

This flexibility, using smart playlists, makes it much easier to listen to large sets of classical music, and allows me to discover a lot more music than I normally would if I were to listen to each CD one after another. It also offers more interesting juxtapositions than the numerical order of the Haydn symphonies or the chronological order of the Schubert lieder.

For some types of music it can be a bit more complicated to set up playlists correctly, since there may be tracks that should be listened to in pairs. I have a set of keyboard music of William Byrd, performed by Davitt Moroney, and some of the pieces are paired. This requires that you check the liner notes before ripping, and join any such pairs together to listen to the music the way it was intended.

So, with the correct approach, the iPod is a great device for listening to classical music, even if you don't use it on the go. Just rip all the CDs you want, create playlists, and plug it into your stereo at home. (Or, of course, if your computer is close to your stereo, you can use iTunes to do the same thing.) You'll be able to listen to all your operas, or your biggest box sets, with greater flexibility by mastering smart playlists.

Buying Music from the iTunes Music Store

have seen the future of music: It's the iTunes Music Store. Or at least something very similar to it. Here's why.

Problem: People want to buy music differently. They don't necessarily want to buy entire albums, since sometimes only one or two songs appeal to them.

Solution: Purchase individual songs, and not on CD-singles, which are too expensive for what they contain.

Problem: People want to get their music now. They don't want to have to go to a store or wait for an online dealer to ship a CD.

Solution: Instant downloads of music over the Internet.

Problem: People are tired of paying onerous prices for CDs, when they know that the artists (the ones who the RIAA claims they are defending) don't get much of the swag.

Solution: Lower prices for downloaded music. You don't pay for shipping, inventory, and all the other expenses. (Though I doubt that the artists get much more at the end of the day.)

DO OR DIE:

>> How the iTunes Music Store (ITMS) is revolutionary

>> Setting up an account and buying music from the iTunes Music Store

>> Managing your purchased music

WANT TO SEE MORE AT THE ITUNES MUSIC STORE?
When you look at the iTunes Music Store in iTunes, you're really looking at Web pages. iTunes just renders the store's Web pages

UNDER
THE
HOOD

ESSENTIAL MUSIC

Frank Zappa

One Size Fits All, Just Another Band from L.A., Roxy and Elsewhere, Joe's Garage, and everything else from his discography, with few exceptions, would make my wish list.

Picking one essential artist (to the exclusion of *all* others) is a very difficult task. Especially to someone who likes *all* music in one form or another. It took me about two days to come to a decision—and even now I am plagued by guilt just thinking about everyone else who has been summarily kicked to the curb by this exercise!

One of my all-time favorite musicians and composers was the final choice because he had so much going for him: classical composition roots, blues inspiration, attention to detail, tremendous catalog, outstanding personal talent on his chosen instrument, complete irreverence (a huge bonus), political wit, and a love for greasy rock as well as highbrow jazz.

One Size Fits All is a perfect example of an album that blends genius composition, technical virtuosity, and wacko humor. To balance all of these disparate elements and actually maintain a career in the music business is amazing to me. I can honestly say that the planet would be a much different place without him.

Thank you, Frank!

➤ Chuck Garvey plays guitar with moe. (www.moe.org).

Problem: People want to do all this legally. (Yes, a lot of people *do* want to pay for their music.)

Solution: An online service such as the iTunes Music Store lets you get music over the Internet and generate good karma.

I'm not trying to tout the ITMS, but Apple's got it right. The first time I used it, I was amazed by its simplicity. I don't buy singles myself, but my 14-year-old son, Perceval, is mostly interested in individual songs he hears on the radio. While he does buy the occasional CD, he is often disappointed by all but a few tracks.

So the first time we went to the ITMS, he bought ten songs. Since we have a fast Internet connection, they downloaded faster than we could notice (while searching for other songs, the first ones were downloading in the background). In less than a half hour of searching and buying, he had ten songs, and I burned a CD for him.

Some people say that iTunes is a Trojan horse. It gives you great functions for managing your music, and especially for getting music to your iPod, but also makes it easy, perhaps too easy, for you to spend money at the ITMS. Perhaps. If you don't want to use the ITMS, you certainly don't have to, but as things are at press time, it's the easiest and most flexible online music service.

Setting Up an iTunes Music Store Account

To enter the ITMS, click the Music Store icon in the iTunes Source list. If you don't have an account with the ITMS yet, you need to set one up. As with any Web site, you need to enter a user name and password, then your address and credit card info. Read the fine print in the license agreement; then, when you've finished the paperwork, you'll have an account (Figure 1-23), and you can enter the store.

and displays them. The ITMS layout is optimized for a 1024x768 screen resolution and assumes that you have your Source list displayed at the left of your iTunes window.

Figure 1-23

After you've entered all the required information, you'll be able to enter the store and start spending your hard-earned money. Click Done to start buying music.

Browsing for Music

When you enter the ITMS, you'll see something like Figure 1-24. This main page (think of the ITMS as a Web site, with a home page and clickable links) shows new releases, specials, and the usual graphics to attract you to featured items.

All you need to do to check out a song is click; you can click album links, graphics, text links, or anything else. It's really a no-brainer.

The best thing about the ITMS is that you can get a 30-second preview of any song. Click a song name to view its page (either you'll see the song alone, or you'll

FAQ

What Can You Do with Your iTunes Music Store Purchases?

Music you purchase from the iTunes Music Store is provided in special AAC files with digital rights management technology. You are allowed to do the following with your music files:

- Listen to your music with iTunes on up to five computers (Macs and/or PCs)
- Copy your music to your iPod
- Burn your music to CD as many times as you want, though you can only burn an unchanged playlist seven times

---

If you have a smaller screen, or if you just want more room for the ITMS window, just double-click Music Store in the Source list. This opens the ITMS in its own window and gives you more room to see its content.

72

Figure 1-24

The main page of the iTunes Music Store, one day in May 2004

go to the page for its album), then double-click its title. iTunes starts playing the preview as soon as enough music is downloaded onto your computer; the faster your connection, the sooner you'll hear the preview.

Nixing the iTunes Music Store

If you don't plan to use the iTunes Music Store and don't want to see its icon in the iTunes Source list, just go into the iTunes preferences, click the Store tab, and uncheck Show iTunes Music Store. You won't see the icon anymore. If you change your mind, you can recheck this option at any time to have access to the store.

There are a few things to be aware of. First, iTunes is set, by default, to use 1-Click purchasing. This means that you click a Buy button next to a song or an album, and you purchase and download the music right away. (You do see a dia-

You can also view any of your sources in this manner—just double-click them to get a wider view of your iPod, your playlists, someone's shared music, or the radio station list.

iTunes

Search Music Store   Browse

Account:

Shopping Cart

Recommendations based on the items in your cart

Feels Like Home	**Me and Mr. Johnson**
Norah Jones	Eric Clapton
Genre: Vocal	Genre: Blues
$12.87 (ADD ALBUM)	$9.99 (ADD ALBUM)

Exile on Main Street
The Rolling Stones
Genre: Rock
$13.99 (ADD ALBUM)

6- and 12- String Guitar
Leo Kottke
Genre: Folk
$9.99 (ADD ALBUM)

The Gospel of the Blues (Re...
Sister Rosetta Tharpe
Genre: Inspirational
$9.99 (ADD ALBUM)

The Lost Tapes
Muddy Waters
Genre: Blues
$9.99 (ADD ALBUM)

Song Name	Time	Artist	Album	Genre	Price	
▶ The Bluebird Recordings 19...		Memphis Slim	The Bluebird Recordi...	Blues	$9.99	BUY
▶ The Bluebird Recordings 19...		Sonny Boy Williamso...	The Bluebird Recordi...	Blues	$9.99	BUY
▶ When the Sun Goes Down,		Sonny Boy Williamso...	When the Sun Goes ...	Blues	$9.99	BUY
▶ When the Sun Goes Down: B...		Blind Willie McTell	When the Sun Goes ...	Blues	$9.99	BUY
▶ Dark Was the Night		Blind Willie Johnson	Dark Was the Night	Blues	$9.90	BUY
▶ Avalon Blues - The Complet...		Mississippi John Hurt	Avalon Blues - The C...	Blues	$9.90	BUY
▶ Personal Standards		The Alan Broadbent	Personal Standards	Jazz	$8.91	BUY

Total: $68.67 + applicable sales tax   (BUY NOW)

127 songs

Source
Library
Party Shuffle
Radio
Music Store
  Shopping Cart
  Purchased Music
60's Music
My Top Rated
Recently Played
Top 25 Most Played

Figure 1-25

When you use a shopping cart, you got to make sure you really want to buy the music you've selected.

log asking if you're sure you want to do this, but if you check Don't Warn Me about Buying Songs Again in this dialog at any time, it won't come back.) So if you slip, and click in the wrong place, you'll end up buying music you may not want.

You can change this to use a shopping cart (see Figure 1-25). Go to the iTunes preferences (iTunes > Preferences on Mac, or Edit > Preferences on Windows), click the Store tab, then check Buy using a Shopping Cart. This uses the standard shopping cart metaphor, and you'll see Add buttons instead of Buy buttons. You'll be able to review your selections before actually purchasing them.

From the shopping cart, click Buy Now to purchase the songs and start downloading them.

Check the other options available in the Store preferences. You can have your songs start playing after download by checking Play Songs after Downloading, and if you have a slow network connection, check Load Complete Preview before Playing. This loads the entire 30-second preview of a song before it starts playing, so you don't get a choppy playback.

After You Purchase Music from the iTunes Music Store

When you buy songs from the ITMS, they are downloaded to your iTunes Music folder and organized by artist, then by album. They are added to your library, and you can see them if you click Library in the Source list and search for them. But they also get added to a special playlist called Purchased Music. (See Figure 1-26.)

Once you've purchased songs, you can do what you want with them (within limits). You can create a new playlist, add them to existing playlists, burn them to CDs, or copy them to your iPod.

It's a good idea to back up your purchased music, and to do it as soon as you can. For if you lose your songs, you can't get them back—Apple doesn't let you download the music again. So you should either burn a CD with your purchased music as soon as you have enough to fill a CD (see Burning CDs and DVDS with iTunes for more on burning CDs and on how to easily back up your purchased music), or copy them to another hard disk or another computer.

Figure 1-26

The Purchased Music playlist contains all the songs you buy from the iTunes Music Store. You can see above that some songs have been downloaded, and others are being downloaded to this playlist.

FAQ

What If You Lose Your Internet Connection While Downloading?

Bummer. You really wanted to hear that new album, but your connection went down while you were downloading the songs. Hey, wait a minute—does that mean you lost the songs?

Nope. Just select Advanced > Check for Purchased Music, when you get your connection back, and iTunes will continue downloading any songs that you've purchased which haven't made it to your computer.

Authorizing Your Computers

As I mentioned earlier, ITMS AAC files contain digital rights management information, which identifies the files as belonging to you, the original purchaser. If you look back at Figure 1-13, which shows information for a purchased track, you'll see that the name and account name of the purchaser are stored in the track.

The ITMS lets you play your songs on up to five computers, and these can be any mix of Macs and/or PCs. The first time you try to play a song on a computer that didn't buy the music, you'll be prompted to enter your account name and password. If you have multiple computers, and you want to play your ITMS music, you need to authorize them in this way.

However, you can deauthorize your computers at any time, as long as you have an active Internet connection. So if you have six computers at home and want to use one to play your ITMS music temporarily, you can deauthorize one of your other computers and authorize the sixth one. (Though not many people have that many computers at home.) To do this, select Advanced > Deauthorize Computer. You'll see a dialog, as in Figure 1-27, asking you whether you want to Deauthorize the computer for your Music Store Account or for your Audible Account. (See Listening to Audiobooks with iTunes for more on Audible.com audiobooks.)

Check which account you want to deauthorize, then click OK. You'll be prompted to enter your password to deauthorize the computer.

The ITMS Doesn't Have Everything

Alas, the biggest problem with the ITMS is that it doesn't have everything I want. I have eclectic tastes, and a lot of my favorite artists are absent. But I give Apple the benefit of the doubt: They tried to get this store off the ground before all the labels were convinced that it would work, and they've got an astounding range of music. I think that, given time, more labels and artists will join the ITMS. I only hope more independent labels make the move, so I can find more music that I like, and so others can discover some great tunes that are hidden behind the stacks of songs by the big names and best sellers.

Figure 1-27
*This dialog
lets you deau-
thorize your
computer so
you can play
your music
on another
computer.*

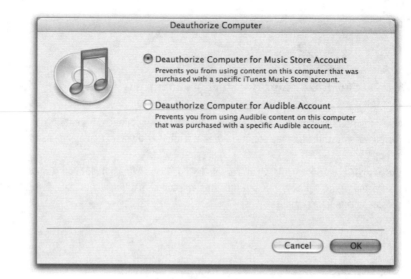

Figure 1-27
*This dialog
lets you deau-
thorize your
computer so
you can play
your music
on another
computer.*

You can easily reauthorize your computer at any time, as long as you can
connect to the Internet. Just try to play an ITMS song, and you'll see a dialog
asking you to enter your account name and password. If, by any chance,
you've already authorized three computers, iTunes will tell you so.

Deauthorize Your Computer Before You Dispose of It

It may seem like a no-brainer, but lots of people sell, give away, or otherwise dispose of their computers and don't consider that these computers may have been
authorized or activated for specific software.

  If you dispose of a computer that has been authorized for the ITMS, you won't be
able to deauthorize it later (unless you can get in touch with the purchaser). While
they won't be able to use your account to buy music, you'll have one less computer
to play your music on.

  Make sure you deauthorize your computer if you give it away, sell it, destroy it,
or even send it for repairs. And if you lose an authorized computer, you'd better get
in touch with ITMS customer service and find out what to do.

Finding Music with iTunes Music Store Links

You'll probably have noticed the pesky little arrows next to your song, artist,
and album names in your iTunes music library. These are iTunes Music Store
links; click one, and iTunes takes you to the Music Store, showing you similar
music. This may be other albums by the same artist or similar artists' music.

This is a good way to discover new music, but these links display all over your library and playlists. If you want to remove them, select iTunes > Preferences, then click the General tab. Uncheck Show Links to Music Store. You'll have to manually search for music, or you can turn them back on if you need some advice on new tunes.

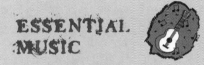

ESSENTIAL MUSIC

Bob Weir: "I'm infatuated with my iPod."

Bob Weir was guitarist with the Grateful Dead for some 30 years, until the untimely death of Jerry Garcia brought that long, strange trip to an end. The group continued as The Other Ones for a while, then morphed into The Dead, its current formation. At the same time, Bob Weir has maintained a solo career, recording and touring with his group Ratdog (http://www.rat-dog.com).

When I spoke with Bob Weir he made it very clear how he feels about his iPod: "I'm infatuated with my iPod," he said, and as he went on to extol its ability to provide random music. He dumps all his music on the iPod and uses the shuffle function to listen. "It's all stuff that I want to hear. You put it on shuffle, and you're almost always pleasantly surprised." And if he doesn't want to hear a song, he just presses the Next button to skip over it.

Weir currently has a 30GB iPod, with about 2,500 songs encoded at a high bit rate, and is planning on buying another one soon to have more music. He likes the ability to have his record collection and his own music on a portable device that he can easily take wherever he wants. Curiously, he's one musician that finds the iPod to be a great tool for his work: He can play songs for his band to introduce them to music he wants them to later play live.

He listens to the iPod everywhere: in his car, with a cassette adapter, when he's running, and when he's traveling, using Bose noise-canceling headphones (see Headphones for Your iPod).

So, what does Bob Weir listen to on his iPod? He shared his iTunes music library with me. While his "essential music" would be "anything by The Beatles from 1964," he's got music by the following: the Grateful Dead, the Jerry Garcia Band, Phil Lesh and Friends, The Beatles, Bob Dylan, the Dixie Chicks, Moby, John Coltrane, Marvin Gaye, Django Reinhardt, Tony Bennett, Louis Jordan, Billie Holiday, Lester Young, Howlin' Wolf, Bill Monroe, Bessie Smith, Ella Fitzgerald, OutKast, Radiohead, and more.

He's also got lots of classical music: Mozart, John Philip Sousa, Janacek, Charles Ives, Prokofiev, Wagner, Bartók, Stravinsky, and many others.

Weir has an eclectic choice of music on his iPod, but anyone who's a fan of the Grateful Dead won't be surprised, because this group found its influences in all types of music. His next step is to transfer all his LPs to his Mac so he can have his entire music collection available 24/7.

Share Your Favorites with an iMix

It's one thing to have your own tunes and listen to them, but one great thing about music is sharing it with your friends (and I don't mean through illegal copies...). With iTunes you can share your favorite playlist—or iMix—with your friends by uploading it to the iTunes Music Store.

Create a playlist with your favorite tunes, then publish it to the iTunes Music Store by clicking the arrow to the right of its name. Enter a title for the playlist, and add any notes you want to describe it. You can then click Tell a Friend to have the iTunes Music Store send an e-mail message to your friends so they can check out your playlist (and maybe even buy the tunes it contains).

Note that only those songs available from the iTunes Music Store will show up on the iMix. If you put a lot of songs in your playlist that aren't sold by Apple, your iMix will be pretty short, so make sure you include enough songs to make it worthwhile for your friends to check out the previews from the iTunes Music Store.

All about Your iTunes Music Library

In addition to being a jukebox, disc burner, and interface to your iPod, iTunes is a powerful organizational tool, and your iTunes music library is the guts of this part of the program. Using the tag information attached to your digital music files (see Tags and Track Info), iTunes maintains a database of all your songs and their locations on your hard disk. Your iTunes music library is like your record or CD shelf, or a box full of CDs. The difference is the voodoo under the hood that lets iTunes know what all your tracks are and where they come from.

By default, iTunes "organizes" your iTunes Music folder. This means that each time you add songs to your iTunes library, the program places them in folders and subfolders named after the artist and album, and iTunes numbers the tracks and adds their names, if these are not already applied to the files.

To maintain this organization, and to record any additional information you've added to your music library, such as ratings, iTunes uses two special files: the iTunes 4 Music Library file and the iTunes Music Library.xml file. (You may not see the file extension, depending on how you have your computer set up.) The former contains a database of all your songs and playlists, as well as some information about songs. If you delete this file, iTunes creates a new one the next time you launch the program, but you'll lose your playlists, song ratings, and some other information. The iTunes Music Library.xml file contains

DO OR DIE:

>> Understand your iTunes music library

>> Manage your library

>> Search and browse for tunes

OTHER THINGS YOU CAN DO AT THE iTUNES MUSIC STORE
Apple has tried to keep control of your eyes by adding lots of interesting things to the iTunes Music Store. It is conceivable that, in

UNDER THE HOOD

some of the information from the first file, but is used to make your music available to other programs. Both of these files are stored in your iTunes folder.

Toolkit: Where iTunes Stores Its Files

iTunes stores its library files in a fixed location, but you can change where your music is stored. Here is where iTunes files are kept on your computer:

Mac OS X:
- /Users/username/Music/iTunes/iTunes Music
- /Users/username/Music/iTunes/iTunes 4 Music Library
- /Users/username/Music/iTunes/iTunes Music Library.xml

Microsoft Windows:
- \Documents and Settings\username\My Documents\My Music\iTunes\iTunes Music
- \Documents and Settings\username\My Documents\My Music\iTunes\iTunes 4 Music Library.itl
- \Documents and Settings\username\My Documents\My Music\iTunes\iTunes Music Library.xml

iTunes stores your music files in the iTunes Music folder, which, as you can see in the Toolkit sidebar, is either in your Mac OS X Music folder or your Windows My Music folder. But this can be a problem for people with lots of music who want to back up their music files. If you have, say, 30GB of music files in your Home or My Documents folder, and store other files there as well, backing up these folders may be time-consuming. For this reason, you can change the location of the iTunes Music folder.

Open the iTunes preferences. (Select iTunes > Preferences on Mac, or Edit> Preferences on Windows.) Click the Advanced tab. As you can see in Figure 1-28, there is an iTunes Music Folder Location section on this tab, showing the current location.

Click Change, then find a new location for your iTunes Music folder. If you have more than one hard disk or partition, it's a good idea to use a second disk or partition for your music files. You'll probably have more space, and it will be easier to back up your files. If you only have one hard disk or partition, you're better off leaving the default setting.

But if you change your iTunes music location after you already have some music in your library, iTunes does not move the existing music. It creates a new library with all your songs linked to the old location, and imports new songs to the new location.

the future, Apple will offer even more content to view and purchase. After all, downloading movies will be easy once people have the appropriate bandwidth.

For now, at least at press time, you can view movie trailers and music videos from the iTunes Music Store. You can also check out Billboard charts

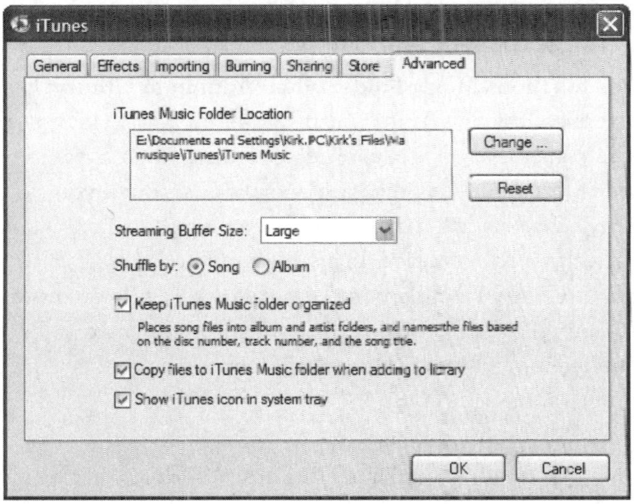

Figure 1-28

You can change the location of your iTunes Music folder, as well as other settings for your iTunes library, on this tab.

If you want to move your entire library, including songs you've already imported, move the iTunes Music folder manually to a new location, then select that folder in the preferences, as shown in Figure 1-28.

iTunes Music Library Settings

As you can see in Figure 1-28, there are other settings for your iTunes music library. It can be useful to uncheck these in some cases.

- **Keep iTunes Music Folder Organized:** When this is checked, iTunes copies all your music files to folders containing the artists' names and subfolders containing album names. If you import music that doesn't have artist and album tags, however, these files go in Unknown Artist and Unknown Album folders. For most people, this is not a problem, but if, for example, you're a fan of live bands whose music is freely (and legally) traded over the Internet, you'll be downloading files without tags. Unchecking this allows you to create your own folders. It takes a bit longer, but it makes it easier to find your tunes. You can always turn it back on when you rip CDs, to ensure that they get automatically organized according to artist and album. (If you're using iTunes for Windows, you may recall that the iTunes Setup Assistant offered to do this already. If you made your choice then, you can change it now, at

as well as charts for radio stations in hundreds of cities around the US. And you can send gift certificates or create monthly allowance accounts for people you want to allow to buy music, but who shouldn't have free rein with your credit card.

least for future music you add to your library. If you're a Mac user, here is where you choose.)

- **Copy Files to iTunes Music Folder when Adding to Library:** If you store all your music files in your iTunes Music folder, it's best to leave this checked. Whenever you double-click a song file, iTunes copies it into your iTunes Music Library folder in the appropriate subfolder. But if you store your files in several places, this will make unnecessary copies. You don't need to have your files in the iTunes Music Library folder; you can drag files and folders into iTunes from any location on your hard disk, but if you move or rename files or folders, iTunes might lose track of them. In my experience, it makes sense to at least keep them in a central location so you can back them up when you need to.

The remaining settings on this dialog are self-explanatory. The streaming buffer size depends on your network connection; the faster the connection, the higher the buffer. If you have a dialup connection, choose Small; a cable, DSL, or other broadband connection, choose Large.

The Shuffle By option lets you choose to have iTunes shuffle music by song or by album.

Finally, if you're using Windows, you have the option to Show iTunes Icon in System Tray for quick access. (As you've seen in Listening to Music with iTunes, this lets you control iTunes from the System Tray, so it's a good idea to leave it checked.)

Managing Your iTunes Music Library

I explained earlier that you have two options for managing your iTunes music library: Either you can let iTunes do everything, or you can do it yourself. If you've chosen the first option, just skip this section.

If you want to manage your library manually, you need to consider where you store your music files, and you then need to manually add them to your iTunes library. You've seen earlier in this topic that you can choose an alternate location for your iTunes Music folder. If you do this, iTunes still manages your music library; it just puts the files in a nondefault folder. But you can also keep your files in another folder or even in several folders. If you do this, you need to manually add your music to your iTunes library.

There are two ways to do this. First, you can click Library in the iTunes Source column, then just drag all your music files from their respective folders into the right-hand section of the window. iTunes records the location of all the files and adds them to your library.

The second way is to add your songs by folder, creating playlists, as explained in Working with Playlists. Dragging a folder into the Source column creates a playlist and adds the contents of the folder (and its subfolders, if any) to your library.

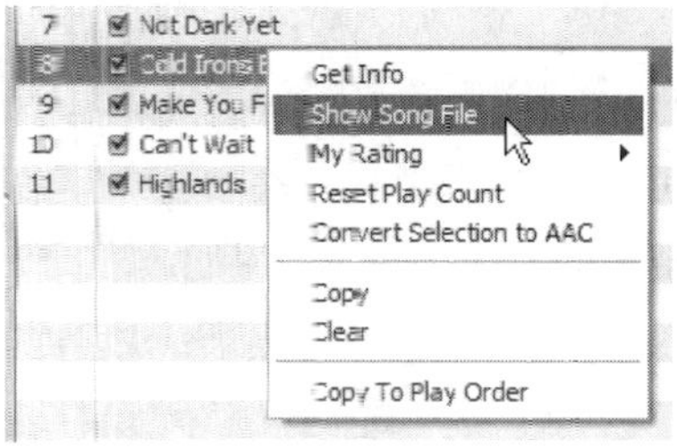

Figure 1-29

To find where a song file is stored, select Show Song File from the contextual menu.

If you store your music files in a central location—a hard disk or partition, or a specific folder—you'll always know where they are, but if you have files in different locations and then drag them into iTunes, you may not remember where they are located. If you ever want to see where a specific song file is located, right-click the name of a song (or Control-click on Mac, if you don't have a two-button mouse) and select Show Song File (see Figure 1-29). This opens the folder containing that file and selects it.

Managing your iTunes music library manually can be a headache, and I only recommend it for people who have a lot of music and who get it from different sources: ripping CDs on different computers, downloading legally shared live music, and so on. There may come a time when you find it easier to centralize all this music. If you want to move it all into your iTunes Music folder, select Advanced > Consolidate Library. This tells iTunes to copy all your song files to the iTunes Music folder, without deleting the original songs. This can take a while if you have a lot of music.

Consolidating your library is a one-way operation—you cannot undo it, and iTunes replaces the original pointers to your files and looks for all your music files in the iTunes Music folder. So make sure you really want to do this before you click Consolidate.

Browsing Your Library

When you want to find music in your iTunes music library, there are several ways you can do this. If you haven't created playlists when ripping your CDs, or dragged folders containing music files into iTunes, you can browse your library (see Figure 1-30), looking for individual songs by genre, artist, or album. Even if you have no playlists and just dumped all your music into iTunes without paying any attention to it, as long as the music has the right tags, it will show up here.

Clicking this button (or pressing Command-3 on Mac, or Control-3 on Windows) displays or hides the iTunes Browse pane (Figure 1-31).

Figure 1-30

To browse your library, click the Browse button.

Figure 1-31

The iTunes Browse pane, where you can browse your music library by genre, artist, or album

The iTunes Browse pane displays only those genres contained in your music library and all the artists you have music by. The Album column displays the albums that your songs come from, not only entire albums; if you only have one song from an album, it's still listed there.

You can find music by clicking any of the genres, artists, or albums. If you click a genre, only those artists and albums that belong to the genre display; you can further narrow down your search by clicking an album. In all cases, the bottom pane displays the songs that meet your selection.

Browsing Preferences

There are a couple of settings you can turn on or off to change the way you see music when browsing. Select iTunes > Preferences, then click General. If you check Show Genre when Browsing, you'll see the Genre column, as in Figure1-31. If you check Group Compilations when Browsing, your compilation albums won't be listed under each artist, but rather as compilations. If you don't check this, you may find hundreds of artists who you only have one song by; each one shows up in the Artists column, even if their songs are on a compilation.

Sorting Songs

Whenever you look at songs in your iTunes library or in a playlist, you see the songs' information listed in columns. In Figure 1-31, for example, you can see columns for Song Name, Time, Artist, Album, and Genre. You can sort your songs by any of these columns by clicking the header above the column. So, in Figure 1-31, you can see that the Album column is selected, and the songs are sorted in the order in which they appear on the albums. To change the sort order, just click the column again; the arrow at the end of the column will change direction, and the sort order will be the opposite. (Instead of alphabetical order, it will be reverse alphabetical order; or if you sort by time, it will sort by shortest to longest, instead of longest first.)

Searching for Songs in Your Library

Browsing is one way to find music, but if your song files don't have the appropriate tags (see Tags and Track Info for more on tags), it won't be listed according to the appropriate genre, artist, or album. Also, if you have a lot of music, it can be quicker to use iTunes' search function to find specific songs.

iTunes has a Search field (Figure 1-32) at the top of its window. Just enter text in this field—a word in a song title, the name of an artist, part of an album name, or a composer—and iTunes finds corresponding tracks as you type.

If you want to limit your search to a specific criterion, click the triangle next to the magnifying glass (Figure 1-33) and select one of the choices: Artists, Albums, Composers, or Songs. As you type, iTunes will only look for matches in the field you select. Note that iTunes can only find songs if their tag info has been filled in.

Figure 1-32

The iTunes Search field. Type a keyword, and iTunes displays corresponding tracks.

Figure 1-33

Narrow down your search by selecting an item from the popup menu.

If you have the Comment field displayed in your library or the current playlist, the popup menu allows you to search in your comments as well.

Deleting Songs

You thought that hard disk would be big enough, didn't you? When you bought your computer, you never thought that you'd want to put 100GB of music on your disk, and, all of a sudden, you're running out of space...

So it's time to do some spring-cleaning. You can easily delete your music by going to your iTunes Music folder, or wherever it's stored, and just deleting the files, but if you do this, they remain in your library. Not the actual files, of course, but pointers to them.

The best way to delete your songs is to do so from the main iTunes library. Either by using the Browse pane or by searching, find the songs you want to delete. Select them, then press the Delete key. iTunes first asks if you're sure you want to remove the selected items. Click Yes. If the music files are in your iTunes Music folder, the program then asks if you want to move the files to the Trash or the Recycle Bin. If you're sure you want to remove the files—if you're sure you have a backup or still have the original CD—you can click Yes. You can still retrieve the files from the Trash or the Recycle Bin, but that's your last chance.

If you're a mouse lover, you can also delete selected items by Control-clicking (Mac) or right-clicking (Windows) and selecting Clear from the contextual menu.

If you want to work without a net, press Command+Delete (Mac) or Shift+Delete (Windows) to delete songs without an alert. They'll get removed from your library and deleted at the same time, so make sure you really want to do this.

TOOL KIT

Finding Songs to Delete

If you need to make space, start by looking for the songs you listen to the least. Click Library in the Source column, then select Edit > View Options, and click Play Count. Click the top of the Play Count column, and you'll sort your songs by the number of times you've listened to them.

You can scroll up and down to see which songs you listen to most, and if you click the Play Count column header again, the sort order changes.

While the number of times you listen to songs is not the only criterion for deletion, when you need to make room on your hard disk, it's a good place to start.

Using the
iTunes Equalizer

As you listen to your music with iTunes, you'll find that there are limits to the sound quality you can get from your computer. Depending on what you use to listen to music—built-in speakers, external speakers, or headphones—you may want to adjust the sound so it sounds better.

iTunes has an equalizer that lets you adjust its output to one of 22 presets or create your own settings by adjusting ten frequency levels. You can use the equalizer for all your music, or you can apply presets to individual songs.

Start by displaying the Equalizer window. Click the Equalizer button (Figure 1-34) to display the Equalizer window.

The equalizer looks a lot like its hardware equivalent: There are sliders that let you adjust the overall volume (Preamp) and individual frequency ranges. If you want to use the equalizer, make sure the On box is checked, then select one of the presets from the popup menu.

iTunes offers 22 equalizer presets:

- Acoustic
- Bass Booster
- Bass Reducer
- Classical
- Dance
- Deep
- Electronic
- Flat
- Hip-Hop
- Jazz
- Latin
- Loudness
- Lounge
- Piano
- Pop
- R&B
- Rock
- Small Speakers
- Spoken Word
- Treble Booster
- Treble Reducer
- Vocal Booster

DO OR DIE:

>> Fine-tune your listening experience

>> Use global equalizer settings

>> Choose equalizer settings for individual songs

Figure 1-34

Click the Equalizer button (top) to display the Equalizer window (bottom).

Flat means that no changes are made to the sound. The Booster and Reducer settings do what they say; they boost the treble, bass, or vocals, or they reduce the treble or bass. These settings are good for specific types of speakers, or when you simply want more bass or treble. The Small Speakers setting is good for when you listen using built-in speakers on a laptop, or other small speakers.

The Manual setting lets you make your own adjustments. If you want to save your settings, click the popup menu and select Make Preset. Enter a name for your settings, then click OK. These settings are added to the popup menu, and you can select them at any time.

To rename or remove any custom settings, or rename or delete presets, click the popup menu and select Edit List. You'll be able to delete or rename any of the presets.

Applying Equalizer Settings to Individual Tracks

When you use the equalizer as I explained earlier, it applies to all your music. But not all your music sounds best with the same equalizer settings. Some music needs extra bass; other songs need mid-range sounds increased for vocals. iTunes lets you apply equalizer settings to individual tracks, and if you do this, these settings override any global settings you use. In addition, settings you apply to individual tracks get copied to your iPod, so the iPod can play the music back using the same settings.

There are three ways to apply equalizer presets to individual tracks. The first is to select a song, then select File > Get Info. Click the Options tab to display advanced options (Figure 1-35).

As you can see in Figure 1-35, you can choose an equalizer preset from the popup menu. You can also adjust the volume for the song using the slider at the top of the window, and you can change the Start Time and Stop Time at the bottom. (This is useful if you have live tracks with spoken introductions, for example.)

Another way to change the equalizer settings is to do so from the library or from a playlist display. You first need to display the Equalizer column. If this isn't displayed, select Edit > View Options, and check Equalizer, then click OK. The Equalizer column now displays, and it shows a popup menu for each song. Click this popup menu and select a setting (Figure 1-36).

Finally, you can easily apply equalizer settings to groups of songs. Select all the songs you want to apply the setting to—say, a playlist, or all songs of a specific album or genre—then select File > Get Info. iTunes asks if you are sure you want to display info for the multiple items. Click OK.

The Multiple Song Information window (Figure 1-37) lets you apply changes to certain tags. You can also choose an equalizer preset from the popup menu at the bottom of the window.

Select your preset, make any volume adjustments you want, and click OK. This is a good way to apply equalizer presets to entire albums or even all the music by a given artist or a given genre. Just search for the album, artist, or genre; select all the songs; and choose your equalizer setting.

Figure 1-37

The Multiple Song Information window lets you apply equalizer presets, and volume adjustments, to several songs at a time.

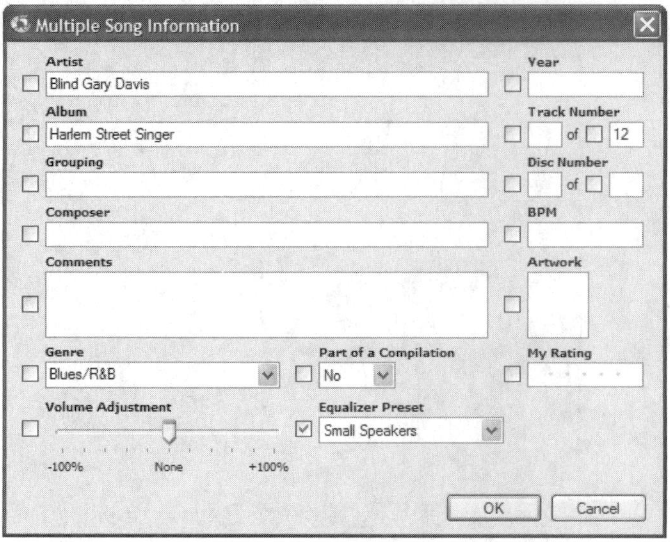

Multiple Song Information

Artist
Blind Gary Davis

Album
Harlem Street Singer

Grouping

Composer

Comments

Genre
Blues/R&B

Part of a Compilation
No

Volume Adjustment
-100%   None   +100%

Year

Track Number
of   12

Disc Number
of

BPM

Artwork

My Rating

Equalizer Preset
Small Speakers

OK   Cancel

Listening to Internet Radio with iTunes

What do you do when you run out of music? Or when you want to discover some new tunes? Or just listen to someone else's playlist? Internet radio is a great way to broaden your horizons and discover tunes and artists you didn't know. In addition to all its other functions, iTunes is an Internet radio tuner. With more than 300 preset radio stations, you can find exactly what you want to hear. And even if you don't like any of these "built-in" stations, you can listen to others as well.

Internet radio offers an eclectic mix of stations, some with annoying commercials and others that are independent and free of ads. The types of programming available range from rock to blues, from rap to ambient, from talk to alternative.

To see which radio stations are available, click the Radio icon in the iTunes Source column. There are about 20 categories. Click the triangle next to one of them, and iTunes checks with the tuning service and displays the stations available in the category (Figure 1-38).

To listen to one of these radio stations, just double-click its name. iTunes will connect to the station, start buffering the stream, then start playing the music, showing the station and the current song in the display at the top of the window. In some cases, if a station has too many listeners, you won't be able to connect. If this occurs, iTunes displays a dialog telling you so.

DO OR DIE:

>> What to do when you're tired of listening to your music

>> Check out new tunes and genres

>> Listen to your favorite radio station when you're on the road

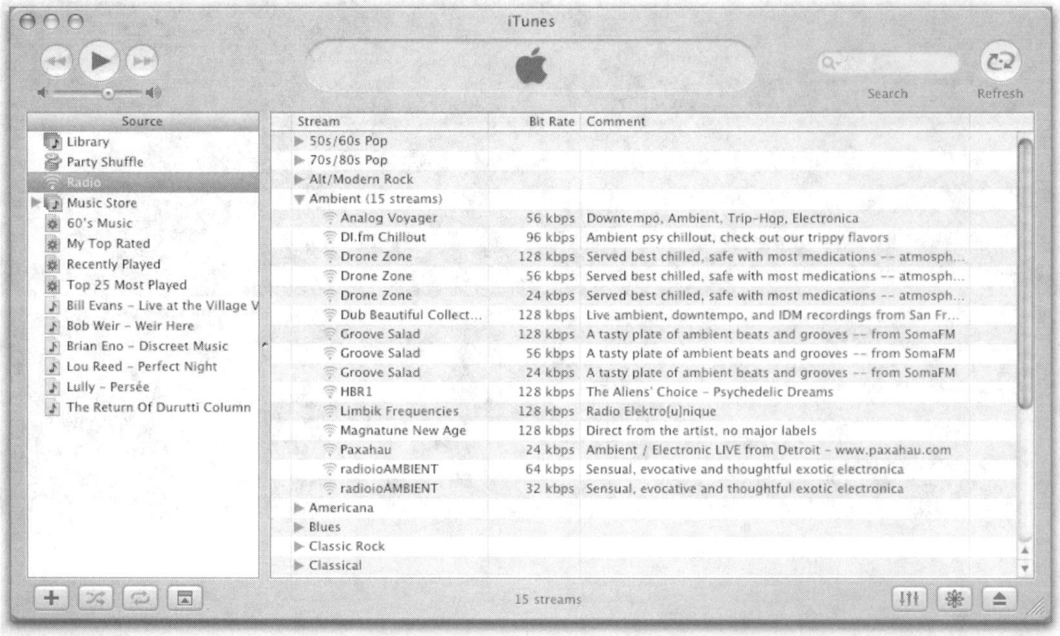

Figure 1-38

iTunes shows the radio stations in the selected category, as well as their bit rates and comments about their programming.

Not Enough Radio Stations in iTunes?

While iTunes offers lots of radio stations, you may find that there are not enough. Your particular tastes may not be well addressed, or you may just want to try out some others.

There are thousands of radio stations that stream music and talk over the Internet, and iTunes can play many of them. To find additional stations, start by checking out the Radio-Locator (http://www.radio-locator.com) or Radio Tower (http://www.radiotower.com), where you can search by format or country, or you can even find out if your favorite AM or FM station offers a stream by entering its call letters. This is especially practical if you're on the road and you want to catch your favorite team's game...

You'll notice, in Figure 1-38, that some stations offer several bit rates. If you're using a dialup connection, 56kbps is the fastest you can receive, and you might not even get that bit rate without some stalling. If you have a broadband connection, go for the highest bit rate available, since the higher the bit rate, the better the music sounds.

iTunes can play MP3 streams, which is just one of several types of streaming audio formats. When you find the radio station you want to listen to, look for an MP3 stream link. (Other formats include QuickTime, RealAudio, and Windows Media Player.)

If you want to listen to another radio station, you might be able to start listening with iTunes by simply clicking a link on the radio station's Web site. For some stations, you need to copy a URL available on the station's Web site. Do this, then go to iTunes and select Advanced > Open Stream. Paste the URL in this dialog, then press OK. You'll start hearing the radio station's stream.

When you start listening to a radio station with iTunes, it gets added to your library, so you don't need to look for the link again later. In fact, if you use iTunes to listen to Internet radio often, you can create a playlist for your radio stations so you can access them more easily.

TOOL KIT

Make a Radio Playlist

I listen to Internet radio stations often, and I have a Radio playlist in iTunes. I've dragged stations from the built-in list to this playlist, and added others from my library after opening streams manually.

In addition, I've set ratings for the radio stations, and sorted the playlist by rating, so my favorites are at the top of the list. If you find enough stations you like, think of creating a Radio playlist to save time tuning to your favorite stations.

Listening to Audiobooks with iTunes

While most people use iTunes and the iPod to rock to the beat, you can also use them to get your daily dose of literature. In fact, many people purchase iPods just for listening to audiobooks; it's probably the best device for listening to spoken word recordings, because you can pick up your listening where you stopped, and because you can store months of listening on even the smallest iPod. You can usually spot these people on the bus or train; they're the ones whose heads aren't rocking or swaying to music, and whose brows may be furrowed as they think while listening.

In case you're unfamiliar with them, audiobooks are recordings of books, read by professional readers, sometimes actors. These books range from abridged texts that last as little as an hour to full-length unabridged books (Tolstoy's *War and Peace*, for example, clocks in at over 62 hours). Some radio shows are also available for download, either directly from radio stations or from providers such as Audible.com.

In fact, Audible has set up a partnership with Apple, selling its audiobooks through the iTunes Music Store. You can choose from thousands of titles either at the ITMS (Figure 1-39) or directly from the Audible Web site (www.audible.com).

Audiobook sound files work the same as any other file purchased from the ITMS. If you buy an audiobook from Audible, you'll need to authorize your com-

---

AUDIBLE OR ITMS?
If you're just interested in listening to the occasional audiobook, the iTunes Music Store might be the easiest way for you to purchase

UNDER THE HOOD

Figure 1-39

The Audiobooks section of the iTunes Music Store looks the same as the music sections.

puter, as you do for the ITMS. You download the audiobook (which may be one or several files, depending on its length) using your Web browser, and you can either double-click it to add it to your iTunes music library, or if you manage your library manually, copy it to your iTunes Music folder, then drag it to your library. If you purchase an audiobook from the ITMS, it goes directly into your Purchased Music playlist, like any tunes you buy, and you can add it to any other playlist.

However, from here on in, things are a bit different. Since audiobook files are so long—up to about eight hours—you need to be able to stop and start listening again from the place you stopped. For this reason, audiobooks use a special type of AAC file that can be bookmarked. When you stop listening and switch to another track or playlist, your position is recorded. When you come back to the audiobook, you pick up where you left off.

Not only does the bookmark work in iTunes, but it also works on your iPod. And if you listen to an audiobook on your iPod and then sync it to your computer, the bookmark location is transferred to the computer. So you can

this content. But if you're a fan of audiobooks, you're probably better off going to Audible.com, where you can take out a monthly subscription.

Subscriptions give you one or two books a month, regardless of their retail price, which generally cuts your bill by about half. In addition, Audible.com

start listening to an audiobook on your computer, sync with your iPod, pick up where you stopped, listen on your iPod, sync again, and listen to more on your computer.

Importing Audiobooks

If you already own some audiobooks on CD you can import them as you do any other kind of music, then listen to them on your computer or your iPod. However, there is a tiny problem—when you import audio files to iTunes, they are not bookmarkable. You need to make a tiny change to the files (see the sidebar Making Bookmarkable Sound Files) so you can save bookmarks.

When importing audiobooks from CDs, you don't need the same fidelity as for music. You can change your import settings to a much lower bit rate—I generally use 64kbps AAC for audiobooks, though you could use an even lower bit rate if you really need to save space. Audible uses 32bps for their highest setting, and their files sound fine. You also don't generally need to have stereo files; this cuts down file size by another 50%.

TOOL KIT

Making Bookmarkable Sound Files

There is only a tiny difference between normal sound files and bookmarkable files. In fact, it's a cinch to make the change. While you wouldn't want to do this to your song files, it's almost essential if you import your own audiobooks from CDs. Note that this only works with AAC files, so make sure your Importing preferences are set to AAC if you want to do this.

If you already have audiobooks in MP3 format, you can convert them to AAC. Check your Importing preferences; make sure they are set to import in AAC format, and, for audiobooks, set the bit rate low, such as 64kbps. Then, select the audiobooks file(s) in iTunes and select Advanced > Convert Selection to AAC. iTunes will decompress the original MP3 files, then recompress them in AAC format. You'll then be able to make the resulting AAC files bookmarkable, as explained next.

If you use Windows, this is easy to do. AAC files have an .m4a extension. To make them bookmarkable, just change their extensions to .M4B. (You'll need to first set your computer to show file extensions; select Tools > Folder options, click the View tab, then uncheck Hide Extensions for Known File Types. You can recheck this after you've made your changes, if you don't want to see these extensions.)

If you use a Mac, you can download a simple AppleScript that makes the change for you. (For more on using AppleScripts with iTunes, see Tools for Doing More with iTunes.) Go to the Doug's AppleScripts for iTunes Web site (http://www.malcolmadams.com/itunes/index.php) and search for "Make Bookmarkable". Follow the instructions, and you'll have bookmarkable files in no time.

also offers more audio formats—these are files recorded at different qualities. If you have an iPod, you won't need to worry about this, since even the smallest iPod can hold several months of spoken word content at the highest quality (Audible's high–bit rate recordings take up about 14MB per hour). But

Some audiobooks on CD are recorded as many short tracks, to make it easier to navigate the CD. When importing audiobooks from CDs like this, you'll probably want to join the tracks. See Ripping Music for more on joining tracks. If you have some older audiobooks on tape, it's a bit more work to get them into iTunes. I discuss importing tapes and LPs in the topic Importing Analog Music.

FAQ

Can You Listen to Audiobooks in Other Formats?

Some Web sites sell audiobooks in MP3 format. You can import these files to iTunes the same way you import any other MP3 files. If you want to join these tracks into one long track, and you're using a Mac, another AppleScript can do the trick. Go to the Doug's AppleScripts for iTunes Web site (http://www.malcolmadams.com/itunes/index.php) and search for "Track Splicer."

If you're using Windows, you can get Twins File Merger, a shareware program (http://www.twins-software.com) which can join MP3 files as well as other types of files, such as text and video files. MP3 Splitter and Joiner (http://www.ezsoftmagic.com) offers similar functions and gives you even more control over the output and the MP3 file tags.

If you want to make these files bookmarkable, follow the instructions in the sidebar Making Bookmarkable Sound Files.

if you have another MP3 player, with limited memory, you can choose lower bit rates, which make for smaller files.

Check both locations, though, if you want to buy a specific book. Some books are cheaper on the ITMS than at the Audible Web site.

BLOG: Jean Shepherd, a Unique Comic Voice

Jean Shepherd was a great American humorist—a genius on a level with Mark Twain and James Thurber. Most people are probably familiar with his holiday movie, A Christmas Story, about a kid who wants a BB gun for Christmas and who nearly shoots his eye out.

Millions of families watch the movie every year on tape, DVD, or cable TV. But most people probably don't realize that it's Shep's voice we hear throughout and that the movie is based on some of the 23 stories he published in *Playboy* magazine. Rock music enthusiasts will find his 1965 *Playboy* interview with The Beatles of interest.

Shepherd was proud of his humorous stories, which were eventually published in his books *In God We Trust—All Others Pay Cash*; *Wanda Hickey's Night of Golden Memories—and Other Disasters*; *A Fistful of Fig Newtons*; and *The Ferrari in the Bedroom*. All of these books are still in print after a few decades and dozens of printings. He also wrote a column for *Car and Driver* and one for *The Village Voice*, and did dozens of pieces for diverse publications such as *Mad Magazine* and *Field and Stream*.

But *A Christmas Story*, his other films, his several television series, his extensive writing, his hundreds of live performances on college campuses nationwide and at Carnegie Hall and Town Hall are merely examples of his great comic talent.

Shepherd's genius was to have created an improvised world of his mind at work, five nights a week and more, without a script, on New York radio. For 22 years, from the 1950s to the mid-1970s, his voice reached the ears of several hundred thousand fanatically dedicated listeners in over 26 states in the eastern half of the United States. (No one knows how many syndicated and pirated shows were broadcast throughout the nation.)

In the '50s he talked for hours on end—in the '60s and '70s, he extemporized for a mere 45 minutes nightly. For Jean Shepherd listeners, each person out there in the dark had the feeling that he or she was the only one engaged with him in the illusion of an intellectual interaction—a dialogue. His fans included Jack Kerouac, major jazz musicians, modernist composer George Antheil, chess champ Bobby Fischer, US Poet Laureate Billy Collins, Shel Silverstein, and hordes of students with their transistor radios under their pillows, listening to his voice in the night.

Shepherd invented "talk radio," decades before Garrison Keillor, David Sedaris, and others followed. Without a script, virtually no telephone calls, only four known guests, and only an occasional bit of funky music as a background, Shepherd talked about whatever crossed his mind: jazzy stream-of-consciousness stories of his childhood in northern Indiana, stories about his life in the army, social commentary, and philosophical musings. In between, he might render "Yes Sir, That's My Baby" or some other silly song on his kazoo, nose flute, Jew's harp, or by thumping it out on his head.

Still available are his improvised narration to bassist Charles Mingus' *The Clown*, several of his comic records now on CD, and, more importantly, some 1,500 of the estimated 5,000 radio broadcasts he made. Hundreds of dedicated fans recorded and preserved his shows for decades, and they can be bought for nominal prices and even gotten free through links at the major Shepherd Web sites, http://www.flicklives.com and http://shep-archives.com, with its archive of more than 1,500 shows.

Excelsior!

➤ Eugene B. Bergmann (ebbergmann@aol.com) is the author of *Excelsior, You Fathead! The Art and Enigma of Jean Shepherd*, the only book about Jean Shepherd's life and work. This book, complete with photos, Shepherd resources, endnotes, and index, is published by Applause Theatre and Cinema Books (http://www.applausepub.com/).

Spacing Out with the iTunes Visualizer

You can use iTunes to listen to music while you work, or you can even use it connected to a stereo as your music center, allowing you to listen to music for hours without ever changing a CD. This is great if you're having a party—just set up a playlist with a few hours' music, and click Play.

But you can also use iTunes to provide visual entertainment, to space out, or just to provide some eye candy and waste time. iTunes' built-in visualizer offers dozens of animated effects that morph and change in time with your music. The iTunes visualizer (Figure 1-40) can display hundreds of thousands of shape/color/effect combinations, and you can either let it run at random or choose your own settings. When you find settings you like, you can save up to ten of them.

To start using the visualizer, click the Visualizer button (Figure 1-41) or select Visualizer > Turn Visualizer On. (You can also press Command+T on Mac or Control+T on Windows to turn it on or off.)

At first, the visualizer displays a white apple in the center of the window, and the name of the track and album at the bottom left of the window; these items fade away after a few seconds. The visualizer then starts displaying its permutation of effects, forms, and colors. Using your music as input, the effects change, dance, flow, and slide across the screen. If the iTunes window isn't enough, fill the screen with these effects by selecting Visualizer > Full Screen (or press Command+F or Control+F). Full-screen effects are great for parties, but you won't be able to get any work done like that.

DO OR DIE:

>> Get iTunes eye candy

>> Turn your computer into a party machine

>> Waste time spacing out to random visuals

Figure 1-40
Tired of watching the same old stuff on TV? Space out while you listen to your music.

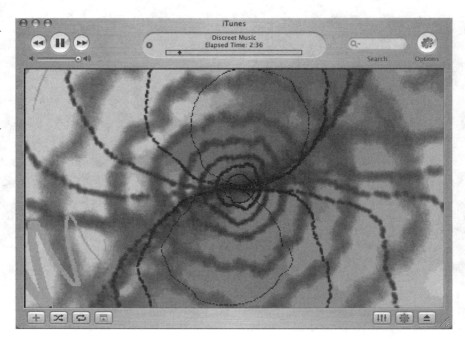

Figure 1-41
Click this button to start using the visualizer.

FAQ

Wouldn't It Be Great to Use the Visualizer as a Screen Saver?

The visualizer is full of great effects—why not use it as a screen saver? If you use a Mac, you can. iTunes Saver (http://www.subsume.com/assembled/iTunes.html) is a Mac OS X screen saver module that displays visualizer effects. You'll only get music with the screen saver if you're listening to music with iTunes when it kicks in, but, hey, you can't have everything.

If you click the Options button at the top right of the iTunes window, you'll be able to set some options controlling the visualizer. You can choose Always Display Song Info, which is good if you're listening to music at random and aren't sure what tracks are playing. You can set it to use OpenGL, if you're using a Mac, which allows 3-D effects; and if you don't have a fast video card, check Faster but Rougher Display. This means that the display won't lag because of your video card, but will be more pixellated.

Controlling the Visualizer

The basic way to use the visualizer is to let it run at random—effects, forms, and colors change automatically. But you can control what the visualizer displays, changing forms, effects, and colors from the keyboard.

Start by pressing R. This tells the visualizer to change to another random setup. Wait a few seconds—it doesn't make a sudden change but flows gradually from one setup to another—and watch the new effect. Each time you press R, the visualizer changes.

If you type N, you toggle between normal and high-contrast colors. And typing C displays information about the current setup.

The visualizer offers 75 forms, 143 effects, and 64 color schemes (that's 686,400 combinations). You can move through these different configurations by pressing different keys.

- **Effect:** Press the A or W keys.
- **Form:** Press the Q or S keys.
- **Color:** Press the Z or X keys.

When you press any of these keys, iTunes displays information about the current configuration in three lines at the top of the screen: The effect name displays on top, the form in the middle, and the color at the bottom. Changes take several seconds to appear on-screen.

If you find a configuration you like and want to keep it on the display, press M twice to "freeze" it without saving it. If you want to save a configuration, press Shift+0 to Shift+9. You can save ten configurations; so Shift+0 saves one configuration, Shift+1 another, and so on. To play back a stored configuration, press the corresponding number key.

For more help using the visualizer, press the H key. You'll see on-screen help that tells you more. And to find out all about the effects available, check out the iTunes Cheat Sheet, at http://doors.stanford.edu/~sr/itunes/.

TOOL KIT

Adding Other Visualizer Plugins

iTunes allows you to add other plugins, both for visualizers and for other features. You can find lots of them by searching the Web for "iTunes visualizer plugin".

A cool visualizer plugin available for both Windows and Mac (most plugins are Mac only) is Goom (http://goom.sourceforge.net/), but a search will turn up more.

Burning CDs and DVDs with iTunes

While iTunes and the iPod are great for listening to music, you may want to burn CDs to listen to in your car or at a friend's house, to make compilation CDs of your favorite tunes, or just to make a backup of your music. Its a good idea to back up any music you buy from the iTunes Music Store, since you can't download the songs again if you lose them.

You also may want to burn CDs just for nostalgic reasons. Music hasn't gone totally digital yet, but who knows? It may no be long before CDs become curiosities, as weird as 8-track tapes. So you might want to make some now to stash away to show your grandchildren.

iTunes includes disc-burning functions, for both CDs and DVDs (depending on your hardware), allowing you to make three types of discs.

DO OR DIE:

>> Burn compilation CDs

>> Back up your music on CD or DVD

>> Burn audio or MP3 discs

- **Audio CDs:** These are standard audio discs that you can play in any CD or DVD player.
- **MP3 CDs:** These are CDs containing MP3 files, that you can play in some CD or DVD players and that you can also use to back up your music. When creating an MP3 CD, iTunes converts your music files from whatever format they are to MP3 files.

- **Data CDs:** These CDs contain the actual data of your files. They are the same as if you burned a CD by simply copying the original song files. Some players will be able to play these discs, depending on the type of files they contain, but the main reason for burning data CDs is to back up your music files.

To choose which format you want to burn, open the iTunes preferences (iTunes > Preferences on Mac, or Edit > Preferences on Windows). Click the Burning tab (Figure 1-42), and choose the format you want to use.

While we're looking at this preference tab, here are the other options available.

- **Preferred Speed:** In most cases, choose Maximum Possible. But if you have problems burning discs, try a lower speed. Also, if you have a fast disc burner, and your blank discs aren't tested for high speeds, you'll generally get fewer coasters by using the maximum speed they specify.

- **Gap Between Songs:** You probably want to have a gap between songs, unless the tracks in your playlist are meant to run together. In that case, select None. You can choose from one to five seconds if you want to have a gap between songs.

- **Use Sound Check:** If you check this, iTunes burns all songs at roughly the same volume.

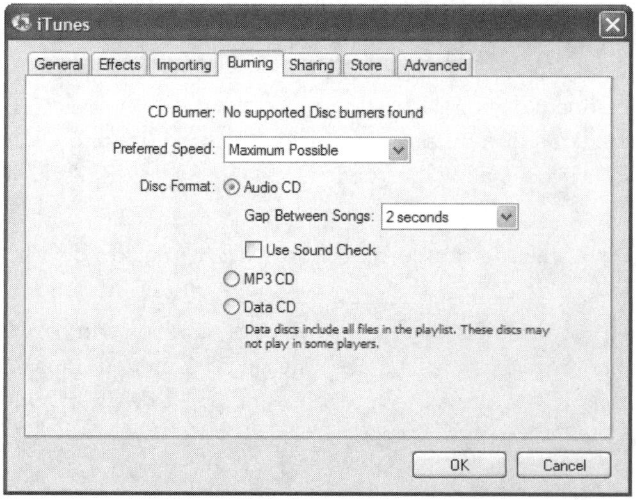

Figure 1-42

The Burning tab of iTunes' preferences lets you set disc-burning options.

Burning a Disc

Its pretty simple to burn a CD or DVD with iTunes. As long as the playlist is no longer than the disc's capacity, just select a playlist, then click the Burn Disc button. iTunes asks you to insert a blank disc (Figure 1-43).

iTunes checks the disc, then asks you to click the Burn Disc button again (Figure 1-44).

As the disc is being burned, iTunes shows you its progress (Figure 1-45).

When the disc is finished, iTunes mounts it as a music CD (if you chose Audio CD), or your computer mounts it as a data CD if it's an MP3 or data disc.

If your playlist is longer than the amount of time available on a CD or DVD, iTunes spits out the first one when it's finished and asks you to insert another blank disc. You can therefore burn as much music as you want, though your last disc might end up being far from full. If you plan to burn playlists that are longer than one disc, check to see if the length lets you burn discs without having a final disc that only contains a couple of songs.

Figure 1-43
After you click the Burn Disc button, iTunes wants a blank disc inserted in your drive to continue.

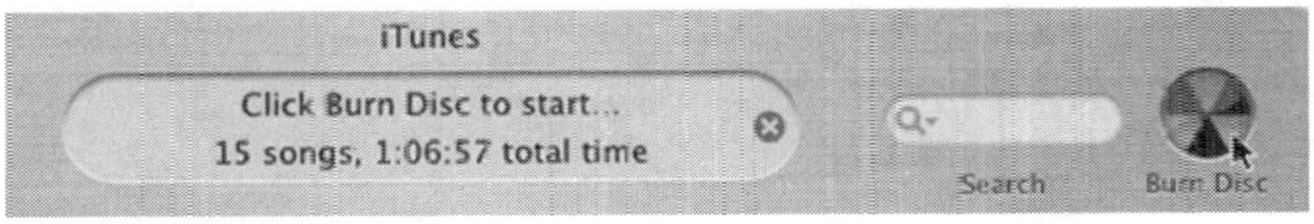

Figure 1-44
When iTunes is ready, click the Burn Disc button to start burning.

Figure 1-45

*The iTunes display shows you the progress
of the burn. The time remaining shown is
not how long it takes to burn the disc, but
how much "music time" remains to be
burned.*

TOOL KIT

Burn a Copy of a CD

If you simply want to burn a copy of a CD, to listen to in your car, for example, and
don't have special disc-burning software that lets you do so, you can use iTunes for
this. But it involves a bit of a workaround and takes a while.

First, change your import settings to import the CD as AIFF or WAV tracks, instead
of compressed tracks. (See Ripping Music for more on this.) Import the CD, then create a playlist from it. (See Creating Playlists from a Selection.)

Next, burn a CD from this playlist as described earlier. This CD will be an exact
copy of the music on the original CD; since you imported it as AIFF or WAV, the music
will not have been compressed and decompressed, which loses quality. It'll take a
bit longer, since you have to both import the music and burn the CD, but you'll have a
perfect copy for your car.

A Smart Playlist to Back Up Your Purchased Music

Since you should have the original CDs for all the music you've ripped yourself, you don't need to back those up. However, you'd better back up any music
you buy from the iTunes Music Store—if you lose your files, you can't download
them again.

Here's a great way to back up your purchased music; it's especially useful
if you buy a lot of tunes from the iTunes Music Store.

1. First, go to your Purchased Music playlist—this contains all the music
   you've bought from the iTunes Music Store. If you don't see it, click the triangle next to Music Store in the Source list.

2. Select all the songs in this list, then select File > Get Info. If iTunes asks you
   if you are sure you want to edit information for multiple files, click Yes.

3. Enter something in the Comments field—this could be anything; you could
   enter ITMS (so you know these tracks were purchased from the ITMS), the
   name of your dog, or simply $. Click OK.

4. Now, create a new smart playlist where you want to match Comment Contains ITMS (or whatever you put in the Comments field earlier). Click OK.

5. Give your smart playlist a name. This playlist contains all the music you've bought from the ITMS. Back this up by burning the playlist, and make a note of the date.

6. The next time you want to back up your music, repeat steps 2 to 4. This adds the same comments to all the files you've bought since your first backup.

7. Edit your smart playlist, adding a second condition: Date Added Is After [the date you recorded in step 5]. Your smart playlist (see Figure 1-46) now contains only those files added since the first backup.

8. Burn a CD using this playlist, make a note of the date, and repeat steps 6 to 8 each time you need to back up your music.

While this procedure works best for your purchased music, you could back up all your music files in this way. Just change the smart playlist to include only the Date Added condition, and get a bunch of blank discs ready.

TOOL KIT

Backing Up Your Music Files

While you still have the CDs you ripped to use with iTunes and your iPod, it would take you a long time to rip them again if you ever lost your files. So make sure you back up your music files. You can either back these files up to an external hard disk, or to CDs or DVDs.

On Windows, your files are stored in \Documents and Settings\username\My Documents\My Music\iTunes\iTunes Music, and on Mac OS X they are stored in /Users/username/Music/iTunes/iTunes Music (unless you've changed your iTunes Music folder location).

Think of backing up these files regularly. It would be a shame to have a hard disk crash and lose not only these files, but also any additional tag information, ratings, play counts, and other information. See a later subsection for a way to back up your purchased music regularly.

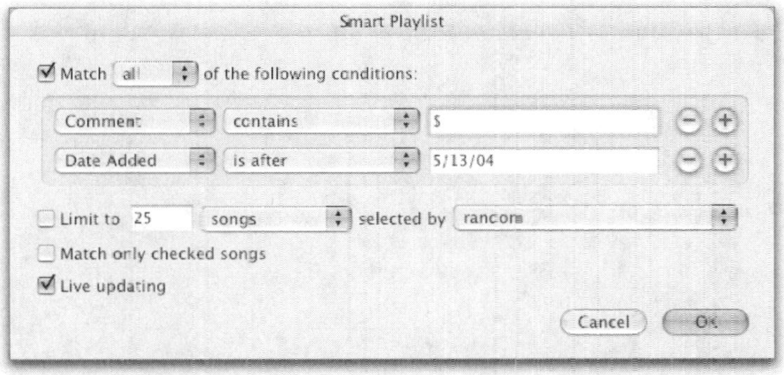

Figure 1-46

This smart playlist shows all songs added since your first backup.

Printing CD Inserts and Labels

Even though you may be digital at heart, and may listen to your music with iTunes or on your iPod, you'll still want CDs occasionally. They're good to listen to when you want to share your music, when you want everyone to hear it. Imagine being at a party where each person has an iPod with earphones stuck into their ears?

In the previous section, you saw how to burn CDs and DVDs, both to create backups of your music files and to create playable plastic discs. You may want to put your special compilation CDs in jewel boxes to carry around with you, and if you do, it's a good idea to have some kind of track list, or even album art to illustrate it.

iTunes lets you print out CD inserts with just a couple of clicks, and offers several types of printouts. Select a playlist, then select File > Print, and you'll see the Print dialog (Figure 1-47). This lets you choose what you want to print and how you want to print it.

In Figure 1-47, I've chosen to print out a CD jewel case insert. This prints album art (if there is any) and a full list of songs with their times. The printed page has crop marks so you can cut the paper to the right size. Just fold it and slip it in your jewel case, and you'll have a custom CD insert.

When printing a CD insert, you can choose from eight themes. Four are in color and four are in black and white. These include a simple text list; mosaics, which include a collage of the album art available for the songs in your

112

Figure 1-47

Print out a CD insert, song list, or album list in color or in black and white.

Printing Labels Directly on Your CDs

If you really want labels, you might want to consider another way of printing them. You can buy special CDs and DVDs onto which you can print directly with certain inkjet printers. While this may involve getting a special printer which is able to print on media as thick as blank discs, it may be the best way to go if, for example, your band wants to print long-lasting CD labels for the CDs it sells at concerts.

One of this book's technical editors swears by the Epson 960, which prints easily and efficiently. While most people won't need such functions, if you do, it's a good way to go to avoid the possibility of labels coming off your CDs.

playlist; or a single cover, which uses only the art from the selected song as the album cover, no matter what songs are in the playlist.

A song listing is a simple list of songs showing the name of the song, the time of each song, the album, and the artist. You can choose from four themes, including one with user ratings, one with dates played, and another custom theme that displays all the information in your iTunes window, according to the columns you have chosen to display.

Finally, an album listing prints albums, with album art if any, from the selected playlist or your entire library. You'll see the artist and album names, the song titles, and their times. This is a good way to print out a list of all your music if you want to have a record on paper or to trade with your friends to show them what you've got in your iTunes music library.

Printing CD Labels

Now that you've got CDs and inserts, it's time to print labels. Well, if you want to. My experience with CD labels is that they eventually come off and sometimes get stuck in CD players. While they can be easy to remove from CD players with drawers, it's a lot more of a headache if you have a slot-loading CD player in your car or laptop. Another annoyance that I've had with CD labels is that they may start curling after a while, with one edge coming off just enough to make a scraping sound inside the CD player. Shoop, shoop, shoop they go, until I finally pull them off.

If you still want to print CD labels, iTunes doesn't do this; you'll need third-party software to do this. For Windows, one good program, especially if you want to print CD labels for more than just music CDs, is Microvision's Surething CD Labeler Deluxe (http://www.surething.com), which comes with thousands of clip-art and background images, as well as tons of templates. Magic Mouse's Discus (http://www.magicmouse.com) is available for both Windows and Mac, and includes templates for CDs, DVDs, audiocassettes, videotapes, inserts and cases, as well as business cards.

You can buy precut CD labels to use with either of these programs from many companies; you'll find these labels in computer stores or stationery stores. Make sure you glue them on as well as possible so they don't come off.

Sharing Music on Your Local Network

When you've got dozens of gigabytes of music in your iTunes library, you don't want to have to copy all that music to another computer at home or at work to listen to it in another location. After all, if Apple's idea is to create a digital hub, you should be able to use iTunes as part of that hub. And you can.

One of the best things about iTunes, for people who have a network at home or at work, is its ability to share music with other computers running iTunes. This lets you stream music from one computer to another. While iTunes doesn't let you do this over the Internet, there are third-party programs that you can use to control or listen to your music from a distance.

Here's the idea: You've got one computer with a huge hard disk, and you rip all your CDs to that computer. You create playlists in iTunes on that computer, and you plug it into your network. Other computers on the same local network can run iTunes with nothing in their music libraries, accessing all the playlists on the main computer.

Think of that main computer as your server, and you'll immediately understand the principle. Each other computer, each client, gets the digital music from the server and plays it. You can have several computers all getting music

DO OR DIE:

>> Pipe your tunes to other computers

>> Share music on your local network

>> Listen to your music from far away

USING M3U PLAYLISTS WITH iTUNES
TunesAtWork streams m3u playlists, which are a special type of streaming MP3 files that allow multiple songs to be streamed

UNDER THE HOOD

from the same server—as long as your network has enough bandwidth—all at the same time.

The best thing about this is that it works out of the box, and the only thing you need to do is check one item in the iTunes preferences. Open the iTunes preferences (iTunes > Preferences on Mac, or Edit > Preferences on Windows) and click the Sharing tab. This displays several preferences for sharing music (Figure 1-48).

Here's what you can set on this preference pane.

- **Look for Shared Music:** Check this to tell your copy of iTunes to look for music shared by others on your network.
- **Share My Music:** Share your music to other copies of iTunes.
- **Share Entire Library:** If you check this, all your playlists are shared.
- **Share Selected Playlists:** You can limit which playlists other copies of iTunes have access to. If you don't want others to know you have a collection of songs by Alvin and the Chipmunks, use this.
- **Shared Name:** Give your library a name, so other iTunes users know whose music they are accessing.
- **Require Password:** You can set a password if you don't want strangers tapping into your library.

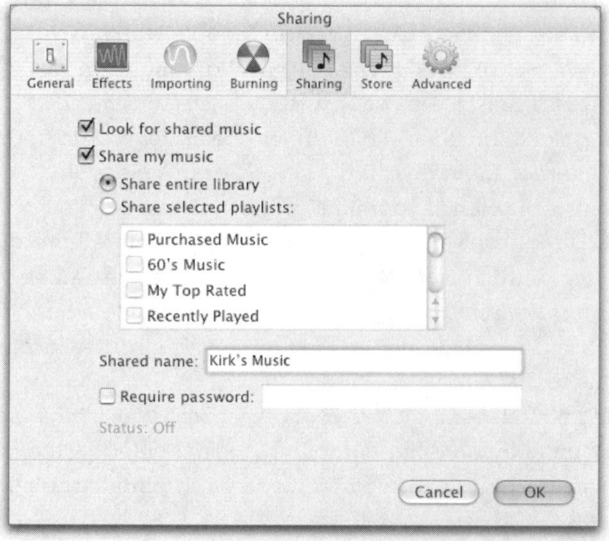

Figure 1-48

The iTunes Sharing preferences, where you set up music sharing for your local network

sequentially. iTunes doesn't recognize these playlists, or, to be specific, doesn't read them correctly. iTunes can start reading m3u playlists, but it stops playing the music after the first song.

The Status section shows whether sharing is on and which other users are connected, if any. Users are considered to be connected if their copy of iTunes has detected your library and displays it in the Source list (Figure 1-49). They don't have to be actively listening to show up as connected.

If you click one of the shared libraries in the Source list, you'll see the entire library; if you click the triangle next to the shared library, you'll see a list of playlists. Unless the user has chosen Share Selected Playlists in their preferences, you'll see all their playlists and be able to listen to all of them.

The beauty of this music sharing is that you don't need to do anything, other than to turn it on. And you can even share between Macs and PCs; as long as the computers are connected to the same local network and have iTunes installed, they can all access any shared music on the network.

Figure 1-49

Two users' music libraries are available to this copy of iTunes.

Controlling iTunes over a Network

Sharing music is one thing: You use one copy of iTunes as a server and another copy as a client, which plays the music. But some people like to play their music into a stereo, in a remote location, such as in an office, where a central stereo pipes music to speakers scattered around the room, or in a store, where the stereo's in a back room. Instead of putting CDs in a player and hitting Shuffle and Repeat, you can control a Mac running iTunes, connected to a stereo, from any kind of computer. Since the interface uses a Web browser, you can even use a WiFi PDA or a cell phone to control iTunes.

Mosey over to http://www.deadendsw.com/Products/webRemote.html and check out webRemote. This shareware program for Mac OS X runs as an interface between iTunes and the rest of the world. Access the program's functions through a Web page, and you can tell iTunes what to play.

FAQ

What About Sharing Music?

To share music or listen to shared music, you must be using Mac OS X 10.2.4 or later and iTunes 4.0.1 or later, or iTunes 4.1 or later on Windows.

Computers sharing music must be on the same local network and on the same subnet. You can share music across a wireless network, a wired network, or a network that combines both of these technologies. You can only listen to music purchased from the iTunes Music Store if the computer playing the music has been authorized to do so.

You can share or see shared MP3, AIFF, WAV, and AAC files, as well as shared Internet radio links. You can't share QuickTime sound files or Audible audiobooks; in fact, audiobooks purchased from Audible.com won't even show up in the shared music you see. You can, however, listen to audiobooks purchased from the iTunes Music Store.

You can only listen to shared music; you can't burn CDs or transfer shared music to your iPod. You also cannot use shared music as a source for the Party Shuffle playlist.

If you're using a Mac, you can download an AppleScript that converts m3u playlists into a form that iTunes understands. Go to http://www.archive.org/about/faq.php?faq_id=173 and download the AppleScript. This is a droplet; you just drag the m3u file on its icon to convert it and open it with iTunes.

Figure 1-50

Using a Web browser to control iTunes with webRemote

webRemote

http://10.0.1.202:2100/?Action=playSong&Show=38

Google

Logout

Currently playing song: "Up With The Lark" by Bill Evans Trio on Consecration (Disc5-1980.9.4).

Bill Evans 9/4/80

Previous Next
Stop Play Pause
Volume Up
Volume Down

Playlists:
Library
*Bach - WTC Random
*Beethoven Piano Sonatas
*Beethoven Quartets
*Bill Evans 1980
*Byrd Keyboard Music
*Dowland Lute Works
*Haydn Piano Sonatas
*Haydn Piano Trios
*Haydn Quartets
*Haydn Symphonies

Up With The Lark	7:15	Bill Evans Trio	Consecration (Disc5-1980.9.4)	0
Mornin' Glory	4:07	Bill Evans Trio	Consecration (Disc5-1980.9.4)	0
Polka Dots And Moonbeams	6:38	Bill Evans Trio	Consecration (Disc5-1980.9.4)	0
Like Someone In Love	7:21	Bill Evans Trio	Consecration (Disc5-1980.9.4)	0
Turn Out The Stars	8:36	Bill Evans Trio	Consecration (Disc5-1980.9.4)	0
Your Story	4:36	Bill Evans Trio	Consecration (Disc5-1980.9.4)	0
Emily	5:10	Bill Evans Trio	Consecration (Disc5-1980.9.4)	0
I Do It For Your Love	6:15	Bill Evans Trio	Consecration (Disc5-1980.9.4)	0
My Romance	8:57	Bill Evans Trio	Consecration (Disc5-1980.9.4)	0
Re: Person I Knew	4:02	Bill Evans Trio	The Last Waltz (Disc 5 Of 8)	0

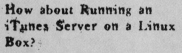

FAQ

How about Running an iTunes Server on a Linux Box?

What if you run a server on your network, but it's neither a Mac nor a Windows PC? If you're running a Linux server, you can still use iTunes music sharing. Here's a link to an article that tells you how to set up a Linux iTunes server:

http://www.whatsinyourbox.org/article28.html

iTunes music sharing uses the daapd protocol. This article tells you how to set up the necessary software to run a daapd daemon on a Linux box, and start sharing music to iTunes clients from a Linux server.

Fire up the program on the Mac that's acting as a server, and make sure to start up iTunes as well. On the remote computer, open a Web browser and enter the network address of the server and the port number specified in the webRemote preferences. You'll see a simple Web page (Figure 1-50) that gives you access to all the playlists on the server and all of iTunes' playing functions.

webRemote can update smart playlists, and you can even use it as a jukebox, where different people can request the songs they want to hear.

Listening to Your iTunes Music from Far, Far Away

OK, you've got all your tunes on your computer at home, and you want to listen to music at work. That seems pretty much impossible, but there is a way. TunesAtWork (http://www.tunesatwork.com) lets you control iTunes running on a Mac anywhere—as long as you can access it over the Internet—so you can listen to your

---

If you use Windows, Musicmatch reads m3u files correctly, as do several other MP3 players. m3u playlists are generally used only for streaming music over the Internet, and some Web sites use them to stream entire albums at low bit rates.

music wherever you are. And you don't even need iTunes on the client computer: You can use any MP3 player to listen.

But there's the rub—TunesAtWork can only stream MP3 files (at least at press time); if you have AAC files, you won't be able to listen to them. But TunesAtWork is a nifty tool. It creates its own miniature streaming server, which feeds MP3 streams over a network. This could be a local network—though with iTunes music sharing, there's little point in using it like this—or over the Internet.

After you launch TunesAtWork, it reads your iTunes Music Library, then displays a dialog showing your IP address (in case you don't know it) and some other information about your music library. All you need to do is enter this address, followed by the port number, in a Web browser that has Internet access. Figure 1-51 shows the TunesAtWork display in the Safari Web browser.

Note: TunesAtWork uses port 12777 by default. If you have a firewall on your home computer, the one serving the music, make sure this port is not blocked.

You can select entire playlists; you can browse by genre, artist, or album; and you can select individual songs for playback. You can also check selected songs and play back only those songs, allowing you to create an ad hoc playlist. However, the one other drawback to TunesAtWork is that it doesn't support smart playlists. But this is a recent project, and the developer plans to add many new features to the program, so if you like it, keep your eye on his Web site for new features.

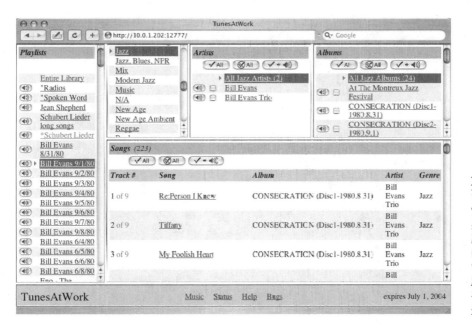

Figure 1-51

With TunesAtWork, access your MP3 collection anywhere, and play your music on any MP3 player.

Importing Analog Music

f you've been around for a while, you've probably got some old analog music stored in your attic or your basement. While you certainly have a CD collection, and a budding digital music library if you buy music online, you may also have a collection of music on older media: vinyl LPs, cassette tapes, or others, such as reel-to-reel tapes. You can still buy cassette players; turntables are available, but harder to find; and reel-to-reel players have gone the way of the dodo, with the exception of high-end units.

So, why not digitize your music so you can burn it to CDs and listen to it on your iPod or on your computer with iTunes? This is not as complicated as you may think. Here's what you need to do to import analog music and convert it to digital music files.

1. First, you need to make sure you have the appropriate sound input. Most computers or sound cards have a line-in jack, which you can use to connect a cable to the output of your record player or cassette deck. If not, you can use a USB microphone, such as the Griffin iMic (http://www.griffintechnology.com/products/imic/), which is a simple adapter that provides audio input and output jacks, allowing you to both record and play music through your USB port.

2. Connect your analog playback device to your computer. You'll probably be running a record player or tape deck through an amplifier, and the best

DO OR DIE:

>> Make those LPs and cassette tapes useful

>> Digitize all your old music

choice would be to connect the amp to your computer using a cable with RCA jacks on one end and a mini-din headphone plug on the other. (Your stereo may require a different cable; check which kind of jack it has.) You can also use the headphone jack on your amp, but you may not have as much control over the sound and volume, and the output is probably not as clean.

3. Now you need software. For Mac, if you're using a Griffin iMic, the company's Final Vinyl software is a simple tool to digitize your music. Another good choice is Roxio's CD Spin Doctor, which comes with its Toast CD-burning program (http://www.roxio.com/en/products/toast/index.jhtml); CD Spin Doctor offers more options than Final Vinyl. On Windows, you could use Roxio's Easy CD and DVD Creator (http://www.roxio.com/adban/creator_6_microsite/index.jhtml) or Microsoft Plus! Digital Media Edition (http://www.microsoft.com/windows/plus/dme/dmehome.asp), which is a low-cost suite of digital media tools, including the Plus! Analog Recorder. There are many other tools—commercial, shareware, and freeware that will record your music—but these two programs have additional features, letting you remove pops and clicks, and cut your digitized recording into individual tracks.

4. Check your sound levels. All the programs mentioned in step 3 provide sound-level meters, and you should set up the levels so the peak volume never reaches the maximum section of the sound-level meters. This is usually a red section. It's all right if the peak volume occasionally hits the yellow section, or the section just below the maximum. Do a couple of tests to make sure the levels result in undistorted transfers.

5. Now, start recording. You'll want to turn on recording on your computer before you start your analog playback. You can cut out the blank sections later. Record each album or tape side completely, and stop recording a few seconds after the end.

6. The next step is to split your recording into tracks. Some software can do this automatically, by detecting silence between songs, but other programs require that you listen to the music or examine the waveform to indicate the split locations. Check the manual for your software to find out how to do this.

7. When you have all your tracks, export the music. Again, different programs offer different options. Most programs let you save your tracks as AIFF or WAV files, which are uncompressed music files. You should probably burn these to CDs right away, unless you don't want to keep uncompressed files. You can use iTunes to burn these files to CDs, or if you are using Toast or Easy CD and DVD Creator, you can click a button to send the tracks to these programs' disc-burning modules. Another thing you could do is edit the tags of the AIFF or WAV files, compress them using Apple

Lossless compression, then burn the resulting compressed files to CDs or DVDs. In this case, you'll save disc space, and you'll still have lossless files, with the appropriate tag information, if you need them later.

8. After you've burned your original tracks to CDs, you can import them into iTunes if you want to have compressed files. Create a new playlist that you'll use temporarily, and drag the files into the iTunes window to add them to this playlist. Select all the tracks, then select Advanced > Convert Selection to [AAC/MP3]. This menu item displays either AAC or MP3, according to the settings you choose on the Importing tab of the iTunes preferences.

9. You can now enter the appropriate information in the files' tags in iTunes, so you can identify the songs. Don't forget to delete the original AIFF or WAV files when you've finished. These files take up a lot of disk space; a CD's worth of files can take up as much as 700MB on your hard disk.

ESSENTIAL MUSIC

Bob Dylan's *Blood on the Tracks*

Much as I love all kinds of instrumental and orchestral music, at the end of the day I'm a word guy, and if you're a word guy, Dylan's your man. We were spoiled by an embarrassment of riches until the infamous motorcycle accident in July 1966, and after the stark surprise of 1968's John Wesley Harding, we seemed to be stranded in a wasteland of ersatz Americana. There were great songs, of course, "Lay, Lady, Lay" and "Knockin' on Heaven's Door," for example, and *Planet Waves* has many fine moments, but nothing could quite match the shock and pleasure of that moment in early 1975 when I set the needle gently on *Blood on the Tracks* for the first time and heard "Tangled Up in Blue." Even better, it wasn't a fluke. Next came "Simple Twist of Fate," "You're a Big Girl Now," and "Idiot Wind," his most vicious song since 1965's "Positively 4th Street." The only disappointment is an overlong "Lily, Rosemary and the Jack of Hearts," which never quite seemed to fit, to my mind, but that's a minor quibble, especially as it's followed by the incomparable melancholy of "If You See Her, Say Hello" and the eerily redemptive "Shelter from the Storm." There may be other contenders, but *Blood on the Tracks* surely remains the classic adult break-up album of all time.

➤ Peter Robinson writes mystery novels and is the author of the popular Inspector Banks series, with 14 titles published (http://www.inspectorbanks.com). Inspector Banks is an eclectic music fan, and in these books, Banks' selection of music—from Hendrix to Britten, from jazz to rock—occasionally annoys his fellow police officers in drives through the English countryside. Peter Robinson's latest novel is *Playing with Fire*.

Tools for Doing More with iTunes

Tunes is a great program, offering lots of features, an easy-to-use interface, and simple controls. Its popularity has inspired a cottage industry with lots of developers creating freeware and shareware programs that allow you to extend iTunes' functions, and control the program and your music playback in different ways.

But first, let's look at the options you have from iTunes. You can start by simply using the iTunes window, or its miniaturized controller window, to play and pause your music and to change the iTunes volume. If you leaf back a few dozen pages and look at Figure 1-9, you'll see that this miniature controller gives you access to the main buttons, but doesn't let you access individual songs or playlists.

You can also use the Dock or System Tray icon to control some iTunes functions. But, again, you're limited to playing and pausing music, moving to the next or previous track, and turning on or off shuffle and random playback.

Menu Bar and Keyboard Tools

Why switch to the iTunes window to change playlists? There are much simpler ways of doing this. You can't do it from the Dock, but M-Beat (http://www.thelittleappfactory.com/software/mbeat.php), a shareware application, gives

Where's All the Windows Software?

Everyone keeps saying that Windows offers more software, but here's an area where Windows is lacking in programs. Of course, part of the problem is Apple's: While a software development kit has long been available for Mac, the Windows equivalent was only released in May 2004 (http://developer.apple.com/sdk/itunescomsdk.html).

I hope our Windows brothers and sisters will start developing additions for iTunes, since, as you'll see in this section, there are many interesting tools available for Mac OS X, tools which extend and simplify the way you use iTunes.

you a control menu and control icons—all customizable—and a menu containing your playlists (Figure 1-52). You can access any of your playlists or their songs from the Playlist menu, or you can click the controls to play, pause, and change songs.

M-Beat also offers a floating window to display track information and album art, and tons of options for which menus it displays and how it displays them.

Synergy, which installs as a preference pane, is another menu bar controller for iTunes (http://synergy.wincent.com/). Like M-Beat, it offers one-click play, pause, next, and previous buttons (Figure 1-53), and its menu (click and hold the Play button to display it) lets you choose playlists, songs, and other iTunes functions. Synergy also lets you set hot keys, so you can control iTunes from the keyboard.

But why even bother with the menu bar when you want to control iTunes? X-Tunes (http://www.pol-online.net/) lets you control iTunes from the keyboard, using its heads-up display (Figure 1-54) that comes to the front when you press a hot key combination.

Just hold down your hot key combination and move your pointer over the X-Tunes display to activate its controls. It doesn't offer as many functions as the other programs I've mentioned; it doesn't give you access to songs or playlists, for example, but it allows you

Figure 1-52

M-Beat offers a customizable set of menus in your menu bar. Left: the main menu. Right: the Playlist menu.

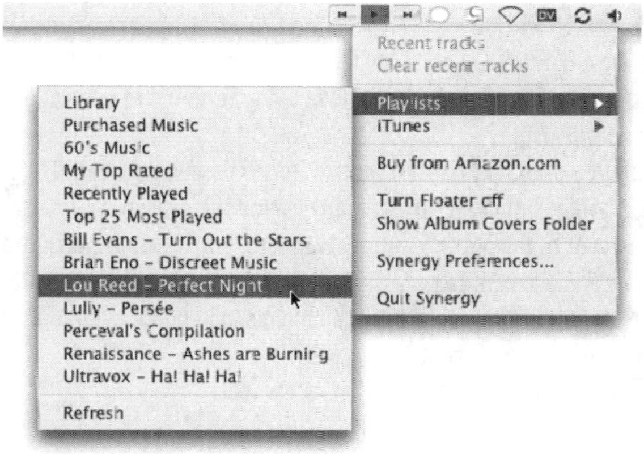

Figure 1-53

Synergy's recessed menu bar buttons are subtle and attractive, and the Play button doubles as a general menu for accessing playlists and other iTunes functions.

Figure 1-54

X-Tunes displays only when you press its hot key combination.

quick access to playing, pausing, and switching tracks within a playlist, as well as volume controls.

Finally, iMote (http://www.mkd.cc/products.html) is even more minimal. While this program lets you access functions from its menu (Figure 1-55), its real strength lies in the ability to use keyboard shortcuts for the main functions of iTunes: play, pause, volume control, next, and previous, as well as rating your songs from the keyboard as you listen to them.

With a bit of practice, you won't need to use the menu, and can even turn it off by selecting Become Invisible. You'll learn the keyboard shortcuts, and you'll be able to control iTunes without switching applications or even using the mouse.

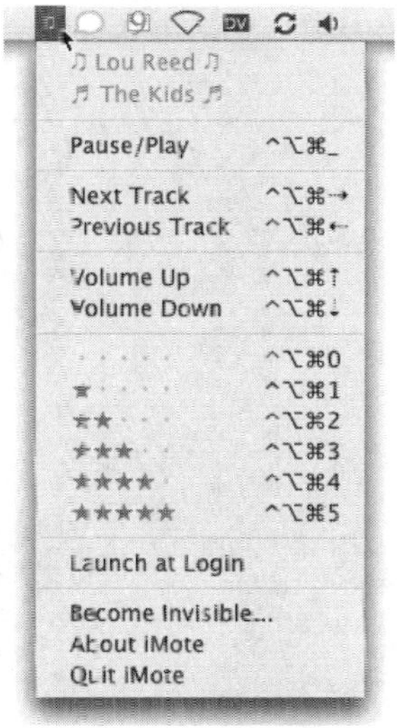

Figure 1-55

iMote's menu shows its functions and keyboard shortcuts.

TOOL KIT

Geek Corner

OK, you're a Mac OS X user, but what you like most about the Mac is the fact that it's built on a version of Free BSD. You love using Terminal to control your Mac from the command line, right?

Well, you probably want to control iTunes that way as well. It's certainly possible, using iTunes AppleScript capabilities and the osascript command from Terminal.

Head over to the Mac OS X Hints Web site, and check out this hint: http://www.macosxhints.com/article.php?story=20011108211802830. You'll find out how to run iTunes with simple commands, and you'll even find a shell script that will take things even further.

Let no one say that Macs don't offer choice!

iTunes Controller Applications

It may seem like overkill to use another application to control iTunes, but the iTunes window is large (at least when it displays enough information to be useful). You can resize the iTunes window so you can still scroll through your sources and access all its functions (Figure 1-56), but it's still larger than many people want. And the minimized version of the window doesn't give you access to any but the basic controls.

So the alternative is to use a controller application, which acts as an interface and passes its commands to iTunes. These applications are generally smaller and offer more functions in a tighter interface. (See Figure 1-57.)

iTunesController Plus (http://itcp.itunescontroller.com/) provides both basic and more advanced functions. It has play, next, and previous buttons; volume controls; and buttons to bring iTunes to the front and to display song information. The Equalizer button lets you choose from six equalizer presets; the Advanced button lets you get lyrics and guitar tabs, set ratings, and convert

Figure 1-56

You can shrink the iTunes window and still have access to all its functions, but this is as small as you can make it.

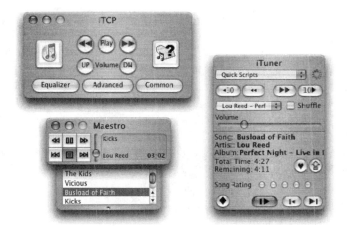

Figure 1-57

*Three iTunes controllers for Mac:
iTunesController Plus, Maestro,
and iTuner.*

digital music files; finally, the Common button lets you select a playlist, update
your iPod, and more.

iTuner (http://people.umass.edu/jlink/) has three different-sized displays.
The smallest window shows only the play/pause, previous, and next buttons.
The medium window also displays song info and lets you set a rating and add
a song to a Favorites list. And the largest window (Figure 1-57) has a popup
menu where you can select playlists and a Quick Scripts menu that offers
advanced functions, such as skipping to the next artist or album, setting equalizer presets, or updating your iPod.

Maestro (http://homepage.mac.com/djodjodesign/) is more minimalist than
the previous two programs. Its window provides only basic functions—
play/pause, previous, next, rewind, fast forward, and volume control—and it
also has a playlist/track button. Click this button to display a drawer with your
playlists, then click a playlist to display its tracks.

Whether you decide to use an additional application to control iTunes is up
to you. All these programs offer small windows with access to all the main functions, so if you want to display a window permanently to control iTunes, they
use less screen space than the iTunes window.

Using AppleScripts with iTunes

The last thing to mention about extending iTunes is AppleScripts. For those
unfamiliar with AppleScript, it's a system-based scripting language that lets
you extend and automate many tasks in Mac OS X. AppleScripts can run
within certain applications, adding new functions or automating others, or they
can run as independent applets, which can tie together several applications.

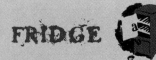

FRIDGE

Just For Fun

Want to tell the world what you're listening to? Check out iChatStatus (http://ittpoi.com/), a preference pane that polls iTunes and adds your current song to your iChat status line.

Or how about putting your current song on a Web site? KungTunes (http://www.kung-foo.tv/itti.php) can do this for you. It retrieves the current song, converts it to a text file, then uploads it to your Web server, so people around the world can find out if you're listening to Alvin and the Chipmunks.

I've already mentioned a couple of AppleScripts in earlier sections. Two in particular are very useful: Track Splicer and Make Bookmarkable, which I examined in Listening to Audiobooks with iTunes. The first script combines several music files into a single file, and the second converts AAC files to bookmarkable files, which keep a record of your position in the file after you stop listening.

As I said earlier, there are two types of AppleScripts: scripts and applets. To use an applet, you either double-click it or drag a file or files onto its icon. But to use scripts from iTunes, you first need to turn on the AppleScript menu in the program.

This is easy. Just navigate to your home folder, then open the Library folder it contains. You'll find a folder called iTunes; open that folder. Create a new, empty folder here called Scripts. This is where you will add scripts you want to run from within iTunes. When you add any scripts to this folder, a new menu displays in your iTunes menu bar (Figure 1-58) showing an AppleScript icon.

To run any of these scripts, just select it from the script menu. If the script requires any input, it tells you what to do. In most cases, scripts you run like this require that you have already selected one or more songs in your iTunes library.

To find what you can do with AppleScripts and iTunes, go to Doug's AppleScripts for iTunes (http:// www.malcolmadams.com/itunes/), the largest compendium of AppleScripts that extend and automate iTunes.

Apple also offers a selection of AppleScripts (http://www.apple.com/applescript/ipod), most of which are for managing notes: creating notes from the clipboard or a Web page, listing and editing notes, and deleting notes.

Figure 1-58

The AppleScript menu displays in iTunes if your Scripts folder contains any AppleScripts.

Window   Help

Make Bookmarkable
Track Splicer

Managing Music with Musicmatch Jukebox

Before iTunes came along, the most popular music management program for the PC was Musicmatch Jukebox. The first iPods for Windows used Musicmatch to manage songs. While iTunes is both free and more powerful, some users may still be using Musicmatch and may prefer it. The program is still out there and being updated; you can download the latest free version from http://www.musicmatch.com/ or upgrade to the paid version for $19.99. The paid version has a number of advantages over the free version:

- Eight times faster ripping from CDs
- Faster CD burning from your music collection
- Automatic song tagging

The free version of Musicmatch lets you manage your music by searching for tracks and creating playlists, and lets you play the songs in a particular order or at random from within a playlist. Figure 1-59 shows the basic Musicmatch program's standard interface.

To create a playlist, drag songs from your library to the Playlist pane at the top right of the window. You can drag songs to new locations in the playlist or remove any songs from a playlist by right-clicking a song and selecting Remove from Playlist. To print a playlist, right-click any song in the play list and select Print Playlist(s).

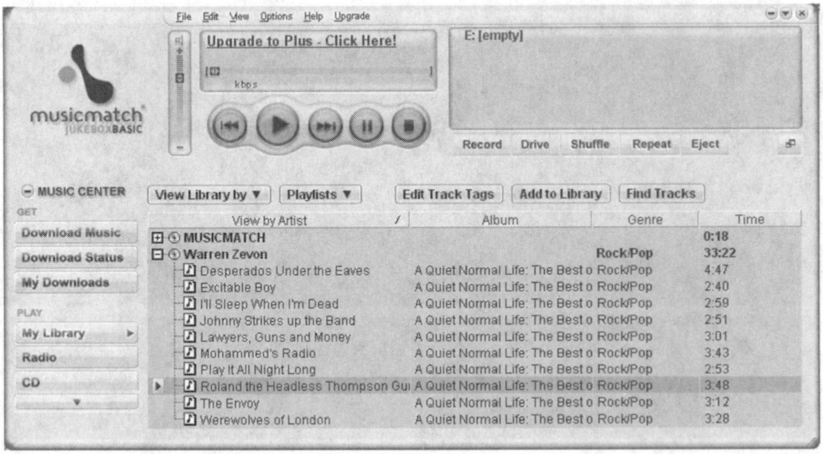

Figure 1-59

The music on your computer is at your fingertips in Musicmatch Jukebox.

One thing you can do in Musicmatch that you can't do in iTunes is to save notes about a song's tempo or mood and the situation in which you'd like to play the song. (In iTunes you'd have to add this information to a song's Comments field.) To enter that information about a song into your library, right-click the song, select Edit Track Tags, and then click the More tab to display the interface you see in Figure 1-60.

The Tempo settings are fairly standard (Fast, Very Fast, Slow, etc.), but the Mood setting lets you choose anything from Wild to Upbeat to Comatose. The Situation setting likewise runs from Party to Dance to Romantic to Drunken Brawl. I'll not make any suggestions about what sort of song fits that last description—I'll leave that to your imagination.

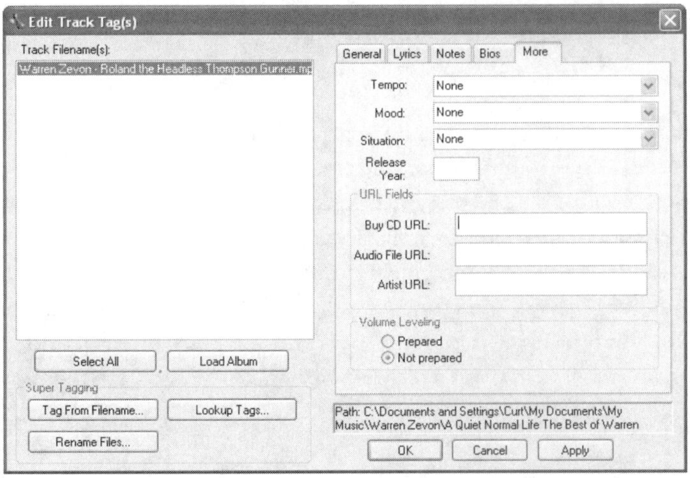

Figure 1-60

Extra options are always handy. In Musicmatch, those options let you record information about a song's overall mood.

Stream Music to Your Stereo with iTunes

Y ou've seen in the previous sections that iTunes is good for lots of things: Not only can you use it to manage your iPod, but you can use it to listen to music. Let's be honest though: Your computer probably has cheap speakers, unless you've gone out and bought something nice (I talk about speakers in Turning Your iPod into a Total Music System).

You probably know that you can connect your Mac or your PC to a stereo, using its audio out jack; you need to get the appropriate cable to do this. But why bother with more wires? Why worry about keeping your computer next to your stereo?

DO OR DIE:

>> Listen to your iTunes playlists on your stereo

>> Stream your music through the air

>> Use iTunes as part of your home media center

Apple's AirTunes

Apple gives you a way to do this through the airwaves. If you have a wireless network (using Apple's AirPort cards, or any other 802.11b or 802.11g WiFi cards or adapters), you can get one of Apple's AirPort Express base stations (see Figure 1-61) and run your music through the ether to your stereo using AirTunes.

As you can see in Figure 1-61, the AirPort Express base station (http://www.apple.com/airportexpress/) is the size of an AC adapter. You plug it into any outlet, and you can use it as a base station to create a wireless network, or you can connect other stuff to it.

Figure 1-61

With Apple's AirPort Express base station, you can play your iTunes music through your stereo or speakers just about anywhere. (Photo courtesy of Apple Computer, Inc.)

Underneath the device you can see three wires. The one closest to the wall is an Ethernet cable, which you can use to connect to any wired network devices. Next is a USB cable, so you can share a USB printer over your wireless network. And finally—this is what interests us here—an analog or optical audio cable, to connect to your stereo or your speakers.

Using iTunes (4.6 or later), you can choose to send your music through the air to any of up to five AirPort Express base stations. You could send music to your living room, family room, kitchen, den, or bedroom. As long as you've got an AirPort Express base station in a room, you can stream music to it. And since the AirPort Express base station is portable, you can carry it to another room when you need to.

Once you've got the AirPort Express base station set up and plugged into your stereo or your speakers (you'll need a mini-din-to-mini-din or a mini-din-to-RCA cable; see Listening to Your iPod on a Stereo for more on cables), fire up iTunes on your wireless-enabled Mac or PC. You'll see, at the bottom of the iTunes window, a popup menu allowing you to select a set of speakers or a stereo (Figure 1-62).

Click the popup menu (Figure 1-62), select a playlist, then press Play. Your music gets sent through the air to the selected stereo or speakers.

You should keep a few things in mind, though. Unless your computer is nearby, you don't have any way of changing what's playing, or even pausing or stopping the playlist. As of this writing, there is no remote control available for this feature. So you should decide what you want to hear and make sure you don't change your mind—if you have to go upstairs to change the music, it's a bit annoying. You can change the volume on your stereo or speakers, say, if the phone rings, but the music will keep playing. If you want to pipe music to a remote location, though, this is a great way to do it.

You can always use a laptop as your music center, with wireless streaming, even if it sits on your coffee table. It's much easier than switching CDs; you get to use all your favorite playlists, and you can use Party Shuffle or even Internet radio stations. That makes for a big remote control, but if you do this you may never use the CD player connected to your stereo again.

What about when you visit friends? If you've got a wireless-enabled laptop and an AirPort Express, take them both, and hook your friends' stereo into the base station—you'll be able to DJ for a party or simply share your favorite music with just a few clicks.

Figure 1-62

Click this popup menu to select a stereo or speakers available with an AirPort Express base station.

◀)) Living Room Stereo ⬍

Music and More with EyeHome

There's another way to get your music from iTunes to your stereo, and also view photos and videos on your TV. Unfortunately for Windows users, it's Mac only: elgato's EyeHome (http://www.elgato.com) is a sleek interface to your Mac's digital content that lets you stream sound and images wirelessly or via Ethernet to a TV and stereo.

The EyeHome is a small box (see Figure 1-63) that you connect to your TV and stereo, then to your Mac. You connect it to a Mac by Ethernet—or you run an Ethernet cable from Apple's AirPort Express base station or an 802.11 adapter—and fire it up.

The EyeHome uses simple software that you install on your Mac. When you turn it on, it finds your Mac (or Macs, if you have several on your network) using Apple's Rendezvous technology. You then use its menus on your TV screen to select iTunes playlists, iPhoto albums, or videos. You can connect the EyeHome to your stereo, so you have top-quality sound; you don't need to listen to your music on the TV. With a remote control, you can select whatever playlists you want from your iTunes music library.

The EyeHome has only one weakness: It can't play AAC files purchased from the iTunes Music Store; it cannot decode the digital rights management (DRM) information in these files. But it can play other formats, including AAC, MP3, and even WMA files. Add to that the ability to view your photos and videos on your wide-screen TV, and your Mac truly becomes a digital media center.

Figure 1-63

The EyeHome, a small box of tricks that streams digital media to your TV and stereo. (Photo courtesy of Elgato.)

iTunes Preference Reference

I n the previous sections of this book, I've looked at all of iTunes' features and functions, and have shown you some of the program's preferences where necessary. In this section, I'll give you a complete overview of all the preferences available in iTunes: There are many things you can change, adjust, and fiddle with in the preferences, and it's good to know what modifications you can make. You don't need to memorize this, but whenever you have questions about what the preferences control, you can come back to this section and look them up.

To open iTunes' preferences, select iTunes > Preferences (Mac) or Edit > Preferences (Windows). This displays the first preference pane, General.

DO OR DIE:

>> A complete overview of iTunes' preferences

>> What to change and what to leave alone

>> Every button you can click, every menu you can select

General Preferences

The General preferences (see Figure 1-64) let you control how iTunes displays information and how the program reacts when you insert a CD into your computer.

Here's what you can adjust in this preference pane.

- **Source Text** and **Song Text:** You can choose between Small and Large for the display of text in the Source column, at the left of the iTunes window, and for song listings, in the main section of the window. If you find you need glasses to read these texts, set them to Large.

- **Show:** You can choose here to not display the Party Shuffle and Radio icons in the Source list. Uncheck these check boxes if you don't plan to use these features. But you'd be missing out on some great stuff.

- **Show genre when browsing:** If this is checked, you will see three columns when browsing your music library after clicking the Browse button. The first column will be Genre. If you don't want to see the Genre column, uncheck this.

- **Group compilations when browsing:** If you check this, you'll see a Compilations entry in the Artist column when browsing, only if you have compilations in your iTunes music library. If you do have compilations, this makes it easier to select these albums.

- **Show links to Music Store:** These are the pesky little arrows that follow artist and album names. If you click them, you go to the iTunes Music Store and see the artist or album in question. If you hold down the Option (Mac) or Shift (Windows) key, you'll see other music by the same artist, or you'll see the album in the Browse pane.

- **On CD Insert:** You can choose from four options.

  - **Show Songs:** The contents of the CD display in the iTunes window.

  - **Begin Playing:** The CD starts playing immediately.

  - **Import Songs:** iTunes starts importing the songs, using your settings from the Importing pane, immediately.

  - **Import Songs and Eject:** iTunes imports the songs, then ejects the CD as soon as it has finished.

- **Connect to Internet when needed:** Leave this checked if you have a permanent Internet connection, such as cable, DSL, or LAN. If not, you might want to uncheck this and tell iTunes to connect when it needs to. iTunes connects to the Internet to access track info for your CDs, to access the iTunes Music Store, and to check for updates.

- **Check for iTunes updates automatically:** iTunes checks automatically to find if a new version is available. If so, it tells you and asks if you want to download and install it. If you don't check this, you can find out if a new version is available by selecting Help > Check for iTunes Updates (Windows) or by using the Software Update preference pane (Mac).

- **Use iTunes as the default player for music files (Windows) or Use iTunes for Internet Music Playback (Mac):** Under Windows, this is a check box; check this to use iTunes by default to play any music files it can understand. On Mac, this is a Set button. Click this to set iTunes to play all music files it can.

Audio Preferences

The Audio preferences (Figure 1-65) let you set some options for audio playback and for using AirTunes (see Stream Music to Your Stereo with iTunes).

- **Crossfade playback:** This lets you set songs to overlap and crossfade; it's kind of like having songs segue into each other. If this is on, songs crossfade, but by default this is set to six seconds; the ends of songs may get cut off, though you'll hear a sort of segue. This works well with some types of music and less well with others. Your mileage will certainly vary.

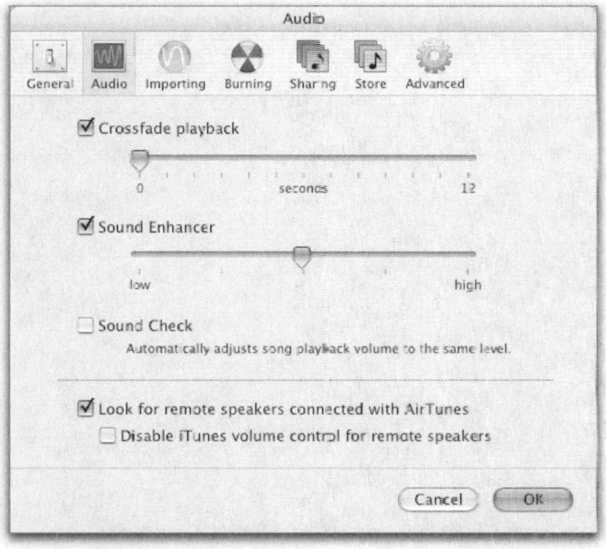

Figure 1-65

The Audio preferences

- **Sound Enhancer:** This is supposed to add depth and richness to your music, but it depends on your speakers. Try it out, and adjust the setting to different levels to see if you can hear the difference. There's some sort of voodoo electronics, probably a lot like the loudness button on a stereo. This is not a surround sound feature, though.

- **Sound Check:** This adjusts song volumes to the same level; if you have songs of different volumes (and we all do), this is good to turn on, especially if you use headphones with iTunes. Going from, say, Mozart to Limp Bizkit could hurt your ears if this setting is not on. This setting lowers the volume of loud songs and raises the volume of soft songs so the levels are similar.

- **Look for remote speakers connected with AirTunes:** If you have an AirPort Express wireless base station, this tells iTunes to search the network for remote speakers. If it finds any, it displays them in a popup menu at the bottom of the iTunes window, so you can send your music to a remote stereo.

- **Disable iTunes volume control for remote speakers:** Check this to override iTunes' volume control and only use the volume on your remote speakers or stereo.

Importing Preferences

iTunes' Importing preferences (Figure 1-66) let you set options for importing music from CDs. (See Ripping Music for more on importing songs from your CDs.)

- **Import Using:** You can select here the type of compression you wish to use. See Ripping Music for more on this, and see Compression Formats—MP3, AAC, Lossless, and the Rest for a full treatise on which format is best for you.

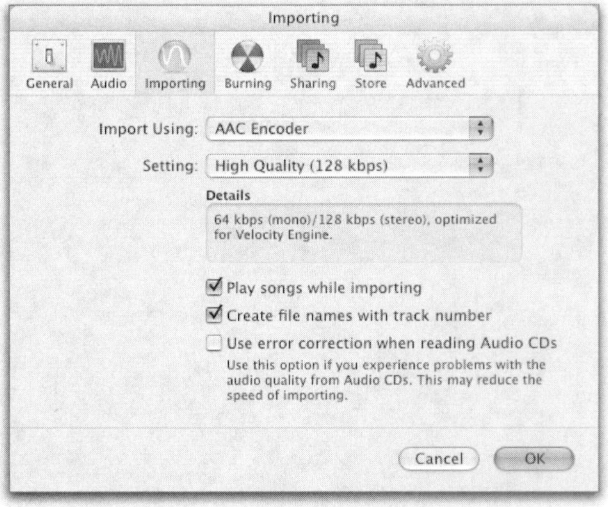

Figure 1-66

Importing preferences let you set the type and quality of compression you want to use.

- **Play songs while importing:** If this is checked, iTunes plays CDs as it imports your songs. This slows down importing, though, so only do it if you really want to listen to your CD and import it at the same time.

- **Create file names with track number:** This adds a track number (01, 02, etc.) to the beginning of your files, making it easier to find which file corresponds to which track in an album.

- **Use error correction when reading Audio CDs:** You should only use this if you have problems with skipping or dropouts when importing CDs. You may need to turn this setting on if you have an older CD-ROM drive, or if you have damaged CDs, but you probably won't need it all the time.

Burning Preferences

The Burning preferences (Figure 1-67) let you set options for burning CDs with iTunes.

- **CD Burner:** This shows your CD burner; if you have several burners, you'll be able to choose which one to use here.

- **Preferred Speed:** You should usually leave this at Maximum Possible, unless you have blank CDs that aren't tested for the speed of your burner, or if you have problems burning CDs above certain speeds.

- **Disc Format:** By default, this is Audio CD with a gap of 2 seconds between songs. If you are burning albums where songs run together, set this gap to 0 seconds. If you want to burn MP3 or Data CDs, select one of these options. See Burning CDs and DVDs with iTunes for more on these choices.

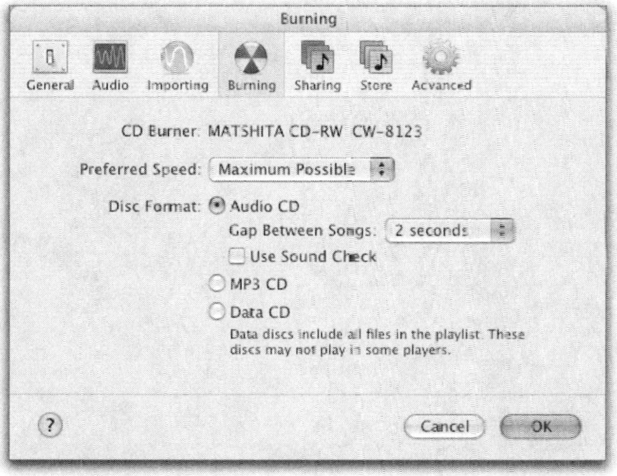

Figure 1-67

The Burning preference pane

- **Use Sound Check:** This is the same as Sound Check in the Audio preferences. In general, you probably *don't* want to turn this on when burning audio CDs; you are better off leaving the volume as it should be. But if you are making a compilation CD, you can turn it on so the volume is more even from one song to another.

Sharing Preferences

The Sharing preferences (Figure 1-68) let you choose whether you share your music across a local network and how you share it.

- **Look for shared music:** This tells iTunes to search the network for other users who have their music libraries shared. Shared libraries display in the Source list.

- **Share my music:** You might as well share your music with others, unless you have limited bandwidth on your local network. Check this to turn on sharing, then select to share your entire library or only selected playlists. Be a sport: Share your music, if you can, and listen to your friends' shared music; you might discover something interesting.

- **Shared name:** By default this is [your name]'s Music, but you can change it to whatever you want.

- **Require password:** If you don't want just anyone to tap into your music, set a password, then tell your friends the secret word so they can listen in.

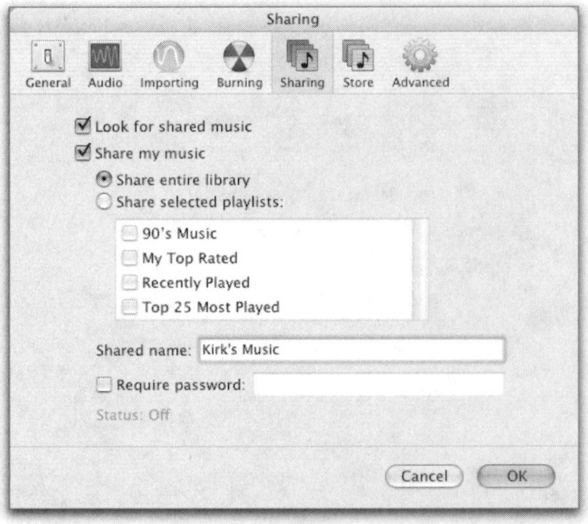

Figure 1-68

The Sharing preference pane

Figure 1-69

*Store prefer-
ences, for set-
ting up the
way you use
the iTunes
Music Store*

Store Preferences

The Store preferences (Figure 1-69) let you set options for using the iTunes Music Store.

- **Show iTunes Music Store:** Don't want to use the store? Just turn this off.
- **Buy and download using 1-Click:** Do you like impulse buying? If this is on, you'll buy stuff instantly, without using a shopping cart. You'll still get alerts, but it's easy to buy too much with 1-Click.
- **Buy using a Shopping Cart:** Better safe than sorry—turn this on so your selections go into a shopping cart before you pay.
- **Play songs after downloading:** This tells iTunes to start playing your new music as soon as you buy it.
- **Load complete preview before playing:** If you have a dialup connection or some other slow Internet connection, choose this; entire previews load before playing, so you'll get to hear them without pauses.

Advanced Preferences

The Advanced preferences (Figure 1-70) let you set some advanced preferences (really).

- **iTunes Music folder location:** This displays the location of your iTunes Music folder, where your music is stored. You can change it here, by clicking Change and navigating to a new folder, or reset it to the default location by clicking Reset. See All about Your iTunes Music Library for more on this.

Figure 1-70

The Advanced preference pane. For setting advanced preferences.

- **Streaming Buffer Size:** This sets the amount of data that is buffered when streaming music. If you have a fast Internet connection, set this to Large. If not, leave it at Medium. If you have problems listening to streamed music with iTunes radio stations, try setting it to Small.

- **Keep iTunes Music folder organized:** See All about Your iTunes Music Library for more on this.

- **Copy files to iTunes Music folder when adding to library:** See All about Your iTunes Music Library for more on this as well.

PART II
iPod

About the iPod

Welcome to the new world of portable music. Well, it's not that new—people have been using the Walkman and similar devices for a couple of decades. But this time it's really a revolution.

When Apple released the first iPod in November 2001, most people didn't realize just how much of a revolution it was. The iPod wasn't the first noncassette or CD-based music player; flash memory players had been around for a while. But compared with the portable music players available at the time, which held 64 or 128MB, the first iPod at 5GB was huge. While flash memory music players could hold 10 or 20 songs, this first iPod could hold nearly 1,000 songs. Steve Jobs, Apple's CEO, who is no stranger to hyperbole, said at the time, "With iPod, listening to music will never be the same again." For once, he was right.

What set the iPod apart was the fact that it was more than just a container for music. Apple combined a tiny hard disk with one of the finest examples of industrial design in a consumer device, providing an attractive object that is astonishingly easy to use. Many people ignored the relatively high price of the iPod and bought the object, at least in part, for its design.

But the iPod is much more than simply the device you carry in your pocket and use to store and play back music. It is part of a whole matrix of hardware

DO OR DIE:

> > Introducing the iPod

> > Which iPod model do you have?

> > A peek inside the iPod

A LOOK INSIDE THE iPOD
Apple's iPod is not only a masterpiece of design on the outside, but it's a fine example of cutting-edge industrial

UNDER THE HOOD

and software elements that combine to provide music to your headphones. Here's what makes the iPod so special.

- **Large capacity:** The iPod holds much more music than most other portable music players, even though some competitors followed and now offer players with similar and even larger storage capacity. Flash memory devices measure the amount of music they can play in minutes or in single-digit hours. The iPod counts its music in the number of days you can listen to it.

- **Fast transfer:** Using its FireWire interface (and, in the latest models, a USB 2 interface as well), you can transfer music from your computer to your iPod much quicker than with any USB 1 device. The competition now offers USB 2 transfers as well, but the original iPod offered the fastest transfer speed at the time.

- **Music management on your computer:** With iTunes (or Musicmatch for Windows, before "hell froze over" and Apple released a Windows version of iTunes 2003), you manage your music directly on your computer: You rip your CDs, create playlists, and organize your music library. The software on your computer is therefore an integral part of the iPod listening experience.

- **Auto-sync:** One of the iPod's strengths is its automatic synchronization with the music on your computer using iTunes (or Musicmatch). No manual transfers are required; you just plug in your iPod, and your music streams from your computer. (You can, however, manage your music manually, if you so desire.)

- **Simple, one-thumb operation:** The iPod is more than easy to use. You can control all its functions with your thumb, or with one finger, while holding it in your hand. You don't need two hands to select playlists, change the volume, play or pause music, or use any of its other functions. Using a plug-in remote control, you can do the main operations without even holding the iPod.

- **Hard disk usage:** You can even use the iPod as an external hard disk to store important files. Carry your important files around with you and access them from any computer.

- **Skip protection:** The iPod offers 20-minute skip protection so you can run, skate, or jump on a trampoline without your music skipping. Just try that with a portable CD player.

- **High-quality playback:** Able to play MP3 files, and VBR MP3 files, at up to 320kbps and later adding AAC (in addition to AIFF and WAV), then Apple Lossless compression, the iPod offers high-quality playback and also has excellent frequency response.

design as well. It's no mean feat to stick all the many components inside an iPod and make them work without heat or interference causing problems.

And the preceding features just concerned the first version of the iPod! Apple has made subtle improvements to both the hardware and software throughout the product's life, changing the controls, adding a dock and a special connector, and extending the iPod's capabilities.

But all this is not without a hefty price tag. The first iPod cost $399, more than any other portable music player at the time. Pundits across the board derided Apple for this price tag, but to the surprise of many, the iPod was more than a hit: It became a cultural icon in just a few years.

The Next Generations of iPods

The first generation of iPods had a "scroll wheel," a rotating wheel with four buttons on its rim. This initial 5GB model was followed by a 10GB model in March 2002, and the larger size helped increase sales. Then came the second generation of iPods, which had a "touch wheel," a pressure-sensitive wheel like a trackpad on a laptop, with four buttons above it for controlling playback, changing tracks, and accessing the menus. Apple went through two versions of this model, with 10GB and 20GB hard drives, before releasing the third generation of iPods.

The third-generation iPod had the same touch wheel and controls but featured a new dock connector at the base of the device. This special 32-pin connector links up to a computer using a special cable—available in either FireWire or USB versions—and allows the iPod to stand in a dock, leaning back gracefully at the correct angle so you can easily see its display. The dock offers several advantages: You can plug the connector cable into the back of the dock, then insert the iPod in the dock to connect it easily to your computer and synchronize its music. The dock also has a line-out jack, which allows you to connect the dock to external speakers or a stereo, providing audio output that is unaffected by the iPod's volume settings.

But the dock connector also allows you to plug other devices into your iPod: Belkin's Media Reader (see Storing Digital Photos on the iPod) lets you use your iPod to download photos directly from a memory card, and you can use it to connect external battery packs and chargers. It seems likely that the dock connector's usefulness will increase as Apple updates the software for the iPod.

First released in April 2003, the 3G iPods came with 10, 15, or 30GB of capacity; by the end of the year, these capacities had increased to 15, 20, and 40GB. In April 2004, Apple introduced Apple Lossless compression, so you

Here's what your iPod contains:

- *A miniature hard drive, ranging from 4GB (iPod mini) to 40GB. This hard drive is silent and only turns on when needed, keeping your iPod from*

could listen to CD-quality sound on your iPod, to the detriment of the number of songs you can carry.

The Incredible Shrinking iPod

Fast-forward to January 2004, when Steve Jobs presented the iPod mini at the Macworld Expo in San Francisco. The press wowed a bit but lamented the $249 price tag. "It's only $50 less than the 15GB model; no one's going to pay that much for the mini." Fooled again. With 100,000 preorders, the iPod mini took even Apple by surprise. So much so that, in March 2004, Apple announced that it was rolling back its international availability, originally scheduled for April 2004, by three months. At the same time, iPod minis were sold out everywhere in the US, as Apple scrambled to get enough hard drives to make more.

The iPod mini is an audacious device: Offering more capacity than any flash memory-based player, it only cost a bit more than 256MB devices. It was not the cheapest hard drive-based player for its capacity at the time of its release, but consumers immediately showed that they wanted this stylish player. With less room on the front of the unit, Apple returned to an all-in-one wheel control: the "click wheel." Like the earliest model, the mini has just one wheel, but the entire wheel tilts when you click on one side, unlike the first iPods, where the buttons were outside the wheel. With a smaller screen than its big brothers, the mini was much lighter and especially much slimmer, being the size of a credit card and not a whole lot thicker.

Apple correctly assumed that there were plenty of people who wanted a stylish device—and were willing to pay for it—but who didn't need 20 or 40GB of disk space. Sure, music freaks with lots of CDs (like me) are happy to have an iPod with lots of disk space, but most people could never even fill theirs up.

Welcome to the Fourth Generation

In July 2004, Apple released the next-generation iPod. This fourth-generation (4G) model includes the best of both worlds: It has the same capacities as the 3G models (at press time, 20GB and 40GB versions are available, but larger capacities should see the day shortly) but abandons the scroll wheel and

overheating, and saving battery life. The hard drive is wrapped in a rubber enclosure or in electrical tape to insulate it from the rest of the iPod's innards.

four buttons for a click wheel, similar to that on the iPod mini. While the Select button in the center of the mini's click wheel has a matte finish, like the rest of the wheel, the 4G model's Select button is a glossy plastic, like the white plastic case.

The 4G iPod introduced some interesting new features. First is increased battery life; the 4G gets up to 12 hours, compared with 8 hours for the previous model and the iPod mini. One of the most surprising new features is the ability to change the speed of audiobooks; you can either slow them down or speed them up, allowing you to listen to audiobooks more quickly, if you're in a hurry to get to the end. The menus changed a bit too, with a Music menu and a Shuffle Songs menu item on the main screen.

4G Corner: What's New in the 4G iPod

Aside from the features presented earlier, in Welcome to the Fourth Generation, the new 4G iPod has a host of tiny changes and additions. Since these changes only affect the 4G iPod—the interfaces and menus for previous models (for 1G and 2G models using software version 1.3, for 3G models using software version 2.2, and the iPod mini) are all the same—it seemed more logical to point them out in special sidebars such as this.

So throughout this part of the book, you'll find "4G Corner" sidebars, which talk about what's new or different in 4G iPods. If you have an older iPod, you won't need to read them (unless you're trying to decide whether you need the new features). If you have a 4G iPod, then read these sidebars along with everything else. Most features are the same, and these sidebars merely point out the details.

TOOL KIT

iPod Models at a Glance

Table 2-1 provides a quick overview of the different iPod models. If you're not sure which generation yours is, you can tell from this table. To find out how much disk space your iPod has, look on the back, near the bottom, and you'll see a number in gigabytes (GB).

- A circuit board containing the processor that runs the iPod, a flash memory chip that holds the iPod's firmware, and a memory cache that holds music after reading from the hard disk (this is how the iPod keeps from

Table 2-1 iPod Model Summary

Model	Date Introduced	Scrolling Device	Hard Disk Size (GB)	Generation	Software Versions Compatible
iPod (5GB)	October 2001	Scroll wheel	5	1	1.0-1.4
iPod (10GB)	March 2002	Scroll wheel	10	1	1.0-1.4
iPod (Touch Wheel 10GB)	July 2002	Touch wheel	10	2	1.2-1.4
iPod (Touch Wheel 20GB)	July 2002	Touch wheel	20	2	1.2-1.4
iPod (10GB with Dock Connector)	April 2003	Touch wheel	10	3	2.0-2.2
iPod (15GB with Dock Connector)	April 2003	Touch wheel	15	3	2.0-2.2
iPod (20GB with Dock Connector)	September 2003	Touch wheel	20	3	2.0-2.2
iPod (30GB with Dock Connector)	April 2003	Touch wheel	30	3	2.0-2.2
iPod (40GB with Dock Connector)	September 2003	Touch wheel	40	3	2.0-2.2
iPod (20GB Click Wheel)	July 2004	Click wheel	20	4	3.0
iPod (40GB Click Wheel)	July 2004	Click wheel	40	4	3.0.1
iPod mini	January 2004	Click wheel	4	NA	iPod mini software 1.1

Note: By the time this book reaches your hands, Apple may have released additional models. The latest software versions at press time are those shown in this table.

skipping when you run and how the iPod can turn its hard disk off). The iPod's connectors (dock connector, headphone jack, and remote control connector) and its Hold button are attached to this circuit board.

BLOG: Steve Wozniak on the iPod mini

I always like to have more of things like RAM and hard disk, where having more doesn't affect functionality. I had lots of use for the 40GB of my iPod-installers, files, photos, backup data, and more. Not to mention that my entire music collection is quite large, so my iPod had to hold a subset of that (I put the rest on a portable FireWire drive, in case).

When the iPod mini was first introduced, I was under the impression that Apple must have made it RAM based, like my early MP3 players (Diamond Rio 500 was one). That's sort of a pure concept, indicative of the day when we'll have every movie ever made on a postage-stamp card the size of today's camera media. So I ordered a few right away. But since this would not really displace my iPod as my music machine, I only got one of them engraved.

Shortly thereafter I found out that the iPod mini was not RAM based, but rather had a smaller hard drive inside. Now I was really sure that it was a backwards step so I nearly canceled my order. I was so busy that I didn't get around to canceling them.

So when my iPod minis arrived, I opened them. I was instantly taken as you can only be with an item right there, atoms, in the palm of your hand.

- A slim lithium-ion battery.
- An LCD screen, which displays menus and information.

ESSENTIAL MUSIC

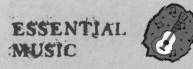

Dylan, Stories, Comedy, and Leonard Cohen

I've listened to about every kind of music for so long, attending all the local concerts of every genre too, that it's hard to talk about one favorite. It would probably head toward Bob Dylan, maybe "Highway 61 Revisited," maybe "Ballad of a Thin Man" or "Like a Rolling Stone," or maybe "Just Like a Woman" on *Blonde on Blonde.* Maybe even earlier, folkier stuff like Bob Dylan's "Dream" or "One Too Many Mornings." Maybe some intermediate stuff like "Mr. Tambourine Man" (possibly my favorite of all) or "I Want You" or "Love Minus Zero/No Limit" or "She Belongs to Me." These are coming out of my head, but the list would have been the same in 1972 for me. So these aren't particular iPod songs.

I figure that if I still ran, I'd take the iPod mini, and my favorite song would be "Silver Stallion," by the Highwaymen, because of its near-perfect running beat.

But these days, my special iPod music is not really music. It's comedy and stories. I have a couple of albums by Kevin Kling on my iPod, and I just love listening to his stories, always short and entertaining, about his own life and family and experiences. Virtually every one comes through with strong mental imagery.

As for comedy, I have an album of XXX-rated comedy by women comedians in a casino, but it's kind of raunchy, like at a comedy club. But more than that, I enjoy the genre of phone prank comedy. I have a number of albums by the Jerky Boys, Big Ant and Lionel, and others. One time I cued up the entire album *The Jerky Tapes* in my car (I use a Transpod for easy iPod use) and called a friend who was in on my joke. I was on a long drive with my assistant, Sharon. So I called Jim, and, as we had previously arranged, he started telling me how he had some comedians at his house who used to play in his nightclub. He told us on the car speakerphone that they would do some phone comedy stuff for us live right there. I deftly switched my phone off and unpaused the iPod, which went into *The Jerky Tapes.* For the first minute or two, it sounds on this CD as though they are setting things up, so Sharon didn't catch on. She heard a number of routines for the next half hour and was laughing hard and had no idea that it wasn't live, even though certain things were beeped out.

It wasn't until weeks later that I played the CD for Sharon so that she'd see how I "got" her, but it still took a *lot* of convincing that it hadn't been live on a cell phone call.

Another song on my iPod is "Vincent," by Don McLean. A couple of years ago, I finally got to see the Vincent Van Gogh painting *Starry Night,* which well represents the words of this song. I took my iPod in and stared at the painting as I listened to the song.

- A touch/scroll/click wheel assembly to control the device. On white 2G and 3G models, four buttons are also part of this assembly.
- Lots of tiny little wires, ribbon cables, and connectors to hold everything together.

> I also was taking my goddaughter and son to this museum, their first time to such a prestigious one, and let them listen to the iPod as well by that painting.
>
> Of all my music, the one that chokes me up the most though is "Suzanne," by Leonard Cohen, which shares the name of my wife.
>
> ➤ Steve Wozniak

These minis were so beautiful and fit my pocket and hand even better than the full iPod. Did I say that they were beautiful?

That night I worked for hours to create a subset of my music that would fit on the mini. Until then I'd been carrying maybe 7GB of music on my iPods and PowerBook. I listened to each of my songs and deleted many to reduce this collection to about 3GB. From then on I was a total convert, even switching between my silver and blue ones to match my clothing.

Status symbol? Well, I still try to wear my iPod minis in ways that they will be noticed, on the outside of my pocket instead of the inside, and on my belt, for example.

I like the feel and design of the iPod mini the best. And just like the original iPod, 1,000 songs, plus or minus, fits my travel needs just fine.

The Altec Lansing portable (battery or AC) travel speakers—which fold up and have excellent bass and a slot for the iPod (the mini works), and audio in/out for connection to other devices, as well as internal volume adjustment—are my most useful and valuable iPod accessory.

I went back and ordered a blue iPod mini with my name engraved, along with "Think Different."

➤ A Silicon Valley icon and philanthropist for the past three decades, Steve Wozniak, aka "Woz" (www.woz.org), is president and CTO of Wheels of Zeus (wOz). Woz, cofounder of Apple, helped shape the computing industry with his design of Apple's first line of products, the Apple I and II, and influenced the popular Macintosh.

Want to see what the inside of an iPod looks like? Don't do this at home...

Here are some pictures of a 3G iPod being taken apart: http:// www.ipodbattery.com/slimipodinstall.htm.

Raintree County: A Great American Novel

The "great American novel" is something that is often spoken of but rarely seen. Critics use that term far too often for books that don't merit more than a passing glance. But occasionally, a novel appears that is a good candidate for that phrase.

Raintree County, "which had no boundaries in time and space, where lurked musical and strange names and mythical and lost peoples, and which was itself only a name musical and strange," by Ross Lockridge Jr., was published in 1948 to critical and popular acclaim. This 1,066-page novel attempted to translate the American experience to paper through the eyes and experiences of a seemingly banal character, John Wickliff Shawnessy, "pagan and Pilgrim, poet and poem, idealist and idea" (Charles Lee, writing in the New York Times in January 1948).

Over a period of 24 hours, as Waycross, Indiana, celebrates the Fourth of July, 1892, Shawnessy looks back on his life since 1848, through a series of flashbacks. He sees his youth, his first experience of feminine beauty, his first loves, then the great American tragedy: the Civil War. As the book goes on, we follow this Leopold Bloom of the Midwest through his peregrinations, until the past rejoins the present and the day ends.

It's hard to sum up such a book, but anyone reading it will find that their life has a new milestone: a before– and after–*Raintree Country*. More than just the characters and narrative, it is the juxtaposition of the simple, idyllic life in Waycross, Indiana, and the chaos of the Civil War or the pandemonium of New York City that remain in memory. Lockridge was seeking simplicity and showed how it did exist, somewhere in the world, in a place not on any map.

While this book is out of print, you can find used copies of it from many online booksellers. See http://www.raintreecounty.com to learn more about this essential American novel.

And here is a full autopsy of an iPod mini. Well, it wasn't intended to be an autopsy, but rather a dissection; it became an autopsy after the doctor pulled too hard on one cable and broke it: http://www.ipodlounge.com/ articles_more.php?id=3059_0_8_0_C.

Setting Up Your iPod on a Mac

So, you finally got yourself an iPod? Or are you thinking of getting one? If you've already got one, you won't need to read this section, since you've probably got it set up and are listening to music on it already.

If not, this brief introduction tells you what you need and how to set up an iPod on the Mac. If you're considering buying a used iPod, you'll find out here whether you can use it on your Mac.

Today's iPods (the fourth-generation white iPods and the iPod mini) require Mac OS X. (Or Windows 2000 or Windows XP; see Setting Up Your iPod on Windows for more on using a new iPod with Windows.) If you're still using Mac OS 9, you can use either the first- or second-generation iPods. But if you want a new iPod, you'll need to be running Mac OS X 10.1.5 or later.

In addition to running Mac OS X, you'll need either a FireWire connector on your Mac or a USB 2 connector. All recent Macs—in fact, just about every model that can run Mac OS X—have FireWire connectors, and some recent models contain USB 2 as well. The FireWire 400 connector is a six-pin port; you'll see the male version of this at the end of the dock connector included with the iPod.

Newer Macs also include a faster version of FireWire called FireWire 800. Its connector is a smaller port. Since today's Macs that provide FireWire 800

DO OR DIE:

>> What you need to use today's iPods on a Mac

>> Installing iPod software

>> Getting your iPod ready for use

A PERSONAL VIEW OF THE iPOD MINI
This book covers all types of iPods, from the first 5GB model to the latest fourth-generation iPod, as well as the iPod mini. Most of the explanations and descriptions are the same for all the models, with

UNDER THE HOOD

connectors also have FireWire 400 connectors, you won't need to worry about an adapter, but if you put a FireWire card into an older Mac, and it only has a FireWire 800 connector, you'll need to get a third-party adapter to use your dock connector cable. You may also have a FireWire card with a four-pin jack; in this case, you can use the included six-pin-to-four-pin FireWire adapter, but bear in mind that this won't charge your iPod. (See Understanding Your iPod's Battery for more on charging your iPod's battery.)

FAQ

What Comes in the Box?

When you buy a new white iPod, you get the following stuff inside its neat box:

- The iPod
- A pair of Apple earbuds
- An iPod Dock Connector to FireWire Cable
- An iPod Dock Connector to USB Cable
- An iPod AC power adapter
- A six-pin-to-four-pin FireWire adapter
- A dock (with some models)
- A CD containing software and PDF files of manuals
- A *Users Guide, Quick Reference Guide,* and warranty documentation

When you buy an iPod mini, here's what you get:

- The iPod mini
- A pair of Apple earbuds
- An iPod Dock Connector to FireWire Cable
- An iPod Dock Connector to USB Cable
- An iPod AC power adapter
- A plastic belt clip
- A CD containing software and PDF files of manuals
- A *Users Guide, Quick Reference Guide,* and warranty documentation

If any of this is missing, contact your vendor! Make sure you know whether your model should come with a dock; as of press time, this is only included with the 40GB white iPod.

the exception of some features that are only available with certain later iterations (third- and fourth-generation iPods, with dock connectors, offer some features, both hardware and software, that earlier models do not).

Installing iPod Software

You may already have iPod software installed on your Mac. If not, use the iPod software installer found on the CD included with your iPod. Double-click the installer file (it will have a name like iPod21.pkg) and follow the instructions.

Make sure you have the latest version of your iPod software. To find out if you do, click the Apple menu, select System Preferences, then click the Software Update icon. Click Check Now, and if there's a newer version of the iPod software, download it and install it. (You should regularly check for updates to Mac OS X; in fact, it's best to have the checks run automatically, which is the default setting on the Software Update preference pane.) You can always check to see if there is an update to iPod software at Apple's iPod support page: http://www.apple.com/support/ipod.

When you first turn on your iPod, you'll see a Language screen. Select a language by using the scroll wheel, then press the Select button (the button in the middle of the scroll wheel).

When you plug your iPod into your Mac, iTunes will open, and the iPod Setup Assistant displays. On the first screen of this assistant (see Figure 2-1), you can enter a name for your iPod. You might simply want to use the name suggested, which is your first name's iPod, but try to be creative. (Don't worry, you can change this name later.) You can also choose to automatically update your iPod, which updates its music from iTunes as soon as you plug it in, and you can click the Register My iPod button to go to the Apple Web site and register it.

After you click Done, the assistant closes, and iTunes begins copying your music. Depending on how much music you have in your iTunes music library and the capacity of your iPod, this may take a while. For example, to copy 30GB of music, it took me just shy of an hour.

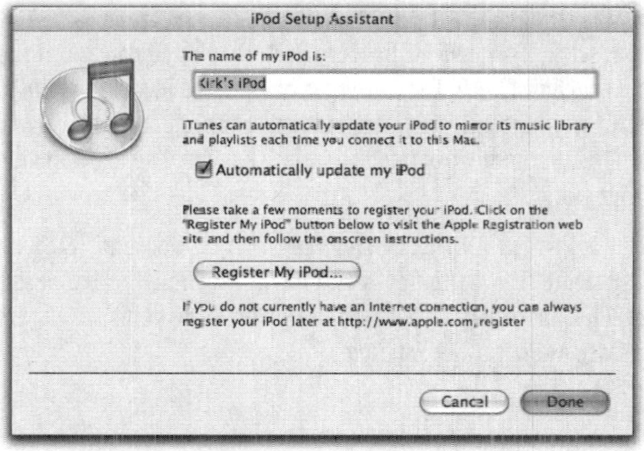

iPod Setup Assistant

The name of my iPod is:

Kirk's iPod

iTunes can automatically update your iPod to mirror its music library and playlists each time you connect it to this Mac.

☑ Automatically update my iPod

Please take a few moments to register your iPod. Click on the "Register My iPod" button below to visit the Apple Registration web site and then follow the onscreen instructions.

Register My iPod...

If you do not currently have an Internet connection, you can always register your iPod later at http://www.apple.com/register

Cancel   Done

Figure 2-1

The iPod Setup Assistant screen lets you set basic options the first time you connect your iPod to your Mac.

There is little difference between the white iPods and the iPod mini, other than the size, capacity, and the way the click wheel works; Apple added the click wheel to the 4G iPod since it was such a popular way of controlling the device. The screen offers the same display (though the iPod mini uses a

160

ESSENTIAL MUSIC

The Beatles

The familiar cliché says that pop music is the soundtrack of our lives. Like all clichés, it's only partly right. Good pop music (which is to say, music that's good at being pop) is actually a series of coded synesthetic experiences, planting itself like a series of little time bombs in our memories.

The opening bars of Stevie Wonder's "I Just Called to Say I Love You" will stop my wife and me dead in our tracks whenever it swims up from...well, in fact from a car radio playing in upstate New York in 1984. Joe Brown's "A Picture of You" takes me back to lying on the summery grass of a tennis court, in 1962 or so, with a radio playing in the clubhouse behind me. The Big Bopper's "Chantilly Lace" reminds me of the inconsolable pangs of generalized adolescent lust at school. The Supremes' "Baby Love" is a bar in a Welsh pub, where I went for lunch every day for six weeks in 1964. "Take These Chains from My Heart" (Ray Charles) and "Come Outside" (Mike Sarne)—the sublime and the ridiculous, side by side—are from the jukebox in the Essex pub where I was a barman when I was 18. And so on, almost endlessly.

Unoriginally too, because we all have similar snapshots lurking away. The tracks and the memories are different for everyone, but the experience is the same. Dinah Washington's "September in the Rain," Maria Muldaur's "Midnight at the Oasis," Billy J. Kramer's "Bad to Me," The Seekers' "Island of Dreams." Classics too: Mendelssohn's Violin Concerto, Bach's First Brandenburg Concerto, Beethoven's Fifth Symphony—all these lie in wait, almost impossible anymore to be listened to purely as music, because their associations are so powerful.

But in the end, the area of music where the memories glare brightest, where the reminders come slyly from every direction, where the sense of a real but ungraspable meaning is the strongest, is in the songs of The Beatles. These hold steam-hammer synesthetics for me: "Eleanor Rigby," "I'm Happy Just to Dance with You," "If I Fell," "Eight Days a Week," all of them music that's perfect at being pop. But if there is one, it has to be John Lennon's "In My Life," where the Sensurround kicks in with the Cinerama memories, and everything outside disappears under the impact of the simple but evocative words, the tinkling baroque of George Martin's keyboard break. Works every time, by heck. Now, where was I?

➤ Christopher Priest (www.christopher-priest.co.uk) is a novelist who writes on the fringes of science fiction. His books include *The Prestige, The Extremes,* and his latest novel, *The Separation.* He has won awards for many of his novels, including the World Fantasy Award for *The Prestige.*

Setting Up Your iPod
on Windows

If you've got an iPod and you use a Windows computer, this section is for you. First, check the sidebar What Comes in the Box, in the previous section (Setting Up Your iPod on a Mac), to make sure you've got everything you paid for. Then, to use an iPod with Windows, you'll need to have certain software and hardware. Apple says you must have Windows 2000 with Service Pack 4 or Windows XP Home or Professional, though, as you'll see later, you can use your iPod with Windows 98. As far as your hardware is concerned, you'll need a PC with a FireWire or high-power USB 2.0 port, or a FireWire or high-power USB 2.0 card.

Not all PCs come with FireWire ports, though several manufacturers, such as Sony, include them (calling the system I-Link or IEEE 1394) to provide connectivity with digital video cameras. If your PC has a four-pin FireWire port, which is common on notebook computers, you can pop the six-pin-to-four-pin adapter on the cable when you want to sync your iPod, and take it off when you want to charge it.

If you don't have a FireWire port on your PC, you can use a USB 2.0 port: Apple includes both a FireWire and a USB cable with all models available at press time (the 4G iPod and the iPod mini).

DO OR DIE:

>> Which version of Windows you need

>> What hardware is required

>> Getting your iPod up and running

But the iPod mini has something that the white iPod doesn't have: cachet. Sure, the original white iPod was a status symbol when it first appeared, but white gets boring after a while. I used the teen-test to find out how each one

Does Syncing Empty Your Batteries?

One of the drawbacks of a four-pin FireWire connection is that your iPod won't recharge; the four pins in the adapter are used for data, while the two missing pins transfer power to your battery. If you have a four-pin FireWire card in your computer and download a lot of songs, you may find that your battery runs down frequently. If so, you can either buy a six-pin FireWire card or pick up a FireJuice power injector from SiK, Inc. You can find the FireJuice injectors for original and third-generation iPods on the Web at http://www.sik.com/firejuice.php.

You can also use your iPod on a computer that has a USB 1.1 port, but your songs will transfer to the iPod at a much slower rate. Here are the numbers:

- USB 1.1: 12Mbps
- USB 2.0: 480Mbps
- FireWire: 400Mbps

"Mbps" means megabits per second, and the preceding numbers are "theoretical," which means they're the top speeds you'll get at optimal conditions. In other words, you're looking at transfers taking anywhere from 30 to 40 times longer if you go through a USB 1.1 connection. FireWire and USB 2.0 cards are cheap—buy one. You'll save time and wear and tear on your iPod, and you won't have to wait all night the first time you sync your iPod.

There is one advantage to Apple's iPod Dock Connector to FireWire and USB 2.0 Cable: You can plug it into both the power adapter (using the FireWire plug) and your computer (using the USB plug), ensuring that you can charge your battery while syncing your iPod. Also, if you have a 4G iPod, it gets power from the USB 2.0 cable, so you can use this cable to charge while you sync. Older models and the iPod mini won't charge when connected via the USB cable alone.

Installing the iPod Software

As you'd expect from an Apple product, getting your iPod up and running is a straightforward matter of popping your iPod CD into your computer's CD drive and walking through the installation wizard. If the installer doesn't launch automatically, display the CD's contents and double-click the Setup.exe file (which displays as Setup if you have file extensions turned off) in the CD's top-level directory. The only decisions you need to make when installing the system software are your preferred language, the

was perceived: My 13-year-old son, Perceval, gave his opinion as I opened the boxes of each one, and as he got to hold them in his hands and fiddle with them.

directory to which you want to install the software, whether to make iTunes the default audio program, and whether you want QuickTime to be the default media player. After the process runs, reboot your computer, connect your iPod, and get going.

Your iPod and Windows 98... Don't Take No for an Answer!

You may have heard that you can't use your iPod with Windows 98. Strictly speaking, that's true: You can't use your iPod with Windows 98, because that operating system doesn't support FireWire or USB 2.0. You can, however, use your iPod with Windows 98 Second Edition, which is usually just called Windows 98SE.

If you are, indeed, running Windows 98SE, you need to buy a FireWire card (if you don't already have one) and then download the Windows 98SE FireWire patch from http://support.microsoft.com/default.aspx?scid=kb;en-us;242975. Install the patch, then install your FireWire card, and get ready to dance around the limitations of the Windows installer.

That's right! There's no problem with the programs that handle the iPod, but the installer doesn't work with Windows 98SE. There is, however, a workaround: All you need to do is start the installer and then run the program that updates Windows separately. Here's how:

1. Run the iPod setup program, which you'll find at the top level of the iPod software CD and which is named setup.exe. You'll see the setup wizard's splash screen.
2. Click Start, point to Find, and then click Files or Folders. Search for "updater", and when you find the file named iPod-for-win-updater-nstlr.exe, double-click it to launch it.
3. Run the updater and click Restore to set up your iPod.

If you have a third-generation iPod, the program you want is named updater.exe, which you can find on your installation CD-ROM in the D:\Program Files\Apple\iPodUpdater\program files\WinRoot\runtime_ipod_updater_dir folder (assuming the D drive is your computer's CD drive).

This is a difficult test, though, because I've had a 40GB white iPod for a while, and it was the first one he saw. When he spotted it the first time, his reaction was: "Cool!" Understated, awe-inspired (while he lives in a house

ESSENTIAL MUSIC

Procol Harum

During my undergraduate years at the University of Pennsylvania, from 1965 to 1968, I sporadically shared a Philadelphia apartment with a talented singer–composer–guitar player named Richard Hogan. Richard suffered from two addictions, one malign—the alcoholism that ultimately killed him—and one benevolent, the British band Procol Harum. Beyond its acoustic delights, the inaugural Procol Harum LP came with a poster reproducing the stark black-and-white album jacket: a wan and wraithlike hippie chick—quite possibly she whose face had turned "a whiter shade of pale" in the group's greatest hit—standing beneath an exfoliating tree that is evidently enjoying an erotic relationship with an alien vegetable. Richard spent much of our senior year seeking a defect-free copy of the first Procol Harum album, acquiring many a poster in the bargain, and in consequence our apartment was papered with that Aubrey Beardsleyesque succubus. By the time I left 443 South 43rd Street, I was probably in love with our ashen apparition, but I was even more in love with Keith Reid's lyrics, reveling in their verbal surrealism, Mervyn Peake–like imagery, and affection for the grotesque.

Although Gary Brooker, the composer and lead vocalist, had a marvelous voice, his enunciations sometimes left you scratching your head. Undaunted, Richard would accost Procol Harum whenever they came to town, asking Mr. Brooker about the mystery phrases and inviting the whole band out to our wraith-intensive pad. (The drummer, B. J. Wilson, sometimes accepted, and to this day I retain vivid images, ominous in retrospect, of B. J. and Richard drinking scotch together.) And so it was that we learned of the peaches that "snuggle closer down into the clotted cream"...of the "two-pronged unicorn" who "plays at relaxation time the rhinestone flügelhorn, while mermaids lace carnations into wreaths for ailing whales"...and how "even Christian scientists can but display marble flags."

Farewell, dear Richard. Good-bye, musical unicorn. *Au revoir, ma belle dame de la figure blanche.*

➤ James Morrow (http://www.sff.net/people/Jim.Morrow/) is an author of novels that are often shelved in the science fiction section of bookstores. He has won the Nebula Award twice, for his short story "The Deluge" and his novella *City of Truth.* His irreverent sequel to the New Testament, *Only Begotten Daughter,* won the World Fantasy Award. His Nietzschean sea saga, *Towing Jehovah,* also won the World Fantasy Award.

with lots of electronic gadgets, he's still not immune to them), and impressed.

But his reaction to the iPod mini was quite different. He first got a glimpse of them while we watched together Steve Jobs' presentation and

iPod Settings and Preferences

nlike your computer—whether Mac or PC—the iPod is a simple device. (Even simpler than any cell phone or VCR, too.) Using it is as simple as navigating hierarchical menus by pressing buttons, and setting it up is easy as well.

There are two types of settings and preferences for your iPod. The first apply to the way iTunes reacts when you connect your iPod, such as whether it launches when the iPod is connected, whether it copies music automatically, or whether you manage your music library manually. The second group of settings is on the iPod itself, and these settings affect its display and playback. Here's an overview of these two types of settings and preferences.

DO OR DIE:

>> Set preferences for your iPod and iTunes

>> Change the display on your iPod

>> Customize your iPod's menus

iTunes Settings for the iPod

I call these "iTunes settings for the iPod" because they control the relationship between your iPod and iTunes on your computer, when you connect your iPod. When you do this, you'll see two special buttons at the bottom of the iTunes window (Figure 2-2). These buttons let you access iPod preferences and eject your iPod.

unveiling of the iPod mini via Apple's Webcast. This was in January 2004, at Jobs' Macworld Expo keynote presentation. Right away, he wanted one. He had techno-lust.

Figure 2-2

These extra buttons display at the bottom of the iTunes window when your iPod is connected.

iPod Preferences   Eject iPod

As you can see in Figure 2-2, the button at the left displays iPod preferences, and the right-hand button ejects your iPod. Click the left-hand button to display the iPod Preferences window (Figure 2-3).

You can choose how you want iTunes to update your iPod in this window.

- **Automatically update all songs and playlists:** If this is checked, iTunes updates your iPod each time you connect it, cloning your entire iTunes music library to your iPod. It adds new songs to your iPod and deletes any songs you've deleted from your library. This is the best way to work if you don't have a lot of music.

- **Automatically update selected playlists only:** You may want iTunes to only update certain playlists. If this is checked, iTunes won't create a carbon copy of your music library on your iPod, but will only update the checked playlists. This is good if you have more music on your computer than you have room for on your iPod, or if you have two iPods, such as a white model and a mini, and have to winnow down your music library to be able to fit what you want on the mini.

Figure 2-3

The iPod Preferences window lets you choose how iTunes acts when your iPod is plugged in, and lets you set several other iPod options.

iPod Preferences

○ Automatically update all songs and playlists
◉ Automatically update selected playlists only:

☑ Allman Bros – 71-6-27
☐ Art Pepper – Among Friends
☐ Art Pepper The Late Show
☐ Bach – Cello Suites
☐ Bach – KdF Hill

○ Manually manage songs and playlists

☑ Open iTunes when attached
☑ Enable disk use
☐ Only update checked songs

Cancel OK

But he was even more impressed when he actually saw one—and a green one, the color he liked best. His reaction this time was: "Awesome!"

So why is the mini more of a crowd-pleaser? Well, let's see what Perceval has to say.

FAQ

Click wheels? I have a Scroll wheel. What gives?

Since we're finally starting to talk about using the iPod, it's a good idea to get some terminology cleared up. Apple has specific names for the different parts of your iPod, so let's review them here.

The wheel you use to move through menus is called the *click wheel*, and the button in the middle of the wheel, which you press to select items, is called the *Select button*. The click wheel is found on 4G iPods and iPod minis.

3G iPods have a *scroll wheel*, which Apple curiously calls the *scroll pad* in the iPod *Users Guide*, but most other Apple documentation calls it a scroll wheel, so I'll use that term. There is also a touch-sensitive Select button in the middle of the scroll wheel.

1G iPods have a scroll wheel as well and have four buttons (see later in this sidebar) around the wheel. Unlike later models, the 1G iPod's scroll wheel actually turns; later models use a touch-sensitive wheel. 2G iPods have a *touch wheel*, with four buttons above it.

The 4G iPod and the iPod mini have four "buttons" built into the click wheel. Located at the north, south, east, and west, respectively, are the *Menu button*, the *Play/Pause button*, the *Next/Fast-forward button*, and the *Previous/Rewind button*. Press the sides of the click wheel to activate these buttons.

1G iPods have the same buttons around the scroll wheel, and 2G and 3G iPods have these buttons between the screen and the wheel, in this order: the *Previous/Rewind button*, the *Menu button*, the *Play/Pause button* and the *Next/Fast-forward button*.

The Menu button doesn't necessarily take you to a menu, but moves you up or back one level in the menus' hierarchy. At times, this might simply be from a song title to a playlist or from a playlist to the list of playlists. The other buttons do as expected.

At the top of your iPod you'll find a *Hold switch*, a small, sliding switch that turns off the wheel and buttons; this is on the right of a white iPod and on the left of a mini. There's also a *Headphone port* and, on some models (third-generation white iPods and iPod minis), a *Remote port*.

Finally, iPod minis and 3G and 4G iPods have a *Dock Connector port* at the bottom; you use this to connect the iPod to its dock or to plug in the FireWire-to-dock connector cable.

(Photo courtesty of Apple Computer, Inc.)

"I like the size; it's small and you can carry it around easily. I like the choice of colors (my favorite is green). I like the buttons on the click wheel; they're easier to press since they're on the wheel, and they're easier to spot, even though they're not lit up like on the white iPod. I don't like the smaller

- **Manually manage songs and playlists:** If this is checked, iTunes does nothing. You must drag your songs and playlists to your iPod to copy them. This is another good way to work when you don't have a lot of room on your iPod. See Syncing Music to Your iPod for more on these three update options.

- **Open iTunes when attached:** Check this if you want iTunes to open automatically whenever you connect your iPod to your computer. If you plug your iPod into your computer to charge it, and you don't really need to update your music often, you might want to uncheck this, since it prevents iTunes from getting in your way. If you don't check this, you'll need to manually launch iTunes whenever you want to update your iPod.

- **Enable disk use:** Check this if you want to use your iPod as an external hard disk. If you check this, you must eject your iPod before unplugging it, or you may damage its hard disk's directory. See Using the iPod as a Hard Disk for more on this.

- **Only update checked songs:** This tells iTunes to only update songs you have checked in your music library; this means that it only copies checked songs to your iPod. This can be a hassle, especially if you have a lot of songs, but it's another good way to manage your music if you have a small iPod and lots of music.

iPod Settings

All your iPod settings are available from—you guessed it—the Settings menu. From the main menu, run your finger clockwise on the scroll wheel until Settings is selected (Figure 2-4), then click the Select button. This moves you to the Settings menu.

The Settings menu contains a slew of menu items that let you turn on or off certain features of your iPod or change its display. Here's what you can access from this menu and what these settings do. Figure 2-5 shows the first six settings.

- **About:** This menu item displays a screen showing you some basic information about your iPod. You'll see the number of songs it contains, its capacity, how much free space is available, and the software version installed. You'll also see its serial number and exact model number. These later items are only useful if you ever need to have your iPod serviced. You'll note that the capacity does not correspond to the size you *think* your iPod is: For example, my 40GB iPod shows only a 37.2GB capacity. This is because there's a differ-

screen, but since you don't use the screen much, it's not a problem. I like the design of the iPod mini, with the rounded edges and the aluminum finish. By the way, I want one too!"

ence between the engineering department's gigabytes (using multiples of 1,024) and the marketing department's version (using multiples of 1,000).

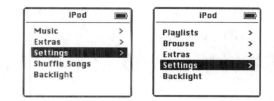

Figure 2-4

From the main menu, scroll to Settings, then press the Select button to access the Settings menu. At the left is the screen as seen on a 4G iPod. At the right is the screen on the iPod mini and earlier models.

- **Main Menu:** This menu lets you choose which items your iPod displays at the top level of its menus. You can turn on or off any of the items here (by default, the 4G shows Music, Extras, Settings, Shuffle Songs, and Backlight; the iPod mini and earlier models display Playlists, Browse, Extras, Settings, and Backlight). Turn on the menu items you use most. If you often browse by artist or genre, for example, turn these menu items on to save clicking through the menu hierarchy. The same is true for menu items like Contacts and Calendar. If you use these functions regularly, it's better to put them at the top-level menu so you can access them with fewer clicks. If you ever want to return the main menu to its default display, just select the last item in this menu, Reset Main Menu, and then select Reset.

- **Shuffle:** This toggles through three positions: Off, Songs, and Albums. See Listening to Music on Your iPod for more on using the shuffle function. The 4G iPod also has a Shuffle Songs menu item at the top level; this starts playing your songs in shuffle mode but does not affect the overall Shuffle setting.

- **Repeat:** This toggles through three positions as well: Off, One, All. See Listening to Music on your iPod for more on using Repeat.

- **Backlight Timer:** Select the amount of time you want the backlight to remain on. If you select Always On, it will never go off, your battery will probably die before you get to the end of an album, and all you'll have done is provided light for the lint in your pocket. If you never use your iPod in the dark, set this to Off. I find the best compromise is ten seconds; this gives me enough time to see what I'm doing and to read a track name or a playlist's contents; then the backlight shuts off without using too much juice.

- **Audiobooks (4G only):** This lets you choose a speed for your audiobook playback. You can choose from Slower, Normal, or Faster. See Listening to Audiobooks on Your iPod for more on this feature.

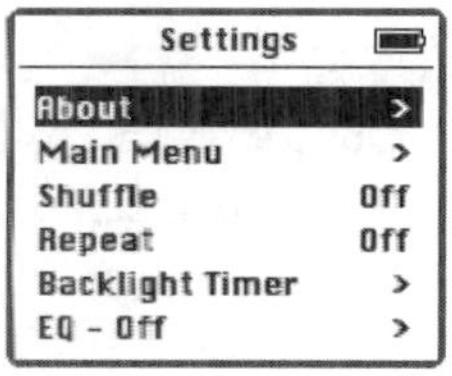

Figure 2-5

The first six settings in the 3G iPod's Settings menu. The 4G iPod has an Audiobooks setting as the sixth item.

You must remember that teenagers don't yet have enough CDs to fill a 40GB iPod (I do, however), so hard disk capacity is less of an issue. They want something that is cool, that is practical, and that is compact. My

ESSENTIAL MUSIC

Tuxedomoon

I'm sorry that there isn't an iPod for art—my preferred medium as an outsider and a consumer: To call up Mantegna, Rossetti, Billy Al Bengston, Callum Innes, and others for immediate gratification would be a sort of paradise.

But I like Schoenberg's *Transfigured Night* in both versions, Miles' *Sketches of Spain,* Pork Records does some wonders... I'm leaving out personal friends except the one CD I still treasure, which is *The Ghost Sonata,* by Tuxedomoon. The title is brilliantly usurped from Ibsen, the CD cover I have from Materiali Sonori a decade ago is a gorgeous matte finish, the booklet is a poignant document of an ensemble's dissolution, the music is haunting: My idea of an art experience.

➤ Harold Budd is a composer and recording artist. His pioneering work in the 1970s, both solo and with Brian Eno, remains the foundation of ambient music. He lives here: http://www.arcspace.com/calif/build/monument.htm.

- **EQ:** This is the equalizer setting. By default, this is Off, but you can choose a global setting from 22 different equalizer presets. If you have applied an equalizer preset to individual songs in iTunes, they override the setting on your iPod. See Listening to Music on Your iPod for more on using the equalizer.

- **Sound Check:** If you turn this on, your iPod plays all songs at the same relative volume. This is good if you listen to a variety of musical styles, and you don't want to keep adjusting the volume for each song. Mellow songs are played a little louder, and loud songs a bit softer.

- **Contrast:** Click this, then turn your finger on the scroll wheel to set your iPod's screen contrast. You'll find the setting that's best for you, but this will depend on whether you are indoors or outdoors. You may want to reset this from time to time, if you change locations. I find that a setting of about two-thirds of the maximum is ideal for both indoors and outdoors.

- **Clicker:** If this is on, your iPod makes a discreet clicking sound, like a slow-motion cicada, as you scroll through its menus. I find this reassuring; it makes it easier to know when you've moved up or down in the menus, and sounds somewhat old-fashioned, kind of like a typewriter clicking. The 4G iPod lets you choose to have the clicker be played through the tiny internal speaker in your iPod, through the headphones, or both. If you set this to headphones, you'll hear the click through your headphones or through external speakers if your iPod is connected to speakers or to a stereo.

- **Date & Time:** Select this to set your Time Zone, the Date & Time, the type of time display (12- or 24-hour), and whether the time displays in the title section of the iPod screen.

- **Contacts:** This lets you choose the sort and display order for your contacts. You can choose First Last (so Steve Jobs shows up at S) or Last, First (so Gates, Bill shows up at G). See Working with Contacts, Notes, and Calendars for more on using contacts.

thoughts on the mini were twofold: First, it's really small. I have enough trouble with cell phones and other small gadgets; would I lose this? Second, how do I choose what to put on the mini? With a music library of well over 40GB (with lots of music on external hard disks) and hundreds of CDs still not ripped, how

- **Language:** If you ever want to change the interface language on your iPod, this lets you choose from 14 languages. You can change to a language you're studying, to keep you on your toes, or you can annoy your friends by setting their iPods to display in a different language. This only changes the actual iPod interface, not the playlists or songs on your iPod. Just make sure you remember where the language setting is (it's third from the bottom) so you can find it again and change it back when they get angry.

- **Legal:** This displays totally boring but obligatory copyright information about your iPod, its software, and compression formats. You won't be tested on this.

- **Reset all Settings:** So, if you've spent an hour adjusting everything and want to do it all over again, select this, then select Reset. Everything goes back to the factory defaults.

TOOL KIT

Changing Your iPod's Name

Remember when you first connected your iPod to your computer, and iTunes displayed an assistant screen? You chose the name for your iPod there. You may have christened it Titanic or Big Phat Pod, or you named it after your current boyfriend or girlfriend, but now this name is wearing thin, or the person you named it after is just a memory. Here's how you can change it.

In iTunes, just select your iPod in the Source list and press Enter. You'll see the name highlighted. Type a new name, then press Enter again. That's all!

In some cases, if you use Windows, you may need to select the iPod in the Windows Explorer, then type over its name and press Enter to save the change.

can I choose a mere 4GB of music to put on the mini? I'd have to whittle down my existing iTunes music library and make some serious choices.

Well, it wasn't that difficult. I mean, even though I've got lots of music, I don't listen to it all at once. I found that the best way was to set the iPod

ESSENTIAL MUSIC

"Dark Star," by the Grateful Dead

As any Grateful Dead fan (aka Deadhead) will tell you, "Dark Star" is the ultimate Dead song. This cosmic symphony of rock psychedalia was the optimal vehicle for the group's improvisations, a template for the moods and feelings that the various musicians wanted to express in their music. Jerry Garcia said, " 'Dark Star' has meant, while I was playing it, almost as many things as I can sit here and imagine," and Phil Lesh called it "the one we tacitly agreed on where anything was okay."

While The Dead jammed many of their songs, "Dark Star" has a special place. It stands aside several other classic tunes that often stretched on for 30 minutes or more—"That's It for the Other One," "Turn on Your Lovelight," "Playin' in the Band"—but always offered a less structured environment for improvisation. The Grateful Dead performed "Dark Star" at least 232 times, according to Deadbase (http://www.deadbase.com).

On an absolute level, there are no Dark Stars, but there is one long, discontinuous "Dark Star," which was proven so adeptly by John Oswald in his "Grayfolded," a melding and morphing of dozens of Dark Stars into a long, single piece that embodies the essence of "Dark Star."

The ur-Dark Star must remain the 2/27/69 version, immortalized on the *Live Dead* album, which was released later the same year. This version has almost chamber-music perfection and subtlety, and its inclusion on The Dead's first live release raised it to a special place in the pantheon of Dead songs. It was the "Dark Star" that Deadheads (other than those who traded tapes) listened to over and over. Every other "Dark Star" flows from that version. Whether it be the raucous 8/27/72 performance, recorded in the scorching Oregon heat, where Jerry Garcia's notes spit from his amps like fire bolts; the sinuous 9/21/72 version (at over 37 minutes), with its long, mellow noodling; or the jazzy Halloween 1971 version, every "Dark Star" has its own character and mood. Other classic Dark Stars include the 2/13/70 Fillmore East recording, which is part of one of The Dead's greatest concerts ever, and the 48-minute 5/11/72 version played in Rotterdam.

"Dark Star" will remain, for aficionados of the Grateful Dead, the hallmark of their work. While The Dead performed hundreds of different songs, the scope and breadth—and length—of "Dark Star" makes it the highlight of almost every live Grateful Dead recording.

mini to update selected playlists, and scroll through the list of playlists, checking the ones I wanted to transfer to it. (See Syncing Music to Your iPod for more on finding the best way to choose how to sync your music.) The

Controlling Your iPod

DO OR DIE:

>> Using your iPod's controls

>> What the buttons do

The iPod is a deceptively simple device. Its minimal interface hides some complex functions, all of which can be managed through a mere six controls. In iPod Settings and Preferences, you saw what these controls are called, and now you'll see what they can do. Your iPod's controls do much more than just play music and pause it. Here's a quick review of your iPod's controls and what they do.

- **Previous/Rewind button:** Press this button to go back to the beginning of the current song. If you're at the beginning of a song, pressing this button takes you to the previous song in the playlist, if any. If you press and hold this button, the song rewinds. If you're at the beginning of the first song of a playlist, pressing this button takes you to the main menu. This is, in fact, the only way to stop the iPod from playing a playlist. Since when you press Pause, your iPod, well, pauses; it doesn't stop the playback. Only by pressing the Previous/Rewind button can you stop the playback and skip to the starting point, the main menu. (You can also get back to the starting point by pressing the Menu button; you can stop playing one song or playlist by choosing another one.)

- **Menu button:** This button takes you to the previous menu, moving up the hierarchy of menus one level at a time until you reach the main menu. If you've set the backlight to stay off, you can turn it on for at least 20 seconds

choice wasn't simple, but I started by choosing the ones I'd been listening to most recently.

I was able to fit 677 songs on the mini—I rip my music at 160kbps and have quite a few long tracks. I didn't put any classical music or audiobooks

(longer if you're moving around in the menus) by pressing and holding this button.

- **Play/Pause button:** As expected, this starts and stops
the playback of the selected playlist, song, or album. If
you press and hold this button for a couple of seconds,
your iPod goes to sleep. (It's not really off, since when
you wake it by pressing any button, you're at the same
place you were when you put it to sleep, unless you
sync it to your computer; in that case, it leaves whatever song was cued and returns to the main menu.)

- **Next/Fast-forward button:** This does the opposite of the
Previous/Rewind button. Pressing this during a song takes you to the beginning of the next song. Pressing it at the beginning of a song skips ahead to
the next song. And if you press and hold this button, you'll fast-forward
through the song. If you press it during the last song of a playlist, this jumps
you back to the main menu.

- **Scroll wheel:** You've already seen that you use the scroll wheel to move up
and down among menus, but this innovative control offers other uses as

FAQ

How Do I Restart My iPod?

Occasionally, you may run into problems with your iPod. You may find that the interface
is frozen, and no matter which buttons you press, nothing happens. As I mentioned earlier, you can't turn your iPod off, only put it to sleep. But if it does freeze, you can force
it to restart.

Turn the Hold switch on, then turn it off again. Press the Menu and Select buttons (on
a 4G iPod or an iPod mini) or the Menu and Play/Pause buttons (on all other models),
and hold them down for about five seconds, until you see the Apple logo display.
Release the buttons. Your iPod will reboot in a few seconds.

After restarting in this manner, you may need to reapply some of your settings. This
seems to affect the Contrast setting often, but usually little else.

If you don't see the Apple logo when restarting, then you've got a problem. Try
restarting again, and if this doesn't work, it's time to have your iPod checked out. (You
can check Troubleshooting Your iPod for some iPod troubleshooting information first.) If
it's still under warranty, or if you have an AppleCare contract, get in touch with Apple
(see www.apple.com for support information).

*on the mini at first, but many of the jazz tracks I have run ten minutes
or longer.*

*As I used the mini, I discovered that I didn't need all my music—in fact, it
was somewhat liberating to be able to choose from a subset of my music*

well. Some of them depend on pressing the Select button first. If you're listening to a song and you press the scroll wheel, you'll see the iPod's display change, showing a volume bar. Scroll to the left or to the right to lower or raise the volume. If you press the Select button, you'll see the display change to show a progress bar for the current song. You can scrub through the song, or rewind and fast-forward, by scrolling the wheel. You'll see the elapsed time and remaining time change as you do this. Finally, if you press the Select button twice while playing a song, you'll see five gray bullets. Scroll to the right, and you'll see these bullets change to stars; this is how you set a song's rating as you listen.

- **Select button:** You've seen earlier how you use the Select button in conjunction with the scroll wheel. You've also already seen how you press the Select button to select items in menus. That's all.

While I don't like to repeat myself, I'll do so here to show the preceding information in a different way. Table 2-2, on the following page, shows the main operations, but from another angle. Instead of telling you what each button does, it shows you what to do to accomplish specific tasks.

ESSENTIAL MUSIC

Discreet Music, by Brian Eno

In 1975, the concept of ambient music was born when Brian Eno released the album *Discreet Music*. The title track of this disc, at just over 30 minutes, remains the ur-recording of ambient music. Eno wanted this piece, containing just "two simple and mutually compatible melodic lines of different duration," to be something "that could be listened to and yet...ignored, perhaps in the spirit of Satie, who wanted to make music that could 'mingle with the sound of the knives and forks at dinner.'"

The music itself was created while Eno was having tea with Robert Fripp in his kitchen: It is as much a process as a piece of music. The liner notes to the album show the "Operation diagram for 'Discreet Music,'" beginning with a synthesizer, going through a graphic equalizer and an echo unit, and then passing through a series of loops and delays to finally result in what is heard on record. Designed to be background music, this piece nevertheless succeeds through synchronicity to be a masterful example of gradual processes.

With a sound like "horns heard through a soft fog," as music critic Mark Prendergast said in his book *The Ambient Century*, the lush melodies rise and fall like breaths becoming still as a body calms down. The timbre of the melodies changes, so they sound at times like flutes, at others like a bass clarinet, and at others like synthesized strings, but these very few notes come and go until they become as familiar as your own breathing.

Perfect music for relaxation, for creating atmosphere, or for conscious listening, "Discreet Music" remains the essential piece of ambient music.

library. While it's nice to have lots of music on an iPod, especially if you're traveling, it makes it harder to choose. Looking at the play counts of some of my music, I realized that I still limited my listening to certain playlists and albums.

Table 2-2 How to Control Your iPod

What You Want to Do	How to Do It
Turn your iPod on	Press any button. If it doesn't go on, check to see if the Hold button is locked.
Put your iPod to sleep	Press and hold the Play/Pause button for a couple of seconds. If your iPod isn't playing any music, it will go off on its own after two minutes of inactivity.
Turn on the backlight	If you have set your backlight to be off all the time, you can turn it on for 20 seconds by pressing and holding the Menu button. If you have set the backlight to be on for any length of time, it goes on whenever you press a button or turn the wheel.
Play a song, an album, or a playlist	Select the item you want to play, then press the Play/Pause button. You can also press the Select button twice to play a playlist or an album. The first press selects the first song in the list; the second press starts playing it.
Pause playback	Press the Play/Pause button.
Go to the next song	Press the Next/Fast-forward button.
Go to the beginning of the current song	Press the Previous/Rewind button when a song is playing.
Go to the previous song	Press the Previous/Rewind button when within the first three seconds of a song.
Go to the main menu	Press the Previous/Rewind button when at the beginning of the first song of a playlist, or press the Menu button several times, until you reach the main menu.
Go to the previous menu	Press the Menu button.
Rewind a song	Press and hold the Previous/Rewind button.
Fast-forward a song	Press and hold the Next/Fast-forward button.
Scrub through a song	Press the Select button, then scroll with the scroll wheel.
Change the volume	Turn the scroll wheel while playing a song or playlist, or while in pause mode.
Rate a song	Press the Select button twice while a song is active (playing or paused), then scroll the scroll wheel to select a rating.
Lock your iPod	Slide the Hold button at the top of your iPod to disable all its controls and prevent it from going on when bumped or jostled in a bag or in your pocket.

And with a smaller library on the mini, I could still change the music from time to time. When I bought new music from the iTunes Music Store, I'd remove one playlist and add the new album. This calls for a bit more work, since it's not automatic, but it's not rocket science.

Listening to Music on Your iPod

K, now that you've gotten through iPod Controls 101, we get to the heart of the matter. Using your iPod is certainly a lot more interesting than fiddling with its settings, transferring music to it, or just looking at it. Sure, it's a beautiful object—whether you have a white iPod or a mini—but let's face it: Beauty is truly only skin deep. If your iPod didn't play music so easily and efficiently, it wouldn't be such a popular item.

So, down to business. There are several ways you can start listening to music. (When I use the word "music" in this section, I include all kinds of audio files, including audiobooks and voice recordings.)

DO OR DIE:

>> Selecting what you want to listen to

>> Browsing your tunes

>> Shuffling, repeating, and equalizing

>> Creating playlists on the fly

Selecting Playlists

The first way to start playing music is by using playlists. As you saw in Working with Playlists, playlists are the main way of organizing your music both in iTunes and on your iPod. Use the scroll wheel to select Playlists (Figure 2-6), then press the Select button.

So while I still feel the iPod mini is a bit expensive, it's a very cool toy. It's sleek and attractive, and unless you really need to carry a lot of music with you, it holds more than enough for you to listen to for plenty of time.

Figure 2-6

Select Playlists, then press the Select button to access a scrollable list of all your playlists.

```
          iPod        ▬
  Playlists          >
  Browse             >
  Extras             >
  Settings           >
  Backlight
```

4G Corner: The Music Menu

Unlike the menu in Figure 2-6, the 4G iPod's main menu has a Music menu. Select this, then select one of its submenus to choose the music you want to play, as described later in Browsing Your iPod's Music. These submenus are Playlists, Artists, Albums, Songs, Genres, Composers, and Audiobooks.

Figure 2-7

When your iPod plays a song, it tells you all about the song.

```
 ►    Now Playing   ▬
 1 of 23
        Dark Star
      Grateful Dead
        Live Dead

 15:37              7:38
```

The list you'll see contains all the playlists you've transferred to your iPod. If you have enough space, and you chose automatic updating, all the playlists you created with iTunes are here. If you've chosen to sync only selected playlists or to manage your iPod manually (see All about Your iTunes Music Library), you'll see the playlists you've chosen for syncing or those you've dragged to your iPod from iTunes.

Select a playlist, then press the Play/Pause button. Or if you don't want to start at the beginning of a playlist, press Select, then scroll to the song you want to start with and press Play/Pause.

When your iPod starts playing a song, it displays the song name, the artist's name, and the album, and, beneath these three lines, shows a progress bar with the elapsed time and remaining time (Figure 2-7).

If the song title is too long to fit on the screen, the iPod scrolls the text from right to left. This can be a pain to read, since it looks blurry, but you'll be able to figure out which song it is.

You can see from the arrow at the top left of the screen in Figure 2-7 that the song is playing. When you press the Play/Pause button, to pause the track, you'll see a standard double-bar pause symbol.

Browsing Your iPod's Music

Another way to start playing music is by browsing your iPod music. Select Browse from the main menu, or select Music if you have a 4G iPod, and press the Select button. You'll see a list of criteria you can use for browsing (Figure 2-8).

When browsing, you can access all your music, even if you've never set up a single playlist. In fact, some people find this a great way to listen to music on their iPods: They just dump all their music into their iTunes Music Library and pay no attention to anything else. They then access it by artist, album, or whichever criteria they prefer. However, if you want to work this way, you need to make sure, when ripping your CDs, that the songs have the correct tags. If not, you won't be able to find them (or at least not easily) on your iPod. (See Tags and Track Info for more on using tags and setting tag information.)

Figure 2-8

You can browse your iPod's music by Artist, Album, Song, Genre, or Composer. The 4G iPod adds an Audiobook menu item to this list.

- When you browse by artist, you see a list of artists' names; then after you select an artist, you see a list of their albums. Select an album, and you'll find which songs are on the iPod. If you have compilation albums on your iPod, you can't choose an entire compilation in this manner; you can, however, access an individual artist's song(s) from this menu.

- When you browse by album, you see a list of your albums' titles. Even if your iPod has only one song from a given album, you'll find that album listed. However, you won't see the entire album name if it's more than 15 to 18 characters. If you have albums with multiple discs, you may not be able to see which disc is which, but as long as the tags are correct, you'll find they're in numerical order (if they are all named Disc 1, Disc 2, or CD 1, CD 2, etc.).

- When browsing by song, you see an alphabetical list of all your songs. Every one of them. If you have a lot of songs, this can be pretty difficult to scroll through, but they are in alphabetical order, which makes it somewhat easier to navigate.

- When you browse by genre or composer, you see a list of genres or composers whose music is on your iPod, then a list of artists. After this point, you browse each artist's songs by album as described earlier.

- No matter which criterion you choose, the first item in the list is All. This displays all artists, songs, albums, or whatever criterion you've chosen. In many cases you may find this the easiest way to access the song or album you are looking for.

To sum up, unless you browse by song, every other criterion leads you to a list of albums—complete or not—which are just sorted differently.

4G Corner: One-Press Random Access

The Shuffle setting is one of the most popular ways of listening to the iPod. Apple made a smart decision by providing direct access to random song playback from the main menu of the 4G iPod. By selecting the Shuffle Songs menu item, you start playing your songs at random—your iPod selects one song after another, with the exception of audiobooks; and if you don't want to hear a song, just press the Next button, and your iPod will play another one.

Mirror, Mirror, on the Wall, Who's the Randomest One of All?

One of the great things about listening to music on the iPod is the shuffle function. It introduces serendipity into your musical library and can surprise you by choosing just the right song at the right time. But to get the most out of random listening, you need to know a few things.

Your iPod plays songs in random order when you turn the shuffle function on (Settings > Shuffle). You can choose from Songs, Albums, or Off. When you choose Songs, it plays one song, then picks another one and plays it. When you choose Albums, it picks an album, plays it all the way through, then picks another.

But the iPod only shuffles what you've selected. This is important, so think carefully. (See the sidebar 4G Corner: One-Press Random Access for a quick way to play songs at random.)

If you want to play songs at random, set the shuffle function to Songs, then find a song. If you want the iPod to choose songs at random from your *entire* library, select Browse > Songs, then select a song. If you press Play right away, the iPod will start by playing the first song in alphabetical order (which is why you hear the song entitled Aardvark so often...). But if you don't like the first song, just press the Next button to go to another random song.

As you listen, you can keep using the Next button to skip songs when you hear something you don't like. This is practical when that audiobook of *War and Peace* comes up, or when you hear the fourth movement of a symphony after a searing guitar solo.

If you select a playlist and start playing a song from it, the iPod will choose songs at random *only from that playlist.* This is important, and I'll come back to it. If you browse your library and select an artist, then select All, the iPod will choose songs by that artist, from all their albums. However, if you select an album, either directly or by selecting Artist first, you'll only hear songs from that album, in random order.

But here's where it gets interesting. You've seen that shuffling songs may bring up *War and Peace* or the fourth movement of Brahms' Third Racket, and you may realize, after a while, that you *never* want to hear certain tracks when listening at random. You can create a special Random playlist and fill it only with the songs you would accept at random. And if this is a smart playlist, it's even easier: Just choose to exclude, for example, audiobooks and classical music by genre, or make the playlist contain only pop and rock, or only jazz and blues. Then when you want to use the shuffle function, you can limit which songs get tossed into the random bucket.

Experiment. Try out different ways of using shuffle, and you may find the iPod is the ultimate radio, where reception is always perfect, and the music always fits your mood.

Using the Repeat Function

As you saw in iPod Settings and Preferences, you can turn on your iPod's repeat function. You can set this to Off, One, or All. When you set this to All, the iPod repeats all the songs in a playlist; at the end of the playlist, it starts over. If you've selected an album to play, it repeats the entire album after it reaches the end.

If you set this to One, the iPod repeats the one song that's playing. If you select a different song, the iPod keeps playing that song until you choose another. Frankly, I don't see why you'd want to do this, but you can, if it turns you on.

Using the Equalizer

You saw in Using the iTunes Equalizer how you can apply equalizer presets to all your music or to individual songs using iTunes. When you sync your music to your iPod, the iPod records these presets and plays back individual songs according to your choices. You can also choose to override individual presets and use the iPod's built-in equalizer to adjust your playback.

There are a few obvious reasons why you would want to do this. First, you may have music that needs bass or treble boosted, especially if you don't have great earphones. Second, if you're listening to your iPod through portable speakers, you might want to adjust the sound. You should try different settings to see which are best for the types of music you listen to.

Apple says that using the equalizer shortens your battery's playback time, but not by how much. I assume that the iPod has to work a bit harder when using the equalizer, but I doubt it makes a huge difference. Of course, your mileage may vary.

Using the On-The-Go Playlist

Third-generation iPods include an *On-The-Go* playlist, which lets you add songs, albums, or all the music by a given artist, on an ad hoc basis, to a special playlist. This is, in fact, the only way you can manipulate playlists from your iPod.

The On-The-Go playlist starts out empty. As you browse your music, either by song, album, or artist, press the Select button and hold it down for a couple of seconds. You'll see the selection highlighting flash, and the selected item is added to the On-The-Go playlist.

You can add single songs, entire albums, playlists, or, if you select an artist, all their music to this playlist. To listen to this playlist, select Playlists from the main menu, then scroll all the way to the end of the list, where you'll see On-The-Go. Start playing this by pressing the Play/Pause button.

The next time you connect your iPod to your computer, if you have automatic updating turned on, iTunes records this On-The-Go playlist and numbers it (the first one is On-The-Go 1, and so on). It then syncs it back to your iPod with this name. You can rename it if you want, or leave it as is. Your iPod then presents you with an empty On-The-Go playlist, so you can make another. With this feature, you can start with no playlists on your iPod and gradually create them

4G Corner: More Power to On-The-Go Playlists

One of the nice features on the 4G iPod is the ability to create and save multiple On-The-Go playlists. Proceed as described for 3G models, then if you want to save your playlist, select Playlists, then scroll to the end of the list to find your first On-The-Go playlist. Select it and press the Select button, then select Save Playlist > Save Playlist. You'll then be able to start over and create another On-The-Go playlist.

If you want to clear the On-The-Go playlist rather than save it, scroll to the On-The-Go playlist at the end of the Playlist list. Press the Select button, then select Clear Playlist > Clear Playlist. If you have saved the On-The-Go playlist, however, you cannot clear it; you can only delete it later from iTunes.

Another 4G addition is the ability to delete songs from On-The-Go playlists. If you haven't yet saved an On-The-Go playlist, scroll to the On-The-Go playlist at the end of the Playlist list, then press the Select button. You'll see the songs you've added to the On-The-Go playlist. Scroll to the song you want to remove, then press the Select button until it flashes. After three flashes, the song will disappear from the playlist.

as you listen to your music. You can rename the playlists in iTunes, giving them more appropriate monikers.

If you want to clear your On-The-Go playlist, select it, scroll to the end, then select Clear Playlist, then Clear Playlist again to confirm.

As I pointed out in Listening to Audiobooks with iTunes, audiobooks that you can listen to on your iPod are digital files containing recordings of people reading books. If you're an audiobook fan, you'll have already read that earlier section, and you'll know all about downloading or importing audiobooks. Now it's time to talk about listening to them on your iPod and using the special features that Apple offers for audiobooks.

DO OR DIE:

>> Listening to words

>> What's special about audiobook files

>> Changing the speed of audiobooks

Finding Your Audiobooks on Your iPod

If you have a 4G iPod, audiobooks that you've purchased from Audible.com or the iTunes Music Store will show up in the new Audiobooks category when you browse your music. To see them, select Music > Audiobooks. But if you've imported your own audiobooks, they may not show up here. The iPod looks for bookmarkable files and adds them to this category. If you have MP3 audiobooks, or if you've imported audiobooks from CDs and haven't made the files bookmarkable, you won't find them here. So you really need to make the files book-

ONE iPOD TO RULE THEM ALL
During the editing of the three Lord of the Rings movies, director Peter Jackson spent long periods of time in London working with

UNDER THE HOOD

4G Corner: Audiobook Features in the 4G iPod

Some of the most interesting new features in the 4G iPod relate to audiobooks, since Apple has realized how popular the iPod is among audiobook listeners. These features include simpler access to audiobooks when browsing your iPod's contents, and the ability to change the playback speed for audiobooks.

If you have a 4G iPod, read the rest of this section carefully to see how to work with these new features.

markable; see Listening to Audiobooks with iTunes for instructions on making files bookmarkable.

If you have an older iPod or an iPod mini, you'll find your audiobooks in the Spoken Word genre: Select Browse > Genre > Spoken Word. Again, this only applies to audiobooks you've bought from Audible or the iTunes Music Store, unless you have set the genre for other audiobooks. You can also search by artist, but some audiobooks are listed by author, and others by reader. It's best to make sure you set the appropriate tags in iTunes before syncing your audiobooks to your iPod (see Tags and Track Info); set the artist to the book's author, and set the genre to Spoken Word.

Some people find it practical to create a Spoken Word playlist and add all their audiobooks to this playlist. It's easier to find them quickly, and you don't need to browse through genres or artists.

Playing Back Your Audiobooks

All of the steps and tips that I presented for listening to music, in Listening to Music on Your iPod, also apply to listening to audiobooks. There's one big difference, however, between audiobooks and music. When you stop listening to an audiobook, you want to pick up where you left off; you rarely want to start over at the beginning, especially if you're reading *War and Peace*.

If you've bought audiobooks from Audible.com or from the iTunes Music Store, this is a snap. These files are a special type of bookmarkable AAC file. Files like this record their location when you stop listening, and transfer this bookmark to iTunes when you sync your iPod. You can even listen to a file on iTunes, picking up where you left off on your iPod, then sync the file and your current bookmark back to the iPod so you never miss anything.

If you have audiobook files in MP3 format, or if you've ripped your own audiobook CDs, see Listening to Audiobooks with iTunes to find out how to make these files bookmarkable.

4G iPods have an interesting new feature for listening to audiobooks: You can change their speed. Select Settings > Audiobooks, then select Slower, Normal, or Faster. Normal is, well, the original speed. But Slower and Faster

composer Howard Shore. But to keep in touch with his editing crew in Wellington, New Zealand, the production team had set up a high-bandwidth secure network so they could transfer digital video files to Jackson for approval.

reduce or increase the speed by 25%. This doesn't make your audiobooks sound as if the reader is sedated, or as if he or she is trying out for the Alvin and the Chipmunks reunion tour; it actually changes the speed without changing the pitch of the voice.

You can also make this change on the fly, while you are listening to an audiobook. Start playing back an audiobook, then press the Select button three times. You'll see a screen showing the name of the audiobook and, beneath this, Speed on the left and the current speed on the right. Use the click wheel to change the speed; scroll to the left to slow it down, and the setting changes to Slower. Scroll to the right, and the setting becomes Faster. This change only affects the current audiobook, so if you don't want to apply the setting across the board, this is the way to do it.

This may all sound futile until you start listening to *War and Peace*. If you have 62 hours to spare, no sweat. But if not, and you want to get Tolstoy moving along a bit faster, you can save more than 15 hours by speeding up the audiobook. In the other direction, slowing it down may be just the right thing if you suffer from insomnia.

Weta Digital's network arrived in a different location from where Jackson was working, however, and to avoid any chance of digital Gollums sniffing the network and intercepting the footage, they needed a simple, portable solution to get the QuickTime files from their network node to Jackson. The

ESSENTIAL MUSIC

The Pearl, by Harold Budd and Brian Eno

One album (among many) which I often feel a need to hear is *The Pearl,* by Harold Budd and Brian Eno. I think this is a landmark album for a number of reasons.

Firstly, *The Pearl* successfully discarded all the recording strategies which had evolved to become unquestioned conventions in popular music—conventions which were intended to grab and hold the listener's attention. It was a great relief to enjoy beautiful, complex, evolving sounds for their own sake again, without all the usual baggage. This discarding also made it possible to address a different emotional and temporal spectrum: one which involves calm, tranquility, contemplation—and slowness.

Even more significantly, Harold Budd, Brian Eno, and Daniel Lanois created a music which plays with our expectations of relative scale. They consciously used recording to fix and explore musical and sonic events which might previously have been overlooked, because they were transient or fugitive.

Experiencing this alters our perspective in the same way that a look down the first microscope must have altered the worldview of someone in the eighteenth century. Suddenly you realize you are experiencing something which was previously overlooked, through a new technology, at a vastly different scale. And for the first time, you can appreciate its true beauty and its real significance.

This album wasn't their first recording of this kind, but I feel that *The Pearl* is the most beautiful and satisfying. (The prototype concept was proposed around the turn of the century by Eric Satie. It eventually became practical to apply these principles in a contemporary domestic context through modern recording techniques. Eno understood the implications of all this and had begun his explorations some time before, as had Budd, from his own perspective.)

The result is a texturally complex, organically unfolding music. It is grown from an interplay between elegant, minimal figures played on a piano and sonic and temporal structures made possible only through the sensitive, intelligent, and perceptive use of recording processes. It stands as a landmark in the history of recorded music. And far above all this contextual stuff, the music is beautiful. An endless delight.

➤ John Foxx (http://www.metamatic.com) is a singer and composer who created the group Ultravox, in the 1970s, and who recorded several solo albums after leaving the band in 1979. He has recently turned to ambient and electronic music, notably with the recent Cathedral Oceans and Translucence/Drift Music, the latter with Harold Budd.

solution was simple: iPods. Using 30GB iPods (the largest available at the time), the editing crew copied the video files and brought them by sneaker-net to Jackson, who plugged them into his PowerBook to view them directly from the iPod.

Understanding Your iPod's Battery

side from the music you put in your iPod, the most important part of the device is its battery. Without a good battery, your iPod would quickly become "that thing in your pocket." It's really a bummer when you want to listen to music, and you find that your battery's dead—it doesn't help much to have 10,000 songs in your pocket when that happens.

As with all portable devices, Apple made a compromise between size, weight, and battery life when designing the iPod. Sure, they could have put a higher-capacity battery in the iPod, making it larger and heavier, but they chose to offer 8 hours of battery life (for 3G and mini models, 12 hours for 4G iPods), in normal conditions, and provide a light, compact device.

But there's a problem: Not everyone gets the expected battery life out of their iPod, and some people get much less. As with every portable device, the battery usage given "varies by use," as Apple says. But this variation depends on a lot of factors, and if you want your iPod's battery to give you as much music as possible, there are ways of doing so.

First, let's look at the battery itself. It's a lithium-ion battery, which is much more efficient than earlier types of rechargeable batteries (such as nickel-cadmium) and much smaller for the same amount of power. This kind of battery is

DO OR DIE:

>> Learn all about your iPod's battery

>> How to extend your battery life

>> Hack your battery display

MELTDOWN WARNING

You might not think of this when connecting your iPod to your computer or AC adapter, but if it's in a case, you should take it out. The battery can get hot when charging, and some cases—especially

UNDER THE HOOD

said to have a life of two to three years, and many factors can affect how long your iPod battery will last.

Unlike nickel-cadmium batteries, lithium-ion batteries don't have a "memory effect," which requires that, for optimal charge, the batteries be recharged when completely depleted. Lithium-ion batteries last longest when partially charged, but only last for about 300 to 500 charge cycles. However, there's a lot of confusion as to what a "charge cycle" actually is. Apple defines a charge cycle like this:

> *A charge cycle means using all of the battery's power, but that doesn't necessarily mean a single charge. For instance, you could listen to your iPod for a few hours one day, using half its power, and then recharge it fully. If you did the same thing the next day, it would count as one charge cycle, not two, so you may take several days to complete a cycle.*

You may find that your battery dies in less than two years, and if you don't have an AppleCare contract or other extended warranty, you'll need to replace it. This is not considered to be a user-replaceable item, and Apple will be happy to replace yours (for $99, at press time), but some vendors sell iPod batteries (for less than Apple) and offer instructions on replacing them. If you're comfortable opening a computer and, say, changing a hard disk, you should be able to change your iPod's battery.

Charging Your Battery

When you take your iPod out of its box, its battery may have a little bit of juice in it, but not much. You'll need to charge it to start using it. The easiest way is to plug it into your computer, via the FireWire cable (if you've got a Mac, or if you have a six-pin FireWire jack on a PC) or via its USB cable (if you have a 4G iPod and a high-power USB port on your PC or your Mac), and let it sit for a while. If you have a dock for your iPod, connect the dock to your computer using the special cable provided, then sit the iPod in the dock.

You can also charge the iPod by connecting it to its included AC adapter. Your battery will charge to about 80% of its capacity in two hours, but it takes about four hours for it to charge fully. Nevertheless, you can start transferring music to your iPod while it's charging; as long as it's plugged into your computer you can use it, even play music with it.

leather or silicone cases—can retain the heat, leading to possible damage of your iPod. Use your judgment as to whether your remove your iPod from its case, but use it wisely.

When your iPod is charging, its display tells you so. It either shows a large, animated battery icon with the word "Charging" above it, or if it's playing music or displaying any of its menus, a small animated battery icon with a lightning bolt through it at the top right corner.

When the charge has completed, the large icon changes, and the word above it says "Charged"; or the small icon changes: The lightning bolt is still there, but the battery part of the icon stops moving. But this is bogus: The iPod never knows when it's fully charged, and after you plug it in, it will say "Charging" for about four hours, no matter how much power was in the battery to start with. When the battery is full, you can unplug the iPod and plug it in again, and another four-hour charging cycle will begin.

The iPod uses a trickle-charge system to ensure that the battery doesn't get overcharged. But that doesn't help the newbie, who thinks their battery isn't getting fully charged, since every time they plug it into their computer or the dock, it starts charging again, or at least says so.

Don't sweat it. It's just one of those unavoidable things, like ants at a picnic. Apple could have given better feedback on battery charging—and on its charge level as well—but decided not to bother.

About That Battery Indicator

An iPod with a dead battery is, well, dead weight. You can't do anything with it. So you'll certainly keep an eye on its battery indicator, to know when you need to recharge it or to have an idea of how much music you can listen to before it zonks out.

If you thought the battery indicator was going to help you, think again.

Let me quote Apple's technical article 61475, laconically titled, "iPod's battery indicator is approximate":

> The iPod battery indicator shows approximately how much charge is left in the battery. You may find that the battery indicator shows a

FAQ

Why Doesn't My iPod Charge?

While I said the easiest way to charge your iPod is to just plug it into your computer, not all computers will charge its battery. Only those computers with a six-pin FireWire jack can charge the iPod; if you use the USB 2 cable or the six-pin to four-pin adapter, the iPod won't charge (though a 4G iPod can charge using the USB 2 cable if you have a high-power USB port).

In this case, plug the six-pin FireWire plug into the power adapter that's provided with the iPod, and let it sit for a few hours to charge it.

If you're using the Apple iPod Dock Connector to FireWire and USB 2 Cable, you can plug the FireWire end of it into your AC adapter, and the USB end of it into your computer. This is the only way you can charge your iPod while updating it if you use the USB 2 connection.

Also, the iPod won't charge if your computer is asleep. On some recent Macs it will charge, but on most computers, sleep mode cuts off all outgoing power through the FireWire port.

Some cases are safe. An open, plastic case like the Showcase, for example (see iPod Cases), provides plenty of air to the iPod's surface both on front and back. But if you have a leather case, remember that leather is an

charge left, but iPod stops playing because the battery is, in fact, empty. In some cases, the battery indicator may show less than a full charge even though you've fully charged iPod for 4 hours.

That's a pretty clear way of saying that the battery indicator is about as reliable as a Ouija board. And that's what it comes to.

I've found that my battery indicator may show no power, even after a charge, show full power then blink off, or anything in between. Users everywhere have the same problem, though this seems to affect 3G models more than the first- and second-generation models. (The 4G iPod is more reliable.)

It's just something you need to deal with. Unless Apple releases a firmware update that corrects this—something that is certainly possible—you'll have to assume that you never know how much time you've got left. However, some users have found the battery indicator to be more accurate following the April 2004 firmware update.

If you really think your battery is gypping you, check out the previously mentioned technical article (http://docs.info.apple.com/article.html?artnum=61475), which describes a procedure to test the battery. If yours doesn't last long enough, and your iPod is under warranty, contact Apple so they can check it and, perhaps, replace the battery.

TOOL KIT.

Changing the Battery Indicator Display

The iPod's battery indicator is not only imprecise, but its display doesn't tell you much more than an approximate level indication. The iPod's software has the ability to display its battery level differently, but Apple doesn't give you a way to do this.

If you have a third- or fourth-generation iPod, there's a simple hack to change the display from a battery icon to a digital display. The maximum is around 500, and the minimum is...well, I've never seen it get down below around 100. Here's how you can make this change.

If you're using a Mac, download a little program called iVolt, which switches the battery indicator from visual to digital and back again: http://homepage.mac.com/billions/ivolt/.

You can also do this from the Finder by pressing Command-G, then entering the following folder path in the dialog that displays:

```
/Volumes/[your iPod's name]/iPod_Control/Device/
```

Press Enter to open that folder.

Next, create a text file with any text editor—such as Apple's TextEdit—called _show_voltage (it's important to keep those underscores) and place it in that folder.

excellent insulator; if your iPod's battery is low, and it needs to charge for a long time, this could raise the device's temperature too much.

If you're a command-line geek, here's the magic command to make the change from the Apple Terminal:

```
touch "/Volumes/[your iPod's name]/iPod_Control/Device/_show_voltage"
```

And to undo the preceding, use this command:

```
rm -i "/Volumes/[your iPod's name]/iPod_Control/Device/_show_voltage"
```

If you use Windows, go to the \[your iPod's name]\iPod_Control\Device\ folder and place a text file (created with NotePad) called _show_voltage in the folder. It's important that this file be named exactly as shown here; its name must not contain any extension.

In all of these cases, you may need to restart your iPod for this change to take effect. Press and hold both the Menu and Play buttons until it restarts.

Extending Your Battery Life

Battery life is the key to happiness, at least with your iPod. As you've seen in the previous section the iPod's battery can be imponderable, but there are ways to tame it. If you want to keep your iPod playing music for as long as possible, keep in mind a few basic rules to extend its life as much as possible.

DO OR DIE:

>> Eleven tips to make your battery last longer

1. Make sure you've got the latest iPod software. If you use a Mac, check for software updates regularly with the Software Update preference pane. If you're on a PC, check Apple's Web site from time to time (http://www .apple.com/ipod/download/). Software updates may improve battery life or, one day, fix that irksome battery indicator.

2. Keep your iPod within its recommended temperature ranges—operating temperature range: 32° to 95° F (0° to 35° C); storage temperature range: -4° to 113° F (-20° to 45° C).

3. If you've left your iPod in the heat or cold for a while, let it adjust to room temperature before you start using it. Don't take it out of a bag that's been in the trunk of your car in winter, or in summer for that matter, and turn it on right away. Let it sit for a half hour or so.

4. Don't leave the iPod in the sun for a long time, and don't leave it sitting on your dashboard in a closed car. The heat could damage the battery. If

you're on the beach, in a boat, or just lying on the grass in a park, think of covering the iPod with something to keep it out of direct sunlight.

5. If at any time your iPod displays its "low battery" icon, plug it into your charger or your computer via its FireWire or USB cable. Make sure your computer's on; the iPod won't charge if the computer's off or asleep. Also, make sure it's not set to go to sleep anytime soon.

6. Use the Hold switch on the iPod and/or its remote to prevent it from being turned on accidentally. If you put your iPod in a backpack, a handbag, or your pocket, it may get turned on by bumping into something. It'll go off after a few minutes—if it hasn't started playing any music—but repeated bumps will use up more battery power.

7. If you don't use your iPod for a while, its battery will run out. At optimal storage temperature it should last from 14 to 28 days. If you're not using it for a long period, you should still charge it every two weeks or so. Try not to let the battery run out completely. But you won't be able to go for two weeks without using it, will you?

8. Try not to use backlighting if you don't need it; this uses a lot of power. If you do, set it to turn off after five or ten seconds. Choose Settings > Backlight Timer to select your backlight settings.

9. The equalizer also uses additional battery power. Choose Settings > EQ to turn it off, if you can live without it.

10. When you change tracks often by pressing the Next or Previous button, the iPod's hard disk spins up. This uses a lot more battery power than if you just let a playlist run on its own. Of course, the iPod was designed for you to change tracks when you want, so don't deprive yourself of the music you want just to get a bit more battery life.

11. Long tracks or large files use more battery life. The iPod's hard disk only spins up when necessary to load music files into its cache. It is designed to work best with songs that are less than 9MB. So if you compress your music at high bit rates or use Apple Lossless compression, you'll have larger files that will deplete your charge a bit faster. But, hey, if that's the way you want to listen to your music, you'll just have to live with slightly shorter playback times.

Many of these tips only affect people who need to squeeze every last minute out of their batteries. If you're really going to try to use it for eight full hours a day (or twelve hours, if you have a 4G iPod), then pay careful attention.

If not, don't worry about things like the equalizer or backlight. Most people get by just fine with a few hours of music between charges.

But if you find that your iPod battery isn't lasting long enough, see Getting More Power to Your iPod for some hardware to recharge your iPod in different places, or for an extra battery pack to help increase your listening time.

Syncing Music to Your iPod

In case you thought we'd finished looking at iTunes, think again. iTunes is the great organizer of your iPod's music, so here's one last section that talks about how it works. In the first part of this book, I showed you how to manage your music library, how to create playlists, and how to edit the tag information for your music files. In most cases, that's all you need to know: You can just plug your iPod into your computer, and let iTunes sync your music automatically.

But that may not be right for you. You may be a control freak: You may want to manage your iPod's music manually, or you may only want to update certain playlists. Or if you have a small-capacity iPod and a lot of music, you might want to be able to choose which music goes on your iPod.

As you see in the sidebar How Much Music Do People Have on their iPods? the question of which is the best way to sync music only interests some iPod owners, since they don't fill up their iPods anyway. If this is the case, your best bet is to use automatic syncing. But if you've got a small iPod and lots of music, or if you've got a white iPod and buy a mini, you'll probably have to decide what you want to put on it.

DO OR DIE:

>> Managing your music automatically

>> Managing your music manually

>> Do you want fries with that playlist?

FAQ

How Much Music Do People Have on Their iPods?

In late March 2004, I asked my friend Rob Griffiths, who runs the Mac OS X Hints Web site (www.macosxhints.com) to run a poll on his site. The question was, If you own an iPod, how many gigabytes of stuff (music and data) do you keep on it?

My thought was that many, if not most, iPod owners didn't have much music on their iPods, and, in fact, that many iPod owners didn't even come close to filling them up.

I'm not surprised at the responses (see Figure 2-9): They show why the iPod mini is so popular.

Now, this poll is hardly scientific; it was a voluntary poll and only ran for 24 hours. However, with 264 respondents, the data is pretty clear: Almost 50% of iPod owners have less than 10GB of music and data on their iPods. Another 36% have 11 to 20GB, and the rest have more data, partly because, well, they have bigger iPods.

So, what does all this tell us? First, that most people either don't need a large-capacity iPod or don't have one. I doubt that the majority of people answering this poll have iPods that only hold 10GB or less. But I can assume that those of us with 40GB iPods are in the minority—unless many 40GB owners don't put much music on their iPods either.

In addition, a more scientific survey carried out by Jupiter Research, published in April 2004, showed that 1,000 songs was just about the right capacity for most owners of digital music players. People found a rechargeable battery, small size, and connectability to be more important than capacity.

Of course, there's an exception to every rule. Fashion designer Karl Lagerfeld recently said, in an interview with the French magazine *Elle*, that he owns 40 iPods! Hold on, let's do the math... If he has 40GB iPods, then that makes about 1.5 *terabytes* of music. Or, according to Apple's calculations, 400,000 songs. If you put all that music end to end, that makes over 20,000 hours of music! How can he listen to all that? And how can he tell what's on each iPod?

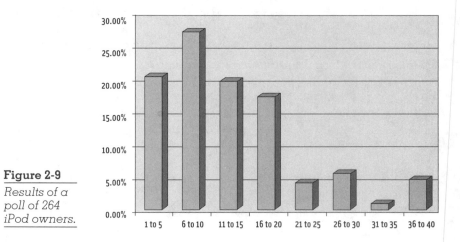

Figure 2-9

Results of a poll of 264 iPod owners.

You have three ways of syncing music to your iPod, and you select this from iTunes, in the iPod Preferences window (see iPod Settings and Preferences):

- **Automatically update all songs and playlists:** iTunes updates your iPod each time you connect it, cloning your entire iTunes music library to your iPod, adding any new tracks and playlists that you've added to iTunes since the last sync, and removing those you've deleted.

- **Automatically update selected playlists only:** iTunes won't create a carbon copy of your music library on your iPod, but will only update the checked playlists.

- **Manually manage songs and playlists:** iTunes does nothing. You must drag your songs and playlists to your iPod to copy them.

Each of these three choices has its advantages and disadvantages. Let's look at them one at a time.

Automatically Update All Songs and Playlists

Most iPod users don't have more music than their iPod can hold, and in this case, letting iTunes handle everything for you is the best way to go. To get the most out of this method of syncing, you should use iTunes to create as many playlists as possible, though you can still browse your iPod (see Listening to Music on Your iPod) by artist, album, genre, or composer even if you have no playlists at all.

The automatic-update option is a no-brainer: Just import your music, plug in your iPod, and you're ready to go. You don't need to manage anything, you don't need to manipulate your music. In fact, when you use automatic updates, you don't even realize that the update occurs. You plug your iPod in, and unless it's your first sync or you've just had a CD-ripping party, it gets updated in a matter of seconds.

Don't Unplug That iPod Yet!

When you sync your iPod to iTunes, by plugging it into your computer, the iPod screen tells you not to disconnect it. As long as the synchronization is going on, don't disconnect it—you might damage the files on the iPod and lose its music. In most cases, this isn't a problem; you can just resync it and get all the music back; but if you use manual updating, you might not have the original files on your computer.

Wait until it says "OK to Disconnect" (on the iPod mini) or shows the main menus (on other models) before you unplug it. And if you have your iPod set to operate as a hard disk, make sure you unmount it correctly (see Using the iPod as a Hard Disk).

Automatically Update Selected Playlists Only

When you choose this option to update your iPod, you get to select which playlists get updated automatically. This is the in-between solution, halfway between automatic and manual. It's the ideal solution if you have two iPods, such as a white iPod and a mini, and want to put only some of your music on the mini. Or if you have more music in your iTunes music library than you can fit on your iPod.

As you can see in Figure 2-10, you check Automatically Update Selected Playlists Only, and the list of playlists becomes active. You then check the playlists you want to update, and click OK. When you do this, iTunes updates the selected playlists, and the next time you connect your iPod, iTunes updates these playlists, and only these playlists, again. If you choose this option, you might want to consider creating playlists for your favorite artists or albums, so you have all the albums you want in their entirety on your iPod.

When you check playlists to update, iTunes first checks your iPod to see if you have enough space to hold the music. If not, you'll see an alert; you can go back into the iPod Preferences window and uncheck a couple of playlists, and see if your music will all fit.

When iTunes updates playlists, it copies any new songs that have been added to them, and syncs rating and playing (play count, date and time) information.

If you add playlists to your iTunes music library and want to put them on your iPod, just click the iPod Preferences button at the bottom of the iTunes win-

Figure 2-10

Select the playlists you want to update on your iPod from this window.

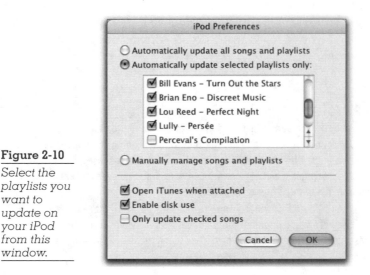

dow and check the new playlists. You can uncheck any existing playlists, and iTunes will remove them, erasing their songs from your iPod.

Manually Manage Songs and Playlists

The manual mode gives you total control over what gets sent from your computer to your iPod, but takes a bit more work as well. When in this mode, you must drag and drop your songs and playlists from the iTunes window to your iPod. Figure 2-11 shows how to drag a playlist. Click the playlist in the Source list, then drag it onto your iPod's icon. Unfortunately, you cannot select multiple playlists to copy to your iPod, so you'll have to do them one at a time, no matter how many you want to copy.

If you copy a smart playlist onto your iPod, you'll only be copying its current contents. Say you have a playlist containing 50 songs you haven't listened to recently. When you copy this smart playlist, you only copy those 50 songs; after you listen to them, you won't get any update to this smart playlist if you manage your iPod manually.

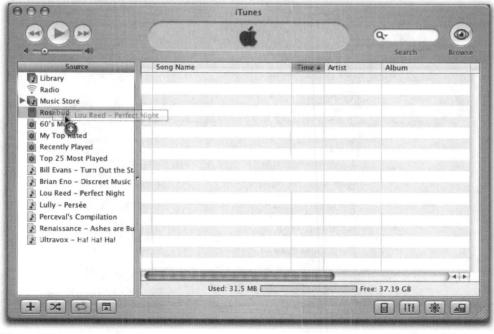

Figure 2-11

Drag a playlist to copy it and all its songs to your iPod

FAQ

Can I Copy Music to My iPod When in Browse Mode?

Unfortunately, the only way you can manually copy music to your iPod is by playlist or by song. You can't copy, say, all the music by a specific artist, or a specific album, when browsing in iTunes. You can, however, search for an artist or album in your iTunes music library, using the Search field, then select all the songs that display and drag them to your iPod.

If you don't want to put entire playlists on your iPod you can also copy individual songs. Just select a song in your iTunes library and drag it onto your iPod's icon (Figure 2-12).

You can create playlists directly on your iPod, if you don't like the playlists in iTunes, or if you want different playlists on the iPod. Just click the iPod icon to select it, then click the New Playlist button. (See Figure 2-13.) An untitled playlist is added to your iPod.

You can then drag songs from your iPod, or from iTunes, into this new playlist. Once you've got music on your iPod, you can move it around into any playlists, even ones you copied from iTunes. You can change the order of songs within a playlist or delete individual songs within one.

Deleting music on your iPod is similar to deleting it from iTunes. Select the songs you want to delete, then press the Delete key. You'll see a warning, then you click OK to remove them. If you delete a playlist on your iPod,

Figure 2-12

Drag individual songs, or select multiple songs and drag them to your iPod.

Figure 2-13

Create a playlist on your iPod by clicking the New Playlist button.

the songs remain there; only the actual list of songs is deleted. You can then create new playlists with the songs the deleted playlist contained.

The only disadvantage to manual management is that none of your rating or playing information ever gets synced to your iTunes music library. You'll see your ratings and play counts when you examine the contents of your iPod, but this information stays on the iPod.

Using Your iPod as a Source with iTunes

When you manage your music manually, you can listen to music from your iPod through iTunes. Say you don't keep all your music on your computer; plug in your iPod and select a playlist or song to listen to through your Mac or PC. Or if you go to a friend's house and want them to hear your latest tunes, plug in your iPod, click No when an alert asks if you want to link your iPod to their computer (if you click Yes, you'll lose all your music), then select it in the Source list. Click the triangle next to the iPod to see its playlists.

If you want to do this, but don't have your iPod set to manual management, this is easy to fix as well. After the iPod mounts in iTunes, click the iPod Preferences button at the bottom of the iTunes window and change to manual management. You're all set to listen to your iPod's music.

Copying Music to Other MP3 Players

If you own a flash memory MP3 player or other hard disk-based MP3 player, you may or may not be able to use iTunes to copy music to it. Some players show up in the iTunes Source list; others don't. If yours does, just drag your songs to it (you won't be able to drag playlists, since only your iPod understands iTunes playlists). If not, you'll need to mount the MP3 player, then drag song files to it from the Mac OS X Finder or from Windows Explorer.

Of course, this begs the question of why you'd want to use another MP3 player if you already own an iPod. You may have a flash memory drive that doubles as an MP3 player, and you find it easier to carry around in some circumstances, or lighter to carry when you're working out. Or you may have a spouse, partner, or child who uses another player—you're certainly not giving them your iPod, right?—who wants to be able to listen to some of your music.

iPod Gripes

Sure, the iPod is a cool device and offers some astounding features. It lets you carry around lots of music, listen to audiobooks, and store files. You can put notes, calendars, and contact information on it, and you can even buy add-on hardware devices to record voice memos and transfer photos from a flash memory card.

But it's not perfect.

While Apple has improved the iPod through its various models and generations, there still remain some areas that provoke frustration, and even ire, among users. I surveyed a bunch of iPod users in forums and mailing lists, asking them what their main iPod annoyances were. While Apple may have corrected some of these problems by the time this book hits the shelves, here are the top iPod gripes.

DO OR DIE:

>> The top-13 list of iPod annoyances

>> Let the ranters have their say...

- **Battery life:** One of the main gripes among iPod users is poor battery life. While Apple advertises 8 hours of playback for the iPod mini and 12 hours for 4G iPods, many users get less than this. In fact, lots of users of 3G models only get 5 or 6 hours of music from their iPods. Naturally, this depends on many factors, and I give tips on improving your battery life in Understanding Your iPod's Battery. Nevertheless, this was long one of the most common criticisms of the iPod, especially since some other hard disk-based MP3 players offer much longer playback, up to 24 hours. The battery can also run down fairly quickly if you're not using your iPod and you don't leave it plugged in to charge, so if you're expecting to just pick up your iPod after a few days of rest, you may find that it's low on juice. But now that the 4G iPod offers 12 hours of battery life, only the mini is handicapped in this area.

- **Battery replacement:** You can't (easily) replace the battery in an iPod, and lots of users think this is a big problem. Especially since your iPod's battery will eventually die. This is unacceptable to many users, even though Apple finally introduced a battery replacement program in late 2003. Why shouldn't the iPod's battery be easy to replace? Most other consumer devices use replaceable batteries, allowing you to carry around a second battery for long trips. I can replace the battery on my iBook, on my cell phone, and on my PDA. A replaceable battery would solve both the problem of batteries that die and the problem of battery life—heavy users could have a second battery to carry around with them on long trips.

- **Totally unreliable battery indicator:** As mentioned earlier (see Understanding Your iPod's Battery), the battery indicator is hopelessly unreliable. The voltage battery hack helps, but even that's not perfect. Apple should have done better, providing a battery indicator that has some relation to reality. 4G iPods seem to have better battery indicators, but they're still not perfect.

- **Scratches:** The iPod scratches easily. Both its white plastic front and its metal back show wear pretty quickly. The iPod mini seems a bit more resistant to scratches, but white iPods age fast. You can get some iPod scratch removing products (see the sidebar Getting Rid of Those Scratches on Your iPod), but it's true that these scratches mar the fine design of the device.

- **Too many button presses to return to the main menu:** There should be a single button (or button combination) to jump back to the top-level menu. It's annoying to have to press the Menu button so many times to get there.

- **Shuffle Songs on the 4G iPod is good, but...:** Yes, it's good. In fact, it's a great idea. There's just one problem: You can't set a specific playlist for this function to choose songs from. While it won't play audiobooks (at least those it recognizes as audiobooks), the iPod still selects from all your songs. For people with classical music, this is a bother; you don't want to listen to isolated movements of classical works. Sure, you can press Next, but it's just not as good as it could be. It would be ideal if it worked like the Party Shuffle in iTunes, where you can choose a playlist as the source.

- **No gapless playback:** Many users mentioned this problem. Unlike iTunes, the iPod does not have a setting allowing you to play music with no gaps between tracks. I find this particularly annoying when listening to operas (even though, using iTunes, there is a workaround; see Ripping Classical and Jazz CDs), but other music, such as live recordings, needs this as well.

- **Font size:** There should be at least one additional font size for the iPod display. When you're playing a track, if the song name is too long to display, it scrolls across the screen, but neither the artist nor the album names scroll. Also, if you name playlists by artist and album, you'll often not even see the entire artist's name. Browsing can be difficult, since many album names are too long to be displayed on the iPod's screen. This font already exists in the iPod; you can see it when you view notes. So there should be a way to choose it for menus and track displays.

- **Can't copy songs to your computer:** While third-party software (see Third-Party Software to Access Your Music Files on a Mac, and see Third-Party Software to Access Your Music Files on a PC) gets around this, it can be annoying that you can't copy music back to your computer. If you lose your original files, through crashes or accidental deletion, you'll have no simple way to get them back. Make sure to back up your files. And back them up again.

- **Only one On-The-Go playlist:** Many users would like to see more than one On-The-Go playlist, which doesn't seem like much to ask. This is now the case on the 4G iPod, but not on the current iPod mini.

- **Doesn't display artwork:** Even though your music files contain any artwork you've added to them, the iPod can't display this artwork, even in black and white. Lots of people would like to see this feature added, but this could lead to a color-screen iPod, which would further limit battery life. Adding album notes and lyrics would also be good, especially if they could be read on-screen like other notes.

- **Can't delete files on the fly:** Many iPod owners want to be able to delete files on the fly, because they don't like the songs, or because they've listened, for example, to parts of audiobooks and have the originals backed up at home.

- **No radio:** It's surprising, with the number of gadgets and hardware accessories, that no company has released an add-on AM/FM radio. Sure, you buy an iPod to listen to music, but why not have the ability to turn on the news or listen to that Yankee game you can't watch when you're on the road?

That's a lot of gripes, but that shouldn't mask the fact that the iPod is a nifty device and does what it is designed for very well. Stay tuned, though. Apple's dominance in this market will certainly inspire them to continue innovating, offering new, enhanced iPods in the future.

iPod Extras

n addition to its music-playing ability, the iPod offers several *extras*, additional features that have little to do with music. You can play games, use your iPod as a clock and set alarms, view notes and calendars, and more. While the extras are certainly not compelling enough to make anyone buy an iPod just for them, they do help you out. Some people find these extras to be useful, but others, who only want an iPod for its music playback, will see them as fluff.

These extras are available from the main menu, by selecting Extras; this displays a submenu showing what's available (Figure 2-14).

In this section, I'll talk about two of these extras: the clock and the games. Since some of the other extras are more important—and more complex to use—I'll devote individual sections to each of them. I'll also talk about two other extras later, since they only show up if you have the required hardware add-ons: If you have a Belkin Voice Recorder or a Griffin iTalk, you'll see a Voice Memos entry in the Extras menu, and if you have a Belkin Media Reader, there will be a Photo Import entry as well. I'll talk about them in Recording Voice Memos on the iPod and Storing Digital Photos on the iPod.

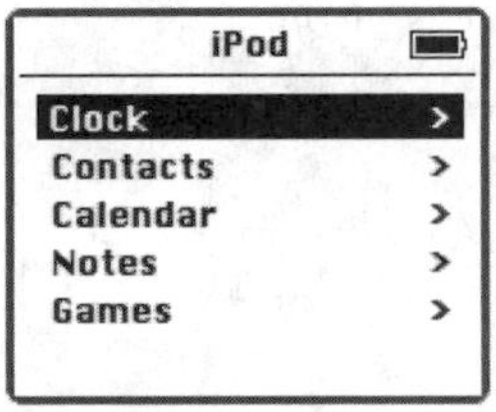

Figure 2-14

Your iPod's extras: useful for some, fluff for others

Figure 2-15

Your iPod's clock and menu items that let you control it and other time functions

Using Your iPod's Clock and Alarm

Your iPod's clock can, well, tell you what time it is. But that's not the most important reason to have a clock on your iPod, though you could put your iPod in a dock and turn the clock on (as in Figure 2-15), using it as a desktop clock at home or at work, even while you listen to music.

You can also use your iPod to display the time in the title section of its display, to set alarms and play your favorite playlist when you want, or to go to sleep after a certain time. It's a full-fledged alarm clock, but not like a clock radio—you'll need an external speaker if you want to have music wake you up, or you'll have to sleep with headphones on, which is pretty difficult.

First, you sometimes want to change your iPod clock's time settings; you should set the date and time when you first set up your iPod, so the last played date and time synced with your computer are correct.

From the main menu, select Extras > Clock. You'll see a big digital clock (Figure 2-15) and, beneath this clock, three menu items: Alarm Clock, Sleep Timer, and Date & Time.

The Date & Time menu item lets you adjust several settings, such as Set Time Zone, Set Date & Time, Time (12-hour or 24-hour), and Time in Title (On or Off). Setting the latter puts the time at the top of the iPod display all the time; this is good if you don't wear a watch, and need to see what time it is. The other settings here are self-explanatory.

Your iPod Clock and Daylight Savings Time

When we switched over to daylight savings time in March, I noticed that I didn't need to make the change on my iPod. I don't know whether the iPod itself knew when to change, or it synced the time with my Mac when I plugged it in. But either way, it did it automatically, so that's one thing you don't need to worry about, at least if you use a Mac.

Setting Alarms

You can use your iPod to wake you up in the morning, or after that mid-afternoon nap, or at any time. You may not know it, but your iPod has a tiny speaker inside it, just big enough to make a strident *beep*, the kind you get from a small electronic alarm clock. You can set the alarm by selecting Alarm Clock from the Clock menu. There are three menu entries: Alarm (On or Off), Time, and Sound.

Set the alarm by selecting Alarm and pressing the Select button. Set the time by selecting Time, pressing the Select button, then scrolling to the time you want.

This can be annoying, since it takes quite a while to scroll a few hours, but you've got no choice.

Finally, set the type of alarm you want to use. You can use any sound you like, as long as it's a beep, or you can set it to any of your playlists. As I said before, this beep is the kind you get on a small alarm clock. When the time comes for you to wake up, your iPod will start beeping; it does this a few times. It doesn't, however, come with a snooze button, so you'd better get up right away.

If you set the iPod to play a playlist, you'll need to have it plugged into an external speaker, and the speaker must be on. I don't see much point in using the alarm like this, unless you want a reminder while you're awake already. If you have a Belkin Voice Recorder or Griffin iTalk, which contain small speakers, and you set the iPod volume up to the max, you'll hear a bit of music seeping from your iPod, but it's not loud enough to wake me up.

Setting the Sleep Timer

The sleep timer helps you save your battery by turning your iPod off after a certain amount of time. You can't set it to go off at a specific time, but it's good if you're listening to music at night, know you're going to fall asleep, and want your iPod to stop playing after you've shut down.

Select Sleep Timer from the Clock menu, then select a time period. By default, this is set to Off. You can choose 15, 30, 60, 90, or 120 minutes. When you wake up in the morning, your iPod's battery won't be dead.

iPod Games

Yep, your iPod comes with a few games. You can access them from the Extras > Games menu. They're not very sophisticated, and, personally, I can't even see the cards in Solitaire well enough to play the game. The brick bash is okay, and my 13-year-old son enjoyed it for about a week. The same is true for the parachute game.

The music quiz can be fun at parties. The iPod starts playing a song and displays five titles. You have to scroll to the correct title and select it. You get points if you're correct, according to how quickly you found the title. But this, too, wears thin after a while.

Some interesting text adventure games have been created for the iPod. They use the iPod's notes feature, allowing you to select which action you take in the story. See Create Text Adventures and Quiz Games with iStory for more on these games.

Working with Contacts, Notes, and Calendars

he iPod is not a PDA, even though Apple has included some basic features to access personal information. And "basic" might even be an exaggeration. All you can do is read certain things, but for many people that's enough. However, others would like to be able to edit their contacts, change appointments on their calendars, and write notes, but, hey, the iPod is a music player, right?

It's pretty easy to view all of these things. I'll talk later about how you get this information into your iPod, since this depends on which platform and software you use. But here's the lowdown on viewing all your non-musical stuff.

DO OR DIE:

>> Viewing contact information

>> Reading notes on your iPod

>> Checking your schedule

Viewing Contacts

This one's simple: From the main menu, select Extras > Contacts. You'll see an alphabetical list of your contacts. (You saw in iPod Settings and Preferences that you can choose a sort order for your contacts.) Scroll to the one you want to see, then press the Select button. Bingo! That's all you get.

To be honest, the contact information the iPod displays depends on what software you've used to store this stuff. Your contacts can include a lot of information, since they use the somewhat standard vCard format. See Syncing Contacts to Your iPod—The Apple Way and Syncing Contacts to your iPod on Windows for more on adding contact information to your iPod.

Viewing Notes

You'll see in Copying Notes to Your iPod how to get notes onto your iPod. It can be as simple as dragging files into a folder, or you can use third-party software to manage notes. Once they're on the iPod, you can view them by selecting Extras > Notes. You'll see an alphabetical list of your notes. Scroll to select one, then press the Select button to view it. You may need reading glasses to read it—the type is pretty small—but notes are a good way to store shopping lists, recipes, directions, or even longer texts. But there's a limit of 4K for these notes, so you can't read books. (Well, actually, you can, and I'll tell you how later, in Reading E-Books on Your iPod.) Also, the iPod can only handle 1,000 notes, and it's incredibly slow to read them; when you want to start reading a single note, the iPod has to read them all internally to present you with a list.

Viewing Calendars

After you've put your calendars onto your iPod (see Syncing Calendars to Your iPod—The Apple Way and Syncing Calendars to your iPod on Windows), you can view them—but not make any changes to them—by selecting Extras > Calendars. You'll see a list of calendars (or perhaps just one, if you only have one); select the one you want to view, then press the Select button. Your calendar displays the current month (see Figure 2-16) and indicates which days have appointments or events set.

Use the scroll wheel to move from one day to another; when you reach the beginning or the end of the month, the previous or next month displays. If you want to view appointments or events for a specific day, press the Select button when that date is selected. You'll see a list of appointments or events; scroll to select one, then press the Select button to see more information, such as the time or any notes you've recorded for the event.

Your iPod will even set alarms for events recorded with some calendar software. See Syncing Calendars to Your iPod—The Apple Way and Syncing Calendars to your iPod on Windows for more on which programs can create calendars that your iPod can use for alarms.

Figure 2-16

A calendar displayed in the iPod. The date in black is the currently selected date. The gray date is today. And any date with an event or appointment recorded shows a small black square, as shown on April 10.

Using the iPod as a Hard Disk

While you may think of your iPod as little more than a music player, it actually contains a small hard disk (if you have an iPod mini, it contains a *tiny* hard disk). This is why the iPod can hold so much music. Many MP3 players contain *flash memory*, a special kind of memory chip that stores data even when the device is turned off. But flash memory is expensive and is only really affordable in small sizes, such as 128, 256, or 512MB.

The iPod (as well as, to be fair, certain other music players) uses a hard disk to store hundreds of times as much music as flash memory devices. Since it is just a portable hard disk, you can use it as such: You can mount it on your desktop, copy files to it, and use it for backups or to simply carry files around with you and move them from one computer to another.

But your iPod is not set to work as a hard disk out of the box; you must turn on a setting to get it to do so. When your iPod is connected to your computer, click the iPod Preferences button at the bottom of iTunes' window to display the iPod Preferences window (Figure 2-17).

Check Enable Disk Use, then click OK. When you do this, you'll see an alert telling you to make sure you unmount your iPod when you've finished using it. If you don't do this correctly, you may damage the data on your iPod (but you won't damage the iPod itself).

DO OR DIE:

>> Copying files to your iPod

>> Using your iPod for backups

>> Is that a hard disk in your pocket?

Figure 2-17

*The iPod
Preferences
window: You
can see the
Enable Disk
Use check box
here.*

Using Your iPod as a Hard Disk on a Mac

When your iPod is mounted as a hard disk, it appears as any other hard disk or volume on your computer. On a Mac running Mac OS X 10.3 (Panther), it appears in the Finder window sidebar (Figure 2-18), and by clicking it, you can see its contents.

If you're using an earlier version of Mac OS X, you'll see the iPod on your Desktop, as in Figure 2-19, though with Panther, you may see it on the Desktop as well, depending on your Finder preferences.

I mentioned earlier that you must correctly remove your iPod when you've finished using it on Mac OS X. There are several ways to do this. If you're working in Mac OS X Panther, you can click the iPod Eject button at the

Figure 2-18

*Under Mac
OS X 10.3,
Panther, the
iPod appears
in the Finder
window side-
bar when
mounted as a
hard disk.*

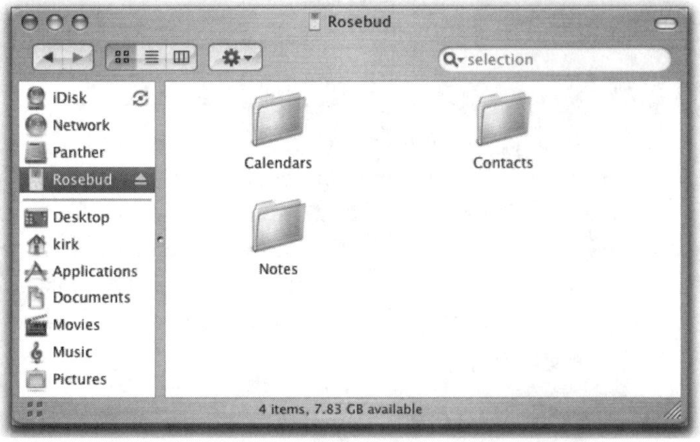

bottom of the iTunes window, or you can click the Eject button next to the iPod in the Finder window sidebar (see Figure 2-20). If you're working in any other version of Mac OS X, or Mac OS 9, you can simply drag the iPod icon to the Trash.

In any case, make sure you unmount your iPod correctly. If you don't, you may damage its hard disk directory information, corrupting your files. While you can recopy your music files to the iPod, using iTunes, you might lose any other files you're carrying around with you. To know whether you need to unmount the iPod, look at its screen; it says "Do Not Disconnect."

Figure 2-19

The iPod displays on the Desktop in earlier versions of Mac OS X.

Figure 2-20

Three ways of unmounting your iPod under Mac OS X: at the top, the iPod Eject button in the iTunes Source list; at the bottom left, the iPod Eject button at the bottom of the iTunes window; at the bottom right, the Eject button in the Finder window sidebar (Mac OS 10.3).

The iPod as Startup Disk on Mac OS X

In the summer of 2003, as Apple was preparing to release Mac OS X 10.3, known as Panther, one of the features announced was "Home on iPod," where users could put their home folders on their iPod, using the files and data in these folders on any Mac. This would allow you to keep your personal data with you at all times as you move, for example, between your Mac at home and another one at work.

But this feature didn't make the cut, probably because the iPod's hard disk heats up too much when it runs all the time. (You can feel just how hot it is if you transfer a lot of music to it.)

Also, on some iPod models, users successfully installed full versions of Mac OS X and used the iPod as a startup disk. While this may be possible, it is certainly not recommended, for the same reason. To quote Apple's technical document 93739, "You can store all kinds of files on iPod, even system software, but you shouldn't use iPod as a startup disk."

I'd follow Apple's advice here. I tried installing Mac OS X on my iPod and had many problems. I could either boot from it or put music on it, but not both. In addition, the constantly spinning hard drive made the iPod really hot—hot enough to inspire me to stick with the iPod's main use: playing music.

Using Your iPod as a Hard Disk in Windows

You don't need any special software to use your iPod as a hard disk under Windows; after the operating system recognizes the device, your iPod will appear as just another drive, as shown in Figure 2-21. You can use My Computer, Windows Explorer, or another file management tool to create folders on and transfer files to your iPod. Formatting your iPod for use with Windows creates a Data Files folder on your iPod by default, but you're under no obligation to use it.

If you want your iPod to be available from the Desktop (and Windows users just love to have everything on their Desktop), right-click the iPod's icon in My Computer and click Create Shortcut. When you're asked if you want to create the shortcut on your Desktop, click Yes. Figure 2-22 shows what the shortcut looks like on a Windows computer.

When you're done using your iPod and want to disconnect from your Windows box, don't just unplug it! If there's any data transfer or syncing going on, you could corrupt your iPod and lose your data. What you need to do is click the Safely Remove Hardware icon in your System Tray, at the right end of the Taskbar, near the clock. The icon looks like a green arrow pointing to the left above a removable disk. When you click the Safely Remove Hardware icon, you'll see a list of devices connected to your computer (shown in Figure 2-23). Click the item representing your iPod and wait for the system's notification that it's OK to unplug it.

You can also use the two methods of unmounting your iPod from within iTunes; see Figure 2-20.

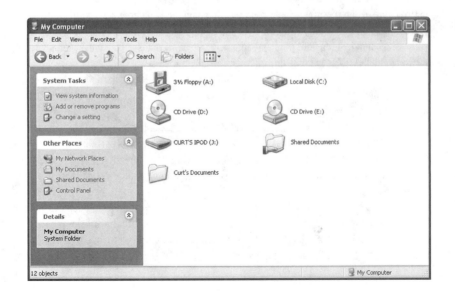

Figure 2-21

Windows sees your iPod as just another drive, but you don't get a cool iPod icon as you do on the Mac.

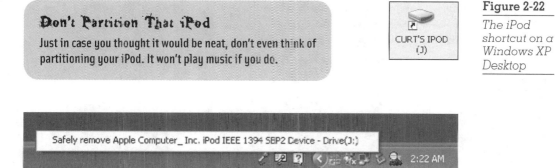

Figure 2-22

The iPod shortcut on a Windows XP Desktop

Don't Partition That iPod

Just in case you thought it would be neat, don't even think of partitioning your iPod. It won't play music if you do.

CURT'S IPOD (J)

Safely remove Apple Computer_ Inc. iPod IEEE 1394 SBP2 Device - Drive(J:)

2:22 AM

Figure 2-23

Windows isn't kidding...be sure to use the Safely Remove Hardware icon before unplugging your iPod.

Copying Files to and from Your iPod

When you use your iPod as a hard disk, whether on a Mac or a PC, you copy files to and from it as you do with any other disk or network volume. Just drag files to the iPod to copy them, and drag them to the Trash or Recycle Bin to delete them. (Make sure you empty the Trash or Recycle Bin, or the files remain on your iPod anyway.)

You can create your own folders on the iPod, but don't rename or delete any of its existing folders: Calendars, Contacts, and Notes. I'll tell you what these folders are for in Putting Other Stuff on Your iPod.

If you want to copy files from your iPod to another computer, you'll find that iTunes may launch on that second computer and display a message telling you that your iPod is linked to another iTunes music library, and asking if you want to change the link and replace all the music on your iPod. Click No! If you click Yes, you'll lose all your music (but not other files) and end up with the music from the other computer.

After clicking No, you'll be able to access the files on the iPod without worrying about your music. Again, make sure you unmount the iPod correctly when you've finished copying your files.

Using Your iPod for Backups

When you use your iPod as a hard drive, you can use it to copy files manually, as described earlier, but you can also use it with backup software as a destination volume for daily or occasional backups. Any backup software can write files to the iPod, as long as you select it as the destination. If you don't have an external hard disk or other receptacle to back up your files, you can use your iPod for regular backups. Of course, if you have a lot of files to back up, you'll have less room for music. See Back Up Your Files to Your iPod, and the following sections, for more on backup software.

Interesting Uses for the iPod

W hile most people use their iPod to listen to music or audiobooks, there are several other ways to make this device fit specific needs. Whether providing music for performances or audio tours of monuments, or helping you find your way in the dark, the iPod is versatile and practical. Here are some unexpected examples of how people use the iPod to provide music, sound, and narrative.

DO OR DIE:

>> What else can the iPod do?

>> Shine the light on me

>> Take a walk with an iPod

Audio Tours with the iPod

In April 2004, the Château de Chenonceau (http://www.chenonceau.com; see Figure 2-24), near Amboise, in France's luxurious Loire Valley, began offering audio tours of the chateau using iPods. Visitors renting an iPod for the tour can choose from 11 languages and can listen to two versions of the audio tour: One is 45 minutes long; the other, 90 minutes. As they stroll through this Renaissance marvel, they hear a presentation of its architecture, its art, its furniture and tapestries, with a relaxing soundtrack of Baroque music in the background.

This is a perfect example of how the iPod can be practical and useful. With plenty of room to store different language files and with an easy-to-use interface, the iPod is far more practical than the portable tape recorders or wireless headsets that museums and other monuments use. Visitors can start and stop the narrative at any time, skip between sections, and go from the short version to the long version if they want to learn more.

Figure 2-24

The Château de Chenonceau: one of the most spectacular examples of Renaissance architecture in France, built over the Cher River in a unique style

The iPod for Stage Performances

Some of you have probably already used your iPods to run music for a party, but you can also use it as a soundboard for a stage show. One improvisational comedy group in Portland, Oregon had to rely on one of the players' iPods to provide music for their show after their minidisc player failed spectacularly. Failed, as in all of the magic smoke that makes electrical devices work came rushing out of the power supply when they plugged it in. If you're running a one-person show, or if you don't have a stagehand, you can use a wireless remote to run your sound cues if need be. The only thing you want to watch out for is phasing, which can happen when you daisy-chain speakers that are a long way apart. Phasing means that your music comes out of one speaker a bit before it comes out of the next speaker in the chain. You can avoid phasing by using a stereo output cable (one plug in the iPod to two outputs) instead of a mono (single output) cable.

Use Your iPod as a Flashlight

Yeah, it sounds weird, but that backlight is pretty powerful. If you ever get lost in a cave or stuck in a staircase during a blackout, the iPod can save your skin. But don't count on it lasting very long. If your battery's not full, set the backlight to go off, say, every ten seconds to make it last as long as possible. This works better with older models; the 4G iPod uses blue light, whereas previous versions used a brighter, white light.

Or you can use Griffin's iBeams (http://www.griffintechnology.com/products/ibeam/) which plug into the headphone and remote jacks on your iPod and provide either a bright flashlight or a laser pointer. The former enlightens the darkness, and the latter is great if you give presentations.

Use Your iPod as a Paperweight

The second law of thermodynamics says that the entropy of the universe increases over time. Entropy is that unexplainable force that causes everything to lose energy and life. One day you wake up and your goldfish is floating belly-up in its bowl; in the same way, you'll go to listen to your iPod one day and find that it has given up the ghost.

Naturally, you won't toss it right away. The first thing is to see if you can replace the battery, but all electronic devices reach a stage, eventually, where it costs more to replace a tiny part than to buy a new one.

So when that happens (and don't worry—you've got time), why not use your iPod as a paperweight? A spare iPod on your desk might impress coworkers and customers. Or it might get swiped.

Troubleshooting Your iPod

n a perfect world, nothing would go wrong with your iPod, and you'd never need to read this section. Alas, as with all electronic devices, things happen. Portable hardware devices are subject to harsh treatment as well (don't tell me you've never dropped your iPod...), and in spite of the iPod's ruggedness, things happen.

While I can't go into all the problems that may occur, I'll look at some of the most common problems and what you can do to resolve them. I'll also tell you where to go for more help when you can't figure out how to fix something, or when you simply have questions about using your iPod. There are nearly 4 million iPod users out there, and you can be sure that whatever problem you have, someone else had it first.

DO OR DIE:

>> What to do when it doesn't work

>> Keeping your iPod in tip-top shape

>> The nitty-gritty on basic iPod maintenance

Keeping Your iPod Up to Date

Apple, like all software companies, releases updates to its programs from time to time for two reasons: to correct bugs and to introduce new features. When you bought your iPod, you got the latest software on a CD. If you're a Windows user, you'll have installed this software, and then you may have just forgotten about it. (I'll get to Mac users in a second.) It's important to check for updates to both iTunes and your iPod software. For iTunes, you can select Help > Check for iTunes Updates to see if a newer version of iTunes is available. For the iPod software, you should visit http://www.apple.com/ipod/ to see if there are any updates to the Windows version.

Now, I left aside Mac users for a moment, because Mac OS X has a built-in software update system that automatically checks for updates to system software and bundled applications, including the iPod software. You can check to make sure this is active. From the Apple menu, select System Preferences, then click Software Update. If Check for Updates is checked, you'll see the frequency in a popup menu; this can be daily, weekly, or monthly. I'd recommend weekly so you don't miss out on any important updates for long. If you don't want updates checked automatically, click the Check Now button. If any new software is available, you'll see a window telling you what's new and letting you install it.

Finally, you can always check Apple's iPod support hub (http://www.apple.com support/ipod/) to see what's new and to get answers to any problems you may have. This page tells you a lot about using your iPod and lets you search the Apple Knowledge Base for answers to your questions.

Updating Your iPod on a Mac

Once you've got an updater, you need to run it to update your iPod's software. (If you update iTunes, you'll usually just download and install a new version of the application.) If you use a Mac, connect your iPod to your Mac, then quit iTunes. Open the iPod Updater application, which is located in the Utilities folder in your Applications folder. (Figure 2-25).

If your iPod is up to date, this application will tell you—see the line that shows the Software Version. If not, click Update to install the latest software on your iPod.

If you're using a version of iPod software before 2.0, quit the updater, disconnect your iPod from your Mac, then connect it again. Your iPod will finish the update after you reconnect it.

Figure 2-25

The iPod Updater application, which you use to update your iPod or restore it to factory settings

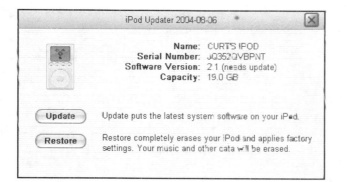

Figure 2-26

The Updater tells if you have the latest and greatest software on your iPod, and lets you restore your iPod to its factory settings.

Updating Your iPod on Windows

There's no automatic updating program for the Windows version of your iPod's software, but you can always go to http://www.apple.com/ipod and download their latest version. Once you have the latest software on your PC, follow these steps to update your iPod:

1. Connect your iPod to your computer and, after iTunes (or Musicmatch Jukebox, if you're using that program) opens and updates your iPod's music and playlists, quit the music program you use.

2. Click the Start button, point to All Programs, point to iPod, and click Updater to open the iPod Software Updater (Figure 2-26).

3. Click Update. If the Update button is grayed out, the software on your iPod is either already up to date or is newer than what's in the updater you downloaded.

4. When prompted, unplug your iPod, then reconnect the FireWire cable to the power adapter and to your iPod so it's getting power. When you plug your iPod back in, it will load the new software.

Restarting Your iPod

Your iPod is like a small computer; it has a miniature operating system and, like any operating system, it can crash. Well, not exactly crash; when the iPod goes haywire, it just tends to freeze. When this happens, you'll find that no matter how many times you press its buttons, and no matter which fingers you use, nothing happens; the screen just stays the same. Your music may be playing, but if the iPod is unresponsive, it has frozen. So the first thing you need to know about troubleshooting is how to unfreeze, or restart, your iPod.

Is My iPod Really Frozen?

It's happened to everyone, so don't feel bad when you get caught. You press your iPod's buttons and nothing happens. You get annoyed, thinking that there's something wrong. But then you realize that you turned the Hold button on. Duh...

Whenever your iPod seems frozen, check the Hold button. If you see a bit of red next to it, that means it's on, and it's protecting your iPod from being turned on accidentally. Also, if you have an Apple wired remote control, it, too, has a hold button. Check that before resetting your iPod (see Restarting Your iPod).

Resetting your iPod is a simple, painless procedure. Do the following:

1. Turn the Hold button on, wait a few seconds, then turn it off.

2. Press and hold the Menu and Play/Pause buttons for a few seconds.

3. When you see the Apple logo on the iPod screen, release these buttons. Your iPod restarts.

Restoring Your iPod to Factory Settings

Restarting your iPod is not a panacea; it will solve some problems, but not all. If this doesn't work, you can try restoring your iPod to factory settings. Think of this as reformatting your iPod's hard disk.

To do this, follow the earlier instructions for updating your iPod, but click the Restore button instead of the Update button. This will erase everything on your iPod, so you'd better have a backup of all your music and files!

When this has finished, disconnect your iPod from your computer and follow the instructions in the Mac setup or Windows setup section. Your iPod will be just as it was when you first unpacked it, and you'll be starting over from scratch, so you'll need to sync your music library and adjust your settings.

Putting Your iPod in Disk Mode

You may sometimes want to put your iPod into disk mode, which allows you to use it as an external hard disk without its trying to update music. This is especially useful if you want to connect it to a computer other than your own. If this computer has iTunes, and you connect your iPod, you'll see an alert asking if you want to link your iPod to that iTunes music library. If you click No, then you won't be able to mount the iPod as a hard disk if you haven't already turned that setting on.

Do the following to put your iPod into disk mode:

1. Turn the Hold switch on, then turn it off again.

2. Press and hold the Play/Pause and Menu buttons until you see the Apple logo. This resets your iPod.

3. When the Apple logo appears, press and hold the Previous and Next buttons until you see the Disk Mode screen. (For iPod Software 1.0 through 1.1, you'll see a FireWire logo on the screen.) If you have a 4G iPod or an iPod mini, press and hold the Play and Select buttons.

When you've finished using your iPod in disk mode, make sure you unmount it correctly (see Using the iPod as a Hard Disk), then restart it, as explained in Restarting Your iPod, earlier in this section, to use it again for listening to music.

Defragmenting Your iPod

Since your iPod contains a hard disk, this disk can become fragmented. This isn't usually a problem, even though some people may worry about it. (Oddly enough, Windows users seem more worried about fragmentation than Mac users.) You shouldn't use any third-party disk software, such as Norton Utilities, Disk Warrior, or others on your iPod. If you really think your iPod's disk is fragmented, the best thing to do is restore your iPod to factory settings—which erases everything—and recopy all your music from iTunes. See earlier in this section for instructions on this.

Checking Your iPod's Hard Disk

If you think you've got hard disk problems, the iPod has a built-in disk scan application. To run this, restart your iPod (see the beginning of this section), then when you see the Apple icon, hold down the Previous/Rewind, Menu, Next/Fast-forward, and Select buttons. (This is easier said than done.) If, however, you have a 4G iPod or an iPod mini, you only need to hold down the Previous and Select buttons to enter diagnostic mode. After you release these buttons, press the Next button until you reach SMRT SCAN (on the iPod mini), or press Play, then press the Next button until you get to HDD SCAN (on the 4G iPod), and press Select to start the scan.

You'll see an icon showing a magnifying glass examining a disc, with a progress bar below it. This test can take a while: It takes about a half hour for a 40GB iPod. Make sure you've got enough battery power when you do this, or plug your iPod into the AC adapter so the battery doesn't run out during the test.

If, when this test is finished, you see a disc icon with a check mark, then everything's okay. If you see a sad iPod, however, you'll need to send your iPod in for service. You can see the other icons that may display after this test here: http://docs.info.apple.com/article.html?artnum=60943. If you think the scan is taking too long, and you're dying to listen to your music, hold down the Select button for a few seconds to interrupt the diagnostic test. If you ever see this test begin on its own when you start up your iPod, the iPod has detected problems. Let it run, since it can repair many of the problems itself.

If you ever put your iPod into diagnostic mode and want to exit, restart your iPod as described at the beginning of this section.

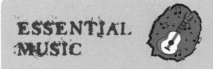

ESSENTIAL MUSIC

"Six Pianos," by Steve Reich

Some music is so surprising that you can never forget when you first heard it. One such piece of music, for me at least, is Steve Reich's "Six Pianos," originally recorded for the Deutsche Grammophon classical label in 1974. On the surface, this piece is not extraordinary, and to many may sound boring: Six pianos play a very repetitive bit of music for about 24 minutes. But that's on the surface. When you start paying attention to the music, you can hear the subtle changes that the different pianos perform as this "gradual music" goes on.

Reich originally wanted to write a piece of music for "all the pianos in a piano store." Each pianist plays the same eight-beat rhythmic structure, yet with different notes, resulting in dense chords of piano music on each beat; but as the piece goes on, the pianists change the notes they play: Two of them play the notes of the fifth beat of one of the pianists as their seventh beat, then his first beat as their third, and so on, until they are playing the same pattern and the same notes, but two beats apart. This "phase" shift is what makes the piece so extraordinary; you don't notice it at first, as you are carried away by the repetitive rhythm, and only start to notice little bursts of melody that stand out before fading into the background. Yet at the end of the 24 minutes, your mind has followed a deeply moving journey through the complexity of this simple music.

I remember first hearing this piece of music at a friend's house in the mid-1970s. (Thanks, Will!) I was totally subjugated by the music's subtle force and intricate detail. It's almost like a musical equivalent of lace, or pianos playing a fractal image. I admit that after that one listening, I became hooked, and have been a fan of Steve Reich's music ever since; but when I want to hear the best example of his music, I return to this piece.

Getting More Info on Your iPod

I hope you don't have any problems with your iPod, but if you do, Apple's iPod support hub (http://www.apple.com/support/ipod/) offers extensive information, including tips, instructions, technical articles, links to downloads, and much more. Check there first if you have problems.

Another place to go is the iPod Lounge Web site (www.ipodlounge.com). You'll find lots of news, tips, articles, and reviews here, and the site's forums are great places to ask questions and find out about new ways to use your iPod. Its Links page (http://ipodlounge.com/links.php) is especially useful, providing links to Apple technical documents about the iPod and iTunes.

The Mac OS X Hints Web site (www.macosxhints.com) also has an active iPod forum, which is not limited to Mac questions, in spite of what the title suggests. Go to http://forums.macosxhints.com and look for the iPod Info Center forum.

BLOG: A Brief History of Recorded Music

Music has changed drastically in the past few decades. Not only has the music we listen to changed, but there have been several revolutions in the way we listen to music as well. And while changes in music are organic, and occur through Darwinian movements as some styles continue, evolving over time, and other styles die a fortunate death, some of the changes in music are due to the media we use to listen to it. As the 78 RPM record changed to 33 RPM LPs, and as the CD has morphed into digital music files, musicians and composers have had new possibilities for recording music. In the beginning, with the 78 RPM disc, you could only fit a few minutes of music on a side; now, you can get up to 80 minutes on a CD, allowing very long compositions to be recorded without pause, if necessary.

So, let's take a stroll down memory lane and look at how the media we use to listen to music has changed. From the 78 to the iPod, it's been a long, interesting trip.

First was the record. (OK, first was the wax cylinder, but I don't go back that far.) It came in a few different sizes: At first, shellac 78 RPM records offered a few minutes of recording time, limiting recorded music to short songs, or requiring that the discs be turned over or changed for longer works. When vinyl records came around, costs dropped, as mass production came into play, quality increased, and, above all, records were much lighter. (Another advantage of vinyl records was that they were unbreakable, at least in normal cropping. And they made good Frisbees too.)

Long-playing (LP) albums turned at 33 RPM and offered about 20 to 25 minutes per side. Singles (usually one song per side, up to about 4 minutes) played

You might be too young to remember vinyl records. For people of my generation, they were more than just musical delivery devices-they also had lots of room for inventive album covers. In the 1970s, artists adorned album covers with unique works, making the packaging of some albums as important as the music they contained. A few classic examples are the Velvet Underground & Nico "banana" album, with its peel-off banana sticker; the Rolling Stones' *Sticky Fingers,* with a real zipper in a pair of pants; or King Crimson's *In the Court of the Crimson King*, with its screaming face across a gatefold album cover.

For those with an aching for the heyday of '70s album covers, one artist stood out by his creativity and the coolness of his work: Roger Dean. This artist was best known for his covers of Yes albums, where his unique style was almost a trademark for the group's music. Roger Dean today sells Desktop pictures of these classic works, from his Web site (http://www.rogerdean.com/wallpaper.php), so you can get your own blast from the past on your computer's Desktop.

at 45 RPM, and EPs, or extended play singles, which were 10-inch 45 RPM discs, could hold more songs than singles, usually four to six songs altogether. Finally, the 12-inch single, played at 45 RPM, offered higher sound quality because of the faster rotational speed, but usually only had one song per side.

Recordings were also sold on different types of tapes. First came the reel-to-reel tape. Very little music was actually sold on this medium, which was used mostly by professionals in recording studios. While they offered excellent quality and didn't skip, these tapes were fragile, and reel-to-reel tape players were large, heavy components. But they had a certain geek factor back in the '60s and '70s; audiophiles purchased them, mostly to make their own recordings of radio shows, and people with quality reel-to-reel tape recorders were somewhat like today's Linux users.

The cassette tape later came along and made these people look like propeller-heads. These compact tapes were a fraction of the size of more expensive reel-to-reel tapes, and were highly portable. Home cassette players became common, as did the concept of "making tapes" for friends. This art form, called the "compilation tape," was an early version of DJ mixes. Music lovers would find the perfect balance for 90 minutes of music that they liked and share these tapes with others.

In between these two types of tape, sometime during the 1960s, a technology that had been around for a few decades reached the mass market. Long used by the movie industry, tape loops were commonly used for advertising and other special uses. But in the 1960s, the 8-track tape started becoming popular, mainly as a way of listening to music in cars. These cartridges, about the size of paperback novels, offered continuous play of music as the player shifted through the four parts of the tape loop. (They are called 8-track tapes because the tapes have four sections of music, each in stereo, hence a total of 8 tracks.)

The heyday of the 8-track tape was in the 1970s, as teenagers used their cars to cruise, hang out, and show off. A powerful car stereo, that could be heard a block away, generally used 8-track tapes to provide the best-quality sound. But the weakness of 8-track tapes was apparent: As the music changed tracks, there was a gap of about a second, often in the middle of songs. ("Baby we were-kachunk, whirrrrrr-born to run.") In fact, only a decade of collective hypnosis allowed people to pretend that these gaps didn't exist.

The death of the 8-track tape came as the quality of cassette tapes improved. Better recording and playback heads, and especially better-quality tape (CrO2 tapes, for example) made the cassette much more practical. Compared with a good car stereo with a cassette player, 8-track sounded almost neolithic.

But the rise of the cassette tape also brought about the first salvos by the RIAA against "home taping." The recording industry felt that they were losing sales because people were copying LPs onto cassettes. (Sound familiar?) The battle raged for quite a while, with the RIAA coming up with nifty slogans ("home taping is killing music"), and they eventually managed to push through taxes on blank recording tapes in many countries.

The final tape technology to appear was the digital audio tape, or DAT. This never really took off for music, since the tapes were expensive and the tape decks even more so. In addition, hardly any music was actually released on DATs, so the only use was to copy analog recordings (cassettes or LPs). Some people used, and still use, DAT to tape live concerts, especially for those bands that allow taping and trading. Portable DAT players are compact and offer excellent quality, but this technology has been surpassed by digital audio recording onto computers.

The DAT marked the beginning of digital audio. When the first digital recordings were made in the late 1970s and released on LPs, this heralded a new age of music media. At first, digital technology was only used for recording, and sometimes for mixing, but the music was released on analog media: LPs and cassette tapes. But when the CD came along in the 1980s, this began to change. Most early CDs were digital only at the final stage of their production, the actual music that listeners heard. They had been made from analog recordings and released or rereleased as CDs. In the early days of the CD (and even now, for some older recordings, such as jazz or classical music) audiophiles checked the CDs they bought for one of three abbreviations.

- AAD: This means the disc was recorded and mixed using analog equipment, and a digital master was made before the CD was pressed, or duplicated. All CDs are digital "pressings," so the third letter is always D.

- ADD: In this case, analog recordings were mixed digitally before being pressed on CDs.

- DDD: The summit of digital technology: digital recording, mixing, and, of course, digital pressing on CDs.

It didn't take a rocket scientist to realize that once the music was digital, it could be rerecorded easily, without losing any fidelity. However, the recording

The Sgt. Pepper Run-Out Groove

For those too young to recall, the final run-out groove of an LP is a circle that keeps the needle in a holding pattern at the end of the music. Generally, this goes "click...click..." until you get up the strength and motivation to raise the record player's arm. But at the end of *Sgt. Pepper* is a few seconds of nonsense chatter, cut up and played backwards. People with automatic record players didn't hear much of this, since the arm lifted on its own when it reached this final groove, but manual record players would play this indefinitely.

industry didn't sweat about that in the early years of the CD. They were too busy counting money as consumers bought record numbers of recordings, even buying CDs of music they already owned (on LP or cassette) to have better-quality sound. No more scratches or pops, no more of that grungy sound as the needle on the record player ran through the first few revolutions of a disc. But also, never again would the run-out groove of a disc contain an infinite loop, as The Beatles' *Sgt. Pepper* album did.

So digital music was around for a long time before computers could do anything with it. While computers with CD-ROM drives could play back CDs, it took a while for them to be able to convert CDs into digital music files. Only in recent years, with the advent of faster processors, cheaper hard disk space, and broadband Internet connections, has digital music become a new way of listening. You can make perfect copies of your CDs—after all, they just contain pits and grooves, representing ones and zeros, the DNA of anything digital. You can take these digital music files and play them back on your computer or on a portable music player; you can burn them to your own blank CDs, making copies of your discs or making your own compilation CDs; and you can share them with others. Oops...

PART III

File Sharing

Copyright, File Sharing, and Piracy

L et us take a brief interlude from our technical discussions about iTunes and the iPod to examine one of the hottest issues related to these technologies. For these tools and devices you use to listen to digital music have opened up a Pandora's box of anger, acrimony, and litigation. The mere act of digitizing a CD that belongs to you—that you have purchased legally—is seen, by some, as a violation of copyright laws, and file sharing runs rampant, as people copy music from peer-to-peer networks with impunity.

On the one hand, you have the RIAA (Recording Industry Association of America, http://www.riaa.com), which claims that file sharing is killing the music industry. This powerful lobbying group, funded by the major record labels and a large contributor to politicians of all stripes, has managed to push through many laws and institute changes in the way we listen to music.

- In the US, as well as in many other countries (the RIAA's influence goes beyond the borders of the US), you pay a tax on every blank CD you purchase, no matter that you may use them all to copy data from your computer or make legal backup copies of your music or software.

- You may pay a tax on hard disks or portable music players, such as your iPod, under the assumption that most of the music you listen to is stolen.

DO OR DIE:

> > Who owns the music you buy?

> > The issues surrounding file sharing and piracy

> > Don't steal music—it's bad karma

SOME THOUGHTS ON COPYRIGHT, BY CORY DOCTOROW
Every successful new medium has traded off its "artifactness"—the degree to which it was populated by bespoke hunks of atoms, cleverly nailed together by master craftspeople—for ease of reproduction.

UNDER THE HOOD

- Most of the major record labels have introduced "copy protection" schemes, which turn music CDs into corrupted, hybrid digital discs, which cannot be played on all CD or DVD players, and which cannot be ripped to use on your iPod or with iTunes.

- The RIAA has also filed lawsuits against people who they accuse of "sharing files," or providing files for download or downloading files from others.

The RIAA claims that the actions in the preceding list are designed to help artists and ensure that they be correctly remunerated for their work. Unfortunately, many artists don't see things this way (see The Internet Debacle—An Alternative View, by Janis Ian), and the music industry has long been criticized for the fact that, other than the best-selling artists, most musicians make a pittance, no matter how many records they sell.

On the other hand, you have myriad groups and associations that are fighting for digital and privacy rights. The most vocal such group, the EFF (Electronic Frontier Foundation, http://www.eff.org), both defends the right to privacy and helps people wrongly accused of file sharing by the RIAA. They are spearheading efforts to make peer-to-peer sharing legal by providing a system by which artists are fairly compensated. In fact, they offer a wide range of solutions to this problem, such as the following:

- Voluntary collective licensing, which is the way artists are remunerated for radio airplay of their music. This system has worked for more than 70 years, and an adaptation of this principle could resolve the problems of uncompensated file sharing.

- Ad revenue sharing, where artists would be compensated by advertising revenue generated by ad views when users download music.

- Peer-to-peer subscriptions, where users would pay a flat fee to download music or would pay a fee per song.

- Bandwidth levies, where ISPs would collect fees from users and funnel them into a rights distribution fund.

File Sharing: For or Against?

It is a moot point whether one is *for* or *against* file sharing. Being for it is supporting the theft of intellectual property, or at best the uncompensated duplication of such content. As guitarist Bob Weir told me, "You've got to honor the music, honor what you love. If you love the music, buy it. Young musicians are all struggling. If they can't make a living, that music will be gone forever."

Piano rolls weren't as expressive as good piano players, but they scaled better—as did radio broadcasts, pulp magazines, and MP3s. Liner notes, hand illumination, and leather bindings are nice, but they pale in comparison to the ability of an individual to actually get a copy of her own.

But being against file sharing is like being against the rain; it happens, and, other than drafting a bunch of jackbooted Internet police, there is nothing to do about it. The problem is that the music industry, when faced with new methods of distribution, decided to put their collective heads in the sand rather than proactively search for a way to leverage this system for their benefit.

This sort of battle is not without precedent. I recall, in the late 1970s and early 1980s, the recording industry fighting against home taping, or using cassettes to record music from vinyl sources. "Home taping is killing music," they declaimed, and then went on to experience the highest level of growth the industry ever knew. Or what about Hollywood, which fought tooth and nail against VCRs and videotaping, then went on to discover, after losing the battle in the courts, that video, and later DVDs, would earn them much more money than theatrical releases.

But these are only the issues that occurred within recent memory. What about the early creators of piano rolls, who were sued for copyright violations by reproducing music that had only been sold in sheet-music form? Or Marconi, sued by vaudeville performers, who felt that the radio would kill their profession? Every change in technology has brought its own series of issues around copyright. As Cory Doctorow (see Giving Away Books) told me, "The history of copyright law is the history of technology. Anyone making a living from copyright today is living off the history of piracy." Not that copyright is all about piracy, but that it is all about finding legal ways to turn piracy into monetary compensation for intellectual property creators.

Now, don't get me wrong; I don't advocate the theft or blatant copying of intellectual property, no more than I advocate the massive copying and sale of software, CDs, and DVDs in some countries where copyright laws are ignored wholesale. After all, I make my living creating intellectual property. I don't think I'd be very happy if this book were copied and sold without my getting any of the money (though I don't get that much per copy, after all the others in the creation and distribution chain take their cut).

But when the remedy is worse than the disease, its time to stop and take a careful look at what sort of world we want to live in. Do we want to live in a world where every time we listen to music we have to authorize our CD player or punch in a PIN number so our music accounts get debited? Do we want to have spiders and bots searching the Internet, trying to implant spyware on our computers so the recording industry (and soon the movie industry) can check out the contents of our hard drives and report back to Big Brother Headquarters? Or do we want to live in a world where people can choose the way they purchase and use the media they like, in freedom and without automatically being branded thieves?

Which isn't to say that old media die. Artists still hand-illuminate books; master pianists still stride the boards at Carnegie Hall, and the shelves burst with tell-all biographies of musicians that are richer in detail than any liner-notes booklet. The thing is, when all you've got is monks, every book

There are legal alternatives to the current state of anarchy, and several organizations (such as the EFF; see The EFF's Point of View) have made viable proposals. Apple's iTunes Music Store is one alternative, and its success shows that people do want to pay for music they download. But above all, it shows that people want another way to buy music, one that today's technology can offer.

It seems to be such a shame, and a waste of time and money, that the industry can't find a better way to distribute music. The Internet offers many new ways to do this, and as time goes by, instead of offering consumers more choice, the recording industry is merely generating bad karma and negative goodwill.

Bob Weir on Music Piracy

Bob Weir was guitarist with the Grateful Dead for some 30 years, until the untimely death of Jerry Garcia brought that long, strange trip to an end. The group continued as The Other Ones for a while, then morphed into The Dead, its current formation. At the same time, Bob Weir has maintained a solo career, recording and touring with his group, Ratdog (http://www.rat-dog.com).

I talked to Weir about his iPod (see Bob Weir: "I'm infatuated with my iPod.") and about music piracy. Bob's thoughts are interesting, since the Grateful Dead was one of the pioneers in allowing concertgoers to not only tape the shows they attended but also trade them, as long as no commercial gain resulted from the trade. For many people, tape trading was an essential part of the Grateful Dead experience, with the music's wide availability exposing people to the group's unique sound.

While many musicians hire security staff to police concert halls and snuff any attempts to tape live performances, Weir thinks differently. "If people paid for a concert ticket, they should be allowed to tape the show." But taping can have its downside as well. "Just about every night we do a ballad, and at a quiet, poignant moment, there's always some drunk guy who shouts or whistles so he can say, 'That was me!'" Nevertheless, Weir is not planning on changing his attitude toward taping.

But when his band, Ratdog, performs, he offers concertgoers another option: instant, live CDs. At the end of each concert, the band sells 150 CD sets of the concert recorded from the soundboard, and burned as soon as the concert ends.

Bob Weir doesn't approve of piracy or file sharing. "Honor what you love," he said. "If you love the music, buy it. Particularly for kids—young musicians are struggling. If they can't make a living, that music ain't gonna be there."

Weir pointed out how this affects his own work. "If I'm going to make a studio recording, it's going to cost me bucks and time. If people are going to rip it off, I'm not going to do it."

takes on the character of a monkish Bible. Once you invent the printing press, all the books that are better suited to movable type migrate into that new form. What's left behind are those items that are best suited to the old production scheme: the plays that need to be plays, the books that

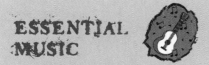

ESSENTIAL MUSIC

Thoughts from a Musician: Vini Reilly of The Durutti Column

The following is included as liner notes for The Durutti Column's latest album, Tempus Fugit *(Kooky Records, 2004).*

This album only exists because you have bought it. The music only has any worth or place in the world because you are listening to it. The loyalty and tenacity you have shown is incredible. The music is as much yours as a listener as it is mine. You give me a role and a purpose in life I would otherwise not have had. You prevent the greedy and destructive world of the record industry from destroying me and you keep cynicism at bay. The only way I can repay such a gift is to persevere, until one day I do actually create a body of work worth your patience. If anyone feels this is over sentimental you are to be mistaken. All I am saying here is truthful and real. Every time anyone listens to my music either on disc or at a gig it is an affirmation of my whole life and that is something no record company could ever put a price tag on.

➤ Vini Reilly is The Durutti Column (http://www.theduruticclumn.com).

are especially lovely on creamy paper stitched between covers, the music that is most enjoyable performed live and experienced in a throng of humanity.

Increased democraticness translates into decreased control: It's a lot harder to control who can copy a book once there's a photocopier on every

ESSENTIAL MUSIC

Rush

Rush (http://www.rush.com.) is one of those bands that people make fun of because they've been around for so long. I was watching *Baseball Tonight,* a sports show on ESPN in the US, and the host made fun of how old a player was by saying that he probably had the stadium sound person play some Rush when he came up to bat. Considering the group celebrates its thirtieth anniversary in 2004, that's a fair joke to make.

Geddy Lee, Alex Leifson, and Neil Peart have done pretty well for a band that got together as a bunch of guys from Toronto in 1974 (yes, OK, the drummer in the band's original 1968 incarnation was John Rutsey, but he fell ill, and left in 1973, and Neil came along in 1974, hence the thirtieth anniversary not happening in 1998). The key is that they're all masters of their instruments. Lee is one of the best bassists around and has been for years; Peart is in the running for best drummer of all time, is the author of two bicycle trek books (*The Masked Rider* and *Ghost Rider*), and is a published poet; and Leifson is one of the most underrated guitarists in the world. When you listen to their live work, such as "A Passage to Bangkok" on *Exit...Stage Left,* you hear so much more than you do when they're in the studio. There's an immediacy and an energy you don't get when something's engineered and produced.

You should spend $2.97 to buy these three Rush songs from the iTunes Music Store: "Subdivisions," "Freewill," and "Driven." Listen to the lyrics...*really* listen to them. There's no end of intellectual and emotional depth in those words and the surrounding music. You'll probably want to buy more of their stuff, but if not, you're still better off for having listened to those three songs.

➤ Curtis Frye (http://www.techsoc.com/contact.htm) wrote some of the sections of this book about using the iPod with Windows. He's a computer book author, an improv comedian, a magician, and much more.

corner than it is when you need a monastery and several years to copy a Bible. And that decreased control demands a new copyright regime that rebalances the rights of creators with their audiences. (Continued on page 246.)

The RIAA's Point of View

Note: I contacted the RIAA several times, by e-mail and by telephone, seeking a spokesperson who would answer my questions about this issue, but no one bothered to get back to me. This blank page is therefore dedicated to their spirit of openness and communication.

ESSENTIAL MUSIC

Sappho Songs, by Sir Granville Bantock

Certain pieces of music have enormous appeal on first hearing. Some stay the course and become indispensable: Walton's first symphony, Shostakovich's eighth quartet, Strauss' Four Last songs, Mahler's Das Lied von der Erde; whilst others do not last the course: Dvorak's cello concerto, Tchaikovsky's violin concerto.

There are other works by 'minor' composers, dismissed by others, that are a mainstay of my listening: the Alwyn, Bax and Arnold Symphonies, It is one of these minor composers whose work I am selecting here: the Sappho song-cycle by Sir Granville Bantock, on Hyperion Records. Sappho is a sensual and voluptuous orchestral song cycle for mezzo voice that has been virtually hidden for 90 years.

The Sappho songs are based on poems written by the Greek poetess, Sappho, who lived on the Island of Lesbos in the middle of the 7th Century. Her poetry was said to be inspired, passionate and also erotic. Very little has survived following the fall of Alexandria. Remaining copies were eventually destroyed, probably because of the lesbian connotations that would have been anathema to the early Christians. What has survived has been mainly due to her work having been quoted in part by other poets and scholars—often only a single line. These still turn up occasionally, with one having been discovered on a strip of papyrus used to wrap a mummified crocodile.

Previous to this recording, only the Prelude was at all well known; it weaves together themes from the songs although not always in the song order. The prelude opens with the harp, which has a very prominent part in this cycle evoking the playing of Sappho who played both harp and lute. There follow nine songs, and the work lasts an hour ending in neither celebration nor resignation. All emotions have been visited during this cycle and Sappho has finally found peace and contentment.

Bantock creates a warm-textured thickly upholstered sound with a perfect balance between a large orchestra (Royal Philharmonic Orchestra/Vernon Handley) and the soloist, Susan Bickley.

➤ Len Mullenger is Founder of MusicWeb, the foremost Web site for classical CD reviews (http://www.musicweb.uk.net).

For example, when the VCR was invented, the courts affirmed a new copyright exemption for time-shifting; when the radio was invented, Congress granted an antitrust exemption to the record labels in order to secure a blanket license; when cable TV was invented, the government just

The EFF's Point of View

The EFF has long fought to "defend freedom in the digital world." They have been active since the early days of the Internet, fighting for people's digital rights. Fred von Lohman, a senior intellectual property attorney with the EFF, answered some of my questions about this thorny issue.

Kirk McElhearn: Isn't file sharing just stealing? Why should you be defending people who prevent musical artists, who already have trouble eking out a living, from making more?

Fred von Lohman: The rhetoric of "stealing" and "piracy" isn't going to solve the dilemma posed by file sharing, any more than rhetoric about the "evils of drink" propped up Prohibition in the US in the 1920s. Rather than heated rhetoric, we need a pragmatic solution that gets copyright holders fairly compensated, while making file sharing legal. The reality is that hundreds of millions of people around the world are using and will continue to use file-sharing networks. There has to be a better way to secure adequate compensation than treating fans like criminals in an effort to drive them into the arms of the iTunes Music Store.

> ### The EFF's White Paper on File Sharing
>
> For a thorough presentation of the EFF's views on file sharing, see their white paper, "A Better Way Forward: Voluntary Collective Licensing of Music File Sharing," at http://www.eff.org/share/collective_lic_wp.php.

ordered the broadcasters to sell the cable operators access to programming at a fixed rate.

Copyright is perennially out of date, because its latest rev was generated in response to the last generation of technology. The temptation

KM: The RIAA likes to say that CD sales have gone down because of file sharing. But I rarely see the press examine these claims. It seems to me that the main reason CD sales have gone down is a greater pressure on consumers to purchase other forms of content, such as DVDs. How does the EFF see the decline in CD sales?

FL: There is far too little reliable empirical evidence from which to draw any clear conclusions about the relationship between file sharing and CD sales. After all, if the RIAA is correct that people are substituting downloads for purchases, given the sheer number of downloads, there should be a catastrophic reduction in sales. Yet we don't see that. There are many variables at play here. More importantly, however, there is no reason that copyright law should have to protect CD sales, when the public clearly demands downloads. Copyright law exists to get authors compensated, not to protect any particular business model.

KM: I'm used to buying music and doing what I want with it. But I recently bought a new Eric Clapton CD, and since it's copy protected, I can't copy it to my iPod. How can anyone tell me I'm only allowed to do what they want with the media I buy?

FL: Copyright owners have never been required to release their works in a format that is the most convenient for you (they could, for example, go back to vinyl, which would be even more inconvenient for you to rip to an iPod). But until the DMCA [Digital Millennium Copyright Act], you were free to take your own steps to manipulate the works you purchased. And technology companies were free to build tools to help you. To some extent, that's what the iPod is—it's a tool designed to help you transform CDs that you own into a format that is more useful to you. The DMCA, however, gave copyright owners the power to prohibit technology developers of the future from building tools like that to help you with "protected" content. It is no accident that next-generation CDs (SACD and DVD-A) are encrypted and therefore cannot be ripped for use on an iPod.

KM: I live in a country (France) where I pay a tax on every blank CD I buy. In addition, I pay a tax on hard drives and related devices, such as the iPod. On the one hand, this tax assumes that I'm already a thief, and on the other hand, it tacitly grants me the right to exercise what that tax pays for, which is copying. Does it make any sense that the RIAA can push through this type of tax and still say I'm not allowed to copy music?

to treat copyright as though it came down off the mountain on two stone tablets (or worse, as "just like" real property) is deeply flawed, since, by definition, current copyright only considers the last generation of tech.

FL: If the public is asked to pay a levy to copyright holders, it should get something for its money—namely, the right to make and use private copies. It is fundamentally unjust that the public would pay and still be forbidden from using these technologies to enhance the value of the music they buy (by digital rights management technologies, for example).

From "Ebooks: Neither E, nor Books," paper for the O'Reilly Emerging Technologies Conference, February 12, 2004, San Diego, CA, by Cory Doctorow, doctorow@craphound.com.

The Internet Debacle–An Alternative View, by Janis Ian

The following is a condensed version of an article originally written for Performing Songwriter Magazine, May 2002, and available on Janis Ian's Web site (http://www.janisian.com) along with a follow-up article, which preceded the unveiling of the iTunes Music Store.

"The Internet and music downloading are here to stay... Anyone who thinks otherwise should prepare themselves to end up on the slagheap of history." Janis Ian, in an interview. September 1, 1998.

Recording industry representatives say that music downloads are "destroying sales," "ruining the music industry," and "costing you money."

Costing me money? I don't pretend to be an expert on intellectual property law, but I do know one thing. If a music industry executive claims I should agree with their agenda because it will make me more money, I put my hand on my wallet...and check it after they leave, just to make sure nothing's missing.

Am I suspicious of all this hysteria? You bet. Do I think the issue has been badly handled? Absolutely. Am I concerned about losing friends, opportunities, and my tenth Grammy nomination by publishing this article? Yeah, I am. But sometimes things are just wrong, and when they're that wrong, they have to be addressed.

The premise of all this ballyhoo is that free music downloading is harming the industry and recording artists.

Nonsense. Let's take it from my personal experience. My Web site (http://www.janisian.com) gets an average of 75,000 hits a year. Not bad for someone whose last hit record was in 1975. When Napster was running full tilt, we received about 100 hits a month from people who'd downloaded "Society's Child" or "At Seventeen" for free, then decided they wanted more information. Of those 100 people (and these are only the ones who let us know how they'd found the site), 15 bought CDs. Not huge sales, right? No record company is interested in 180 extra sales a year. But...that translates into $2,700, which is a lot of money in my book. And that doesn't include the ones who bought the CDs in stores or who came to my shows.

I've found that every time we make a few songs available on my Web site, sales of all the CDs go up. A lot. And I don't know about you, but as an artist with an in-print record catalogue that dates back to 1965, I'd be thrilled to see sales on my old catalogue rise.

Now, the RIAA (Recording Industry Association of America) and NARAS (National Academy of Recording Arts & Sciences), as well as most of the entrenched music industry, are arguing that free downloads hurt sales. (More than hurt—they're saying it's destroying the industry.)

Alas, the music industry needs no outside help to destroy itself. We're doing a very adequate job of that on our own, thank you.

The Recording Industry's Take

Here are a few statements from the RIAA's Web site.

1. "Analysts report that just one of the many peer-to-peer systems in operation is responsible for over 1.8 billion unauthorized downloads per month." (Hilary B. Rosen letter to the Honorable Rick Boucher, Congressman, February 28, 2002)

2. "Sales of blank CD-R discs have...grown nearly 2-1/2 times in the last two years...if just half the blank discs sold in 2001 were used to copy music, the number of burned CDs worldwide is about the same as the number of CDs sold at retail." (Hilary B. Rosen letter to the Honorable Rick Boucher, Congressman, February 28, 2002)

3. "Music sales are already suffering from the impact... in the United States, sales decreased by more than 10% in 2001." (Hilary B. Rosen letter to the Honorable Rick Boucher, Congressman, February 28, 2002)

4. "In a recent survey of music consumers, 23%...said they are not buying more music because they are downloading or copying their music for free." (Hilary B. Rosen letter to the Honorable Rick Boucher, Congressman, February 28, 2002)

The Other Side of the Story

Let's examine these points one by one, but let me first remind you of something: The music industry had exactly the same response to the advent of reel-to-reel home tape recorders, cassettes, DATs, minidiscs ("Why buy the record when you can tape it?"), VHS, BETA, music videos, MTV, and a host of other technological advances designed to make the consumer's life easier and better. I know because I was there.

1. Who's to say that any of those people would have bought the CDs if the songs weren't available for free? I can't find a single study on this, one where a reputable surveyor, such as Gallup, actually asks people that question. I think no one's run one because everyone is afraid of the truth—most of the downloads are made by people who want to try an artist out or who can't find the music in print.

   And if a percentage of that 1.3 billion is because people are downloading a current hit by Britney or In Sync, who's to say it really hurt their sales? Soft statistics are easily manipulated. How many of those people went out and bought an album that had been overplayed at radio for months, just because they downloaded a portion of it?

2. Sales of blank CDs have grown? You bet. I back up all my files onto CD. I go through 7 to 15 CDs a week that way, or about 500 a year. New computers make backing up to CDs painless; how many people are doing what I'm doing? Additionally, when I buy a new music CD, I make a copy for my car, a copy for upstairs, and a copy for my partner. That's three blank discs per CD. So I alone account for around 750 blank CDs yearly.

3. I'm sure the sales decrease had nothing to do with the economy's decrease, or a steady downward spiral in the music industry, or the garbage being pushed by record companies. Aren't you? There were 32,000 new titles released in the US in 2001, and that's not including reissues, DIYs, or smaller labels that don't report to SoundScan. (Our "Unreleased" series, which we haven't bothered SoundScanning, sold more than 6,000 copies last year.)

   A conservative estimate would place the number of "newly available" CDs per year at 100,000. That's an awful lot of releases for an industry that's being destroyed. And to make matters worse, we hear music everywhere, whether we want to or not—stores, amusement parks, highway rest stops. The original concept of Muzak (to be played in elevators so quietly that its soothing effect would be subliminal) has run amok. Why buy records when you can hear the entire Top 40 just by going shopping for groceries?

4. Which music consumers? College kids who can't afford to buy ten new CDs a month, but want to hear their favorite groups? When I bought my nephews a new Backstreet Boys CD, I asked why they hadn't downloaded it instead. They patiently explained to their senile aunt that the download wouldn't give them the cool artwork, and more important, the video they could see only on the CD.

Why Do People Download Music?

Realistically, why do most people download music? To hear new music, or records that have been deleted and are no longer available for purchase. Not to avoid paying $5 at the local used-CD store, or taping it off the radio, but to hear music they can't find anywhere else. Face it—most people can't afford to spend $15.99 to experiment. That's why listening booths (which labels fought against, too) are such a success.

You can't hear new music on radio these days; I live in Nashville, "Music City USA," and we have exactly one station willing to play a non-Top-40 format. On a clear day, I can even tune it in. The situation's not much better in Los Angeles or New York. College stations are sometimes bolder, but their wattage is so low that most of us can't get them.

In the hysteria of the moment, everyone is forgetting the main way an artist becomes successful: exposure. Without exposure, no one comes to shows, no one buys CDs, no one enables you to earn a living doing what you love.

In 37 years as a recording artist, I've created over 25 albums for major labels, and I've never once received a royalty statement that didn't show I owed them money. So I make the bulk of my living from live touring, playing for 80 to 1,500 people a night, doing my own show. I spend hours each week doing press, writing articles, making sure my Web site tour information is up to date. Why? Because all of that gives me exposure to an audience that might not come otherwise. So when someone writes and tells me they came to my show because they'd downloaded a song and gotten curious, I am thrilled!

Who gets hurt by free downloads? Save a handful of super-successes like Céline Dion, none of us. We only get helped.

It's difficult to convince an educated audience that artists and record labels are about to go down the drain because they, the consumer, are downloading music. Particularly when they're paying $50–$125 apiece for concert tickets and $15.99 for a new CD they know costs less than a couple of dollars to manufacture and distribute.

The Next Generation of CDs

What's the new industry byword? Encryption, or copy protection.

They're going to make sure no one can copy CDs, even for themselves, or download them for free. Brilliant, except that it flouts previous court decisions about blank cassettes, blank videotapes, and so on. And it pisses people off.

How many of you know that many carmakers are now manufacturing all their CD players to also play DVDs? Or that part of the encryption record companies are using doesn't allow your store-bought CD to be played on a DVD player, because that's the same technology as your computer? And if you've had trouble playing your own self-recorded copy of O Brother, Where Art Thou in the car, it's because of this lunacy.

The industry's answer is to put on the label: "This audio CD is protected against unauthorized copying. It is designed to play in standard audio CD players and computers running Windows O/S; however, playback problems may be experienced. If you experience such problems, return this disc for a refund."

Now I ask you. After three or four experiences like that, schlepping to the store to buy it, then schlepping back to return it (and you still don't have your music), who's going to bother buying CDs?

If you think about it, the music industry should be rejoicing at this new technological advance! Here's a foolproof way to deliver music to millions who might otherwise never purchase a CD in a store. The cross-marketing opportunities are unbelievable. It's instantaneous, costs are minimal, shipping nonexistent...a staggering vehicle for higher earnings and lower costs. Instead, they're running around like chickens with their heads cut off, bleeding on everyone and making no sense.

The Real Problems Facing Recording Artists

I object violently to the pretense that the RIAA is in any way doing this for our benefit. If they really wanted to do something for the great majority of artists, who eke out a living against all odds, they could tackle some of the real issues facing us.

- The normal industry contract is for seven albums, with no end date, which would be considered at best indentured servitude (and at worst slavery) in any other business. In fact, it would be illegal.

- A label can shelve your project, then extend your contract by one more album because what you turned in was "commercially or artistically unacceptable." They alone determine that criteria.

- Singer-songwriters have to accept the "Controlled Composition Clause" (which dictates that they'll be paid only 75% of the rates set by Congress in publishing royalties) for any major or subsidiary label recording contract, or lose the contract. Simply put, the clause demanded by the labels provides that (a) if you write your own songs, you will only be paid three-fourths of what Congress has told the record companies they must pay you, and (b) if you cowrite, you will use your "best efforts" to ensure that other songwriters accept the 75% rate as well. If they refuse, you must agree to make up the difference out of your share.

- Congressionally set writer/publisher royalties have risen from their 1960s high (2 cents per side) to a munificent 8 cents.

- Many of us began in the '50s and '60s; our records are still in release, and we're still being paid royalty rates of 2% (if anything) on them.

- If we're not songwriters, and not hugely successful commercially (as in platinum-plus), we don't make a dime off our recordings. Recording industry accounting procedures are right up there with films.

- Worse yet, when records go out of print, we don't get them back! We can't even take them to another company. Careers have been deliberately killed in this manner, with the record company refusing to release product or allow the artist to take it somewhere else.

- Because a record label "owns" your voice for the duration of the contract, you can't go somewhere else and rerecord those same songs they turned down. And because of the rerecord provision, even after your contract is over, you can't record those songs for someone else for years, and sometimes decades.

- Last but not least, America is the only country I am aware of that pays no live-performance royalties to songwriters. In Europe, Japan, Australia, when you finish a show, you turn your set list in to the promoter, who files it with the appropriate organization and then pays a small royalty per song to the writer. It costs the singer nothing, the rates are based on venue size, and it ensures that writers whose songs no longer get airplay, but are still performed widely, can continue receiving the benefit from those songs.

So What's the Future Going to Be Like?

There is zero evidence that material available for free online downloading is financially harming anyone. In fact, most of the hard evidence is to the contrary.

Free exposure is practically a thing of the past for entertainers. Getting your record played at radio costs more money than most of us dream of ever earning. Free downloading gives a chance to every do-it-yourselfer out there. Every act that can't get signed to a major, for whatever reason, can reach literally millions of new listeners, enticing them to buy the CD and come to the concerts. Where else can a new act, or one that doesn't have a label deal, get that kind of exposure?

I am not advocating indiscriminate downloading without the artist's permission. I am not saying copyrights are meaningless. I am objecting to the RIAA spin that they are doing this to protect "the artists" and to make us more money. I am annoyed that so many records I once owned are out of print, and the only place I could find them was Napster. Most of all, I'd like to see an end to the hysteria that causes a group like RIAA to spend over $45 million in 2001 lobbying "on our behalf," when every record company out there is complaining that they have no money.

We'll turn into Microsoft if we're not careful, folks, insisting that any household wanting an extra copy for the car, the kids, or the portable CD player has to go out and "license" multiple copies.

As artists, we have the ear of the masses. We have the trust of the masses. By speaking out in our concerts and in the press, we can do a great deal to damp this hysteria and put the blame for the sad state of our industry right back where it belongs—in the laps of record companies, radio programmers, and our own apparent inability to organize ourselves in order to better our own lives—and those of our fans. If we don't take the reins, no one will.

Giving Away Books

Cory Doctorow is a strange guy. He's a novelist, short story writer, and journalist, and he gives his books away. For free. You can go to his Web site (http://www.craphound.com) and download his two novels and lots of his short stories, as well as tons of articles he's written.

Now, this doesn't have anything to do with music, or with iTunes, but it does have a lot to do with the issues of copyright and file sharing. (Actually, this does have something to do with the iPod, since you can download iPod-readable versions of his books. I'll talk about them in Reading e-books on Your iPod.)

After Cory Doctorow had written a bunch of short stories, he came up with an idea for a novel. Now, for science fiction writers, novels are about the only way to make money. When they publish short stories in the pulp magazines, they get about 6 cents a word, roughly the same amount Hugo Gernsback paid in the 1930s. Taking an average short story of about 5,000 words, that means $300 for several weeks' work. Not very promising for the bottom line.

But when Doctorow wanted to write this first novel (*Down and Out in the Magic Kingdom*, Tor, 2003), he suggested to his editor that he give it away as a free download from his Web site. Surprisingly, the editor agreed—most people in the publishing business don't think this way—and Doctorow started giving his stuff away.

It was a huge success. People who had never heard of him downloaded his novel and liked it enough to buy it. Others downloaded it and maybe didn't like it, or didn't end up buying a paper version, but that didn't matter: Doctorow got the exposure he wanted, while doing a Good Thing, and generating positive karma.

Doctorow didn't see this as much of a risk; after all, as I pointed out earlier, science fiction writers don't make much money. He makes a lot more from his nonfiction writing; he says that "Really successful writers are *sui generis*. They make their livings in ways that are as distinctive as fingerprints," and, for him, this involves a complex combination of writing, consulting, and entrepreneurship. He saw this as a short-term way of getting recognition and selling more books, a way of creating positive goodwill, and, over the long term, discovering new ways of making sales.

So far, so good. Doctorow has been successful at selling his books, in part because they're good books, but also in part because he's found a unique way to promote himself. Giving away books attracts attention from the media, and he's been discussed in all sorts of media, from Web sites to magazines and newspapers.

PART IV

iPod Software

Putting Other Stuff on Your iPod

W e're inundated with pocket and handheld devices: cell phones, PDAs, music players, and other electronic devices. Sometimes you just want to trash them all; they take up space, they're not all that usable, and they wear out your eyes with their tiny screens. Phones are good for talking, but as they shrink to become easy-to-lose devices, rather than easy-to-use, they become less practical. PDAs are good for certain things, but you need to have the right mindset to adapt to them; they don't adapt to you. Perhaps the world would be a better place without all these electronic gadgets, which offer their share of frustration and cost more and more of our hard-earned money. But then how would you listen to music on the go?

You've seen in previous sections that your iPod can hold more than just music. While it's not a PDA, you can store contact information, calendars, and notes. Sure, the iPod's not designed primarily for this; these functions seem more like an afterthought. They're not very flexible, especially since this data is read-only; you can't make any changes to it. But it can save you some time if you don't own a PDA and want to be able to carry around some basic stuff, like phone numbers, notes, and calendars.

That's the way Apple sees it. Unfortunately, Apple doesn't provide many ways to get this "other stuff" onto your iPod. If you're a Mac user, you're in luck: Apple's iSync can transfer contacts and calendars (together with to-do lists). If you're a Windows user, well, there's nothing Apple can do for you. iTunes is still

DO OR DIE:

>> More than just music

>> What's that number?

>> Carry a digital shopping list

Think about Security

If you transfer personal data to your iPod, think about what might happen if you lose your iPod, or if it gets stolen. This personal data is not protected in any way, and anyone who finds your iPod—or even anyone who picks it up to fiddle with it in your home or office—can access your contacts and calendars. If your data is sensitive enough that this could be a problem, don't sync it to your iPod. There is no way to protect this data from prying eyes.

the only real software Apple's ever made for Windows (with the exception of QuickTime, which is more a behind-the-scenes media player).

But third-party software developers have picked up the gauntlet and come up with a surprising selection of programs. Some use the notes feature and take it further, allowing you to put e-books, or other types of information, such as news and weather on your iPod. And others have provided solutions for syncing data from specific programs, such as Outlook Express on Windows, or Entourage on Mac.

Read on to see how you can put more than just music on your iPod.

Syncing Contacts to Your iPod—The Apple Way

The iPod's ability to store and display data is basic. Really basic. In fact, you couldn't get much more basic. Nevertheless, as long as you have your iPod with you, why not add your contact info, your calendars, and a few notes? After all, unless you've got the entire New York City phone book, all this data will take up less space than one song.

As you can expect, Apple offers an excellent interface with its own programs for syncing this kind of data. (You'll see later, in Syncing Contacts to Your iPod on Windows, Syncing Calendars to Your iPod on Windows, and Anapod Explorer: The All-in-One iPod Manager for Windows, how you can sync personal data to your iPod if you're running Windows.) Apple provides a way for Mac users to sync data from two programs that manage personal information, both of which are included with Mac OS X:

- **Address Book:** A contact management program, which interfaces directly with Mail (the OS X e-mail program) and other software
- **iCal:** A powerful calendar program, which offers multiple calendars, alarms, calendar sharing, and more

To synchronize data from these two programs to your iPod, you use the iSync program (located in your Applications folder). iSync lets you synchronize data between two Macs, if you have a subscription to Apple's .Mac online service, to certain cell phones and PDAs, and to your iPod.

When you open iSync, you'll see the devices that you can sync to (Figure 4-1).

Figure 4-1

iSync shows which devices you have set up for synchronization. In this figure, you can see that iSync is ready to synchronize data with .Mac and with an iPod.

Click the icon for your iPod to see the synchronization options (Figure 4-2).

If you want to sync data to your iPod, you need to check Turn On [your iPod's name] Synchronization. You can set iSync to automatically update this data by checking Automatically Synchronize when iPod is Connected. This means that your Mac updates the data you've selected in the lower section of the iSync window each time you connect your iPod, at the same time it updates your iPod's music, so you've always got the latest information.

When you've decided what you want to sync (see the following subsections), just click Sync Now to have your Mac transfer all your stuff to your iPod.

Syncing Contacts Automatically

iSync lets you synchronize contact information from Address Book, which is a contact management program included with Mac OS X. You can choose All Contacts, which is the default, or if you have created groups in Address Book,

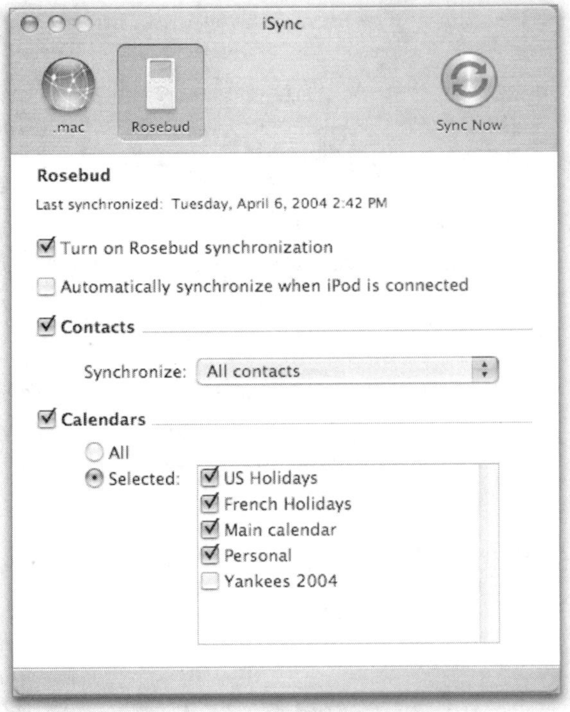

Figure 4-2

Synchronization options for an iPod

you can select a specific group from the popup menu. Since your contact information is not password protected (see Think about Security in Putting Other Stuff on Your iPod), you might want to set up a specific group of iPod contacts, ones you wouldn't be worried about other people discovering. (You can find out more about creating groups in Address Book by checking its online help.)

iSync copies all the contacts you select, and you can then view them on your iPod. See Working with Contacts, Notes, and Calendars for more.

If you don't use Apple's Address Book program, you need to jump through a couple of hoops to get your contact information into Address Book. Just open whatever program stores your contact info (your e-mail or PIM program), and save your contacts as vCards. This is a special type of file that is becoming more common on the Mac (it was originally used by Windows programs), which contains all the information in your contact record. (For example, if you use Palm Desktop, which many Mac users find valuable even if they don't have a Palm PDA, you can export your addresses as vCards.)

You can import vCards into Address Book by selecting File > Import and selecting vCards. If your program doesn't offer vCard export, you can usually just display all your contacts, drag them to your Desktop to create vCards of them, then drag them into Address Book.

Syncing Contacts Manually

Well, when you do it manually, it's not really syncing, is it? But since the iPod recognizes vCards (see the previous subsection), you can just drag them into your iPod's Contacts folder.

First, your iPod needs to be set up to allow disk access. (See Using the iPod as a Hard Disk for more on this.) When you mount your iPod on the Desktop, click its icon in the Finder window sidebar (or if you're using a version of Mac OS X before 10.3, just double-click its icon on the Desktop). You'll see its contents, as in Figure 4-3.

If you've got vCards for your contacts, from any program other than Apple's Address Book, just drag them into the Contacts folder. These could be individual vCards, one for each contact, or they could be larger vCards containing a group of contacts. (When you use iSync to synchronize your Address Book contacts, for example, only one file is copied containing all of them.)

When "manually" syncing your contacts, you'll need to repeat this operation each time you update your info. This can be a drag, but unless you use Address Book or import your stuff into this program, it's (almost) the only way. I say almost, because, as you'll see in Put More Stuff on Your iPod—Mac Tools, there are some great third-party programs that give you much more control over the stuff you sync and let you sync info from many other programs as well.

Figure 4-3

When you look at the contents of your iPod, all you see are three folders: Calendars, Contacts, and Notes.

O

n the Windows side, getting contacts to your iPod is a question of converting them into vCards. The most commonly used e-mail programs, Outlook and Outlook Express, are the main programs you can use to create vCards for your contacts. In Outlook, follow these steps to create a vCard for a contact:

1. Select File > New > Contact and use the dialog box (shown in Figure 4-4) to create the contact you want to save as a vCard.

2. Select File > Export to vCard File.

3. Type a name in the File name box and click Save.

In Outlook Express, follow these steps to create a vCard for a contact:

1. Select Tools > Address Book to display the Address Book.

2. Select New > New Contact.

3. Type in the contact information for your vCard and click OK.

It's interesting to note that some Web-based phone directories let you create a vCard for a contact that you find after searching. For example, if you go to the Prince Edward Island (Canada) provincial government phone book site at http://www.gov.pe.ca/phone/ and perform a search, every result returned in the search will include a link you can click to create a vCard for that person. Also, if you're a Java programmer, you can find a description of the vCard class

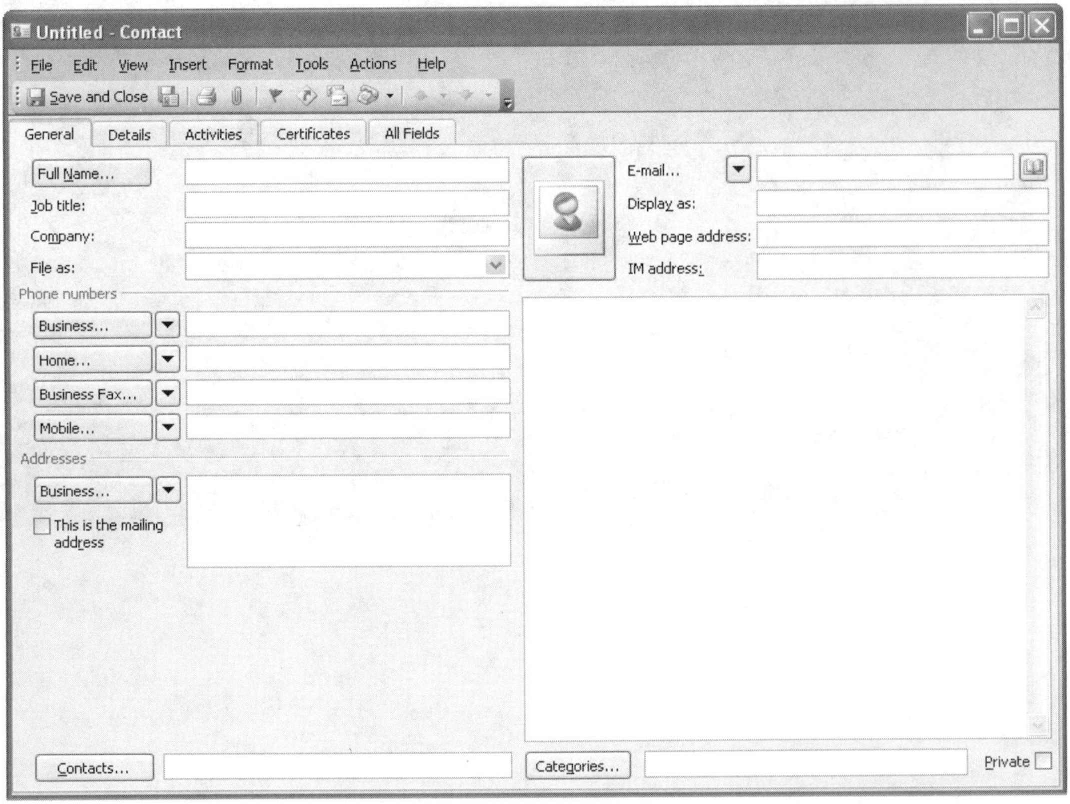

Figure 4-4

The Contact dialog box has room for everything you need to know about your contact.

at http://www.noctor.com/doc/api/ie/ncl/sms/nbs/VCard.html. You can use the properties and methods of that class to create your own vCards.

Once you've created a vCard, you can drag it from your hard drive to your iPod's Contacts folder in Windows Explorer, My Computer, or whatever other file manager you're using.

If you want to automate this process, you can use a program called iPodSync that lets you synchronize your contacts from Outlook to your iPod (Outlook Express isn't supported). You can download this shareware program from http://iccnet.50megs.com/iPodSync/ and try it for 15 days for free. iPodSync's contact synchronizing interface (shown in Figure 4-5) is friendly and intuitive.

iPodSync also handles tasks, and syncs them as contacts. You can keep your iPod load light by only syncing incomplete tasks, or you can sync everything and bask in the glory of what you've done. Figure 4-6 shows you your options for syncing tasks with iPodSync.

If you're looking for a simple program to copy your contacts to your iPod, you can download OutPod from http://www.stoer.de/ipod/ipod_en.htm. OutPod is a lightweight program that reads the contents of your Outlook Contacts

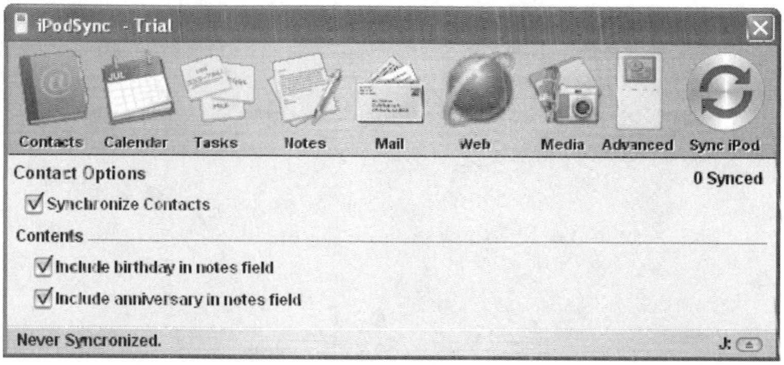

Synchronizing contacts is straightforward in iPodSync...just select the options you want, and click Sync iPod.

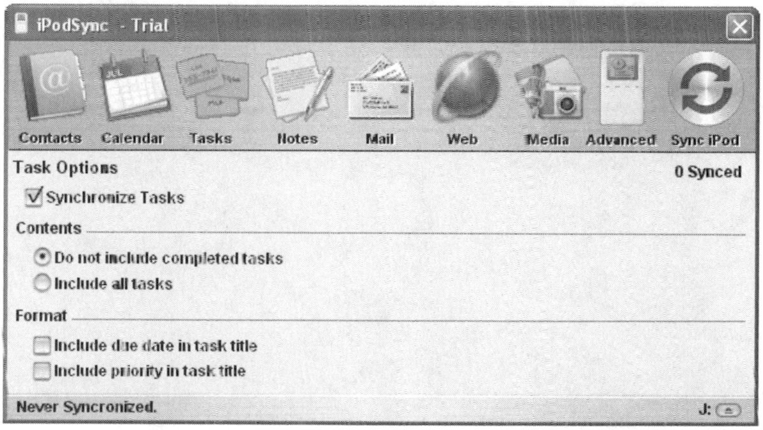

Figure 4-6
iPodSync handles tasks as if they were contacts, so you can sync your to-do list at the same time you export your contact list.

folder (the interface is shown in Figure 4-7) and writes the contents to a series of vCard files or, if you prefer, a single file. When you run OutPod, you may see a dialog box telling you that an unknown program is trying to read your Outlook Address Book. In this case it's OK—it's OutPod—and you can give the program access without fear of a worm or virus spreading by e-mail.

So, even on Windows, whether manually or with one of the preceding programs, you can get your contacts onto your iPod easily.

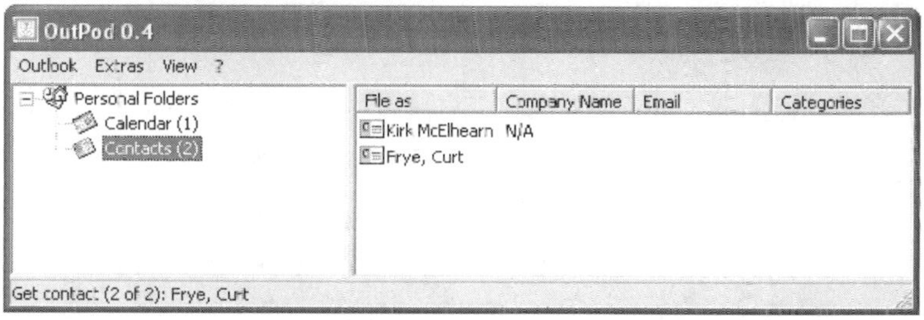

Figure 4-7
Keep it simple. OutPod is free and it does something Outlook doesn't do: it copies multiple vCards into a single file.

Syncing Calendars to Your iPod–The Apple Way

f you're like most people in the iPod demographic, you've got a busy life. You've got work, a family, sports or leisure activities, dates, meetings, and appointments. You can't manage all these without some sort of calendar; otherwise, you'll get mixed up and go to the dentist when you're supposed to be at your yoga class. It happens to the best of us. Modern technology has helped by providing new, efficient ways of managing our time: If you use a calendar program on your computer, you know how much easier it is than writing, erasing, and changing appointments in a paper date book.

DO OR DIE:

>> Your iPod as your personal majordomo

>> Putting your appointments and events on your iPod

>> Ring! You've got an appointment.

For this reason, Apple lets you sync calendars to your iPod, just in case you don't have a PDA that keeps you on time. The iPod reads calendar files and displays their info, and also rings if you have alarms set for your events. It even records to-do lists you've created with iCal, so you can see how much more you need to do before you can call it a day.

As you can see in Figure 4-2, shown in Syncing Contacts to Your iPod—The Apple Way, you get to choose between All Calendars or selected calendars. If you have more than one calendar and don't want or need them all on your iPod, uncheck the ones you don't want to transfer. It's that simple.

If you don't use iCal—say you use Microsoft Entourage or another PIM program—you still may be able to sync your calendars automatically. But the trick is to use iCal anyway as an intermediate step in the process. Entourage doesn't let you export your calendars; however, iCal can somehow dig into your

Updating Subscribed Calendars

One of the powerful features available in iCal is the ability to subscribe to other peoples' calendars. You can do this using Apple's .Mac service, or subscribe directly via links on Web pages. However, when you sync your calendars to your iPod, only the current events are recorded. If you do subscribe to other calendars, think of regularly syncing your iPod with iSync to make sure those calendars are always up to date. And check before you set out on a big trip, to make sure that the person you're meeting hasn't changed their schedule.

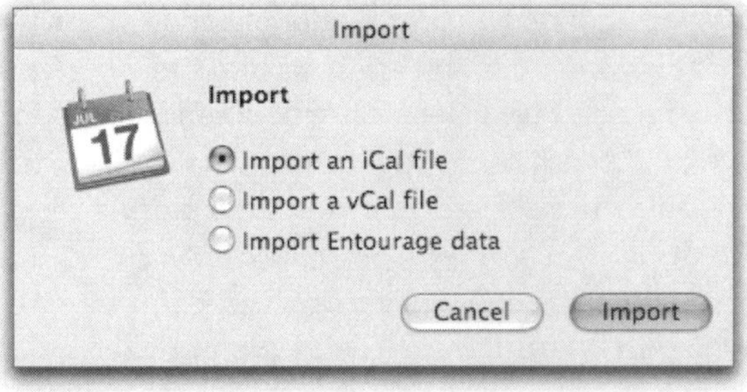

Entourage database and import its calendars. Open iCal—even if you don't usually use it—and select File > Import. You'll see a dialog asking what you want to import (Figure 4-8).

Select Import Entourage Data, and iCal automatically finds your Entourage database and imports your calendar as a new Entourage calendar. (If you have more than one Entourage identity, select the one you want to import.) You can then go ahead and sync this calendar to your iPod with iSync. The only problem is that you need to reimport this calendar each time you want to update your iPod.

iCal can also import vCal files, which are used by many programs, including Palm Desktop. If you have calendars in this format, click Import a vCal File, then click Import. But as with Entourage data, you'll need to regularly reimport these calendars to keep them up to date.

As you saw in Figure 4-3, your iPod contains a Calendars folder. You can manually add any iCal calendars that you may have saved, or received from others, or downloaded from the Internet, to this folder. They'll be accessible in the same way as those you sync automatically.

To find out how to view calendars, see Working with Contacts, Notes, and Calendars. To find third-party solutions for syncing calendar info, see Put More Stuff on Your iPod—Mac Tools.

Figure 4-8

iCal lets you import calendars even from programs that can't export them.

Syncing Calendars to Your iPod on Windows

I don't know if there's anything cooler than keeping appointments on a gizmo that plays your favorite music—cool for some, vital for those with short-term memory deficiencies. You can be jamming to your favorite tunes on the subway while you check your calendar to make sure the meeting of the day does indeed start at 10:00 AM and not 9:00 AM. The trick is getting your appointments from Outlook or another application to your iPod. There are a couple of programs you can pick up for next to nothing, or nothing at all, to make it happen.

iPodSync, which you can also use to sync your contacts to your iPod (see Syncing Contacts to Your iPod on Windows), also works for your Outlook calendar and task entries. When you click the Calendar button, you'll see the list of options that control which entries you want to ship over to your iPod. Figure 4-9 shows you what that options screen looks like.

The Include Recurring Appointments option is important because Outlook uses a rule to fill in the dates of recurring appointments, such as a meeting that occurs on the first Tuesday of every month. If you don't select the Include Recurring Appointments option, iPodSync will only copy over the first appointment in that pattern, and you'll miss all the others (at least if you're so busy listening to music that you don't check your calendar on your computer!).

iPodSync comes with another handy alternative on the Advanced tab (shown in Figure 4-10), which is the option to remove all Outlook data sent to your iPod by iPodSync. If you use more than one management program and

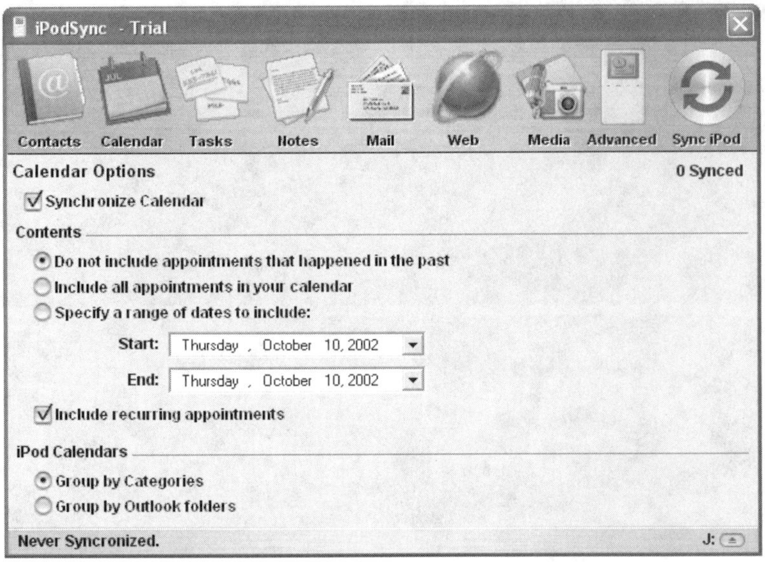

Figure 4-9

Pick the appoint- ments to sync by date range and type.

Figure 4-9

Pick the appoint- ments to sync by date range and type.

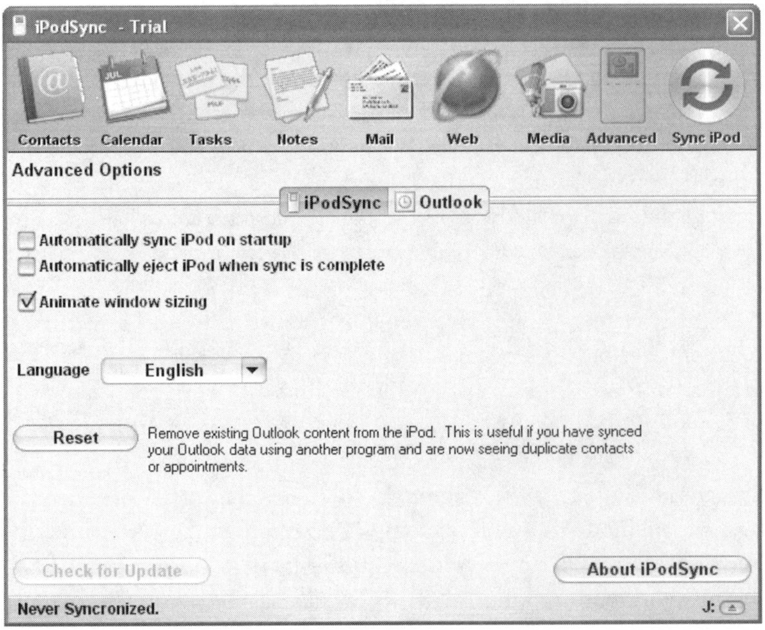

Figure 4-10

Duplicating your efforts? Click the Reset button to get every- thing back in line.

inadvertently copied a second set of appointments to your iPod, just click the Reset button to remove data exported using iPodSync.

You can also use OutPod, a free program created by Oliver Stör and downloadable from http://www.stoer.de/ipod/ipod_en.htm, to synchronize your calendar to your iPod. You can't save by date or control recurring appointments in OutPod—you're limited to copying an entire calendar at once. You can, however, exert a bit of control over the process by selecting Extras > Options to display the Outpod Options dialog box, shown in Figure 4-11.

While OutPod is more limited in its ability to sync calendars, it's a perfect solution for people who don't have busy schedules.

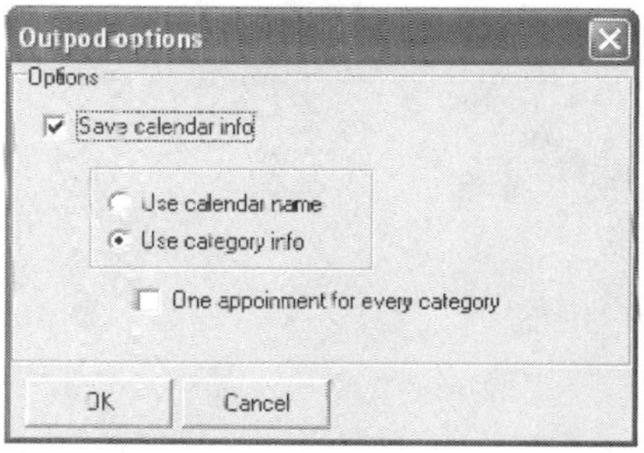

Outpod options

Options

☑ Save calendar info

    ○ Use calendar name
    ● Use category info

    ☐ One appoinment for every category

[OK]   [Cancel]

Figure 4-11

Select whether to use the calendar name or the Outlook category information as the sorting criteria for your exported calendar.

ESSENTIAL MUSIC

"Children on the Hill," by Harold Budd

In 1980, I first heard the music of Harold Budd. The only thing I heard then was a single piece of music on an obscure sampler from a little-known Belgian label called Les Disques du Crépuscule. This cassette contained music by many other musicians and groups that I have come to love—such as The Durutti Column, John Foxx, Michael Nyman, and Gavin Bryars—but what stuck with me most about this tape was the one piano piece by Harold Budd.

Deceptively simple, subtly emotional, this is an austere piano piece about five minutes long where the right hand plays a haunting melody over a simple rhythmic left-hand part that, for most of the piece, plays just four notes. It's hard to describe the beauty of this piece and its understated melody that rises and falls like the eternal breath of life. But when I first heard it, I was so taken by the music that I copied it to an endless loop cassette tape and would spend hours listening to it. Even today, hearing this piece brings tears to my eyes.

I later discovered other music by Harold Budd, including his albums *The Plateaux of Mirror*, released the same year; *The Pavilion of Dreams*, released in 1978; and his 1984 classic *The Pearl*, recorded with Brian Eno, who produced much of his work (for more on this album, see the sidebar by John Foxx on page 272) and his recent recording *The Room*.

Budd's music has always retained this naïve simplicity, yet his seemingly simple melodies hide a powerful ability to move and transfix the listener. His music exudes stillness and quiet, and speaks to each listener in a unique way. Unforgettable, like a sunset on a lonely beach, Harold Budd's music is inimitable.

Copying Notes to Your iPod

DO OR DIE:

>> Keeping track of snippets

>> Taking notes on the road

Never trust your pockets for paper snippets, such as shopping lists, recipes, or directions. You'll lose the paper: It's the seventh law of the variegation of matter. And if you don't lose them, the universe's natural entropy will cause them to get wadded up into unreadable balls of wood pulp.

Of course, some of you are organized and can handle such things, but I for one end up losing anything that's not nailed down, or not on my computer or iPod. Hence the iPod's notes feature, which lets you put snippets of text onto your iPod for later use. You can put shopping lists, recipes, directions, or even lists of CDs you want to buy or books you've been looking for. You can access them quickly and read their contents while you listen to your music.

To get notes onto your iPod, well, you just have to put them there. Apple doesn't have any special software that syncs notes to your iPod, other than some AppleScripts they offer (see the sidebar Using AppleScripts to Manage Notes). If you really want powerful note management, I look at some third-party programs that can sync notes in Put More Stuff on Your iPod—Mac Tools.

Make sure your iPod is set up to be used as a hard disk. (See iPod Settings and Preferences for more on this.)

If you're using a Mac, when your iPod is mounted on the Desktop, click its icon in the Finder window sidebar (or if you're using a version of Mac OS X

> ## Using AppleScripts to Manage Notes
>
> If you're a Mac user, you've seen how you can use AppleScripts to extend iTunes' functionalities (Using AppleScripts with iTunes). Apple also offers a selection of AppleScripts for the iPod (http://www.apple.com/applescript/ipod), most of which are for managing notes: creating notes from the clipboard or a Web page, listing and editing notes, and deleting notes.
>
> These AppleScripts don't run on the iPod, they run on your Mac, but allow you to manipulate notes on your iPod when it's mounted as a hard disk. If you want a simple solution for transferring notes from the clipboard or from Web pages, these AppleScripts are a perfect way to manage your notes.

FAQ

Is There a Limit to the Size of iPod Notes?

You can drag files of any size to your iPod's Notes folder, but the iPod can only display 4K of text. If your shopping list gets cut off, you'll know why. If you have notes that are longer than 4K, split them into multiple notes, perhaps numbering them Note1, Note2, and so on, so you can be sure to keep them in order.

Some third-party software can get around this limitation by splitting your notes automatically.

before 10.3, just double-click its icon on the Desktop). You'll see its contents, as in Figure 4-3 earlier.

If you're using Windows, double-click the iPod icon on the Desktop to open the iPod as a folder (shown in Figure 4-12).

To add notes, just drag text files to the Notes folder. These files must be .txt or plain text files. You can put other files in that folder, but the iPod won't be able to read them. To find out how to access your notes, see Working with Contacts, Notes, and Calendars.

When you're finished and you want to take your iPod with you, make sure you remember to unmount it correctly. See Using the iPod as a Hard Disk for more on unmounting your iPod.

Figure 4-12

To Windows, the iPod is just another hard disk.

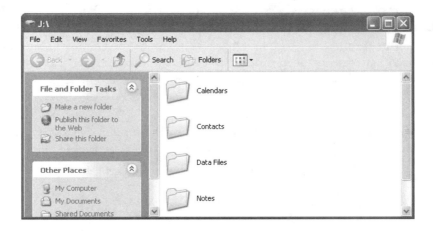

Loading e-books on Your iPod

Words may seem boring when compared with the music you can buy and listen to on your iPod, but good storytelling never gets old. Whether you're reading a book for a class or your own edification, you can load it onto your iPod and read it at your leisure, as long as you have it in a text file. And you don't even have to turn off your music to do it.

The size of the iPod's hard disk—even the smallest version, the iPod mini—is such that you can carry around the contents of an entire library. While the iPod's screen isn't the best for reading books, the sheer amount of disk space is impressive. You could have, in your pocket, more books than most of the world's great thinkers or writers have ever owned. Sure, you'll need time to read them, but the ability to carry around hundreds, even thousands of books is awe-inspiring.

The only problem with reading texts on your iPod is that they are limited to 4K, as I pointed out earlier when talking about notes. But don't sweat it; several third-party developers have found ways to get around this and to get around another built-in limit, that of having no more than 1,000 notes on an iPod. This only works with third-generation iPods and later, though, so if you have an older model, you're stuck with paper for now.

DO OR DIE:

>> Put a library in your pocket

>> Get e-books for free!

Copying e-books in Text Files

I'll soon explain how you can actually read books on your iPod. But first, think of how many files you can put on your iPod. Even if you don't want to read them on your iPod, you could put thousands of e-books on it in text format and then copy these files to your or another computer to read them. You've seen in Using the iPod as a Hard Disk how you can copy files to it. You could create an e-book folder and copy as many books as you want, having them available for reading on any computer you can connect the iPod to.

Loading e-books on Your iPod from a Mac

To read e-books on your iPod, you need to get them there and in the appropriate format. Since notes are limited to 4K, you need to use special programs to format e-books so you can read them on your iPod. To do this on a Mac, you can use Book2Pod (http://www.tomsci.com/book2pod), a free program that formats large text documents so you can read them on your iPod using its notes feature. Book2Pod works with 3G iPods and later, supports documents larger than the 4K note limit, and works around the 1,000 note limit as well, so you can even put *War and Peace* on your iPod.

You launch Book2Pod, connect your iPod, then click the + button to add a book. Navigate to find a plain text file of an e-book (such as one downloaded from Project Gutenberg), then click OK. You'll see the book listed in the Book2Pod window (Figure 4-13).

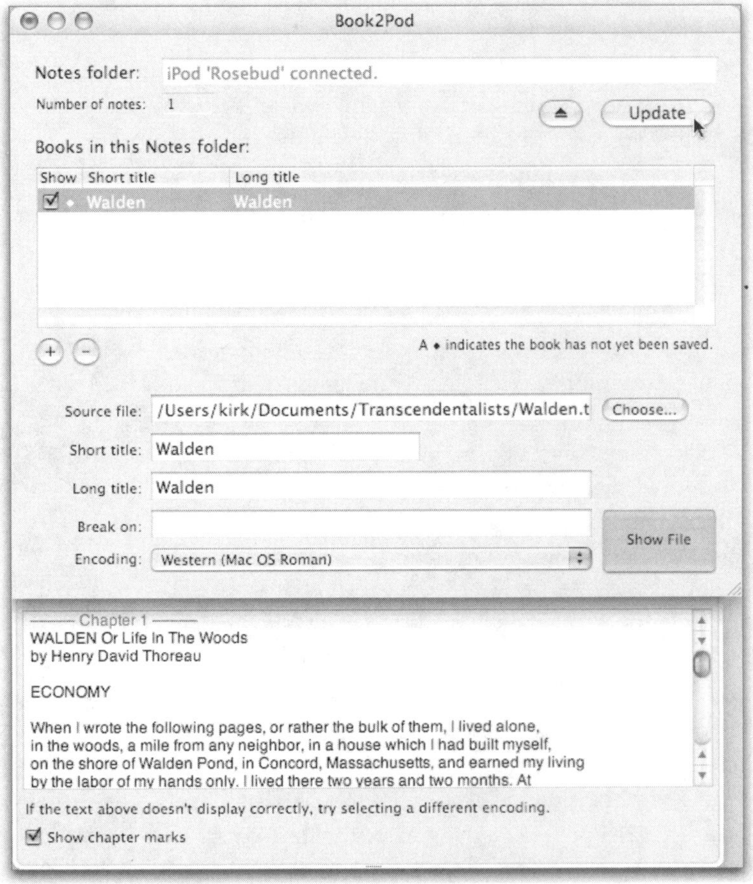

Figure 4-13

Putting Henry David Thoreau's Walden on my iPod to read in the woods

Click the Update button, and Book2Pod splits the text file into notes, formatting them for you to read on your iPod. You can put lots of books on your iPod this way, and you can use Book2Pod to delete the ones you've finished and manage your portable library.

Loading e-books on Your iPod from Windows

If you use Windows, the best way to get e-books on your iPod is with iPodLibrary (http://www25.brinkster.com/carmagt/ipodlibrary), which you can use to transfer your e-books to your iPod quickly. iPodLibrary can also, under certain circumstances, bypass the 1,000-note limit inherent in your iPod.

When you install iPodLibrary, you may see a couple of error messages complaining about missing DLL files, or a warning that you don't have the Visual Basic 6.0 runtime executable on your computer. DLL files are dynamic link libraries, which are files that contain routines the program needs to run. You can find the following download links on the iPod Library site:

- mscomctl_dll.zip (which contains the mscomctl.dll file)
- MSFlxgrd.zip (which also contains the MSFlxgrd.ocx file)
- A link to a Google search that lists places you can go to download the VB6 runtime (if you get an error that says, "Couldn't find MSVBVM60.DLL")

After you've installed iPodLibrary, connect your iPod to your computer and run iPodLibrary. You may see an alert telling you that your iPod doesn't appear to be connected to your computer. Click OK to clear the alert and display the program's iPod Library screen (shown in Figure 4-14).

To let the program know which drive letter your iPod is assigned to, click the Settings button and then click the iPod Drive down arrow. You'll see your iPod's name assigned to a drive letter. If you don't see your iPod in the list, you can disconnect and reconnect the iPod to give your computer another chance to detect it.

You can download an e-book to your iPod by clicking the Import eBook button at the top of the iPod Library window and then using the controls on the Import eBook page to pick the book you want. The Import eBook page is shown in Figure 4-15; the Library title entry is the name the iPodLibrary program uses to refer to the book, while the iPod title entry is the name displayed in your iPod's Notes list.

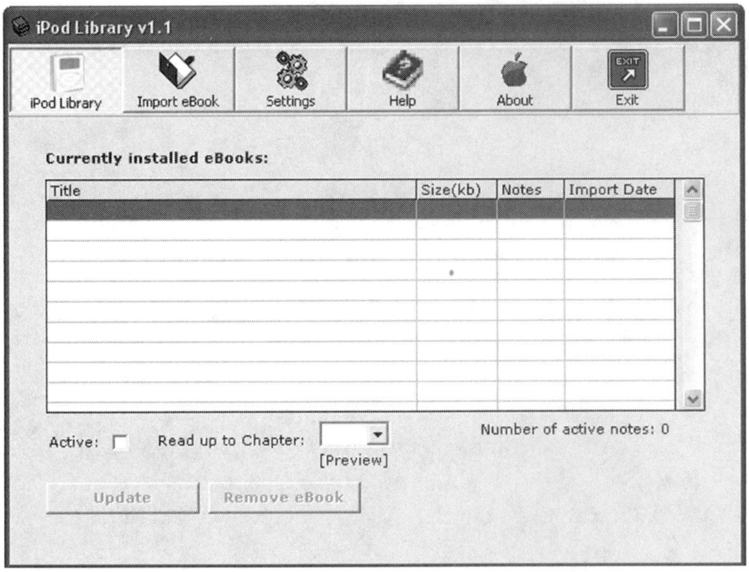

Figure 4-14

The iPodLibrary main screen shows you which e-books you've copied onto your iPod.

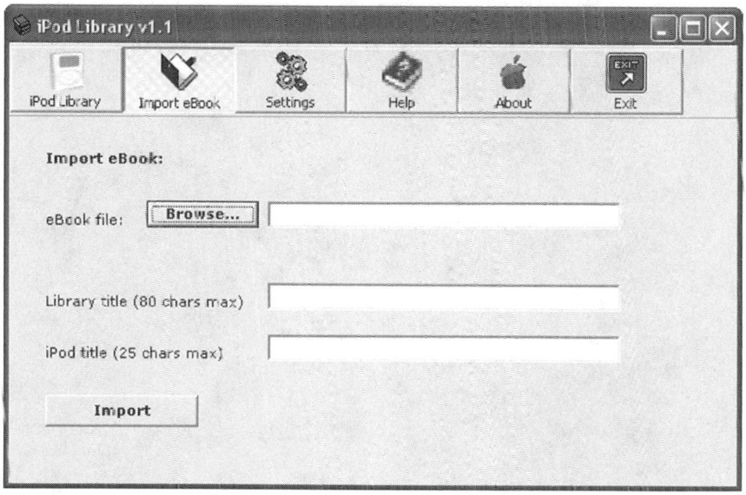

Figure 4-15

The Import eBook page lets you add new e-books to your iPod.

iPodLibrary works with all four major formats for e-books: plain text (*.txt), Adobe's Portable Document Format (*.pdf), Hypertext Markup Language (*.htm), and the Microsoft Reader format (*.lit). If you see HTML tags in your e-books, click the Setup button on the Settings page to configure your iPod to read e-books.

Inactive e-books Don't Take Up Notes Space

The iPod comes with a limit of 1,000 notes, each of which can have a maximum size of 4K. If you're banging up against the 1,000-note limit but want to download another book, iPodLibrary lets you leave an existing e-book on your iPod, "hiding" it from the system so it won't take up space. To do that, click the title of the e-book you want to hide, clear the Active check box, and click Update. iPodLibrary will hide your e-book, clearing space in the Notes menu for your new books. You won't be able to read the inactive e-book, but you can delete or make inactive another book to free up space for it when you do want to read it.

BLOG: Henry David Thoreau: An American Original

Best known for his book *Walden*, Henry David Thoreau had little success as an author during his lifetime, but is now considered one of the emblematic writers of the American Renaissance of the late nineteenth century. *Walden*, a nonfiction account of his life in a hut by Walden Pond, near Concord, Massachusetts, remains one of the most original statements of American literature. Thoreau's importance has far exceeded that of his friend, mentor, and fellow transcendentalist Ralph Waldo Emerson, and *Walden* has become a cultural icon.

The idea of living by a pond or lake is part of the American mythos. Millions of Americans go, each year, to spend vacations in wooden huts by lakes around the country, fishing, barbecuing, and enjoying life in the woods, as Thoreau did. Henry "went to the woods to live deliberately"; most of us only go for a short vacation, but on a starlit night, amidst the silence of the forest, you can feel what drew Thoreau to seek out the solace of solitude, and revel, if only for a moment, in the same peace and oneness with nature.

Thoreau would be called a Luddite, if he were around today. And many of his comments on advances ring true; he saw many advances as bringing little to the appreciation of real life. Would Thoreau use an iPod? Probably not. But his message is worth reflecting on, as we burden ourselves with ever-increasing numbers of gadgets and devices As Thoreau said in *Walden*:

> *"Our inventions are wont to be pretty toys, which distract our attention from serious things. They are but improved means to an unimproved end, an end which it was already but too easy to arrive at; as railroads*

lead to Boston or New York. We are in great haste to construct a magnetic telegraph from Maine to Texas; but Maine and Texas, it may be, have nothing important to communicate."

But to better reflect on this, why not buy an audiobook version of *Walden*? Check out the iTunes Music Store or Audible.com; there are several versions available: An abridged version, read by Archibald MacLeish, at just over one hour, gives you a taste of Thoreau through some of the best parts of the book. This version is only available from Audible.com. An unabridged version of *Walden* is available from both sources and, at over 12 hours, will give you plenty of time to mull over Thoreau's message.

Or if you'd rather just read *Walden*, go to http://www.gutenberg.org and search for "Walden". Download the text and read it on your computer, your iPod, or a PDA. Or you could even go for one of those artifacts called "books," which require no batteries. You'll find many editions of *Walden* in your local bookstore or library.

Recommended music to listen to while reading *Walden*: Charles Ives' Concord Sonata, which contains a movement entitled "Thoreau," Beethoven's Sixth Symphony, anything by Harold Budd, some acoustic Grateful Dead, Johnny Cash's *Unearthed*, anything by Iron & Wine, or Bill Evans' *Live at the Village Vanguard*.

Reading e-books
on Your iPod

Now that you've put a few e-books on your iPod, it's time to see how to read them. This is pretty simple, but you need to be patient, at least the first time you go to check out what books your iPod library contains, or whenever you've updated your notes or e-books. The iPod has to read all the notes it contains before it can display anything in the Notes menu, so if you have a lot of books, this takes a long time. If you do want to read *War and Peace*, go make yourself a cup of tea and make sure your iPod's not low on battery power.

To view e-books, whether you've transferred them from a Mac or Windows computer, go to the main menu, then select Extras > Notes. You'll see a list of any notes you've added manually (see Copying Notes to Your iPod), as well as different folders, depending on how you transferred your e-books. If, for example, you copied Cory Doctorow's *Down and Out in the Magic Kingdom* (which I heartily recommend: go to http://craphound.com/down/download.php and look for the file formatted for the iPod Notes Reader), you'll see a folder for that book. Select this folder, then select the first file in the folder. You can't read the entire note name in this list, so just select the one at the top.

As you read, use the scroll wheel to move down in the text. Unfortunately, there's no way to jump down one screen, so you're stuck (for now) with this slightly annoying need to keep the text moving to read it. Since the iPod (at least white iPods) only displays eight lines per screen, if you read at a normal pace you'll do as much scrolling as you do reading.

DO OR DIE:

>> Read while you listen

>> Read all kinds of books

Deleting e-books in a Snap

If you ever get tired of reading or have finished some of your e-books, you can delete
them easily without using any special software. The programs mentioned in the previous
sections are necessary for formatting e-books,
but you can delete them by just mounting your
iPod as a hard disk (see Using the iPod as a
Hard Disk), opening the Notes folder, and
deleting the folders containing your e-books.

When you get to the end of a note——at least if
your e-book was formatted correctly using one of
the programs mentioned previously—you'll see
what looks like a link: a bit of text, usually Next,
underlined like a Web link. Scroll to the bottom of
the note, then press the Select button to activate
this link and jump to the next note.

It's all very simple, but the problem of scrolling all
the time can be hard on your eyes. However, if you
want to keep up on your culture while listening to
music on the bus or train, this is a good way to do so.

Create Text Adventures and Quiz Games with iStory

Back in the days of text-only computing, computer users wanted to play games, but gaming was much different from what it is now. Programmers built what were called text adventure games, the most famous of which was the Zork trilogy.

If you've ever seen a "pick your path" adventure book, it's the same idea. You, the player, are given a situation and a number of choices, and those choices lead either to other pages in the book or to another situation in a computer program. It's a lot like creating a Web site—each page has links to other pages, unless you've reached the end of the game, and then your only choice is to start the game again or turn off your computer.

Well, you can create text adventure and quiz show games for the iPod if you use Windows. Download the Windows program iStoryCreator and sample iStory games from http://www.ipodsoft.com/iCreator.aspx. iStory is part of the iPodSoft effort, which aims to bring more and more useful iPod programs to the PC. Figure 4-16 shows the main interface for iStoryCreator.

iStoryCreator is easy to use: The online help file is complete, and the interface makes it easy to enter your choices and create links. You can also choose to play songs when a player reaches a given page. The author of the "Millionaire" game in the figure even uses a well-known host's voice as the sound for this page.

iStoryCreator runs on top of the .NET Framework 1.1, which you can download from http://msdn.microsoft.com/netframework/technologyinfo/howtoget/default.aspx.

DO OR DIE:

>> Text games on your iPod for more fun

>> Do you want to do this or that?

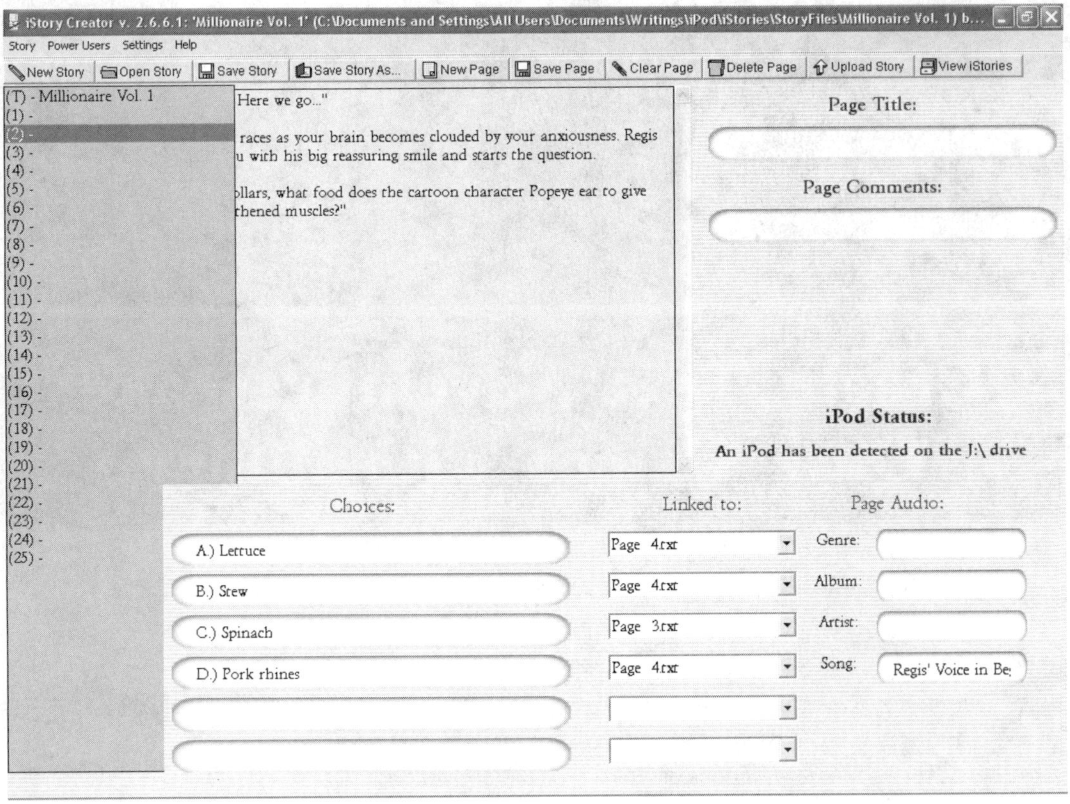

Figure 4-16

You don't need to know any HTML to create your own games and quizzes for the iPod.

Anapod Explorer: The All-in-One iPod Manager for Windows

s of this writing, the all-singing, all-dancing iPod management program for Windows, that puts all types of information onto your iPod, is Anapod Explorer (http://www.redchairsoftware.com/anapod). Not only can Anapod Explorer manage your extra stuff—contacts, notes, and so on—but it can also manage your music and create playlists.

You need Windows 2000 or later to run it, and this neat program looks and acts exactly like Windows Explorer. As shown in Figure 4-17, every subdirectory on your iPod is presented as a folder, and you can use the built-in Structured Query Language (SQL) database to view your music by artist, album, or genre. You can also view your Notes and Outlook Contacts, but not your Outlook Calendar.

Double-clicking the Artists, Albums, or Genres icons displays a corresponding list from the Anapod Explorer database (songs in the case of Artists and Genres, album names in the case of Albums); double-clicking the Playlists, Contacts, or Notes icons changes the right pane so you can view, edit, create, or delete the corresponding items on your iPod.

For example, double-clicking the Playlists icon displays your Playlists. Unless you've created your own playlists, the only playlists that will appear are the smart playlists that iTunes creates for you, but you can create your own playlist by clicking the New Playlist button (located just below the Folders button

DO OR DIE:

>> Manage everything on your iPod

>> Sync notes, contacts, and music with the same program

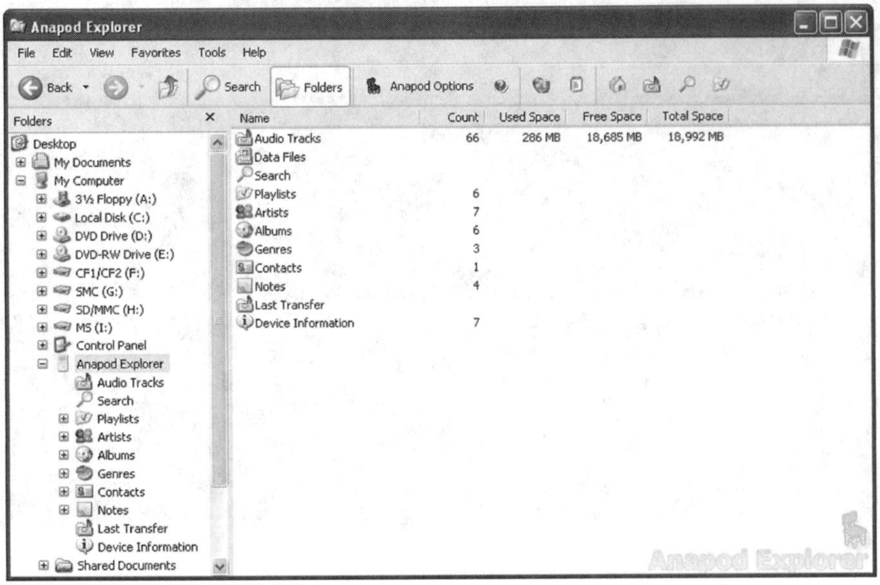

Figure 4-17

Anapod Explorer's interface hands you the keys to the iPod kingdom.

on the main toolbar) and typing a name in the dialog box that appears. You can then add songs to the playlist this way:

1. In the left pane of the window, click the Expand icon (the plus sign) next to the Playlists item.

2. Again in the left pane, click the Audio Tracks item to make the available songs on your iPod appear in the right pane. If you know the artist, album, or genre of the songs you want to add, you can restrict the number of songs that appear on-screen by double-clicking the corresponding icon in the left pane and displaying the songs from the desired category.

3. Drag the songs you want to add to your target playlist in the left pane. It's the same thing you do in Outlook when you want to file an e-mail message in a folder.

Editing a playlist is pretty straightforward as well:

1. In the left pane, click Playlists. Then, in the right pane, double-click the playlist you want to edit.

2. The playlist appears in the right pane of Anapod Explorer, as shown in Figure 4-18.

3. Drag the track you want to move to the desired spot in the order.

There are two limitations to reordering songs in a playlist: You can only move one song at a time, and you can't move a song to the end of the list. To put

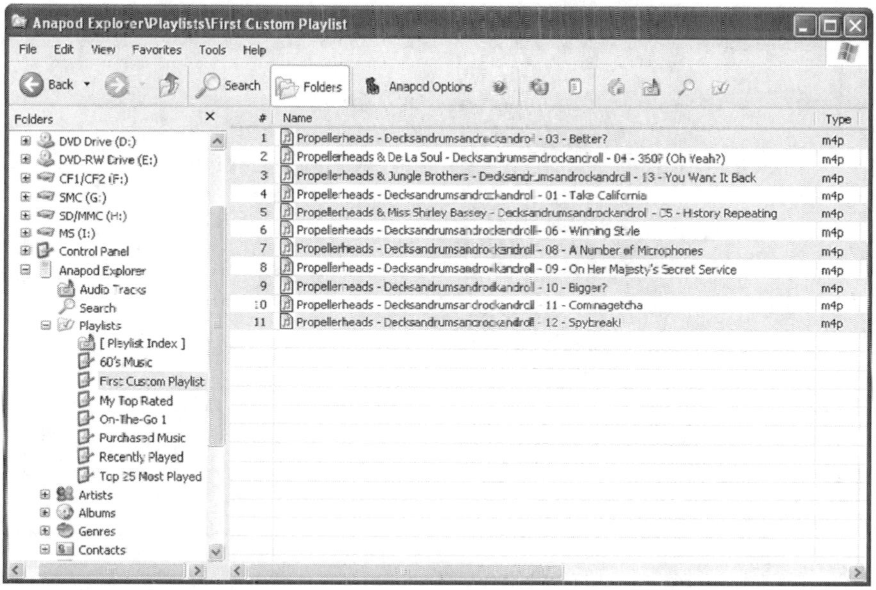

Figure 4-18

Displaying a playlist gives you the opportunity to edit it.

a song in the last position, you must move it to the next-to-last position and then move the last song above it. Neither quirk is a deal-breaker in what is an otherwise great program, however. (iTunes still takes the palm for the best music management program.)

Managing Contacts and Notes with Anapod Explorer

It's actually not easy to notice that Anapod Explorer handles contacts and notes when you're looking at the main Anapod Explorer window (shown earlier in Figure 4-17), but there are entries in the Folders pane for Contacts and Notes. The Contacts and Notes interfaces are very similar to the Playlists interface, which makes Anapod very easy to use to put all your stuff onto your iPod. When you click Contacts, you see the rich contact management environment shown in Figure 4-19.

Anapod Explorer shows the contacts you've created on your PC, which you can then sync to your iPod. As with other programs of this type, you can decide whether to export the contacts from the default Outlook folder or from another folder where you've saved your contacts' vCards. As you might expect, clicking New Contact opens a dialog box into which you can enter all of the usual information about your contact. It's doesn't look exactly the same as the Contact dialog box in Outlook, but it has the same fields and exports your contact info into the same format.

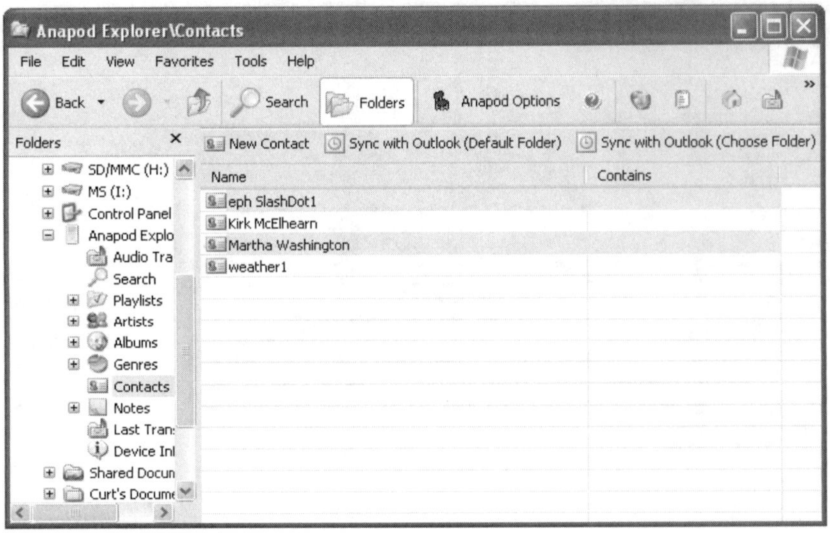

Figure 4-19

Once you know where to look, you can manage your contacts in Anapod Explorer.

Right below the Contacts item in Anapod Explorer's Folders pane is Notes, which you can click to display the notes environment shown in Figure 4-20.

What's cool about Anapod Explorer's note-handling tools is that you can create new Notes folders from its interface without going through Windows Explorer or My Computer. Yeah, it's a little thing, but it's a nice touch not to have to switch between program windows when you're in mid-flow.

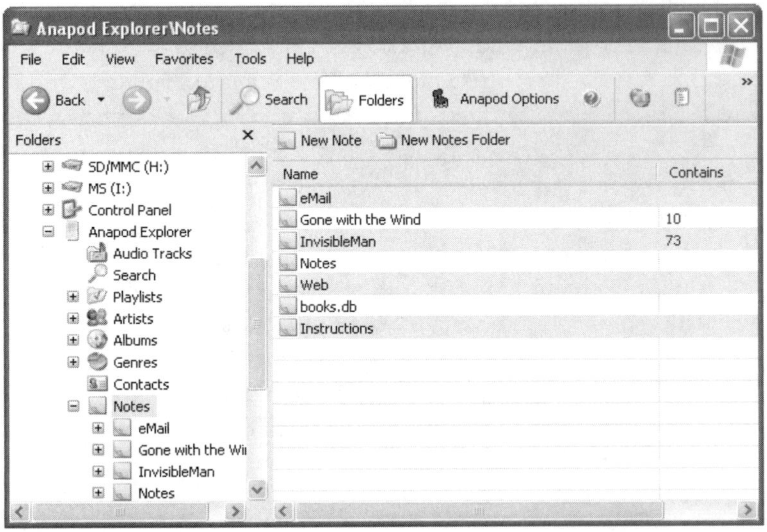

Figure 4-20

Managing notes comes easy in Anapod Explorer.

Managing Your iPod on Windows with XPlay

DO OR DIE:

>> Another way to manage your stuff with Windows

>> Use a Mac-formatted iPod on Windows

he battle between Apple and Microsoft has raged for years, and there's no sign of it settling down anytime soon. For a long time, transferring files between Macs and PCs was difficult, if not impossible, even when you were running the same program on both computers. But over time, floppy disk and CD formats were reconciled to the point where it's almost always possible to transfer files from a Mac to a PC and back. Almost. But is it possible to use a Mac-formatted iPod with a Windows computer? Yes, if you get a copy of XPlay from http://www.mediafour.com.

XPlay lets you manage the contents of your iPod using the familiar Windows Explorer interface, as shown in Figure 4-21. The difference between XPlay and other programs is that it incorporates Mediafour's MacDrive technology, which lets your Windows computer read Macintosh disks, including Mac-formatted iPods, as if they were formatted for Windows.

When you double-click one of the icons in the main XPlay window, you're taken to a new window with specific tasks listed in the XPlay Music Tasks pane. For example, if you double-click Playlists, you'll see a list of existing playlists in the main window and a clickable task for creating a new playlist in the XPlay Music Tasks pane. Creating a playlist is as easy as clicking the Create a Playlist task and typing in a name when you're prompted to do so. After you create your playlist, you can add songs to it by right-clicking the song you want to add, pointing to Add to Playlist, and then clicking the playlist to which you want to add the song.

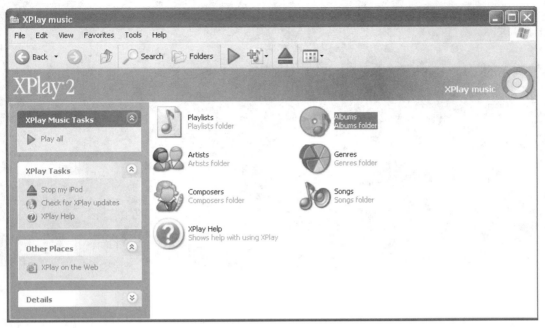

Figure 4-21

The main XPlay screen will be familiar to any Windows user.

After you've created a playlist, you can change the order of the songs by double-clicking the playlist and dragging your songs to the desired spot in the list. If you want to play the songs in a random order, right-click the playlist and click Shuffle Playlist.

If you move up a folder level while you're viewing the music on your iPod, you'll see a Windows Explorer window that displays the folders on your iPod (as shown in Figure 4-22). XPlay doesn't have a built-in calendar or contacts editor, but you can drag iCal, vCal, and vCard files to and from the existing folders from within XPlay.

If you want to transfer calendars to your iPod with XPlay, use your PIM program to export them in iCal format, if possible. This format is more widely used than the vCal format, so you should use iCal if you have a choice.

Editing the Uneditable

Unlike other programs, XPlay lets you add songs to smart playlists (such as the Recently Played list).

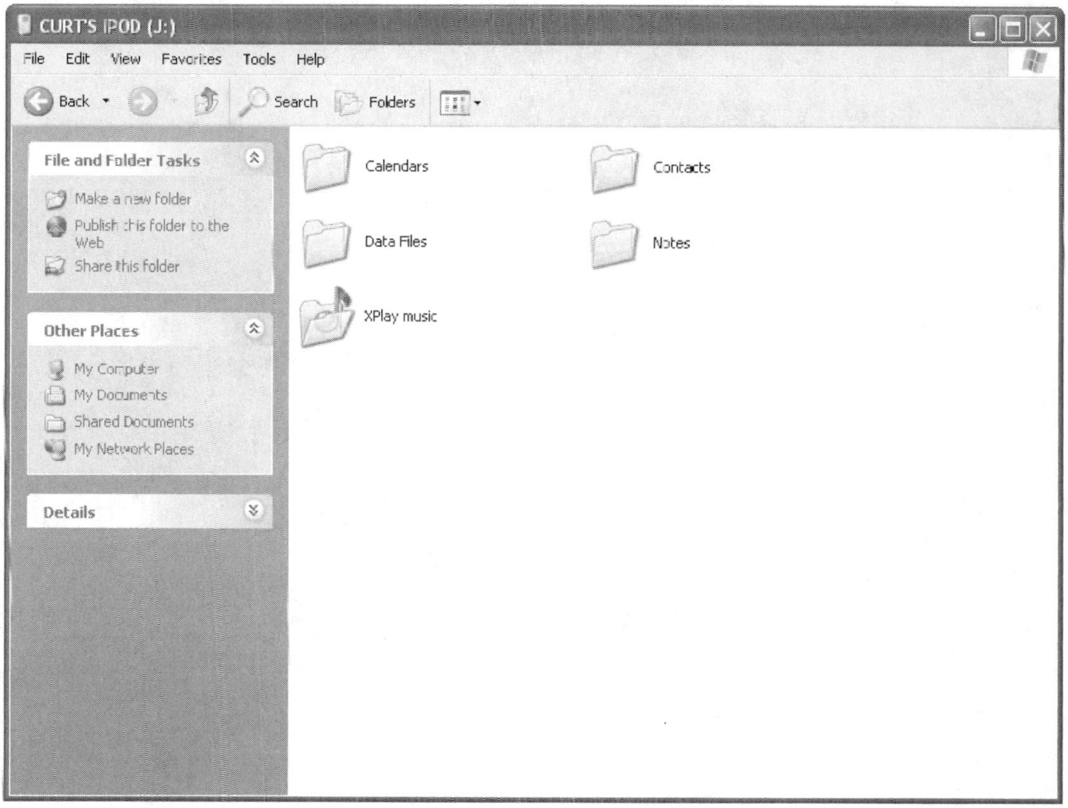

Figure 4-22

Transferring files, contacts, appointments, and notes to and from your iPod is as straightforward as copying any other files in the Windows file system.

Put More Stuff on Your iPod—Mac Tools

O. K, I've said that your iPod isn't a PDA, but if you don't own a PDA, why not take advantage of your iPod and use it to copy much more stuff from your Mac? With Apple's software, you can put notes, contacts, and calendars on it, as you've seen earlier. But there are third-party programs that offer you far more functionality, letting you put contacts and calendars from other programs, e-mail, sticky notes, and even news briefs on your iPod.

iPod It--The All-Purpose Transfer Tool

The first problem with using Apple's method of transferring your contacts and calendars to your iPod is that iSync only transfers data from Apple's Address Book and iCal. (See Putting Other Stuff on Your iPod.) If you use other programs, you're out of luck. While you can still get your contacts into Address Book, it can be annoying, especially since you need to export and import them each time you want to update the contacts on your iPod.

iPod It (http://www.zapptek.com/ipod-it) offers a solution for some users, those who work with Microsoft Entourage—the e-mail client and PIM tool included with Microsoft Office—letting them transfer contacts and calendars from its database, and transferring e-mail, notes, and tasks as well. As you can see in Figure 4-23, iPod It also lets you transfer e-mail from Apple's Mail and

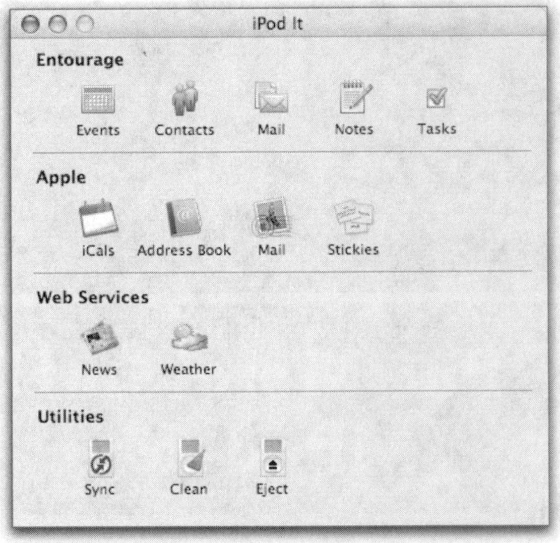

Figure 4-23

iPod It lets Mac users put lots of stuff on their iPods.

transfer the contents of your Stickies, and it provides an interface with Address Book and iCal. And as icing on the cake, you can get news and weather information from the Internet and put that on your iPod as well.

Since iPod It syncs the same type of information as iSync (iCal calendars and Address Book contacts), it can easily replace the Apple tool. With the ability to transfer e-mail from Mail and Entourage, and the rest of your Entourage data, it is the ideal tool for users of these programs, letting you store a full range of info on your iPod.

iPod It is easy to use. Just click one of the icons on its main window (Figure 4-23) to access options for one of the types of stuff it manages. For Entourage, you can choose events, contacts, mail, notes, and tasks by category, or you can choose to transfer specific e-mail folders or notes. For Apple programs, you have the same options as you do with iSync—choosing which calendars to transfer or which groups of contacts—with the addition of being able to transfer e-mail and sticky notes. Finally, the Web Services section lets you add news headlines and summaries, and weather for a selected area.

Just click the Sync icon to sync all the selected info to your iPod. If you want to erase everything, click Clean. And you can even eject your iPod from the iPod It window by clicking the Eject icon.

Pod2Go--Transfer Stuff from the Web to Your iPod

Like iPod It, Pod2Go (http://www.kainjow.com/pod2go) can duplicate the functions of Apple's iSync. This program doesn't transfer e-mail onto your iPod, but offers a variety of features to move lots of other stuff onto your iPod. Pod2Go can transfer your Address Book contacts and iCal calendars, as well as your Safari bookmarks and sticky notes. But it goes a lot further than that: It provides an interface with certain Web sites, allowing you to download information from the Internet and transfer it to your iPod.

Pod2Go's popup menu (see Figure 4-24) gives you access to nine types of information: news, weather, movie info, stock quotes, horoscopes, song lyrics, notes, directions, and application data from Address Book, iCal, Safari, and Stickies.

Just select one of these categories, and you'll see a window allowing you to choose, for example, which news you want to receive, what your star sign is, or what your zip code is to get movie info. If you have a 3G iPod or later, you can save your info as notes, organized by subfolders to make it easier to navigate, but if you have an earlier model (or if you'd rather save it this way), you can save all this as contacts. In the latter case, you'll see on your iPod new contacts containing the info added by Pod2Go.

Pod2Go is a great way to get additional stuff to put on your iPod. Since it does the downloading for you, you can set up, for example, a selection of news sites, and every time you connect your iPod, Pod2Go refreshes the latest headlines and syncs them to your iPod. Get movie schedules so if you decide to go see a flick at the last minute, you'll know what you can see. Song lyrics are cool to have as well—turn your iPod into a karaoke machine! (Well, sort of... People will look at you funny if you walk down the street, staring at your iPod screen and singing...)

Figure 4-24

Pod2Go lets you download information from the Web and transfer it to your iPod.

Download News from Google Using GoogleGet

For those of you who want to have the most recent news available as notes on your iPod, you can download GoogleGet for Windows from http://mesmerized.org/teki/extra/googleget/. The interface is very simple to use. After you install the program, all you need to do is identify the drive letter assigned to your iPod and then click News Options (the News Options tab is shown in Figure 4-25) to pick the Google variant from which you want to download your news and select the news to get.

GoogleGet is written in Visual Basic 6, so you'll need to have both mswinsck.ocx and tabctl32.ocx installed on your computer for the program to run. Most systems already have these files installed; however, if you need either, then download the appropriate file from a site such as http://www.santanacreations.com/needed_files.html.

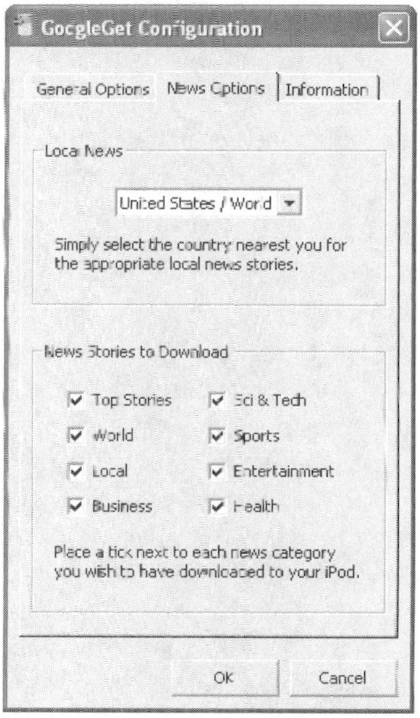

Figure 4-25

What kind of news do you like? You can download it from Google to read on your iPod.

Off-Topic: Nick Hornby

While music is really important in my life, as you've seen throughout this book, words are perhaps even more so. I make my living writing them, and spend a lot of time reading other people's words. I've talked about a couple of authors here—Henry David Thoreau and Ross Lockridge Jr.—both of whom could be considered "highbrow" authors, but now it's time to opine about a wordsmith who's closer to today's climate.

Nick Hornby has written a half-dozen novels, and Hollywood has put two of them on screen (so far; a third is in the works). He writes stories about real people in real situations; more or less. One thing that stands out in his books is his love of music, and his use of music as not only a glue holding his characters together (or keeping them apart), but his use of music as a character, in his novel *High Fidelity*.

There's something uncanny about this book. First, I wonder who told him about my late teenage years. You've got to be suspicious of a guy who's from a different country and who writes a novel so close to your experience. But Nick (I feel I know him, through his writing, well enough to call him by his first name) shows in *High Fidelity* that my experience was not isolated—I guess I'd be pompous to assume that it was.

When, in my late teens, I became friendly with a guy who worked in a record store, and a few other music-lovers who hung out there, I lived through a lot of the events that Nick portrays in *High Fidelity*. Music for us, back then, was everything: we loved discovering new music, sharing our favorite albums and violently criticizing the lame tastes of others, and making compilation tapes of all the obscure stuff that only we, and a handful of others, not only liked but had actually heard of. And the guy who worked in the record store, Stu, had a few thousand LPs, and spent a lot of time worrying about the best way to organize them. *High Fidelity* frames this record-store culture in a larger story of love and loss, the kind that we've all lived through.

More recently, Nick penned *Songbook* (called *31 songs* in the UK), a collection of essays about (you guessed it) 31 songs that he likes for one reason or another. In the paperback edition, you get extras (though you don't get the CD that comes with the hardcover): discussions of 14 albums (well, four, actually, plus a top-ten list), expanding on the highly personal, overly introspective discussions of well-known and little known music. In this book, Nick (and here he really sounds first-namable) rambles on like one of my cohorts from the record store after three Tsing-Tao beers during one of our Friday night Chinese dinners. He writes as though he's talking to you over fortune cookies, telling you about his latest discovery. If you're really into music, you have to read this book, and then—like me—you'll probably go out and buy some of the songs he talk about.

Nick Hornby (here I get serious, so I use his last name), also mentions that his son, Danny, is autistic, and, in one essay, talks about how Danny reacts to different kinds of music. As the father of an overly-normal son (though his musical tastes make me wonder every now and then), I cannot but shed tears thinking about what it must be like to raise a child like Danny. Nick points out that he's made enough money to ensure Danny's future, but he also co-founded TreeHouse, a school in the UK for autistic children, to which he has made substantial donations. Why don't you go to their Web site (http://www.treehouse.org.uk) and give them a donation to help the many autistic children whose parents can't afford to ensure their future; all those kids who may never be able to appreciate music like you and me.

Copying Music from Your iPod to Your Computer

You *did* remember to back up the music files on your computer, right? I mean, I've reminded you a few times already, especially about the ones you've purchased from the iTunes Music Store. If you lose them, you can't get them back.

So your computer crashed... And you lost all your data... Bummer.

But you do have a backup, right?

Kirk's rule number one of computing: Back up your data now; you will lose your original data one day. It's not a question of *whether* you will lose it or not, it's a question of *when* you'll lose it. Computers are sensitive objects, and your files are merely positive or negative charges in microscopic sectors of hard disks.

Things happen, and they can delete your data. Or if you have a serious system problem, the only way to get your computer working again may be to reformat your drive, reinstall Windows (or Mac OS X, though that happens less frequently), and start from scratch. If you don't have a backup, well, you're sunk.

But even if you don't have a backup of your music files, you should be able to copy them from your iPod back to your computer, right? After all, the iPod has the files on its hard disk? So that should be easy...

Not.

Apple doesn't give you a way to copy files from the iPod, because that would open the floodgates of people sharing music too easily. But there are ways to get at these files, and it's certainly reassuring to know that if you lose

DO OR DIE:

>> Oops, I deleted those songs...

>> How do I get them back?

>> Um, what do you mean I can't?

the music on your computer, you can get it back. Read the next few sections to find out how to access your music files on your iPod.

Don't use these methods to share music illegally, though. That's bad karma.

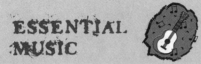

ESSENTIAL MUSIC

Anything by Jorma Kaukonen

This time I'm not talking about a song or an album, but an artist. And to be honest, I shouldn't really say "anything," because I've had some frightful experiences listening to Jorma's music performed live, but, overall, he is one of the few artists whose music gets my feet tapping and my face smiling, and this for over 25 years.

Jorma Kaukonen (http://www.jormakaukonen.com) was guitarist for Jefferson Airplane, when he and bassist Jack Casady formed Hot Tuna, and, in 1970, released the first eponymous album under this name. With ten blues songs played on acoustic guitar and bass, this down-tempo album set the stage for a more than three-decade career playing the blues: old blues songs and original blues-influenced tunes as a solo performer, and loud versions of these songs with the electric version of Hot Tuna and in a variety of other configurations.

I've seen Jorma perform in many places: from New York's Palladium theater, a venue with a couple of thousand seats, to the Lone Star Café, a bar in Manhattan which holds a couple of hundred at best. I've seen him perform outdoors, in theaters, in concert halls, and in bars. And just about every performance contains the magic of his love for the blues.

Note the use of "just about" in that last sentence. There was actually one performance I walked out of, at the Palladium in New York. It was in 1981, to the best of my recollection, and Jorma was playing with a band he called Vital Parts: guitar, bass, and electronic drums. It was so loud that I couldn't put up with it; it was one of the few concerts I walked out of. Jorma had dyed his hair pink, and I remember walking to the subway station after leaving, as fans were coming to the Palladium for the late show. My friend Jay and I would tell them, "Jorma's pink, man," and delight in the looks of perplexity on their faces. They got their comeuppance at that late show...

But that's forgiven. Because most of the shows I saw Jorma perform were solo acoustic gigs, and brilliant examples of musicianship. I'll never forget the 11/11/78 show at the University of Pennsylvania, where Jorma sat in a chair onstage for about three hours, playing all his great tunes, and held the audience entranced throughout. I've got a tape of this show, recorded right next to where I was standing, and can even hear some of my friends talking at times...

Jorma is one of those rare musicians who not only played the blues but lived them. He brought one of the great blues musicians, Reverend Gary Davis, out of obscurity, and performed classic songs by Jelly Roll Morton, Lightnin' Hopkins, Blind Blake, and many others. An acoustic Jorma concert is a magnificent event, as he uses his virtuosity and great voice to bring to life the music of yore.

Accessing Your Music Files from a Mac

If you have a Mac, you've got several ways to access your music files. Some of them are easy and only require Mac OS X; others use third-party software. The former let you copy your music files, but not playlists, and when you copy them to your Mac, you'll have a bunch of files in no special order; but at least you'll have them.

DO OR DIE:

>> Copy files you've lost to your Mac

>> Find where your music files are hiding

Since the iPod is just a hard disk, all you need to do is mount it and access the music files. When you mount your iPod and double-click its icon, though, you don't see any music—you see several folders, such as Contacts, Calendars, and Notes (Figure 4-26), but none of them contain music. This is because the music folders are hidden.

With Mac OS X, it is easy to hide files or folders. But if you know where to look, and how to look there, you can easily find these hidden folders and access their contents.

Let's first use the geek method to see what's on an iPod. If you are familiar with working in Terminal and using the command line, you can issue the following command (don't type the $; that's the shell prompt character) to get to where your music is stashed:

```
$ cd /Volumes/[your iPod's name]/iPod_Control/Music
```

In the preceding command, replace [your iPod's name] by the actual name of your iPod; if its name contains one or more spaces, put double quotes around

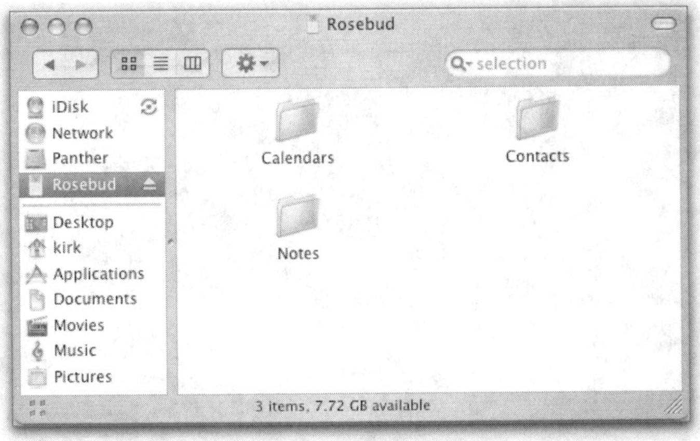

Figure 4-26

*So, where is
that music
hiding?*

the name. Press Enter. Then type `ls` (that's the letter l, not the digit 1) and press Enter. You'll see something like this:

```
$ ls
F00   F02   F04   F06   F08   F10   F12   F14   F16   F18
F01   F03   F05   F07   F09   F11   F13   F15   F17   F19
```

Each of these folders contains some of your music files. Try looking inside the first one by issuing these commands:

```
$ cd F00
$ ls
01 Am Fenster D. 878.mp3          1-09 I_ll Be All Right Som.m4a
01 Fidelity.m4a                   1-12 Prelude and Fugue in F.m4a
01 First Light.m4a                1-12 Serpent of Dreams.m4a
01 I_ll Be Your Mirror.m4p        1-13 nr_13 Mit dem gru_nen.m4a
01 Marc Minkowski _ Acis _.mp3    1-14 No. 7_ Eb major. Fugue.m4a
01 Our Lady Of The Angels.m4a     1-14 The Moon Was Yellow.mp3
01 Part VI.m4a                    1-16 No. 8_ D_ minor. Fugue.m4a
01 Re_ Person I Knew.m4a          1-23 Well-Tempered Clavier.m4a
[etc.]
```

As you can probably see, none of these songs look like they go together. iTunes copies your music in some obscure way to these 20 folders, maintaining a database in your iPod so it can find the right songs for any of your playlists.

If you want to open any of these folders and access the song files from the Finder, just type the following command when inside the folder:

```
$ open .
```

You'll need to go to each of the music folders (F00, etc.) and run the open command; if you run this command on the Music folder itself, you won't see any of its contents. These F folders are invisible.

If you're allergic to the command line or have never used it, don't fret; there's another way to access these files. In the Finder, select Go > Go to Folder, then type `/Volumes/[your iPod's name]/iPod_Control/Music/F00` and press Enter. You'll see a Finder window with your song files (Figure 4-27).

Finally, there's another way to access these files, which can even be easier to use. Marcel Bresink's free program TinkerTool (http://www.bresink.de/osx/TinkerTool.html) lets you access lots of hidden functions in Mac OS X. While we'll only look at one of them, TinkerTool is a great program for customizing your Mac in many ways. What you can do with it to work with your iPod's hidden music, is simply turn on a setting that displays hidden files in the Finder. When you open TinkerTool, click the Finder icon in its toolbar (Figure 4-28), and look for the Show Hidden and System Files option.

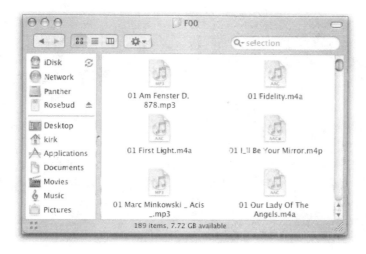

Figure 4-27

Ah, so that's where they're hiding!

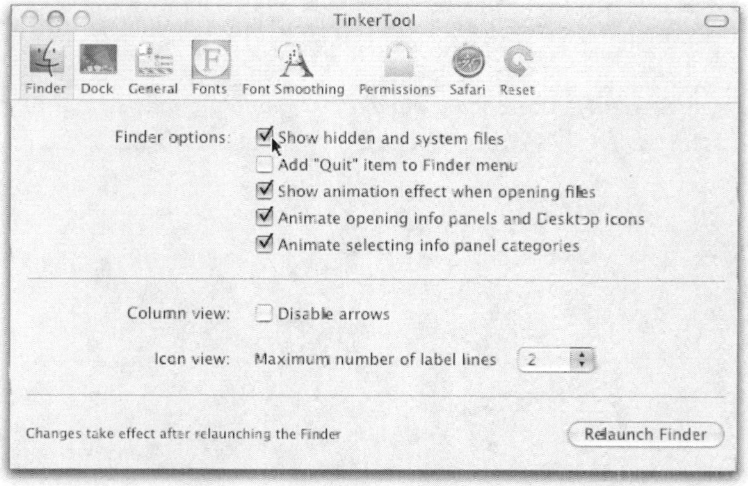

Figure 4-28

Checking this option displays all your Mac's hidden files, even the ones on your iPod.

Check this option, then click the Relaunch Finder button at the bottom of the window. This quits the Finder and restarts it. (Don't worry, it doesn't do any harm.) Now, click your iPod's icon in the Finder window sidebar, or double-click its icon on the Desktop. You'll see a bunch of icons that weren't there before (Figure 4-29), including some dimmed folder icons.

Double-click the iPod_Control folder, then double-click the dimmed Music folder. You'll see all the F folders hiding in the shadows. Double-click any of these folders to see their contents.

Using any of the three preceding methods, you can copy your music files back to your Mac and drag them all into your iTunes music library. You'll have to re-create your playlists, and you'll have lost any additional information, such as ratings or comments, but you'll at least have all your music files intact.

Now, you going to back them up?

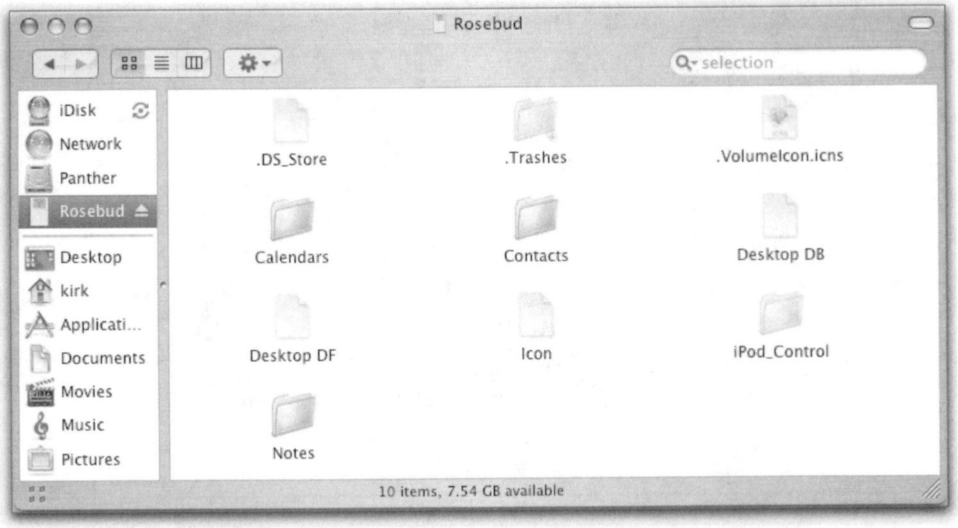

Figure 4-29

You can see the dimmed iPod_Control folder icon after applying the secret setting in TinkerTool.

Because of the occasional need to copy music files from your iPod to your Mac, as you saw earlier in Copying Music from Your iPod to Your Computer, many developers have written programs that let you do this and even more. The basic operation these programs offer is to copy individual songs; some programs let you copy playlists as well; and others provide advanced features, such as syncing your music or even playing it directly from your iPod.

DO OR DIE:

>> Programs to copy music from your iPod

>> Copy music files and playlists

Copy Music and Notes with iPod2Mac

The freeware program iPod2Mac (http://www.daniele.ch) puts a pretty face on the operations you saw in Accessing Your Music Files from a Mac. It's a simple program and offers two functions: You can copy music files from the hidden folders on your iPod, and you can view and manage text notes it contains. To copy music files, connect your iPod, then open iPod2Mac. On its main window, click the Find iPods button. The program finds your iPod and displays some information about it.

Next, click the Music Files tab, and select one of the F folders (F00, F01, etc.) to see the songs it contains. You can select whichever music files you want to copy (Figure 4-30), or click the Select All button, then click Copy to copy the files to a folder on your Desktop.

iPod2Mac's Text Notes feature is very useful as well. Instead of creating text files and copying them to your iPod, you can create them directly with this program, and either type them or paste text into them. Select any you want to save to your Mac, or delete the ones you no longer need. This and the music file copying make this a great program that's free, to boot!

Copy Your iPod's Music to Your Mac or to Another iPod

I did suggest you back up your music, right? Well, here's a great program— another freeware—that can back up your iPod to your Mac's hard disk, or even copy its contents to another iPod. Pod2Pod (http://www.ifthensoft.com) does this with just a few clicks.

When you open Pod2Pod, you'll see a window with two wells where you can drag two iPods (Figure 4-31). If you want to back up the music on your iPod, drag it to the well on the left; if you want to clone your iPod to another one, drag its icon onto the other iPod on the right. (This requires that you be able to connect them both to your Mac.)

If you want to back up your iPod's music, click the Backup Music to HD button. To copy to a second iPod, click Copy Music to iPod 1 or 2; you can copy in either direction. If you can't connect two iPods, copy first to your hard disk, then use the Restore Music from HD button.

Copy, Back Up, and Sync Your Music

While the preceding programs are simple tools for recovering your music in the event of loss on your Mac, iPodRip (http://thelittleappfactory.com) is a full-featured program that copies music from and to your iPod, syncs music with your iTunes music library, and even plays songs directly from your iPod on your Mac. iPodRip is one of the only programs that not only recovers songs, but also additional information, such as ratings and playlists.

iPodRip has an interface similar to that of iTunes (Figure 4-32). It contains two Source lists (one for your iPod and one for your iTunes music library) and displays their contents just like iTunes, with a Browse section at the top and a list pane at the bottom.

To recover songs from your iPod, select the iPod Source, then select an artist, album, or individual song and click Recover Songs. A window displays (Figure 4-33) showing your options.

The biggest difference between iPodRip and the other programs I've discussed earlier is its ability to recover playlists, ratings, and play counts. And since it can recover your songs and put them directly in your iTunes music library, it's almost as though you hadn't lost them in the first place.

Oh, by the way, did I remind you to back up your music?

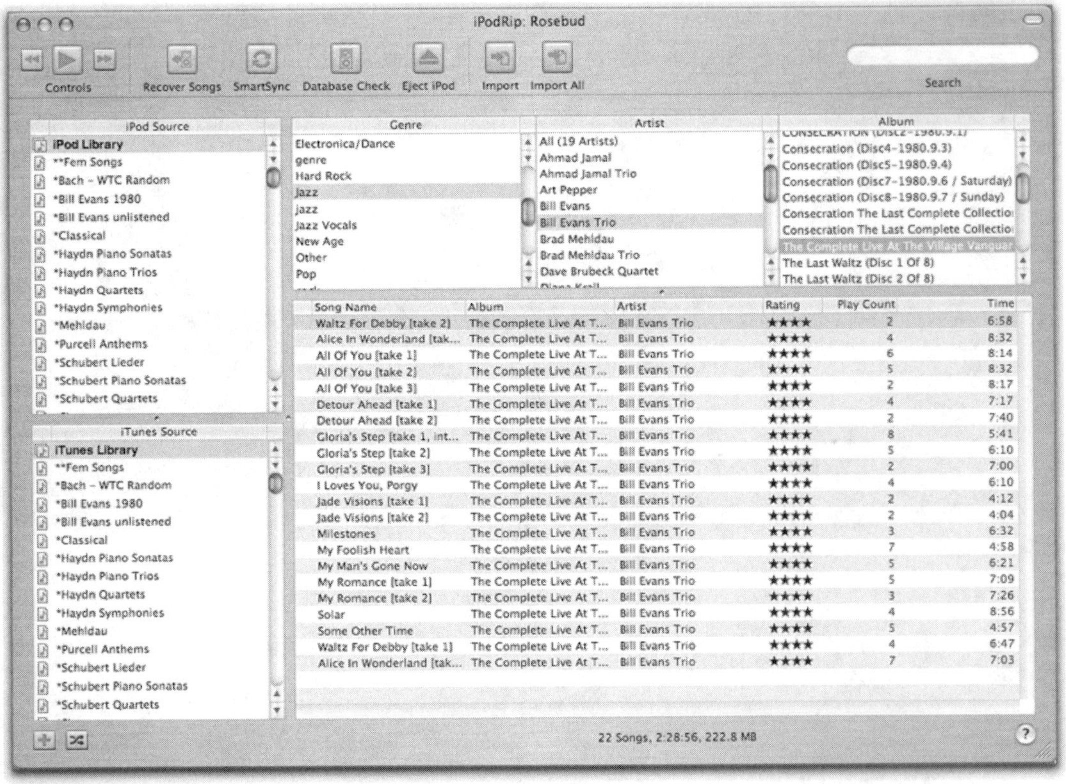

Figure 4-32

iPodRip provides more than just song recovery— you can even use it to sync with your iTunes music library.

Figure 4-33

The many options available when recovering songs with iPodRip

Accessing Your Music Files from Windows

An iPod formatted for Windows tries the same data-hiding schemes as Mac versions, but there's actually an easy way to show the hidden iPod_Control folder and the Music subfolders where the goodies are stored.

If you skimmed through Accessing Your Music Files from a Mac, you saw that there is a hidden folder called iPod_Control that contains all your music files, as well as some other files. If you want to access your music files and copy them back to your PC, you need to get to this hidden folder.

To display hidden folders on a Windows computer, select Start > Control Panel > Appearance and Theme > Folder Options to display the Folder Options dialog box, shown in Figure 4-34.

Click the Show Hidden Files and Folders option button and click OK. Now, when you open your iPod in My Computer, you'll see the elusive iPod_Control folder (see Figure 4-35).

See Accessing Your Music Files from a Mac for more about the folders in the iPod_Control folder and how your iPod stores music here.

DO OR DIE:

>> Copy files you've lost to your Windows PC

>> Third-party tools to copy your music

While You're at It...

Now that you have the Folder Options dialog box open, you should also make sure the Hide Extensions for Known File Types check box is cleared. One of the methods virus writers use to befuddle Windows users is to give files names such as "yourinfo.zip.exe." All the user sees is "yourinfo.zip" until it's too late.

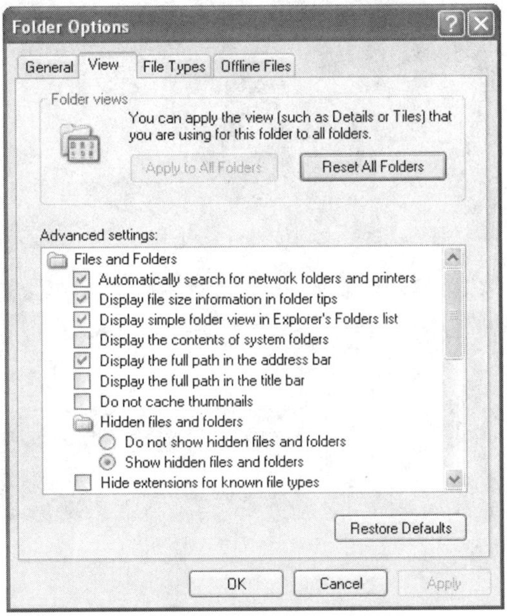

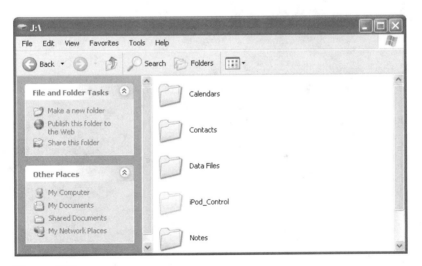

Figure 4-34

*The well-hidden Folder Options dialog box
lets you see all of the files and folders on your
computer.*

Figure 4-35

*Open the iPod_Control folder, and you can
navigate through the Music subfolder and its
subfolders, which contain your music files.*

Third-Party Software to Access Your Music Files on a PC

t can be tough to bring in the songs you want from your iPod, mostly because the songs are spread around a bunch of subfolders with no rhyme or reason. However, there are, as the French say, ways to correct fate. EphPod, the free iPod management program you can download from http://www.ephpod.com/, lets you download songs by following this procedure:

1. Create a folder to store the copied songs.

2. Display the songs in the Songs pane, select the songs you want to copy, right-click any selected song, and select Copy Songs to Directory.

3. Use the Browse for Folder dialog box to identify the target folder, and click OK.

As a test, I copied the song "Take California," by Propellerheads, with the default settings, which created a folder named Propellerheads and a song file named 01 - Take California.m4p. That's fine, but the name doesn't store the genre with it, which could make a difference if I want to view my music by genre on my PC. Here's the procedure to change the file name and directory structure EphPod creates when you copy your songs:

1. Run EphPod and click the Configure EphPod button just below the menu bar.

2. In the Configuration dialog box, click Advanced Options to display the Advanced Options tab (shown in Figure 4-36).

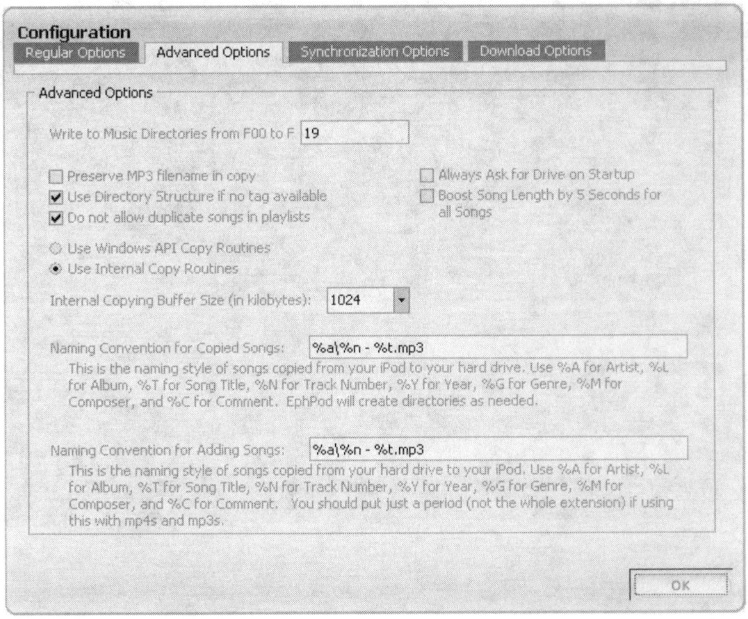

Figure 4-36

*EphPod. It's
free, and it'll
save your
behind if your
hard disk
crashes.*

The default options for saving a file will work fine, but you might want to change how the copied songs are named on your computer. The default string, found in the Naming Convention for Copied Songs box, is "%a\%n - %t.mp3". Let's break that down.

- **%a** creates a new folder from the artist's name (if it doesn't already exist).
- **%n** puts the track number in front of the song's title.
- **[space] - [space]** adds those characters to the file name.
- **%t** adds the song title to the file name.
- **.mp3** adds the file type extension for an MP3 file.

There are other characters you can use to add the genre or year to the file name. Those controls are:

- **%m** for composer.
- **%y** for year.
- **%g** for genre.
- **%c** for comment.
- **%l** for album.

While other programs offer additional song download capabilities, there's nothing out there that justifies getting another program or spending any money for this task, especially given the other features that come with EphPod.

ESSENTIAL MUSIC

Sandinista! by The Clash

By 1980, after only a few years changing the world of popular music, The Clash was at the height of glory, after releasing the hugely successful *London Calling*. Punk had become almost mainstream, fighting in the streets with the sounds of disco and the earliest rap songs (at least in New York City). At the end of this year came *Sandinista!* an odd mix of punk, reggae, dub, ska, and even rap–"The Magnificent Seven," one of the album's few hits, became a boom-box anthem in the streets of New York in 1981.

While this three-LP set, which the band fought their record company to sell for the price of a single LP, marked the beginning of the end for the band, it remains the group's most daring album and, in some ways, is the testament of this punk band, more so than their first two albums, which are much more guitar and leather.

Sandinista! is both a political statement (in support of the Nicaraguan revolution) and a musical statement. As the latter, it allowed The Clash to show their diverse musical roots and influences, and create their most audacious music. Opening with "The Magnificent Seven," the album quickly shifts tone with "Hitsville U.K." an almost ABBA-like pop ballad, designed to climb the charts. Next comes "Junco Partner," a dub/reggae song, then "Ivan Meets G.I. Joe," a song about the Cold War, with lots of pinball-machine-type sounds in the background. In these first few songs, the tone is set: This album covers everything, every type of experimentation and musical directions that the band wanted to follow.

This album is not without weaknesses—what band could come up with 36 great songs all at once?—but some of the tracks stand out for their unique sound and style: "Something about England," a nostalgic ballad; "Lightning Strikes (Not Once but Twice)," a bass-driven rap song which sounds like an alternate version of "The Magnificent Seven"; the powerful "One More Time," and its follow-up "One More Dub"; the classic "Charlie Don't Surf"; through the closing song, "Shepherd's Delight," a down-tempo dub.

While this album might have been better with fewer tracks, its originality lies sometimes in the minor songs, the versions and dub mixes of other tracks. It shows a powerful band willing to take risks and willing to share with its listeners exactly what was going through its musical mind in that crucial period when punk was breathing its last gasps.

Back Up Your Files to Your iPod

You've already seen that your iPod is essentially a pocket-sized hard disk (see Using the iPod as a Hard Disk) and that you can copy and back up files to it as to any other type of computer media. I talked about the importance of backing up your music files earlier, but what about the rest of your files?

Say you're working on that really important PowerPoint presentation—the one that'll let you IPO your startup for many millions of dollars. And it's got to be finished tomorrow. And your computer crashes, turning your hard disk into digital gobbledygook...

But you've got a backup, right? Huh? You mean you didn't back it up? Oh my...

I said it before, and I'll say it again. Kirk's rule number one of computing: Back up your data now; you will lose your files one day It's not a question of whether you will lose it or not, it's a question of when.

The days of the floppy disk are gone. Apple tolled the death knell when it released the first iMac, and PC manufacturers have since realized that this was not just hubris. What can you put on a floppy disk? A one-minute MP3 file? A few PowerPoint slides? Some Word documents, as long as they're short and contain no graphics?

Backups now require larger-capacity media. Most computers sold today have built-in CD writers, but do you always have a blank CD handy to make a copy of your stuff? What about other types of backups, using Zip disks, external hard disks, or other media? You need to have them available to be able to back up your stuff.

But your iPod can be your savior. As long as you haven't stuffed it full of music, you'll have a little bit of room (or maybe a lot) to put your files there. While you're working on that presentation, think of copying it to your iPod every couple of hours. After all, if you lose the PowerPoint file, you may lose that IPO, a business deal, or your job.

The easiest way to back up files is to just drag them onto your iPod (see Using the iPod as a Hard Disk for more on copying files to it). But that only works for a few files or if all your files are in the same folder. Nevertheless, it's a quick and safe way to make sure you've got at least one more copy of those important files.

In the next few sections, I'll look at some software that helps you make backups of your important data quickly and painlessly. And so I don't have to mention it again, you'll need to set up your iPod to work as a hard disk to do any kind of backups, whether manual or automatic using special backup software. See Using the iPod as a Hard Disk to find out how to do this.

So, have you backed up your stuff yet?

Free Windows
Backup Software

O ne great use for your iPod is as an emergency backup hard disk for your laptop when you travel. Even a 10GB iPod has enough space to hold plenty of music and still have room for your data, so you should take advantage of it. Just remember that if someone grabs your iPod and knows that you can store regular files on it, your data becomes their data. There's no such thing as "security through obscurity."

DO OR DIE:
>> Back up your files on Windows

>> Do it for free

>> Do it now!

If you just want to back up a few files, you can copy them over from My Computer or Windows Explorer. If, however, you want to back up a lot of data or you want to only back up those files that have changed since you made your last archive, you'll need a specialized program. One program that fits the bill is Microsoft Backup, which is included with Windows. Backup is available for your use in every version of Windows since Windows 98SE, but you'll probably need to install it from your Windows CD. Here's how you do it in Windows 98SE or Windows Me:

1. Insert your Windows CD into your computer's CD drive, click Start, point to Settings, and then click Control Panel.

2. Double-click Add/Remove Programs and then click the Windows Setup tab.

3. In the Components list, click System Tools and then click Details.

4. Select the Backup check box and click OK twice.

5. Remove your Windows CD and restart your computer.

You follow a different procedure to install Backup on a Windows XP computer:

1. Put your Windows CD in your computer's CD drive, open My Computer, right-click the Windows CD, and click Open.

2. Double-click the Valueadd folder, double-click the Msft folder, and then double-click the Ntbackup folder.

3. Double-click Ntbackup.msi to run the installation program. When it's done, click Finish.

Once you have Backup on your computer, you should back up your files immediately. When you run the program, you'll use the interface shown in Figure 4-37 to select the files you want to back up.

The dialog box indicates which files you've selected to back up, using a series of codes that appear in the check box next to a drive, folder, or file:

- A blue check means that the entire contents of the drive or folder will be backed up.

- A gray check means that at least one file in the drive or folder, or one of its subfolders, will be backed up.

- An empty check box means that no files in the drive or folder will be backed up.

To back up your files follow these steps:

1. Click Start, point to All Programs (just Programs in Windows 98SE and Windows Me), point to Accessories, and then click System Tools. Click Backup. If you don't have a backup device (such as a CD burner) con-

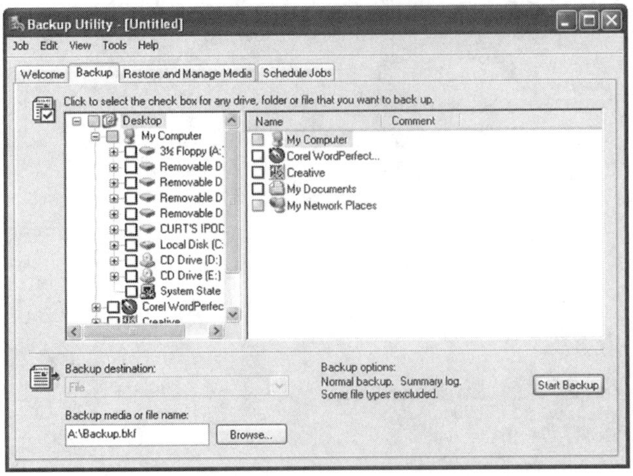

Figure 4-37

The Backup interface lets you specify which files to archive.

nected to your computer, a message box will appear asking if you want Windows to look for such a device. To back up your files to a hard disk on your computer or elsewhere on your network, click No.

2. Select Create A New Backup Job and then click OK.

3. Select Back Up Selected Files, Folder, And Drives and then click Next.

4. In the left-hand pane of the dialog box, use the controls to select the folders containing the files you want to back up.

   - Click an Expand control (a plus sign) to display the contents of a hard disk or a folder.

   - Click a Contract control (a minus sign) to hide the contents of a hard disk or a folder.

   - Click a folder icon to display the contents of the folder in the right-hand pane.

5. Select the check box next to a folder to back up the entire contents of that folder (including all subfolders), or select the check box next to a file (in the right-hand pane) to back up only those files you select within that subfolder. Click Next. If there are certain files within a folder you don't want to back up, you can select the check box next to the name of the folder, display the contents of the folder in the right-hand pane, and clear the check box next to the name of any file you don't want to back up.

6. Select All Selected Files and then click Next.

7. Click the Folder icon next to the name of the file to which Backup will archive your files.

8. Use the controls in the Where To Back Up dialog box to pick the folder to which you want to write the backup file, type a name for the file in the File Name text box, and then click Open. Click Next. If you click the Look In down arrow, you'll see your entire computer as well as Network Neighborhood displayed in the list of drives.

9. Leave both check boxes selected so Backup will compress the files to save space and verify that the files were backed up successfully. Click Next and then click Start.

10. If you are asked to save your backup job, type a name for the job and click OK.

11. In the Backup Progress dialog box, click Report to view a report summarizing what went on during the backup or click OK.

12. Open the Job menu and click Exit.

Changing Your Backup Type

If you have a lot of files to back up and it takes too long (you decide how long is too long), you might want to back up just those files that have changed since the last time you made a backup. If so, you can make a differential backup, where you back up only those files that have changed since you last made a complete (*all files*) backup, or an incremental backup, where you back up only those files that have changed since the last all-files backup or your last incremental backup.

In Windows, files have an *Archived* property, which is set to true when a file has been backed up, and another property that records the time and date the archive was made. If you do a differential backup, the Backup program doesn't change the Archived property to true, so the file will be backed up every time. If you do an incremental backup, Backup does set the Archived property to true, so the file will only be backed up in later jobs if it has changed since the last incremental backup. In other words, modifying a file changes the Archived property to false.

If you do a differential or an incremental backup, Backup doesn't archive all of your files, so you may need to restore files from more than one archive to get everything back. Differential and incremental backups are faster than all-files backups, but unless you're really pressed for time or are down to your last few megabytes of disk space, the safety of backing up all of your files in every job will probably outweigh the space and time savings of partial backups.

To change the type of backup you perform with Backup, follow these steps:

1. Run Backup, click the Backup Job down arrow, select the backup job you want to edit, click Options, and then click the Type tab.

2. Select New And Changed Files Only, and then either:
   - Select Differential Backup Type to back up only those files that have changed since the last All Selected Files backup.
   - Select Incremental Backup Type to back up only those files that have changed since the last All Selected Files backup or the last Incremental backup. (Note: You can always revert to backing up every file you selected by selecting All Selected Files.)

3. Click OK and then choose Save from the Jobs menu.

Scheduling Backups in Windows XP

ne great feature of the version of Backup that comes with Windows XP (see the earlier section Free Windows Backup Software) is that you can have Windows run backup jobs on a regular schedule. What's more, you can schedule several types of backups so you don't have to wonder how long it's been since you did your last full backup.

To schedule a backup job in Windows XP, follow these steps:

1. Click Start, point to All Programs, point to Accessories, point to System Tools, and then click Backup. If the Backup Or Restore Wizard appears, click Advanced Mode.

2. Select the Schedule Jobs tab and click the day you want your files backed up. Click Add Job and then click Next.

3. Select the option button representing the files you want to back up and click Next. If you selected Back Up Selected Files, Drives, Or Network Data, a dialog box will appear that lets you specify the data you want to back up. Do so, and then click Next.

4. Click Browse. In the Save As dialog box, select the directory in which you want to store the backup file, and click Save. Click Next and then click Finish.

5. Click the Select The Type Of Backup down arrow and specify the type of backup you want to perform:

- Normal, which backs up all files and marks the files as archived
- Copy, which backs up the files but doesn't mark them as archived
- Incremental, which backs up any files that were modified or created since your last backup
- Differential, which backs up any files that were modified or created since your last backup but doesn't mark them as archived
- Daily, which backs up only those files that were created or modified on the day the job is run

6. Click Next.

7. Select the Verify Data After Backup check box to have Backup check your archived data to be sure it can restore the files from the archive. If necessary, clear the Disable Volume Shadow Copy check box so Backup can back up any files you are editing when the job is run. Click Next.

8. Select Append This Backup To The Existing Backups and then click Next.

9. Select Later, type a name for the job in the Job Name text box, and click Set Schedule.

10. Click the Schedule Task down arrow and select the schedule on which you want the backup to be performed. Depending on the schedule you select, you'll be able to give Backup more details about when you want it to run the backup job. For example, selecting Daily lets you choose whether you want to run the job every day, every two days, and so on. Click OK when you've made your selection.

11. Type your password in the Password text box and type it again in the Confirm Password text box. Click Next and then click Finish.

Back Up Your iTunes Music Library on Windows

he only thing I hate more than doing work twice is buying the same thing twice. And if I had to replace any songs I'd bought from the iTunes Music Store because I'd neglected to back them up, I'd probably go crazy. I wouldn't be very happy if I had to rerip all my CDs either.

Of course, running a program such as Backup may seem like a pain, but there is a simple solution: Copy the files from your iTunes music library to a hard disk or an external drive, or even burn them to a bunch of CDs or DVDs.

Copying these files is the same as copying any other files. On Windows, your iTunes music library is stored here: \Documents and Settings\username\ My Documents\My Music\iTunes\. You'll want to back up the entire iTunes folder, since it contains not only your music files, but also other special iTunes library files. If you ever have a serious crash, you can just replace this folder, if you've got a recent enough backup.

DO OR DIE:

>> Back up your music files

>> Find your iTunes folder

ESSENTIAL MUSIC

Ege Bamyasi, by Can

What albums can I still listen to, day in, day out, without tiring of the music? Only four albums met this test. Of the two from Can that made the cut, *Ege Bamyasi* (from 1972), sounds like it was recorded yesterday—I have to show the album sleeve to young people I play it to, because they can't believe it's not vintage 2004!

Like all great albums, it has not one dud track on it, but the music is unlike any other album (even by Can). Moods vary widely from track to track, and even within each track. Its range is astonishing: from lyrical to obsessive-compulsive (Can does that better than anyone else), through desperate and bouncy bopper music. The whole album is punctuated with "How did they do that?" sounds, which intrigue and delight.

Two things are never far away on this album—the first is haunting melody, such as "Sing Swan Song," and the other thing is a driving beat, like on "Vitamin C." But it can also be very uncompromisingly avant-garde electronic sounding. I remember playing "Soup" once, and had to leave the room. My father called out, "Come quick—the hi-fi has caught fire!" When I came and told him it was meant to sound like that, he gave me a look that I'll never forget! But "I'm So Green" comes next to soothe any frazzled ears and reassure worried Dads.

Can is deceptive—if you think you hear Michel Karoli's guitar, you can probably hear Irmin Schmidt's virtuoso keyboards, and vice versa. Jaki Leibezeit's drumming is both complex and driving, and has made him one of the world's most respected drummers. And Holger Czukay's obsessive bass is, as ever, interspersed with sounds no one else has been able to make, before or since. Vocals are provided by Damo Suzuki, whose amazing range goes from threatening whispers to amazingly babylike whimpering, via desperate howling and a thousand other forms—a kind of Noh-inspired Japanese Jimi Hendrix of the voice.

In terms of sheer electronic technique, these guys are unique—they shunned synths and had their instruments built to their unique specs! They would ring modulate radios to produce weird ethnic chants from political speeches and dance-band broadcasts—live! In *Ege Bamyasi* you witness the constant subtext of pops, squiggles, and backing noises to the music, and a mastery of echoes and sound environments unrivalled on any record since. Legends about Can are almost as many as the musicians who claim to have been inspired by this album.

As for what the album title means (the sleeve is illustrated by a can of okra shoots), more than thirty years after I bought it on first release—I have absolutely no idea!

➤ Mark Willan, one of the book's technical reviewers, is a chartered surveyor and technical translator who trained as a classical musician before deciding to earn a living. He now lives happily on the French Riviera with a small family of iPods.

Backing Up Files on a Mac

Well, here's one area where Windows has an advantage: Windows XP includes free backup software, as you saw earlier in Free Windows Backup Software. Mac OS X doesn't provide you with a free backup tool, but if you're a subscriber to Apple's .Mac online service, you'll be able to download Apple's Backup program for free.

Backing Up Files with Apple's Backup

If you do have a .Mac account, you can use Apple's Backup application to back files up to your iPod. (Make sure you have version 2.01 or later; if not, go to www.mac.com and download a newer version.) Backup offers a simple way to make sure all your important files get backed up, letting you check QuickPicks that cover certain locations and file types.

But first, make sure your iPod is set to work as a hard disk (see Using the iPod as a Hard Disk). Then, connect it to your Mac and open Backup. Click the popup menu at the top of the program's window (Figure 4-38) and select Back Up to Drive, then click Set. In the alert that displays, click Create if you want to create a new backup, locate your iPod, then give a name to the backup file. Click OK.

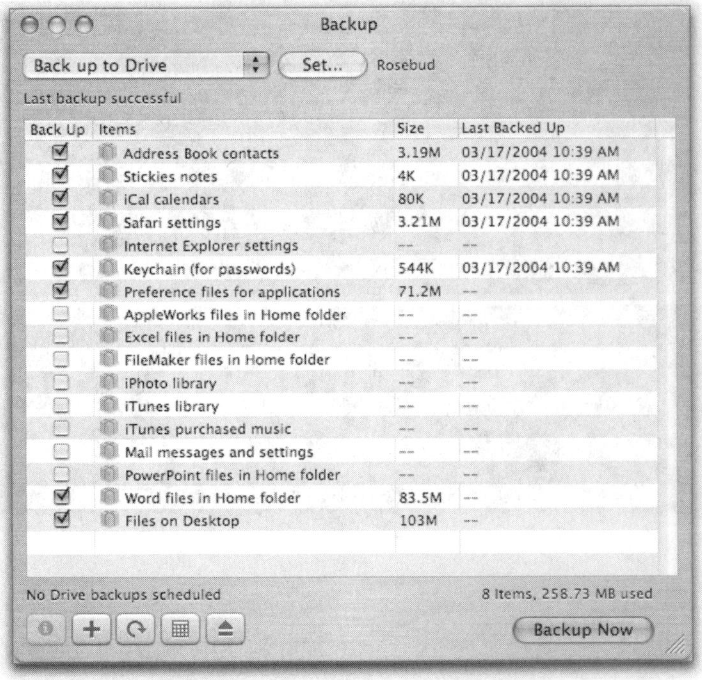

Figure 4-38

Apple's Backup, ready to back files up to an iPod

Back Up	Items	Size	Last Backed Up
☑	Address Book contacts	3.19M	03/17/2004 10:39 AM
☑	Stickies notes	4K	03/17/2004 10:39 AM
☑	iCal calendars	80K	03/17/2004 10:39 AM
☑	Safari settings	3.21M	03/17/2004 10:39 AM
☐	Internet Explorer settings	--	--
☑	Keychain (for passwords)	544K	03/17/2004 10:39 AM
☑	Preference files for applications	71.2M	--
☐	AppleWorks files in Home folder	--	--
☐	Excel files in Home folder	--	--
☐	FileMaker files in Home folder	--	--
☐	iPhoto library	--	--
☐	iTunes library	--	--
☐	iTunes purchased music	--	--
☐	Mail messages and settings	--	--
☐	PowerPoint files in Home folder	--	--
☑	Word files in Home folder	83.5M	--
☑	Files on Desktop	103M	--

Back up to Drive Set... Rosebud
Last backup successful

No Drive backups scheduled   8 Items, 258.73 MB used

Backup Now

Apple's .Mac—Is It Worth $99 a Year?

I've mentioned Apple's .Mac online service several times in this book, and it's time to take a brief look at it and especially to tell you whether I feel it's worth shelling out $99 a year for.

.Mac offers a number of services and functions: a mac.com e-mail address; easy-to-create home pages using templates; an online iDisk, which gives you 100MB of storage and which is accessible from Mac OS X with just a click; free software (including Backup and the Virex antivirus software); and many more features.

.Mac was free when it first came out, but in the tried-and-true tradition of bait and switch, Apple started charging $99 a year for this service after it had been around for 12 months. Many Mac users complained, but others are less upset at the idea of paying for this service. It's true that you could get many of the features cheaper, or even for free, but the bundle Apple gives you is tempting. I have a .Mac account, and while my mac.com e-mail address is not my main address, it lets me have a backup address in case of need. I've also used the iDisk and created file-sharing Web pages to get files to people when other avenues don't work.

Apple tries to spice up the stew every couple of months by offering free software or special offers. You get free games, discounts on other programs, free training on certain Mac OS X features, and more. If you don't have a .Mac account, you can try it out for free for 60 days (open the System Preferences and click the .Mac icon to find out more). Check it out to see whether you think it's worth the money.

You can see several lines with check boxes that you can select in Figure 4-38. These are called QuickPicks and let you choose specific types of files to back up. Say you want to back up all your Word files, Mail messages, and Safari settings—just check those boxes. You can click the + icon to add specific folders as well, but these QuickPicks cover most of your important stuff.

When you're ready to back up your files, click Backup Now. This will be pretty quick, since the files copy to your iPod over its FireWire cable. You can back up lots of files in a jiffy, as long as you've got room on your iPod.

Scheduling Backups

It's not enough to back up your files once; you need to do it regularly in case disaster strikes. Apple's Backup lets you schedule backups so they run daily, at a specific time, or weekly, on a specific day at a specific time. Click the Schedule button (see Figure 4-39), to display the Schedule sheet.

Choose whether you want to schedule daily or weekly backups, then choose the time (and the day, for weekly backups). Click OK to save this schedule. You can quit Backup; it will launch when it's time for it to get to work.

Just make sure that your iPod, or your hard drive, is connected at the time the schedule is due to run. And if your Mac's not on, the schedule won't run; it

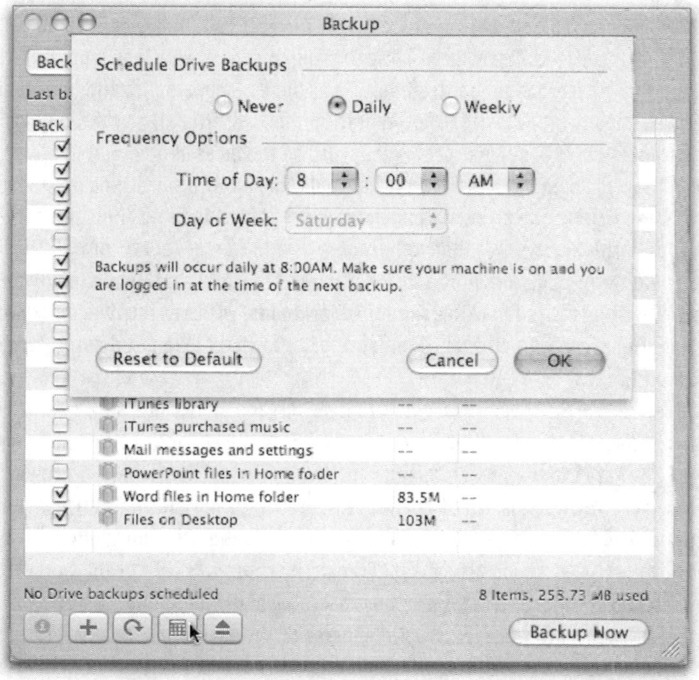

Figure 4-39

Click the Schedule button, at the bottom of the window, to display the Schedule sheet and set up automatic backups.

won't run when you turn it on later, at least not until the next scheduled backup is due to run. So find a day and time when you can be sure that your Mac will be up and running.

And don't forget, you can always run your backups manually, even if you have a schedule set. Just click the Backup Now button.

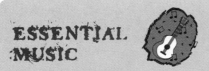

ESSENTIAL MUSIC

Discipline, by Throbbing Gristle

I wasn't going to write about Throbbing Gristle, the scion of industrial music of the 1980s. Really. But when I was almost finished writing this book, I read Nick Hornby's *Songbook* (released in the UK as *31 Songs*), which is a lot like 31 Essential Music sidebars. (I promise, Nick, I had the idea of using these sidebars before I read your book...)

Hornby talks about a song that is "ten and a half minutes of genuinely terrifying industrial noise": "Frankie Teardrop," by Suicide. I haven't listened to that song, and don't plan to, but it made me realize that essential music is not just what you keep listening to, but it's also what you've grown out of.

So, it goes like this. In the wasteland of post-punk, a lot of new types of music sprouted from the undergrowth. New wave was the most popular and got lots of radio play, but other types of music got sold under the counter in New York City record stores that specialized in British imports. I had always been intrigued by "different" types of music, out of curiosity, and sometimes because I had discovered so many interesting records by being open-minded.

So, Throbbing Gristle: The name is a British slang term for...well, look it up; I'd rather not get a Parental Advisory label on this book. I was about 20 years old, and had clearly not experienced enough of the world to not want to be shocked; after all, at that age, you're still in adolescent mode, and you like seeing the looks on the faces of your parents (well, I didn't live with them anymore) and friends when you come up with something off-the-wall.

Throbbing Gristle (http://www.mute.com/tg/) played industrial music; harsh, loud music combining electronics, heavy bass beats, and noise—lots of noise. There were vocals as well, ranging from ecstatic to paranoid. The song that best exemplifies their music is "Discipline": a song with a rhythm of jackboots, with a repetitive beat going Dum Dum Dum-Dum...Dum Dum Dum-Dum, and lyrics such as "We need some discipline." Primal stuff, what.

Suffice it to say that I've grown out of that music (and did so long ago, after I attended a concert by Psychic TV, one of the descendants of Throbbing Gristle), and I no longer have any desire to listen to their music again. Ever. Nevertheless, it's all part of growing up, of learning where the boundaries of music are, and of figuring out that music often hides much more than it presents in its notes and lyrics. Actually, Nick Hornby puts it into the proper perspective in his chapter about "Frankie Teardrop": "...what would we rather listen to? Blood-curdling re-creations of our miserable and unbearable existence, or something that offered a brief but precious temporary respite?" I think the answer is obvious.

Back Up Your iTunes Music Library on a Mac

I know, I'm starting to get annoying, reminding you to back up your stuff, especially your music files, but one day you'll thank me. You really want to have extra copies of your music files, just like all your other important files, in case your hard disk gives up the ghost. But to do this, you'll generally need an external hard drive (other than your iPod; after all, these songs are already on the iPod, so there's not much point in copying them there again).

External FireWire hard drives are affordable, fast, and easy to use. You just plug one into your FireWire port and start copying. I've got three of them; anyone who has files of any value should have at least one, and it should be larger than the size of your computer's hard disk, if possible.

If you want to back up your iTunes music library, there are two easy ways to do so. The first is to just drag its folder onto your external hard drive. This folder is located here: /Users/username/Music/iTunes. You can get there easily by opening your home folder, then double-clicking the Music folder.

Backing up this folder will take a while if you have a lot of tunes, and the next time you do so, you'll replace the existing folder and you'll have to copy everything again.

The second way is to use Apple's Backup. As you can see in Figure 4-38, one of its QuickPicks is iTunes Library and another is iTunes Purchased Music. If you choose the former, this includes the purchased music; but if you only want to back up the purchased music, choose the latter.

Just create a new backup set, saved to your external drive, and back up your iTunes Library. The first time, as for a manual backup, may take a while, but subsequently Backup only copies files that have been added or changed. This includes any files whose tags you've changed, but your play counts, ratings, and other info are stored in separate files, so not all your music gets copied.

You can do the same with other backup software: See the next section, Other Backup Software for the Mac, for more on programs that you can use to back up your files.

You have no excuse, now. I've harped at you to back up your files and told you how to do it. So back up your files!

Other Backup Software for the Mac

f you don't have a .Mac membership—and therefore cannot use Apple's Backup program—you should consider
getting software to back up your files. I won't tell you
again how important this is; you've probably gotten tired of it
by now. But I will give you a few ideas and tell you which programs you can use. Here are a few choices for good Mac
backup software.

Intego Personal Backup

I use Intego Personal Backup (http://www.intego.com), which is one of the
simplest backup programs available for Mac. You can simply drag and drop a
source and destination (see Figure 4-40), and run a backup with a single click.

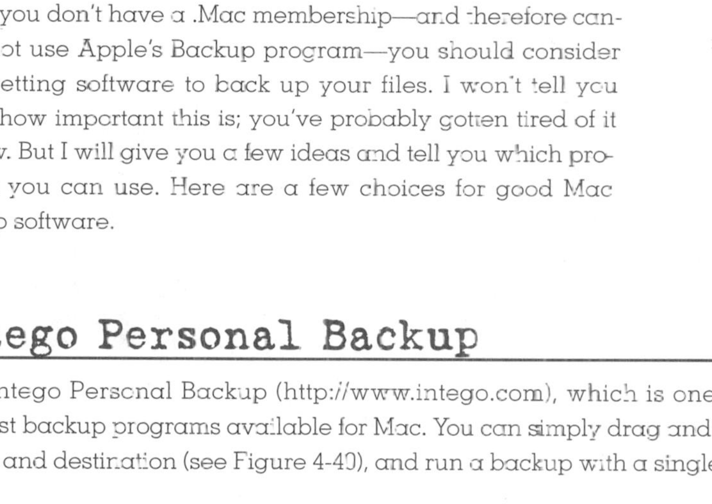

Figure 4-40

*Intego
Personal
Backup ready
to back files
up to an iPod*

Intego Personal Backup also lets you schedule backups, select multiple sources, filter which files get backed up, and much more. It's a great and easy-to-use program for protecting your data, and you can set up a backup in seconds.

Dantz Retrospect

Available in many sizes and flavors, Dantz Retrospect (http://www.dantz.com) is one of the most powerful and complex backup programs. It runs on Mac, but Dantz also offers Windows and network versions of its software. With a relatively high level of complexity, Retrospect can nevertheless run backups of many computers at once, copying files to a central server, for total protection. Retrospect Desktop, a simpler version, is ideal for home and small office use.

La Cie Silverkeeper

For a free program, Silverkeeper (http://www.lacie.com/silverkeeper) is pretty good. While it lacks scheduled backups and multiples sources, it's sufficient for many users, who only have a couple of folders to back up. Just select a source and destination folder, and run your backup. It's simple, but efficient.

Other Backup Programs

There are many other commercial, shareware, and freeware backup programs available. You can find others by searching MacUpdate (http://www.macupdate.com) or Version Tracker (http://www.versiontracker.com).

Linux and the iPod

This book assumes that you use a Mac or a PC running Windows. But what if you don't? What if you're a Linux user? Granted, the Linux user base is even smaller than the Mac user base, but many people extol the use of open-source software, partly out of their beliefs and partly because of the price. So what can you do if you see a penguin when you boot up your computer, and want to use an iPod?

First, a word of warning: This is not for the faint of heart. Using your iPod with Linux can entail some serious hacking—in some cases, you'll have to configure your kernel yourself, then compile it. So if you're not at home with this type of work, skip ahead.

However, there is always a sense of satisfaction after making something like this work, and many people want to try it just "because it's there." So here are some pointers that can get you on the road to using your iPod with Linux.

You can start by checking the "Using an iPod with Linux" Web page (http://pag.lcs.mit.edu/~adonovan/hacks/ipod.html), which gives tips and pointers as well as links to software, including some of the programs mentioned in the following subsections.

DO OR DIE:

>> Use your iPod with your penguin

>> Let Tux take control of your music

>> Put a penguin in your iPod

gtkpod--A GUI for the iPod under Linux

gtkpod is a *nix GUI for the iPod. Bearing a great deal of similarity to iTunes, it "allows you to upload songs and playlists to your iPod. It supports ID3 tag editing, multiple charsets for ID3 tags, detects duplicate songs, allows offline modification of the database with later synchronization, and more." This open-source software, available from http://gtkpod.sourceforge.net, is a great way to get the most out of your iPod if you're using Linux or another Unix-based operating system. gtkpod doesn't do everything, at least not yet, but it's certainly powerful enough to do most of what you need to get music from your *nix box to your iPod.

myPod--A Java GUI for the iPod

Able to run on most platforms, at least those with Java, myPod (http://mypod .sourceforge.net) provides a graphical user interface for the iPod. While it only manages music, it lets you create and synchronize playlists and edit MP3 tags. It might be a bit out of date, so your mileage may vary as to whether it works with your iPod and on your platform.

GNUPod--A Complete System to Control Your iPod

GNUPod (http://www.blinkenlights.ch/cgi-bin/fm.pl?get=ipod) is described as "a collection of Perl-Scripts which allow you to use your iPod under GNU/Linux and many other Operating Systems with a useable Version of Perl 5 (+Modules)." If you understand what all that means, then you're the perfect type of person to try it out. This free software lets you—with a bit of work—sync and manage your iPod from any *nix-based operating system, as long as you have the appropriate version of Perl.

Have a look at the GNUPod manual (http://www.blinkenlights.ch/gnu-pod/gnupod.html) to see exactly what this involves. It's not easy, but if you're comfortable with configuring Linux from the command line, you'll be able to get this to work in a snap.

Why Not Just Use Wine?

Wine (an acronym for Wine Is Not an Emulator) lets you run Windows programs on Linux. Wine doesn't emulate Windows; it just provides the Windows API. This means that you need a Linux distribution running on a Windows-compatible processor, but, unlike emulation, Wine runs applications as fast as they would on Windows.

Check out Wine here: http://www.winehq.com. The interesting thing about using Wine is that you can run iTunes or other Windows iPod software, such as

Anapod Explorer (see Anapod Explorer: The All-in-One iPod Manager for Windows), on your Linux box and have the same functions as you would when running Windows.

Put a Penguin in Your iPod

Want to run Linux on your iPod? Yes, you read that right... You can actually run a Linux distribution on your iPod. (Note: This may invalidate your warranty, so do this at your own risk!)

I'll be honest—this isn't for me. I think the iPod's software is fine, and I don't see why I'd spend my time trying to get a Linux operating system running on it. But there are people who may want to do this, just as a project or a challenge. The "Linux on iPod" page (http://ipodlinux.sourceforge.net/) tells you all about setting up a Linux distro for your iPod and how to work with it. Check out this site and see if you're the kind of person who would enjoy hacking this on a rainy day.

PART V

iPod Hardware and Accessories

Get More Stuff for Your iPod

t would be no understatement to say that the iPod has spawned a veritable cottage industry of accessories and hardware extensions, as well as cases, chargers, earbuds and headphones, cables, and much more. There are literally hundreds of accessories available for your iPod, whether it's a white model or a mini. Go into any store that sells iPods, or check Apple's online store, and you'll see dozens of them. Check the ads in computer magazines, and you'll see even more.

This huge number of accessories attests to the iPod's overwhelming market share. With around 3 million iPods sold in just a few years, this music player has gotten a foothold in the marketplace for a long time to come. You'll be able to find plenty of stuff to extend and protect your iPod, and if you're a gadget freak like me, you'll have lots of choice when you want another device to fool around with. Best of all, if you've got a friend, spouse, or significant other who owns an iPod, you'll always be able to find something for their birthday or Christmas.

But it's more than just market shar—it's also the affective relation people have with their iPods. They *like* this device, much more so than other electronic devices. Maybe it's the way that music soothes the savage in us; maybe it's the almost magical way that you can carry around so much music in your pocket. But the iPod is enticing. As Bob Weir, guitarist with the Grateful Dead, Ratdog, and The Dead, told me, "I'm infatuated with my iPod." When you feel like that, you want to buy things for it.

DO OR DIE:

>> More gadgets for your favorite gadget

>> Choose the right stuff for your iPod

So how can you sort the wheat from the chaff when there is so much stuff available? Well, I've tried to do some of the work for you by testing and using as many accessories and hardware add-ons I could get my hands on. Some accessories are truly essential (see Essential Accessories), and others are just more cool toys. Many things you can buy for your iPod will help you keep it safe and scratch-free (see iPod Cases), and others let you connect your iPod to different output devices (see Listening to Your iPod on a Stereo).

So have a look through the next few sections and see what kind of stuff you can get for your iPod. You may not want to buy any of it; you may want to buy it all. It's up to you and your bank account.

What Your iPod Wants Most: Music

No matter how many gadgets you buy for your iPod, it's still all about music. If you really want to change your iPod, try getting some new music. Don't stick with the same old artists; try something new. Check out new genres, new artists, independent labels, and lesser-known musicians.

One of the biggest problems in discovering new music is hearing it the first time. You may listen to a local radio station or watch MTV, where you're limited to the handful of popular songs they play. Open your mind to new music: Your tastes may not be as eclectic as some, but with iTunes and the iTunes Music Store, you can listen to previews of more than 700,000 songs.

Music is magical: It "soothes the savage beast" and is the "food of love." As Shakespeare said:

The man that hath no music in himself,
Nor is not mov'd with concord of sweet sounds,
Is fit for treasons, stratagems, and spoils;
The motions of his spirit are dull as night,
And his affections dark as Erebus.
Let no such man be trusted.
(Merchant of Venice)

I've got a few thousand CDs and listen to a wide variety of music, but the way I've discovered the most new music is through friends with tastes that differ from mine. Ask your friends what they like, and plug your earbuds into their iPod every now and then to hear what they groove to. *Vive la différence.*

Essential Accessories

f all the accessories, gadgets, and add-ons you can get for your iPod, there are a few that I really consider essential. In fact, I couldn't imagine not having these accessories for my iPod—they are so useful that they should be included with all iPods (and a couple of them do come with some iPods). While your taste may be different, and, especially, your usage may be unlike mine, I think you'll find that these items are part of the must-have iPod kit.

DO OR DIE:

>> What you really need

>> The accessories you can't live without

The iPod Dock

The dock is probably the most essential and useful accessory for the iPod. Available in different sizes—one for white 3G iPods, one for 4G iPods, and a smaller version for the iPod mini—the dock provides several valuable features.

- It's a stand.
- It's a charger.
- It's a connector to speakers or your stereo.

The dock is a simple device: It's a small weighted stand with a well, which holds a connector and keeps your iPod standing at a slight angle (see Figure 5-1). On the back is a plug for the dock connector cable, and a line-out jack to connect the dock directly to portable speakers or to a home stereo.

Figure 5-1

When your iPod stands in the dock, it is at the perfect angle for viewing its display and pressing its buttons. (Photo courtesy of Apple Computer, Inc.)

Available in any color you want (as long as it's white), the dock makes it easy to sync your iPod. If you've got it connected to your computer all the time, just slip the iPod in its well to sync your music. The line-out jack lets you play music from your iPod directly to your stereo or to portable speakers, without the music being processed by the iPod's built-in amplifier. This results in louder sound and provides clearer music to your stereo.

4G Corner: Can You Use a 3G Dock with a 4G iPod?

Yes. My 40GB 3G dock will hold my slightly slimmer 40GB 4G iPod; and my 4G dock holds my 3G iPod as well, though it's a snug fit. The same is the case for old slim white iPods (15 or 20GB) and new ones (20GB); even though there is a difference in thickness, you can still use their docks. So if you've got a dock and buy a 4G iPod, you won't need another one (unless you want a second dock—a good idea, in fact, as I mention later).

You may even find that it's a good idea to have two docks: one next to your computer, plugged into its FireWire or USB port, for quick syncing and charging, and another where you listen to your stereo. All you need to listen to music through its line-out port is a cable that connects to your speakers or stereo (see Listening to Your iPod on a Stereo for more on connecting an iPod to speakers).

Using an iPod mini with a Maxi-Dock

If you've got a white iPod and bought a mini as well, you can get by with your maxi-dock as long as you're careful. The dock connector you see in the dock, which slips into your iPod, is the same size, so either iPod can connect to the dock. However, the dock's well is naturally larger on the maxi-dock than it is on the mini version. If you're *very* careful, you can just slip your mini into the maxi-dock, but there is a risk of your bending the dock's connector. Also, if the mini is not seated perfectly in the maxi-dock, your mini might lose its connection—this can be a problem if your mini is set up to work as a hard disk. Since you shouldn't unplug it without correctly unmounting it, you can lose data if the connection is lost.

The iPod mini can sit in the maxi-dock if you slip a piece of plastic or rubber behind it, as long as it's the right thickness. Try it out, but be forewarned: Using a mini in a maxi-dock can damage both the iPod mini and the dock, since the connectors may get twisted. If you really like the dock, think of buying a mini dock for your iPod mini.

The iPod Remote

The second essential accessory, at least for me, is the iPod remote (see Figure 5-2). This wired remote plugs into your iPod, in both its headphone jack and its special remote jack, allowing you to plug your headphones into the jack on the remote itself.

Figure 5-2

Apple's iPod remote lets you control your iPod even when it's in your pocket. (Photo courtesy of Apple Computer, Inc.)

As you can see in Figure 5-2, the remote has four buttons: a Volume button, which allows you to raise or lower the volume; a Previous button; a Next button; and a Play/Pause button. It also has a spring-loaded clip so you can clip it on your shirt, your pocket, or your shorts. Even when your iPod is in your pocket or your backpack, you can still control it using the remote. You can't, however, choose any playlists from it; you can only control music within a selected playlist or album.

The remote acts as an extension cord for your headphones, but it's most useful because you can use it to control your music without having to open your iPod case, remove the iPod from your purse, or take it in your hand at all. Since you may want to—and need to—pause your music as you walk or jog, or you may want to change tracks or volume quickly, this is the best way to do so.

iPod Cases

The third essential accessory is a case for your iPod. In fact, cases are so important that I devote an entire section to them (see the next section, iPod Cases). While you can use the Apple iPod Carrying Case with Belt Clip, included, like the dock and remote, with the two larger-capacity white iPods, or you can use the iPod mini armband or belt clip to secure your mini to your body, there is nothing like a good, sturdy case to protect your iPod and provide solace and peace of mind.

Smartwrap

Why didn't Apple think of this?

If there's one thing that's annoying about the iPod, or at least about its earphones, it's the cable. It's often too long, especially if you use Apple's wired

Figure 5-3

Sometimes the best ideas are the simplest: the Smartwrap, which keeps your earphone cable from getting tangled.

remote. So you end up winding the excess cable in a skein and wrapping an ugly cable tie around it to hold it together.

Enter the Smartwrap (Figure 5-3). This simple plastic device lets you wrap your excess earphone cable and keep it the perfect length.

Sumajin's Smartwrap (http://www.sumajin.com) comes in eight yummy colors, from staid white and black; to translucent plastic; to bright orange, red, and green. This inexpensive device will keep your cords untangled and will make you look cooler as well. If you get a few of them, you can choose the one that matches your clothes. And if you have a remote, you might want to use two of them: one for your earphone cable and one for the remote cable.

iPod Cases

Your iPod is an attractive object and an expensive one too. You want to do your best to protect its gorgeous finish and keep it from becoming besmirched by scratches and blemishes. Naturally. But your iPod (at least if it's a white one) is pretty fragile. Don't plan on keeping it scratch-free for long, unless you leave it in its box; and what would be the point of that?

iPod minis are sturdier, and their brushed-aluminum finish is more scratch-resistant than the white plastic of the larger models. But time will tell; the color might get worn off after a while. It's too soon to tell.

In any event, a good case for your iPod is as essential as headphones. Sure, you can get by without one, but just wait until the first time you drop one. Kirk's first law of gravity states that "Your iPod will eventually succumb to attraction from a celestial body," and I don't mean Meg Ryan...

I've dropped mine—maybe twice, in fact. The first time, I stood there stunned, wondering if I had killed it. I started to shiver, then picked it up like a wounded bird. But fortunately it was still working fine, though there's a tiny scar on one corner of the white plastic face.

The second time I dropped my iPod, I had it in a case. Saved by the miracles of modern technology!

A good iPod case should meet several criteria.

- It should be sturdy.
- It should be practical.
- It should look cool.

DO OR DIE:

>> Wrap your iPod in a cocoon

>> Protect your investment

>> Show off your fashion consciousness

Well, maybe the third point is less essential for some people, but the first two should be your main criteria for choosing a case for your iPod. Sturdiness means that it not only protects the outside of your iPod, but also offers a shock-absorbent surface, so when your iPod does fall to the ground, the case absorbs a lot of the gravitational pull. Practicality means that you should be able to plug your headphones (and remote, if you have one) into the iPod easily; that if you have a 3G or mini, you should be able to plug the dock connector into the iPod without removing it from the case; and that you should be able to open the case to access the iPod's controls when you need to.

So, here's a selection of what I find to be the best cases. Some are inexpensive and others cost a bit more; they range from silicone to leather, to metal and plastic. Some have belt clips, making your iPod easy to carry and move around with, and others are merely protective covers. The case, or cases, you choose depends on your needs and usage. You might find the Apple iPod Carrying Case with Belt Clip sufficient if you have a white iPod, but that doesn't meet the practicality test; you can't access any of the iPod's controls when it's in this case. It doesn't really meet the sturdiness test either; it leaves the top corners of the iPod exposed a bit too much. You might find the mini's armband or belt clip sufficient; but, again, they don't meet the sturdiness test: They leave the iPod's surface open to the elements. However, they let everyone see your iPod mini, and the mini sure is a fashion statement.

In any case (no pun intended), you should get a case for your iPod, if only to protect it. But with the huge number of choices available, get one that looks cool or that matches your wardrobe, as well.

4G Corner: New Cases for 4G iPods

As this book goes to press, manufacturers are scrambling to get new product to market. Don't think that Apple told all the purveyors of accessories that they were planning to release a 4G iPod in July 2004. By the time this book gets to your hands, most manufacturers will have released 4G-compatible cases. So, in the following subsections, when I mention cases for "white iPods," you should assume that vendors have released 4G models by the time you read this book, even though I don't talk about them specifically. I've only been able to see 3G models at press time, though, so I can't be sure that all these cases will be updated.

If you have a case for a 3G iPod, it might work with a 4G model. The main difference is the lack of the four touch buttons below the screen, and the higher position of the click wheel on the 4G iPod. If the case has an opening for the 3G touch wheel, the 4G click wheel will not lie exactly under that opening.

However, you'll find that many 3G cases work fine with 4G iPods. In addition, you'll even find that some older cases work well—since the earliest iPods had a single wheel, some old cases will be nearly perfect for the 4G.

Soft Cases and Sleeves

The simplest kind of case you can get is a silicone or plastic sleeve. This kind of case is light and provides scratch protection for your iPod, and can also protect against mild shocks. Many companies provide this kind of case, and at such a low cost, it's almost criminal (at least for your iPod) to not buy one. There are lots of silicone and plastic sleeves and protectors, but here are a few that are worth checking out.

The iSkin Evo and iSkin mini

iSkin (http://www.iskin.com) provides a full range of iPod protectors for iPods and iPod minis in yummy colors, some of which glow in the dark. With a screen protector, a dock connector protector, and a rotating belt clip, iSkin protectors are a great way to keep your iPod from getting scratched. These protectors have holes so you can access the iPod's buttons and wheel, so they're not weatherproof. But they are made of a soft plastic material that makes your iPod easier to hold on to if you're jogging with one in your hand.

The Speck Products iPod Skin and Mini Skin

Speck Products' iPod Skin and Mini Skin (http://www.speckproducts.com/) are rubberized protectors that are sold individually and in three-packs, so you can change the color of your iPod when you want it to match your outfit. The Mini Skin comes with a detachable lanyard so you can wear your iPod mini around your neck.

Brando Silicone Jacket

This silicone sleeve for white iPods (http://shop.brando.com.hk/) also comes with a plastic film to protect your display screen and a special film to protect the scroll wheel. Light and snug, the Silicone Jacket, like other silicone protectors, provides minimal shock protection, but keeps your iPod safe from scratches.

The PodSleevz

RadTech makes a nifty plastic sleeve, the PodSleevz (http://www.radtech.us/Products/Podsleevz.aspx), which fits snugly around your white iPod and protects it from the elements. It's got a clear plastic pane that allows you to see the iPod's display, and, unlike most sleeves and cases, it completely covers the buttons and scroll wheel. Nevertheless, you can activate the iPod's controls while the sleeve is on. There's even a die-cut knock-out at the bottom of the sleeve that you can remove so you can plug in your dock connector. You can't put the iPod in the dock when the sleeve is on, but it will fit in Apple's iPod Carrying Case with Belt Clip.

ESSENTIAL MUSIC

Live at the Village Vanguard, by Bill Evans

For the first live recording of his trio, Bill Evans accepted to be taped at the Village Vanguard on June 25, 1961, playing with Scott LaFaro on bass and Paul Motian on drums. This was a Sunday, and the trio played five brief sets, all of which were recorded by Orin Keepnews, a producer Evans had worked with in the past and would do so again many times. The recordings were released on several albums: First, *Sunday at the Village Vanguard,* then *Waltz for Debby* showed the full range of songs from that day, and later *More from the Vanguard* was a collection of alternate takes. In 2003, a definitive set, *The Complete Live at the Village Vanguard 1961,* was released, which contains all the music from these three albums, including one interrupted track that had not been released.

It's easy to look back and judge history through hindsight, but the patrons of the triangular basement room at the Village Vanguard probably had no idea that they were witnesses to a historical recording. From the very first notes of "Gloria's Step," a piece composed by LaFaro, you can hear the perfection that Bill Evans and his various trios would bring to jazz over the next two decades, and the magical rapport that these three musicians had on stage. But the recording equipment lost power during this first song, leaving a partial take with a dropout in the middle. Those who read symbolism into the vagaries of life might see this as a premonition of Scott LaFaro's death only ten days later in a car accident.

But the recordings remain one of the most powerful live recordings of any jazz music. Evans plays with the detachment and subtlety that made him such a great artist, allowing the other members of his trio to be creative performers and not mere accompanists. Evans would record many albums throughout his career in this lineup, which became his preferred way of playing, but the one to return to is this sacred 1961 recording.

It's almost a shame to hear the crowd mingling and talking behind the musicians, as though they were impervious to the beauty of the music; Evans would say, "I just blocked out the noise and got a little deeper into the music," but Paul Motian claims that the crowd is what he likes best about the recording: "The sounds of all those people, glasses and chatter—I mean, I know you're supposed to be very offended and all, but I like it."

Each of the pieces played that day is a masterpiece, from the jaunty "Gloria's Step" to the heart-rending "My Foolish Heart," to the delicate "Waltz for Debby," one of Evans' most beautiful pieces. When they finished their last set, with only a handful of people still listening, playing LaFaro's "Jade Visions" twice, they all went home leaving history behind them.

(You can read a moving article about this famous performance, by Adam Gopnik, from *The New Yorker,* here: http://www.billevanswebpages.com/gopnik.html).

Plastic Cases

Different from the preceding soft cases and sleeves, plastic cases offer more protection from shocks, and many of them cover your iPod completely. With belt clips and solid protection, plastic cases are sturdy and hold your iPod securely, though they aren't as attractive as leather cases.

The Contour Design Showcase

This is my favorite plastic case. The Showcase (http://www.contourshowcase.com) is light and sturdy, and its hinged opening makes it a snap to insert and remove an iPod. (See Figure 5-4.)

The Showcase has a clear plastic façade with holes to provide access to the buttons and scroll wheel, and its removable belt clip lets you wear it or carry it. When you use the belt clip, the Showcase sits horizontally on your hip, making it easier to walk or jog with the Showcase. The Showcase comes in eight delicious colors, so you can jazz up your iPod while you protect it.

The Belkin iPod Clear Case

Belkin's iPod Clear Case (http://www.belkin.com) for 1G and 2G iPods is a light-weight, see-through case that provides easy access to the click wheel, and full view of your iPod's display. With a 360-degree swivel clip, the case can be worn on your belt or pants at any angle you want, and it has a snap to prevent your iPod from falling out as you move around.

The Monster iSportCase

Yet another plastic case, but this one has an extra advantage. Designed to hold your iPod when you're on the move, the iSportCase (http://www.monstercable.com) holds your iPod firmly by its corners, giving you full access to its controls and displays. But the extra plus is its self-adhesive dashboard mount, so you can slip its belt clip into the mount when you're in your car. You get both a case to hold your iPod when you're active and a mount to keep your iPod accessible when you're on the road.

Figure 5-4

The Contour Design Showcase, one of the best plastic cases

The Xtremity iPod Case System

More than a simple case, the Xtremity iPod case system from XtremeMac (http://www.xtrememac.com) is a set of parts that you assemble as you want. This sounds like Lego bricks, but it's actually quite practical. The Xtremity has a basic case/holster piece made of plastic, which has rubber strips to hold your iPod firmly, and a rubber dock protector at the bottom. In its basic use, this case protects the outside of the iPod, but not the front; you have full access to its controls and display.

Add a belt clip, and the case rides on your hip; add a clear plastic cover, and the case protects the front and top of your iPod as well. You unsnap the cover to access the iPod's controls, but you can see the display at all times. Finally, stick the included dash mount on your car dashboard, and you'll be able to slip the case onto the dash mount for easy car listening. The package includes all the pieces I mentioned here, and you can use the ones you want to customize your case.

Marware iPod mini Cases

Marware, a company that makes cases for all iPods, from the original models forward, has a great line of products for the mini (http://www.marware.com/Overview_iPodMini.html). Its neoprene cases, some with belt clips, others with armbands or wristbands, give your iPod mini total protection while you're on the go. The Sportsuit Sleeve is a neoprene pouch with room to store your earphones as well, and Marware cases work with the Multiadapt clip system, giving you a wide range of choices for clipping your case to your belt, your pants, or even your car's dashboard.

Leather Cases

Ah, now we get to the chic part of this section. Unlike the first two types of cases, leather iPod cases are made to impress as much as they are to protect. A bit more expensive than plastic or silicone cases, leather cases offer many advantages: They absorb shocks very well, they feel nicer when you hold them, they come in attractive colors that match your shoes, and they smell nice. And they're cooler.

The Incase Leather Sleeve and Leather Folio

Incase (http://goincase.com) is a manufacturer of cases for laptops, cameras, guitars, and much more. Their iPod cases are elegantly crafted, yet sturdy and tough. Two of their cases, the Incase Leather Sleeve and Leather Folio, are excellent and practical, and protect your iPod against shocks and scratches. The Leather Sleeve is a belt-clip case that provides a clear plastic screen protector and an open space so you can access the buttons and scroll wheel.

The Leather Folio is a bit more original: You slip your iPod into it, and the cover folds over the front of your iPod. But the belt clip is on the cover, which snaps firmly to the case, and when you unsnap it, your iPod folds down so you can see its display in the correct direction. No more twisting to read your display. When you've changed songs or selected a playlist, just snap it back up for total protection. The Leather Folio even has a small protection plug for the dock connector.

Covertec's Luxury Leather Case

The name of this case is no exaggeration—it's made of really nice, luxury leather. Not only that, it's really practical. This soft leather case (http://www.covertec.com) fits any white iPod (see Figure 5-5), and its cover closes with a snap, making it easy to open and close.

Figure 5-5

The Covertec Luxury Leather Case is made of fine leather and is meticulously crafted.

The case has an opening for your headphones and/or remote, and if you get a model with Covertec's "WIPS" belt-clip system, there's a small screw hole, in which you screw a round piece of plastic. This in turn slips into the belt clip, which holds it firmly (you need to press two buttons on each side of the clip to release it) and allows you to spin the case 360 degrees.

Vaja's Handcrafted Leather Cases

The Argentinean company Vaja (http://www.vajacases.com) sells a full line of cases for PDAs, cell phones, and iPods. These handcrafted cases use fine Argentinean leather, with smooth grain and a very soft touch. These are beautiful objects, and if you're looking for a case that is more attractive than protective, this is for you.

The iVolution (Figure 5-6) is made of leather over a sturdy frame, with a clear plastic front. Holes in the plastic provide access to the buttons and scroll wheel, and the top of the case is open so you can plug in your headphones and remote. The bottom of the case has an opening that is the right size for your dock connector cable, so you don't need to remove the iPod from the case to sync it or charge it. This case comes with or without a belt clip, so you can wear your iPod in style.

Figure 5-6

The Vaja iVolution case—a masterpiece of workmanship

The AP51 and AP52 cases are more traditional cases, with leather covers that protect your iPod more thoroughly, but still retain the same level of design and quality. And the iVod mini is a luxurious case for the iPod mini, similar to the iVolution, which protects and enhances minis.

Available in a wide range of colors—more than 25 colors, as well as many two-tone combinations—these cases are luxurious and feel great when you hold them in your hands. The perfect gift for a fashion-conscious iPod lover.

Krusell's Handit Multiadapt

The main advantage to this case, which is made of fine leather, is the use of Krusell's Multiadapt system to provide a wide range of belt clips and other ways to hold the case. The Handit (http://www.krusell.se) is a sturdy leather case with a snap-on cover. The back of the case holds a small plastic connector, onto which you can click many different clips and adapters. From small belt clips to 360-degree belt clips, from a car dashboard mount to a lanyard, this system lets you get the perfect clip to keep your iPod where you want it. You can buy a case and several clips to use in different situations, giving you a full range of ways to protect and access your iPod.

For Those Who Have Everything--The Gucci iPod Case

One sign that a tech gadget has made it out of its geeky niche is when fashion companies start making accessories for it. Don't expect them to make designer earbuds or cables, but cases are the perfect area where luxury goods companies can make a fashion statement.

Gucci (http://www.gucci.com) released an iPod case, showing that even the fashionable want to listen to music. At $195, it's not for everyone, but if you can afford it, and you want to impress a friend, you couldn't go wrong.

Other Cases

There are some other kinds of cases that are useful to consider owning, whether for traveling or for using your iPod with other hardware. Let me examine two of these and tell you why they are so essential.

The Monster iCase

All of the cases I've looked at earlier are great when you're walking, commuting, skateboarding, jogging, or working out. They hold your iPod securely and protect it from shocks and scratches. But what about when you're traveling, when you might not be listening to your iPod, but when you want to keep it safe *and* keep all your other accessories with it?

Monster's iCase (http://www.monstercable.com/computer/mac.asp) is simply the best travel case I've found for a white iPod. It is about the size of a hardcover book and unzips to open like a book. This case not only lets you slip your

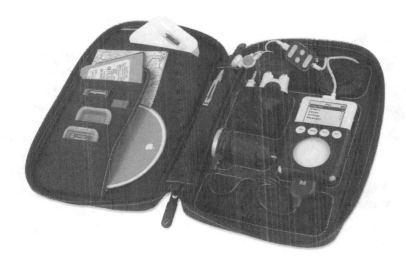

iPod into a special holder, but also has pouches and pockets to put all your other stuff in (Figure 5-7).

As you can see in Figure 5-7, the iCase holds much more than just your iPod. You can stick your earphones and remote in it, and you can also store your dock, your charger, a few CDs, and lots of other stuff. But it's not designed just to sit in your suitcase. You can listen to your iPod while it's in the case, by running its earphone wires out through the top of the case (just leave a space when you zip it shut). And the iCase comes with two great accessories: a Monster iCharger, which lets you charge a 3G iPod or iPod mini from a car's cigarette lighter, and a Monster iSplitter, a special cable that lets you plug two sets of earphones into your iPod. The iSplitter is perfect for long plane trips—you can invite your neighbor to listen to your tunes with you (as long as you've got a second set of earphones).

Travel Cases for the iPod

While there aren't many travel cases designed specifically for the iPod, like the Monster iCase, another way to pack all your gear for a trip is to get a camera bag. These come in all shapes and sizes, are well padded, and are full of pockets and dividers. Check out a local camera store to see what they've got. You might find just what you need to store your iPod and its accessories when you're on the road.

The HeadRoom GigaBag

Designed to hold a white iPod and an AirHead or BitHead portable headphone amplifier (see The HeadRoom AirHead and BitHead), as well as your cables, earphones, and remote, the HeadRoom GigaBag (www.headphone.com) is a great accessory for carrying extra stuff with your iPod. If you have an AirHead, it fits right behind the iPod in this bag (see Figure 5-8), and you can access the iPod's controls through the clear plastic front of the bag; and with a little unzip on top of the bag, you can access the AirHead's controls.

Figure 5-8

The GigaBag with an iPod and with lots of other stuff hidden inside

The GigaBag is a little bigger than the iPod; it's designed not only for the iPod, but to hold other music players as well. But the big advantage to this bag is that you can put other stuff behind the iPod. It's designed for HeadRoom's AirHead and BitHead headphone amplifiers, but if you don't have one of these, you can store an extra battery pack (see Getting More Power to Your iPod) and all kinds of other accessories in this bag.

You can wear the bag over your shoulder, with its shoulder strap, or use its belt clip to wear it on your hip. The GigaBag is a great bag for when you've got more than just your iPod to carry around with you.

TOOL KIT

Getting Rid of Those Scratches on Your iPod

No matter how much you've protected your iPod, it gets scratched. Bummer... The white iPod is fragile; not that it breaks, but its plastic and metal case is prone to scratching. At first, you'll look at this with wistful remembrance, but after a while, you'll start to want to do something about it. While you can't get rid of serious scratches—like the time it fell down the stairs in the subway station—you can remove a lot of the tiny surface scratches that besmirch the glossy finish of the pristine plastic.

Two products, combined with elbow grease, let you do this. RadTech's Ice Creme (http://www.radtech.com) is a set of polishes and special polishing cloths that works in three steps. The first polish, Ice Creme A, wipes out the deep scratches, while Ice Creme B does a final polish. Ice Creme M is designed for the metal back of the iPod, though this is less efficient; there are limits to what can be done without ruining the chrome finish. The entire process takes time—about an hour for an iPod—and when you have finished, your iPod looks much newer, though any serious gouges will remain to haunt you.

iCleaner (http://www.ipodcleaner.com/) works in a similar way. The Ultra Pro Scratch Remover Kit comes with three polishes, two types of polishing cloths, and gloves for use with the metal polish. iCleaner Scratch Remover gets rid of deeper scratches, and iCleaner Maintenance Polish puts the final sheen on your iPod and is good for polishing it from time to time before scratches get too pronounced.

One final advantage for some Mac users: Both these products work on iBooks as well, which use the same type of plastic as the white iPods.

ESSENTIAL MUSIC

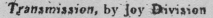

Transmission, by Joy Division

In the late '70s, amidst the rubble of punk rock, a group of angry young men came onto the scene in Manchester, UK. It all began at the Factory, an old factory converted into a performance venue. Joy Division, whose name I'll let the reader research on the Web, was fronted by deep-voiced singer Ian Curtis, and their music was, at best, gloomy, dark, and depressing. Yet it was a different kind of depression than the "no future" of the punk rockers; this was the depression of absolute despair and ultimate nothingness, rather than unemployment and the dole.

Originally called Warsaw, the group changed its name in 1978, and during that year recorded what would be their first LP: *Unknown Pleasures.* This album was released in June 1979 and quickly helped develop the cult following that the group would have throughout its short life.

Ian Curtis suffered from epilepsy, but also from depression and stress. The group had to deal with high expectations from the public and from critics—high for an independent band—and wasn't really the typical pop band. On top of that, Factory Records, while a dis-coverer of talent, was not a marketing powerhouse, and Joy Division's records sold far less than they could have.

In May 1980, Ian Curtis committed suicide, shortly after the release of what would come to be Joy Division's most popular song: "Love Will Tear Us Apart." The group went on to popularity after changing their name to New Order and becoming a new-wave band.

But what remains of Joy Division's original works, limited though they may be, are a few dozen intensely powerful songs that are not to be listened to during lonely, dark nights. Curtis' lyrics are morose and, at times, can be overwhelming. Combined with his deep, rough voice, which sounds as if it comes from beyond the grave, this is the kind of music that parents don't want to discover their teenage kids listening to.

"Love Will Tear Us Apart" is not a good example of Joy Division's music, though it is arguably the most popular song they recorded—if one can call any of their music "popu-lar." What stands out as perhaps the vintage Joy Division song is "Transmission," the A-side of the band's first single. This song sounds as though it was written and performed by a group of boys who barely knew how to play their instruments—the dominant music in the song is a bass riff that could be played with one finger and a guitar riff of about five notes played repeatedly. As Curtis begins singing, he sounds as though he's pushing his voice to the bottom of its range:

> Listen to the silence, let it ring on
> Eyes dark grey lenses frightened of the sun

But as the song goes on and the energy builds, his voice moves up to higher climes:

> Well I could call out when the going gets tough
> The things that we've learnt are no longer enough

continued

No language, just sound, that's all we need know
To synchronize love to the beat of the show

Curtis reaches a summit of both range and emotion as he screams, in the final verse, as the cataclysm approaches:

And we could **dance**
Dance, dance, dance, dance, dance to the radio

I've put the word "dance" in bold, on the first line; that's where the scream comes. This is one of those screams that you never forget, one of the great rock-and-roll screams, almost as good as Roger Daltry screaming in "We Won't Get Fooled Again," but of a different tone. Daltry screams in ecstasy, but Curtis is a man reaching his limits, howling at himself, his life, his situation, but at anything but the moon. The essence of Joy Division is contained in this one word, this cry for help, understanding, and relief.

Curtis was no Dylan, but there were people who listened to Joy Division for the lyrics; I suspect this was similar to buying *Playboy* for the articles. Yet these lyrics sounded the way his life would end: lonely, painful, like shards of words gouging your skin. You don't need to listen to the lyrics; some of the song titles are enough to give you an idea of where Curtis was coming from: "Atrocity Exhibition," "She's Lost Control," "I Remember Nothing," "Isolation," "Something Must Break," "Dead Souls."

While Joy Division's music was gloomy, Ian Curtis definitely entered rock-and-roll history with "Transmission," one of the rare songs where the singer's tone mimics the story being told in that song. Where a primal scream is the ultimate crescendo. Where life is all about dancing to the radio.

Headphones for Your iPod

I f there's one item that is truly essential for your iPod, it's headphones. (I'll use the word "headphones" in this section to include any type of listening equipment that goes on your ears: earbuds, earphones, or headphones.) Headphones provide the most important link between a musician's instrument or a singer's voice and your ears. Needless to say, good headphones are indispensable to enjoying music, whether with an iPod or any other portable music player.

There are several types of headphones, and their prices can range from a few dollars to a few hundred, or even more. In fact, you can buy headphone systems—headphones and specially designed amplifiers—that cost as much as a small car. But most people don't want to spend more for their headphones than they do for their iPod, though as you'll see later, if you're a real music lover, you might be tempted.

DO OR DIE:

>> Music to your ears

>> Mainline sound to your brain

>> Headphones for every taste and budget

Earbuds

Your iPod naturally comes with headphones: a pair of Apple earbuds that slip into your ears and offer decent-quality sound. But these earbuds do not please everyone. First, many users find they are too large or too small. If you're out of the designers' bell curve for ear size, these earbuds will either be uncomfortable (if your ears are small) or they'll fall out, especially when you're on the move (if your ears are large).

> ## Learn Absolutely Everything about Headphones
>
> Headphones are a vast subject, and there are many types of headphones, as well as many reasons to buy a particular model rather than another. Depending on the type of music you listen to, where you listen to it, and your sensitivity to the quality of the sound you hear, you'll want to consider different headphones. If you're a music fanatic, you'll probably want different headphones for, say, listening outdoors and indoors.
>
> So, to learn everything about headphones and find out about all types of headphones, go to HeadRoom's Headphone Buying Guide (http://www.headphone.com/layout.php?topicID=2). The guide is divided into logical sections, such as Headphones by Type, Cheap Headphones, and Portable Listening. You'll find out everything you'd ever want to know about headphones and which ones are best for using with your iPod.
>
> You can also check out the forums at Head-Fi.org (http://head-fi.org/), where audio extremists talk about the best headphones and offer tons of tips on getting the most out of the ones you have.

You'll find dozens of earbuds in audio stores or computer stores, and it's very hard to know which are worth buying. Let me put it this way: While many people find the sound of the Apple earbuds to be disappointing, you ain't heard nothing yet. Many cheap earbuds sound little better than telephones. The best way to find a pair that you like—both for size and sound—is to find a friend who has some and try them out.

One drawback with earbuds is that many people find they fall out when they exercise. Again, this depends on your ears and how much you sweat. If you have this problem, you'll probably want to look at in-ear headphones or over-ear headphones, which may or may not stay on better. Of course, if you try to listen to music while scuba diving or boxing, I don't think any of these will help...

In-Ear Headphones

This type of headphone is different from earbuds, because they go directly into your ear canals and stay in position because of the ear caps or tips on the ends of the headphones. This is a tricky thing to get right, however, since you must get a perfect seal to get good sound. If you don't get a good seal, even the most expensive in-ear headphones sound terrible.

Apple In-Ear Headphones

Apple sells a set of in-ear headphones, which are reasonably priced and which are a good deal for most listeners. They offer good isolation, which not only enhances the quality of the sound, but also cuts out a lot of ambient noise, such as when you're on a bus, train, or plane. However, you've got to get the hang of inserting them correctly.

Apple has a technical document about these headphones, offering tips on getting the best sound. This document, "iPod In-Ear Headphones: Tip—Getting Optimal Audio Quality" (http://docs.info.apple.com/article.html?artnum=93655), says the following:

> To aid in the proper positioning of the ear bud, open your ear canal a little wider when you insert the ear bud. Everyone's ears are different, but you can usually do this by grasping either the upper or lower part of your ear and pulling gently away from your head with one hand while slowly inserting the tip of the ear bud into the ear canal with the other hand. In some cases, wiggling the ear bud into place can also help. Let go of your ear when you feel a good seal. The ear bud should remain securely in place when there's a good seal. Repeat the process until the desired fit is achieved.

You may want to try using other ear caps if the standard ones don't fit well. The Apple in-ear headphones come with three sizes of ear caps, so try them all. Also, you may find that your ears are not the same size. If so, use one size ear cap for one ear and a different size ear cap for the other.

Shure In-Ear Headphones

Shure (http://www.shure.com) has long served audiophiles by providing quality products in all areas of sound recording and reproduction. The company sells everything from microphones to recording studio equipment and has an impressive line of in-ear headphones designed for use with portable music devices like the iPod.

Shure's E series of in-ear headphones represents some of the finest headphones you can get for your iPod, though the top-of-the-line model, the E5c, will cost more than your iPod itself. But if you have demanding ears and an uncompromising attitude toward sound, you owe it to yourself to check these out.

The E5c contains two micro-speakers with extended frequency response, in-line crossover, and a level attenuator, to provide near-studio-quality sound.

FAQ

How Good Can the Sound Be?

This is an important question when considering the purchase of expensive headphones. Remember, when you use your iPod, your music is compressed (unless you're a real audiophile and you use Apple's Lossless compression, or an uncompressed format such as AIFF or WAV; see Compression Formats—MP3, AAC, Lossless, and the Rest for more on this). So no matter how good your headphones are, your music quality is limited by the sound of the music itself.

An iPod is not designed to provide perfect sound; it's designed to provide sound on the go. While you can use it as part of a home stereo system—and many people won't notice the difference between compressed music and CDs—the default compression setting just doesn't cut muster. Using 128kbps compression, even with AAC files, is not good enough, and even the most expensive headphones won't improve the sound very much.

At best, when you're listening to compressed music, good headphones will give you an extended dynamic range, richer bass, and crisper treble, but they can't iron out the weakness of the original music.

So if you're tempted by an expensive set of headphones, consider ripping your music at a higher bit rate, or reripping your CD collection if you've already used the default. You'll make your investment much more worthwhile.

They come with more than half a dozen different types of ear caps, so you're guaranteed to find the perfect fit. (They come with foam, rubber, and silicone ear caps, in several sizes.)

If you don't want to go whole hog, you can opt for the E3c, which have only single micro-speakers, but which, for most listeners, will still sound great. And at the low end of the scale, the E2c is an excellent compromise, providing great sound and noise isolation at a lower price.

Etymotic In-Ear Headphones

Another great brand for in-ear headphones is Etymotic (http://www.etymotic.com). The Etymotic ER-4 and ER-6 in-ear models offer quality comparable to that of the Shure E series earphones. In addition, the ER-4 and ER-6 come with a full set of tools and adapters, to make your listening experience better. The Etymotic ER-4 comes with both foam and three-flange rubber ear tips so you can adjust the amount of noise isolation (foam cuts off 41 dB of sound, and rubber 33 dB), and also includes a headphone plug adapter and a set of tools to clean the earphones.

Ear Monitors

The final step up the in-ear headphone ladder is ear monitors. Originally designed for musicians, these are earphones that are created to the most exacting standards, offering crystal clear sound, and, in many cases, are molded to your ears. To do this, you visit an audiologist, who makes silicone impressions of your ear canals; then you send them off to the manufacturer, who creates the ear monitors in plastic molded to the exact shape of your ears.

Ultimate Ears

The Rolls Royce of ear monitors is the Ultimate Ears UE-10 pro (http://www.ultimateears.com). (See Figure 5-9.) With a frequency response from 20Hz to 16,000Hz, and triple drivers, these cans let you discover a whole new world of sound. You can hear every subtle sound, every harmonic, every tiny quaver in a singer's voice. The music you hear is total, complete, unadulterated. The perfect sound—at least as perfect as your source—is mainlined into your brain, and you hear concerts in your head. They also filter out about 26 dB of external sound, so you can hear your music unblemished by street noises or airplane ventilation. You really hear all the music, and nothing but the music, with these monitors.

This is not without cost. At $900, these ear monitors are not for everybody. But Ultimate Ears offers other models that are substantially less expensive, though still more than your iPod cost.

To get the most out of these ear monitors, you should use a high bit rate when ripping your music, or use the Apple Lossless compression codec (see Compression Formats for more on lossless compression).

There's only one disadvantage to these ear monitors: Since they are molded to your ears, no one else can use them, and you can't even show your friends how great they sound. But when you listen to them, you'll understand why so many professional musicians use them when performing.

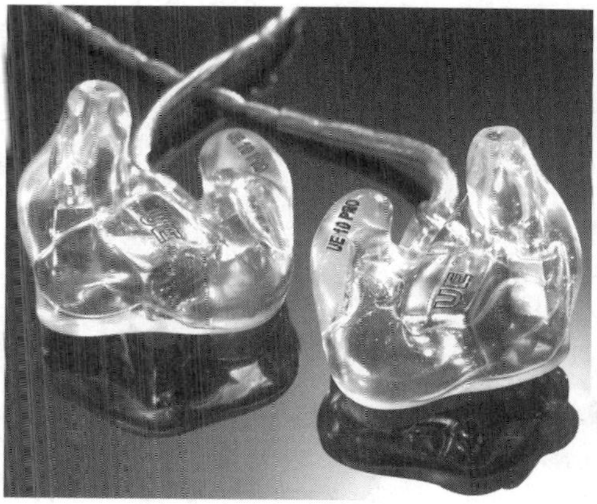

Figure 5-9

Ultimate Ears UE-10 ear monitors—custom molded for perfect fit and perfect sound.

Over-Ear Headphones and Light Headphones

Now you get out of earphone/earbud territory and start looking at what are more commonly called headphones. With two earpads and a headband, or with clips to hold the earpads on, this type of headphone is a good compromise for people who find earbuds and in-ear headphones uncomfortable. As with earbuds, many such headphones are available—hundreds, maybe even thousands of different models.

Clip-on headphones offer large earpads, but are small enough that you can carry them in your pocket. The thing to look out for with clip-on headphones is comfort. The clips that go over your ears may hurt your skin or may not be the appropriate size for your ears.

Light headphones, with thin spring-steel bands that go over or behind your head, can be more comfortable than clip-on models and are adjustable to fit any size head. Some of them can be folded or twisted to make them more

---

Watch Out for That Bus!

In-ear headphones and ear monitors are dangerous—don't wear them when walking down the street. They block out enough sound that you won't hear cars, trucks, buses, or cyclists approaching. If you start crossing the street, open your eyes and look both ways. Seriously.

That reminds me of a song that accompanied a public service announcement for street safety when I was a kid growing up in New York City:

Don't cross, don't cross,
In the middle, in the middle,
In the middle, in the middle,
In the middle of the block.

The words are a bit repetitive, but it did the trick. Ah, the power of public service announcements...

portable, but they generally don't fit in your pocket. If you don't carry a purse or knapsack, these headphones will get in the way when you're not using them.

Unlike with earbuds and earphones, you can often try out this kind of headphone in electronics or audio stores. But many of them are low-priced and sold in blister packs, so you won't be able to check out their sound. A good place to get some comments and reviews on these and other headphones is the forums at Head-Fi (http://www.head-fi.org).

Full-Size Headphones

Aka "real headphones," at least for purists, these are headphones with full-size ear cups, and come in two styles: sealed and open. Sealed headphones isolate you from ambient sound, cutting off around 10 dB of outside noise. This isn't enough for a train or a plane, but it's enough to cut out the sound of people talking in a waiting room, for example. (You may also find them to be a bit uncomfortable: They tend to apply more pressure on your head to optimize the seal, and they can get warm over time.) Open headphones let you hear almost everything around you, and some people find these more comfortable, since they don't like the feeling of being shut out from the world. (And they're safer in traffic.)

Full-size headphones cost anywhere from around $30 to several hundred dollars, not to mention some systems with special amplifiers that cost thousands of dollars. But in the intermediate price range of $200 to $300, you can get headphones that will sound great and will last a long time. In fact, few people can really appreciate the difference between headphones at this price and more expensive cans.

Many companies offer full-size headphones: from the big names in consumer electronics, such as Sony, Panasonic, and JVC; to companies more specialized in headphones, such as Koss and Bose; to the headphone specialists like AKG, Beyerdynamic, Grado, and Sennheiser.

One advantage to this type of headphone is that you can almost always try them out in any good audio store. If you're planning to buy full-size headphones, I'd recommend you do this: Go to a good audio store with your iPod, and talk to a salesperson. People who sell headphones are often audio fanatics, and they'll help you find what fits best with the music you listen to and the way you listen to it.

If you do want to use your iPod for home listening, I strongly recommend getting a set of full-size headphones. The only problem is that if you do, you'll be disappointed when you go out on the street with your earbuds or other portable phones. But don't wear full-size headphones on the street; they are mugger magnets, and you'll probably get ripped off pretty quickly.

If you use full-size headphones with your iPod, you may find that you need to turn the volume up really loud, not to hear the music as such, but to drive the headphones. The bigger the ear cup, the more power is generally needed to get sound out of them. So, the ideal accessory for a good pair of full-size headphones is HeadRoom's AirHead or BitHead portable headphone amplifier. (See Headphone Accessories.)

I'll make just one recommendation in this area, since I have what may be the best bang for the buck in full-size headphones: the Sennheiser HD580. Sold for around $200, these headphones offer just about the purest, most transparent sound possible for this price. Often compared with headphones costing several times as much, the HD580s are a comfortable open headphone, where the music seems to float around your ears, offering subtle details and a rich palette of sound. While they slightly lack bass, you can adjust the equalizer setting on your iPod (or turn up the bass on your stereo). Wearing these headphones is like floating in a cloud of music. The soft, velour ear cups give you no feeling of weight, and the music flows from them with no extraneous force. The only drawback to these headphones is the length of the cable: They come with a ten-foot cable, which is great for home listening, but if you ever want to wear them when walking or traveling, you need a cable tie to wind it up.

Noise-Canceling Headphones

As a subset of full-size headphones, or of light headphones, several companies make noise-canceling headphones, which use technological magic to eliminate ambient noises. Put these cans on when flying, and you'll be able to hear your music without turning up the volume, and much of the airplane's ventilation noise will disappear. The same is true on trains and buses: Much of the ambient noise that annoys you just fades away.

These headphones have tiny microphones that pick up ambient noise, then send signals into the headphones to cancel this noise by matching the outside sounds' waveforms. You can use them to listen to music, or you can even just put them on and turn on the noise-canceling function to get some peace and quiet without listening.

Two professional musicians told me how much they love the Bose QuietComfort noise-canceling headphones (http://www.bose.com). While not cheap, these headphones provide excellent sound and reduce the fatigue that occurs when you're flying. But both of these musicians told me they use these headphones all the time, even with the noise-canceling function turned off.

Wireless Headphones

The final type of headphones you can use is wireless headphones. These are less useful for the iPod than they are for listening to music from iTunes on your computer, but you could use them with the iPod, if it's your main music center. Wireless headphones are exactly what they sound like: headphones with no wires, so you can move around without worrying about pulling the wires out of them. The newest models use the same frequency bands as digital phones or WiFi (802.11) networking systems, and while this provides clean sound, it is also their weak point. If you have a phone or wireless network in the same band, it may interfere with the headphones.

But wireless headphones are great for moving around. Say you work at a desk but move around a lot. If you want to listen to music—even in another room—you can use wireless headphones to keep yourself connected to your iPod or to your computer. One model worth checking out is the Amphony Model 1000 digital wireless headphones (http://www.amphony.com/), which use a 2.4GHz transmitter to provide CD-quality sound. This, however, is the same frequency range as WiFi networks, and you'll get interference if you use the two of them together. Amphony is working on a 5.6GHz system that will alleviate this problem.

Headphone Accessories

So you've got your iPod and your new headphones, and now you want to start listening to some serious music. Well, there are a couple of accessories that will make some headphones sound even better, let you share your music with friends, or both. Have a look at these gadgets that'll improve your music and help you share it as well.

DO OR DIE:

>> Make your headphones sound better

>> Amplify and purify your sound

The HeadRoom AirHead and BitHead

HeadRoom (http://www.headphone.com) makes a variety of accessories for headphone fanatics, including the AirHead and BitHead portable headphone amplifiers. These lightweight devices, about the size of an iPod, make the music that comes out of your iPod sound sweeter and more realistic. If you have any full-size headphones, this is the perfect portable device to make them shine.

The AirHead (Figure 5-10) has an audio input jack that connects to your iPod via a short male/male cable. The BitHead also has a USB connector, so you can use it with a computer. Both devices offer two headphone jacks so you and a friend can share your music as it's enhanced.

These amps offer about 40 hours of battery life, using four AAA batteries. You can turn down your iPod, using the AirHead or BitHead to provide more power, extending your iPod's battery life. And they sound sweet, especially when you use good-quality headphones that need that extra punch to deliver.

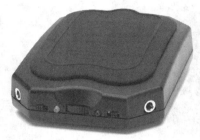

Figure 5-10

*The AirHead portable head-
phone amplifier—more power
to your headphones*

However, these amps have one
weakness. Some high-end headphones,
such as the Shure in-ear headphones,
are so sensitive that they pick up some
background noise from the amp, resulting in a slight hiss. (You can reduce this
hiss by putting the iPod's volume up to
the max and lowering the amp's volume.)
This isn't the case with larger headphones that need more power, or with
low-end headphones, which do sound a
lot better with one of these devices.

Boost Your iPod

So, you want to save battery time on your iPod and share your tunes? The
Boostaroo (http://www.boostaroo.com/) is what you need. This portable headphone amplifier and splitter gives your music an extra kick. While it's not an
audiophile product like the AirHead or BitHead (see earlier), it uses two AA
batteries to boost the volume of its source, which could be an iPod or any other
device that produces sound, as long as it uses a mini-din jack.

In addition to its volume amplification, the Boostaroo has three headphone
jacks, so you can share your music with two of your friends. Or carry it around
with you, and when you meet someone who has an iPod, let them plug in and
hear what you're listening to.

Share Your Music

Well, the two previous devices I discussed come with extra audio jacks so you
can share your music with others. But they use batteries to amplify the sound
coming from your iPod. If you don't need to amplify your
sound, or you don't want to worry about extra batteries,
you can still share your music. Get a Monster iSplitter
(http://www.monstercable.com; see Figure 5-11), which
lets you connect two sets of headphones to your iPod.

Share your music. When you're commuting, for
example, invite your neighbor to listen to your tunes. A
great way to break the ice and meet new people.

Cheaper Splitters

Since the iPod uses a standard mini-
din plug for its headphones, you'll
probably be able to find cheaper
cables allowing you to split the output
and share your music. Check your local
Radio Shack, electronics, or hi-fi store.

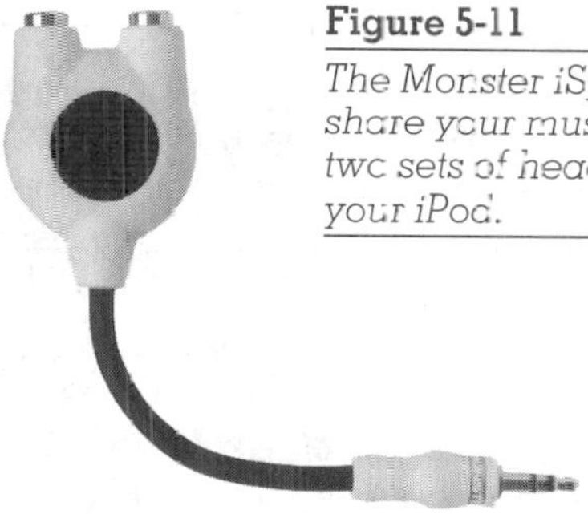

Figure 5-11

The Monster iSplitter lets you share your music by plugging two sets of headphones into your iPod.

ESSENTIAL MUSIC

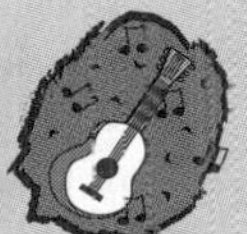

The Return of The Durutti Column

For those who weren't around or listening to music in 1979, it's hard to imagine how different the world of "popular" music was. Critics and retailers hadn't fragmented music into the many genres you see today in stores, and many of today's genres didn't even exist. Rap was taking its first steps, ambient and electronic music were considered avant-garde, new age was just budding, and punk and disco were battling it out in the record bins. New wave was just following in the footsteps of punk, as progressive rock was in its final death throes.

Amidst the punk and new-wave music that came out of England, as part of the late-'70s independent music scene, was a now-legendary record label based in Manchester: Factory Records. Its first two groups were Joy Division (which, after the suicide of lead singer Ian Curtis, morphed into New Order) and The Durutti Column, but Factory released many other records by little-known groups, and the Factory concept, together with other independent labels in the UK, such as Rough Trade, revitalized a moribund music scene.

In January 1980, when *The Return of the Durutti Column*, the first album by The Durutti Column, was released, it was not only a breakthrough record but a surprising sound amidst the angst and anger of the punk years. This 33-minute record, a collection of instrumental songs by Vini Reilly (credited on the album as The Guitarist; Martin Hannet is credited as The Producer, though there are also some bass and drum parts on the record), had such a unique sound that I was instantly smitten, as were thousands of other listeners.

Vini Reilly has one of the most original styles of playing the guitar, with a pulsing, crystalline sound that weaves layers of guitar chords, riffs, and arpeggios throughout his music. On this record, full of overdubbed guitar parts showing off Reilly's understated virtuosity, Reilly set down the foundation for the music that he would play over the coming decades, but also put a nail in the coffin of punk rock. With a record as brash as this—such mellow, melodic music, confronting the ambience of punk and angst—Vini Reilly forever marked popular music.

continued

Vini Reilly later talked about recording this album. "The idea of doing very personal guitar pieces, pre-1977, would be a joke really; you'd be a big old fart and generally be stale and boring, consigned to the folk/rock thing or whatever. But post-punk, it was something else, it became something other, and so it fits in to a degree with all the other mishmash of strange things that were going on."

While The Durutti Column is not very well known, the band quickly developed a cult following. As critic Mark Prendergrast wrote, "The Durutti Column remain very much a mystery. Discs become immediate collectors' items on release, rare concert appearances are always packed to capacity..." Performing sporadically, The Durutti Column (the group is basically Reilly and whoever he works with on a given album or gig, with the exception of drummer Bruce Mitchell, who has long been a part of The Durutti Column both in the studio and on stage) has regularly released albums over the past 25 years, and is still producing fine, distinctive music for a limited coterie of dedicated fans.

Vini Reilly is a craftsman, often recording his work on small, portable multitrack recording devices, building his songs layer by layer into one-of-a-kind creations. A photo used on the cover of a special album for fans who are members of the Durutti Column Subscription Group shows Vini in a large living room, sitting on the floor, a guitar in his lap, listening to something he's just recorded on a small recording device. This photo sums up The Durutti Column: one man who writes the music he wants to, plays it his way, and releases it without the music industry getting in the way.

Find out more about The Durutti Column at http://www.thedurutticolumn.com.

Getting More Power
to Your iPod

What's one of the most common gripes about the iPod, at least from heavy listeners? It's battery life. (See iPod Gripes.) While the 4G iPod gives you a whopping 12 hours of playback time, the iPod mini and older iPod models are designed to provide 8 hours of melody. In spite of these "your mileage may vary" estimates, many users get lower battery time. So if you're in this group, you should consider ways of increasing your iPod's playback time. There are a few ways you can do this: adding a battery pack, charging your iPod in your car, or using some unorthodox ways to provide power to your iPod.

DO OR DIE:

>> Lengthen your iPod's battery life

>> Use your iPod in the wild

The Belkin Backup Battery Pack

When your iPod's running out of juice, you need to get it charged as soon as you can. If you can't charge it, you need an extra battery. But unfortunately, the iPod does not allow you to carry a second battery and change it when you need to, as most laptops and many other portable devices do.

There is a solution: Use a backup battery pack, such as the one sold by Belkin (http://www.belkin.com). Designed for 3G iPods with dock connectors, this battery pack (see Figure 5-12) works like a camel's hump, providing additional juice for days when you run out.

You slip four AA batteries into this battery pack and stick it on the back of your iPod, using its suction cups. It makes your iPod a lot bulkier and a bit

Figure 5-12

The Belkin Backup Battery Pack piggybacks on your iPod with a couple of suction cups.

Harness the Sun's Energy

Why not use solar power to keep your iPod spinning? If you're planning to go hiking for a while, that's probably the only way you can get extra power for your iPod (though you might find it nicer to enjoy the sound of nature). But, hey, it's your choice.

The iSun (http://www.icpsolar.com) is a portable charger and power source that harnesses the sun's energy so you can listen to your iPod while climbing Mt. Everest or while skiing across Antarctica. It can provide power to all kinds of portable devices, so if you go out in the wild often, you'll find it indispensable to make sure you can power your GPS device, radio, cell phone, laptop, or other electronic device.

You can also use a wearable solution to get power for your iPod, as well as other devices. The Solar Scott eVest (http://www.scottevest.com) has solar panels built into its shoulders, so you can power an iPod, a PDA, or a digital camera when you're away from a power grid. The solar panels convert the sun's rays into energy that is stored in a hidden battery pack. Then you just need to plug into your iPod and charge it.

heavier, so you won't be able to use your favorite case. Plug the cable into your iPod's dock connector, and you've got additional power—up to 15 hours of extra music. If you use rechargeable batteries, you'll get a bit less playback time, but you'll save on your power bill. With a battery pack like this, you'll be able to fly halfway around the world and have music for the entire trip.

Car Chargers

If you listen to your iPod in your car, either on the way to and from work or school, or when taking longer trips, it's almost a no-brainer: You need a car charger. Not only does this charge your iPod's battery, but it powers your iPod as well, so you can listen with it plugged into the charger, knowing that when you get out of the car, your battery will be full (depending on how long it was charging and how low it was when you plugged it in). A car charger is an essential accessory for anyone using the iPod when driving. There are lots of them, and they aren't very expensive. Here are a few of them.

Monster iCharger and XtremeMac Car Charger

The Monster iCharger (http://www.monstercable.com) and the XtremeMac Car Charger (http://www.xtrememac.com) each comes in two models: one for iPods with dock connectors, and one for older iPods with FireWire connectors. Plug them into your car's cigarette lighter and they charge—as simple as that. The Monster iCharger is also included with Monster's iCase (see iPod Cases). And Monster's iCarPlay Wireless (see FM Transmitters in the section Listening to Your iPod on a Stereo) is both a charger and an FM transmitter; if you want both, this is a good choice.

Belkin Auto Kit

Belkin's Auto Kit (http://www.belkin.com) is a bit different. It's more than a charger, offering a headphone jack and a volume control. Only for iPods with dock connectors, it's a great charger to use with an FM transmitter in a car (see FM Transmitters in the next section). The adjustable volume makes changing your sound level easier when driving—its volume wheel is simpler to access than the iPod's scroll wheel. Belkin's Mobile Power Cord for iPod with Dock Connector is a similar adapter that also offers a 6V DC out jack, which you can use to power Belkin's TuneCast II FM transmitter (see FM Transmitters).

ESSENTIAL MUSIC

Born to Run, by Bruce Springsteen and the E Street Band

It seems almost facile to choose this album as "essential," given the career that followed the success that Springsteen has experienced since this album was released in 1975. Having become a stadium-filling rock star, Springsteen is very different from the Jersey kid he was before *Born to Run*, yet his music and his performances (three-hour concerts are the norm) haven't changed all that much.

What was so important about this record was its theme: suburban angst, the boredom of cruising on Saturday nights, and the loneliness of the youth of the 1970s, mired in the end of the Vietnam era and the waning years of the Cold War. Released in August 1975, *Born to Run* came just in time to serve as a soundtrack for the GIs returning from 'Nam, and for those of us who dreaded the prospect of turning 18 around then and having our numbers come up.

While Springsteen's first two albums, *Greetings from Asbury Park* and *The Wild, The Innocent and the E Street Shuffle*, were Dylanesque in their lyrics and music, *Born to Run* was a whole new ball game. The lyrics still were similar—highly personal poetry that somehow burrowed its way into the souls of teenagers—but the music had more oomph, more power, more anger. From the haunting opening notes of "Thunder Road"—arguably one of Springsteen's greatest songs—to the angry scream "Hiding on the backstreets" at the end of the first side of this album, these first four songs alone would give the album the status of classic.

But then comes side 2, with the driving beat of "Born to Run," sounding like a '73 Camaro revving up, waiting to jump out and roar down the street when the light turned green. Next are "She's the One" and "Meeting across the River," two more lyrical songs, that turn down the energy for a moment, before the final crescendo of "Jungleland." It's hard to imagine a more powerful song than this almost ten-minute epic, or a more moving moment of rock and roll, as the music begins with a syncopated piano riff that gets you going, then revs up ("Outside the street's on fire in a real death waltz"), ending with the total annihilation of all the hopes and dreams that you could ever have imagined. This is not the "no future" of punk, which would burst onto the music scene in the following years, but the angst and fears of blue-collar kids, the ones living on the outskirts of cities and life, trying to get by, wondering what would come next.

Popular music has a powerful ability to set a soundtrack for an era, a year, a summer, or a month. And in the late summer of 1975, and for the next few years, *Born to Run* was just that—the soundtrack for the confused youth of the suburbs.

Listening to Your iPod on a Stereo

Y ou don't have to listen to your iPod through head-phones; in fact, I know some people who never use them at all. An iPod can easily connect to a stereo, either at home or in a car, and with a few additions, it can be a portable music system of its own.

You need two things to use your iPod this way: First, you need a stereo or speakers to pipe the sound to your ears. Second, you need something to connect the iPod to the stereo. Let me tell you three ways of getting music to your stereo, and in the next section, Turning Your iPod into a Total Music System, I'll tell you about using standalone speakers so your iPod can be your total, portable music system.

Connecting Your iPod to a Stereo with Wires

Wires and cables, the bane of the computerized home or office. If you're like me, you've got far too many of them: adapters, transformers, connectors, network cables, and more. Well, if you want to listen to your iPod on a stereo, you'll need yet another cable. There are generally two types of cables you can use to connect your iPod to a stereo: The first is a male/male mini-din cable. A mini-din plug is the kind of plug on your iPod's earbuds, and it is a standard sized,

Another Reason to Buy the Dock

If you plan to listen to your iPod on a home stereo, you can't do without a dock. It does two useful things: It presents the iPod at the right angle so you can see its display and access its controls, and it has a mini-din line-out jack, which you can use to plug into your stereo. The sound that comes from this jack is unadulterated by the iPod's internal amplifier and volume control, so it's louder and clearer. However, when listening this way, you can't change the volume by spinning the scroll wheel; since the output volume is constant, you need to change the volume on your stereo.

one-eighth-inch or 3.5-mm plug that is used for many consumer electronics devices.

If your stereo has a mini-din plug for you to connect external devices, you can use a cable like this. However, not many home stereos have this kind of jack.

The second kind of cable is a mini-din-to-RCA cable. This has the familiar mini-din jack on one end and two RCA jacks on the other end. RCA jacks are used to connect to stereo amplifiers and receivers; if you've got a stereo, you've got things connected with RCA jacks: your CD player, tuner, tape deck, and so on.

You can find both of these kinds of cables in any audio or computer store; they're common enough that you'll even find them in other stores that sell audio products. If you want a really good, gold-plated mini-din-to-RCA cable, check out Monster's iCable for iPod (http://www.monstercable.com), which uses high-quality cables and 24k gold-plated tips.

Since many people want to connect their iPods to stereos, several companies sell connection kits, which include several types of cables, adapters, and chargers. XtremeMac's Get Connected Audio Kit (http://www.xtrememac.com) comes in two versions, one for original iPods with FireWire connectors and another for 3G iPods with dock connectors. The kit includes a charger, a splitter (so two people can listen to your music at the same time), a male/male audio cable, a male/female audio cable, a mini-din-to-RCA cable, and a cassette adapter (I'll tell you about them later in this section). All the cables are gold-plated, and you'll have everything you need to connect to any kind of stereo or speakers.

Dr. Bott (http://www.drbott.com) sells a Universal Connection Kit for the iPod. Similar to the XtremeMac audio kit, Dr. Bott's kit comes with all the same cables, a cassette adapter, an auto-charger, and a pouch, and also includes a PocketDock, a useful adapter that lets you connect any six-pin FireWire cable to a dock connector iPod.

Listening to the iPod in a Cassette Deck

I mentioned cassette adapters earlier; these are interesting gadgets that look like cassette tapes with a wire coming out of them (see Figure 5-13). The wire, which has a mini-din plug, connects to your iPod, and you slip the cassette adapter into your tape deck. This lets you easily listen to your iPod's music on a car stereo with a cassette deck or on a home stereo with a tape deck.

You can get cassette adapters with the many connection kits available, such as those I talked about earlier, but if you don't need all the other cables, Belkin (http://www.belkin.com) sells a Mobile Cassette Adapter. This is probably one of the easiest ways to pump your music into your car stereo, and it doesn't need batteries. In addition, cassette adapters provide your music with no interference, unlike FM transmitters (see next), whose sound may not be as clear.

Figure 5-13

Belkin's Mobile Cassette Adapter, an easy way to listen to your iPod in a car stereo

FM Transmitters

The third way you can get music from your iPod to a stereo—at least one with a tuner—is to use an FM transmitter. While many of these are designed to work in cars, you can also use them at home. They stream your music across a specific frequency, and you tune in to pick it up. As long as there are no powerful radio stations on the same frequency, the music generally sounds good, though not as good as through a direct connection.

All these transmitters offer multiple frequencies so you don't get stuck on the one frequency that pounds out talk radio at a million megawatts. You choose which one sounds best—you should take the time to try them all—and the rest is easy.

Naturally, any of these devices that connect to the iPod's headphone jack can be used for other audio devices as well—your computer, a portable game console, or anything that puts out sound to a mini-din jack. Unfortunately, these transmitters are not perfect, especially for car listening. You may get interference with them, depending on where they are in your car, where your antenna is, and how many radio stations are in your area.

Monster iCarPlay Wireless

This FM transmitter from Monster (http://www.monstercable.com), for iPods with a dock connector, has strengths and weaknesses. Since the iCarPlay Wireless (see Figure 5-14) plugs into your car's cigarette lighter, it powers and charges the iPod while you're listening, making it the most practical transmitter for car use.

But since it only plugs into your cigarette lighter, you can't use it with your home stereo. If you only want to listen in your car, this is your best bet—you don't need batteries, which you need for most other FM transmitters.

Figure 5-14

Get power for your iPod and music on your car stereo with the iCarPlay Wireless.

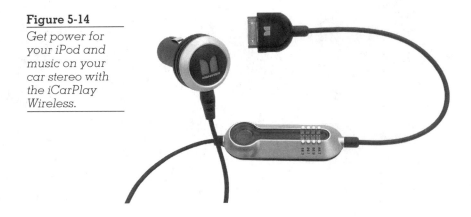

Arkon SoundFeeder

The SoundFeeder, from Arkon (http://www.arkon.com), is a small, egg-shaped device that works with two AAA batteries. You choose from eight frequencies (four in the 88MHz range and four in the 107MHz range) and just turn on your iPod. With either a car stereo or a home stereo, you'll get decent sound, but you'll need to remember to have backup batteries in case it runs out.

Belkin TuneCast II Mobile FM Transmitter

With a broader range of frequencies (from 88.1MHz to 107.9MHz), Belkin's TuneCast II (http://www.belkin.com) can memorize up to four of the frequencies you use most. It turns on and off automatically when you plug it into your iPod or other device, and provides up to ten hours of battery life. It also comes with a DC cable, so you can plug it into Belkin's Mobile Power Cord for iPod, a car cigarette lighter adapter. If you do this, you'll have a lot of wires, but you won't need batteries.

Turning Your iPod into a Total Music System

Now that you've made your first steps into going digital, at least for your music, why not go all the way? With an iPod and some good speakers, you can have a pretty good music system on your desk, in your bedroom, or even in your living room. While audiophiles may snort at the idea, such simple systems, using your iPod as the center of your music system, are the way of the future.

Look at what you use to listen to music today: You may have a stereo in your living room, which you also use to give yourself great sound with a home theater system. You might have another stereo in a family room, playroom, or bedroom; this may be a full-size system, a mini-stereo or a boom-box. What about the basement, or outdoors, or your office, or any other places you listen to music? If you're a real music fan, you may have several systems of varying size and quality.

Think about the headaches involved with this. If you want to listen to a certain CD, you need to remember where it is, then bring it to where you want to listen to it. A minor annoyance, certainly, but an annoyance all the same. Or if you have a spouse or partner who likes the same music as you, you'd need to make copies of any CDs that you both listen to in different places.

Fast-forward. Put the music you like on your iPod, and connect it to a set of speakers. Keep your iPod with you, and carry it from one place to another. Whenever you want to listen to music, just select a playlist and press Play. If you've got several people in your family with different tastes, they can all have their own iPods with their individual music libraries

Using Standalone Speakers

There is no shortage of standalone, self-powered speakers, mainly designed for use with computers. This is the perfect way to set up an iPod music system: Just plug the speakers into the iPod, either to its headphone jack or to the dock's line-out jack. You can get great sound out of some of these speakers, but do shop around and check out the Web. A good place to look is in the forums at Head-Fi (http://head-fi.org), where audiophiles talk about and review their favorite hardware.

One set of speakers that's worth checking out is JBL's Creature (http://www.harman-multimedia.com), a three-speaker set with a subwoofer and two tiny tweeters. The speakers surprise listeners—you tend to assume that tiny speakers equal tinny sound, but the Creature speakers have a full, rich sound that is unexpected for their price range.

You can use these speakers with your iPod by plugging them into either the headphone jack or the dock's line-out jack, and you can also use them on your desk to listen to music from your computer—after all, you might as well just use iTunes to play your music when you're using your computer.

The Rolls Royce of Mini-Speakers

If you've tried some mini-speakers, designed to be plugged into your computer, you may be disappointed. While some systems offer surprisingly good sound—such as the JBL Creature speakers mentioned earlier—most of them offer muddy sound with poor depth and resolution. While this type of speaker is acceptable for playing games on a computer, it's a shame to listen to music on them. You get so used to poor-quality sound that you no longer realize what you're missing.

Enter the Eclipse TD 307 (http://www.eclipse-td.com), a set of mini-speakers with maxi-sound (see Figure 5-15). These speakers, little brothers of the company's 512 studio-quality speakers, will astound you with the clarity and purity of the sound they offer. Listening to these speakers makes you realize just how much you miss when listening to systems designed for their small size.

I confess to having been totally blown away by the sound that comes out of these speakers. Never before have I heard compact speakers that reproduce *all* the music on a recording. It's not only that they have pure and true sound, but they bring out all the instruments and sounds that you often don't hear on your stereo and probably never hear on your earphones or headphones. These speakers use *Time Domain Theory* to create a soundscape that astounds with every note. Time Domain Theory "aims to reproduce the original audio waveform, which contains the amplitude/phase frequency characteristics,

through the speaker, without change." Part of the magic occurs because of the shape of the speakers, but the rest is the result of voodoo electronics inside the speakers.

There are some caveats, however. First, like X-ray glasses, these speakers show you what is *truly* behind the music. If a CD is recorded poorly, or if you listen to an old CD that was not remastered. you're likely to hear something that you don't like. These speakers are unforgiving to such recordings; any CD with hiss in the background will be hard to listen to, and any muddy recordings sound, well, even muddier. Good live recordings sound great; Peter Frampton's *Frampton Comes Alive*, with its judicious use of crowd noise to enhance the live atmosphere, makes you feel as if you're in the middle of the arena during the show. Stan Getz's final recording (*People Time*, recorded with pianist Kenny Barron), recorded live in Copenhagen, sounds as if it's being performed in your living room, and ascends to a new level of emotion. Or listen to Bill Evans' live recordings from the Village Vanguard in June with your eyes closed, and you might think you're sitting at one of the tables with a cigarette in your hand and a drink in front of you. Somehow the music envelops you and seems to come from all around, even with just two speakers.

Studio recordings get even more of an improvement, as long as they were recorded well. Put on any of Pink Floyd's classic albums (*Dark Side of the Moon* or *Wish You Were Here*, for example), and take a trip into musical space. Or if you're a classical music lover, listen to a good recording of a string quartet. Close your eyes, and your mind can situate the location of each performer in the space in front of you. One of the most astounding recordings I listened to with these speakers is Brad Mehldau's studio version of "Exit Music (For a

Film)," from his album *Songs—Art of the Trio, Volume Three*. Jorge Rossy's subtle drum and cymbal playing is brought out in front of the speakers, making it sound as if the kit is in the middle of the living room.

The system is much improved by the addition of a subwoofer; the basic setup is two speakers and an amplifier. If you don't listen to bass-heavy music, you can get by without one, but just about everything sounds better with a subwoofer.

These speakers aren't cheap, but if you want to hear what music should sound like, you owe it to yourself to check them out.

Mini-Speakers for Portable Listening

If you do take the plunge and turn your iPod into your music center, you'll want to use the best possible speakers in a large room, such as a living room, but in smaller areas, like a bedroom or a small office, you'll probably want something more compact. But you may also want something you can take with you when you're on the move—to listen to outside or in places where you don't have any other speakers around. After all, music is much better if you can share it with others.

Altec Lansing inMotion

Designed to provide stereo sound in a compact package, Altec Lansing's inMotion (http://www.alteclansing.com), compatible with any iPod with a dock connector (even an iPod mini, using an adapter supplied with the unit), folds up to the size of a hardcover book so you can take it anywhere. With two speakers (see Figure 5-16), battery or AC power, and a dock connector, you just slip your iPod into the unit and play.

When you use four AA batteries, the inMotion provides up to 25 hours of music; when you plug it into an AC outlet, it charges your iPod while it's playing; and if you plug in your dock connector cable, you can sync your iPod while it's sitting in the inMotion. Think of this device as a dock with speakers. You can even plug other devices into it to use the speakers for older iPods, your computer, or another MP3 player.

Tivoli Audio iPAL

You wouldn't think it by looking at this small radio with a built-in speaker, but it's got a huge sound. The Tivoli Audio iPAL, or Portable Audio Laboratory (http://www.tivoliaudio.com/ppalbrn.htm), surprises by the richness and full range of its output. Designed initially as a radio, it comes with a mini-din jack so you can plug in an iPod or other portable music player, and it pumps out sound that'll make you think twice. For the iPAL (see Figure 5-17) has only one speaker. But this speaker is so good that you won't notice the difference. After all, if you have two speakers and they're too close together, you won't really hear the stereo separation. So Tivoli Audio decided to go for a single speaker with high-quality sound and amplification.

But it gets better. The iPAL is recharge-able and weather-resistant, and its case is rubberized. While you can use it on your deck or near a pool, I'd hesitate about using it in the rain—I'd hesitate even more about having my iPod out in the rain. But you won't have to worry about the occasional splash or those first drops of rain at a picnic.

Figure 5-16

The inMotion waiting for an iPod to start playing music for everyone

The iPAL shines in its powerful, rich bass, an area where most small speakers suffer. Unlike a boom-box with artificial bass enhancement, the iPAL's bass is realistic and even, without the common booming that you hear in cheaper units. For many uses, whether at home, in the office, or outdoors, the iPAL is a great way to listen to your music. (And it's got a built-in AM/FM radio, with a very accurate tuner, so when you're tired of listening to music, or you want to catch that Yankee game, you can do so.)

Figure 5-17

The iPAL provides awesome sound indoors and out.

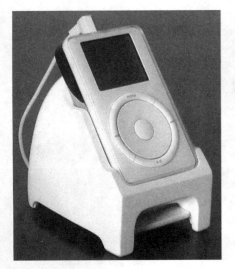

Figure 5-18

The Rockin Chair displays your iPod and plays its music.

The Rockin Chair iPod Speaker Stand

While not for audiophiles, this little stand with a built-in speaker ranks high on the coolness meter. Tim Craig wanted to listen to his iPod without more wires cluttering his desk, and still have access to it so he could see its display and activate its controls. So he built the Rockin Chair (http://www.ipodspeaker-stand.com; see Figure 5-18) just for himself. His friends all wanted one, and he eventually turned his idea into a small business.

This stand is simple but unique. Tim's idea was great: Make a stand with a built-in speaker so the iPod can play music easily. As you can see in Figure 5-18, there's a cable to connect the speaker to the iPod's headphone jack. There are three models: for older iPods, as in Figure 5-18; for the newer models, with a space for the dock connector to plug into the iPod; and the Rumble Seat, designed for the iPod mini. They are all handmade of plaster of Paris, with several colors available.

The stand has a small speaker, which provides mono sound, but the practicality of this stand outweighs its sound quality. Sometimes you may want to listen to music simply without worrying about getting the best possible sound. Also, if you listen to audiobooks or radio shows on your iPod, you won't need stereo anyway. The Rockin Chair is a great accessory for casual listening and easy access to your iPod, and looks cool on your desk.

Recording Voice Memos on the iPod

he iPod is great for playing music, but what if you could use it to record things as well? While it's not a full-fledged tape recorder, you can use your iPod, if you have the right hardware add-on, as a personal Dictaphone to record voice memos. Or with a microphone adapter, you can even use it to record interviews or lectures.

DO OR DIE:

>> Turn your iPod into a Dictaphone

>> Hold on to that thought

There are two devices that work with the iPod: Belkin's Voice Recorder (http://www.belkin.com) and Griffin's iTalk (http://www.griffintechnology.com). Both of these gadgets offer a microphone and tiny speaker, and the iTalk also lets you plug in an external mike. The iTalk also has a louder speaker and a headphone jack; you can play back your voice memos or your music through the speaker, or your can use the pass-through headphone jack to monitor your recordings. Belkin also offers a Universal Microphone Adapter, which lets you plug in an external microphone and adjust its gain, but this adapter does not include a microphone, like the Voice Recorder or iTalk.

These devices use a special function available in 3G and 4G iPods, though not for iPod minis. When you plug them in, the iPod displays a Voice Memo screen. It shows a timer, to time the recording, and two menu items: Record and Cancel (see Figure 5-19).

Select Record to start recording. Speak into your microphone, and record as long as you want (or as long as you have room on your iPod). As you

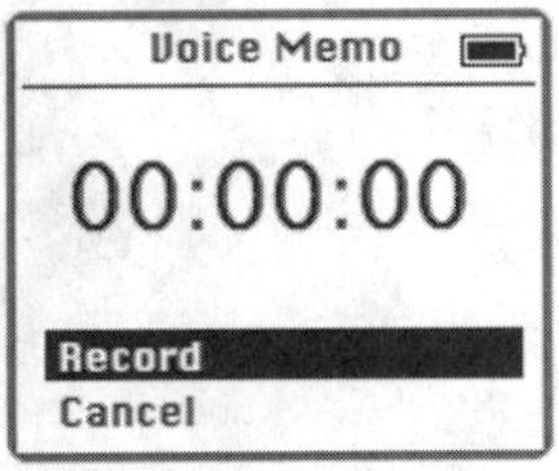

Figure 5-19

The Voice Memo screen displays when you plug in a voice recorder.

Figure 5-20

You can see how long you've been talking, and you can pause or stop and save your recording.

record, the iPod flashes the word "Recording" beneath the timer, and the menu items change to Pause, and Stop and Save (Figure 5-20).

Select Pause to pause your recording, then Record to start again, and select Stop and Save when you've finished. When you finish recording a memo, your iPod displays the Voice Memos menu, with a Record menu item followed by a list of your memos, named by the date and time you've recorded them. To record more, select Record. To listen to a memo, select it, then select Play. To delete a memo, select Delete, then select Delete Memo to confirm the deletion.

You can access the Voice Memos menu from the iPod's main menu by selecting Extras > Voice Memos. But if you've never connected a microphone to your iPod, you won't see this menu item.

Note that voice memos are recorded in WAV format and can take up a lot of space—about 650MB per hour. But there's probably plenty of room on your iPod to store memos and recordings.

Voice Memos and iTunes

Voice memos you record on your iPod don't just stay on the iPod. When you next connect it to your computer and sync the iPod, you'll find a new playlist in iTunes called Voice Memos. Each "song" is named according to the date and time you recorded your memos, and iTunes shows their duration and the size of the files. You can delete them in iTunes, or copy them, burn them to CDs, or do anything else you do with music. You can even make a playlist of your favorite voice memos. Well, maybe not...

Storing Digital Photos on the iPod

Yes, the iPod is just a miniature hard disk (well, with some special audio processing circuitry), and you can use it to store all kinds of stuff. You've seen in Using the iPod as a Hard Disk that you can copy files to your iPod. Well, digital photos are just another kind of file. With a special accessory, you can take advantage of a feature built into 3G iPods and move digital photos from your camera or its memory card onto your iPod for easy storage.

Say you're out on a trip taking pictures, and you use the highest resolution for your digital snapshots. Your camera's memory card lets you store a bunch of photos, but since the digital film doesn't cost anything, it's easy to fill it up. If you've got your iPod with you, wouldn't it be great to be able to transfer the photos to your iPod, free up space on your memory card, and shoot more pictures?

Well, that's exactly what you can do with Belkin's Media Reader (Figure 5-21) or Digital Camera Link for iPods with dock connectors. (These accessories only work with white iPods, though, not with the iPod mini.)

The Media Reader is basically a memory card reader that connects to your iPod's dock. It supports CompactFlash (Type 1 and 2), SmartMedia, Secure Digital (SD), Memory Stick, or MultiMediaCard (MMC) memory cards. The Digital Camera Link is a USB adapter that serves as an interface between your camera and your iPod. Plug a USB cable into the camera, then into the Digital Camera Link, which is, in turn, connected to your iPod's dock connector.

Once you've got either of these devices connected, they work the same way. Your iPod automatically launches the Photo Import function, and you'll see a screen telling you how many photos are on the memory card, how much space they take up, and the type of card. Select Import to transfer them to your iPod. A progress bar shows you the status of the import.

When you've finished, you can select Done to keep your photos on the memory card, or select Erase Card to free its space so you can shoot some more.

Your iPod stores your photos in "rolls." When you click Done, you'll see the Photo Import menu (which you can also access from the main menu by selecting Extras > Photo Import). This menu lets you import more photos or examine each roll, which is numbered like this: Roll #1 (37). The number in parentheses is the number of photos in the roll.

Select a roll to view its contents. You'll see its type (Photo roll), the date and time you imported it, the number of pictures, and the size. You can delete these pictures by selecting Delete Roll; but make sure you really want to delete them or that you've already transferred them to your computer.

Transferring Photos to Your Computer

Once you've got your pictures on your iPod, you now need to get them onto your computer. There are a few ways to do this, some of which depend on which platform you use.

If you use a Mac, just connect your iPod and open iPhoto or Image Capture. Both of these programs recognize your iPod and see that it contains photos. Check the documentation for these programs for more on importing your photos.

If you use Windows, you have two choices: You can either use a photo program to import your photos, if it recognizes your iPod, or you can simply copy them from the iPod if it is set to be used as a hard disk. (See Using the iPod as a Hard Disk to find out how to do this.) Your pictures are stored in a folder called DCIM at the top level of the iPod; just copy them into your My Pictures folder.

Naturally, Mac users can also copy photos directly from the iPod if it's set up to work as a hard disk.

ESSENTIAL MUSIC

Warren Haynes Live at Bonnaroo

OK, I lied—sosumi. I said earlier that all the music in these essential music sidebars was from the previous millennium; this is the exception that proves the rule.

Why should I consider this recording, of a solo live performance by a guitarist-singer-songwriter at a music festival in 2003, to be essential? Well, Warren Haynes is one of the most exciting guitarists around. In addition to performing solo and with his band, Gov't Mule, Haynes plays with the Allman Brothers Band, The Dead, and Phil and Friends. But this recording is just him—his guitar and his voice. Most of the songs are played on acoustic guitar, but even the ones where he plays electric are just Haynes strumming and picking.

So, another rhetorical question: Why is this essential? It's hard to say, but there is something timeless about this performance. Haynes got up on stage in front of tens of thousands of people during the Bonnaroo festival in June 2003 and sang 16 songs: Some were his own, others were covers, such as "To Lay Me Down" and "Stella Blue," which Grateful Dead fans will recognize, or the Eagles' "Wasted Time" or Radiohead's "Lucky." In these days of mammoth concerts sponsored by companies that make sneakers or sell sugared water, the Bonnaroo festival (http://www.bonnaroo.com) remains a place where jam bands, independents, and little-known performers can rock and jam for a few days, and where fans can listen to their favorite bands and discover new music.

Haynes' performance is riveting: Here is an ace of the electric guitar going back to his roots, singing and strumming, playing simple songs, and doing so with emotion and energy. Just about all of these songs are memorable, but the most powerful is the closing song, "Soulshine," a Haynes original sung as a duet with South African singer Vusi Mahlasela. This song has the sound of a classic, of one of those country-rock anthems. Haynes has performed it with Gov't Mule, the Allman Brothers Band, Phil and Friends, and on his own, and this acoustic version, while devoid of Haynes' blistering solos, is an

continued

understated masterpiece. This is definitely a song that others will cover in the years to come (something that's already begun, in fact).

Let your soul shine
It's better than sunshine
It's better than moonshine
Damn sure better than rain

There's something refreshing about hearing a performer like this sing alone with his guitar. This is the ultimate raw performance, where there is no slick production, no over-dubs, just the words and music. Maybe there's some nostalgia involved—this is the kind of music I used to play with friends, sitting cross-legged in Cunningham Park, when I was a teenager. We only had acoustic guitars and our voices, and while we probably sounded bad, it really was the thought that counted.

I've listened to this set over and over, and while it's too recent to call it essential, I have a suspicion that it's one of those recordings that I'll be listening to often in the years to come.

Last Word—A Talk
with Professor iPod

D r. Michael Bull is a professor of sociology at the University of Sussex in England (http://www.sussex.ac.uk/mediastudies/profile119032.html). His studies of personal stereos led him to examine the role of the iPod in society; this in turn has earned him the sobriquet of "Professor iPod," since he seems to be the only such scholar examining this device and the effects it has on our actions and interactions. I chatted with Dr. Bull and asked him how the iPod is changing our lives.

Kirk McElhearn: Why did you choose to study the iPod?

Dr. Michael Bull: The iPod is the newest piece of technology that has transformed the way that people listen to music. Its a qualitative leap from the early generation of Walkmans, and I wanted to study exactly what this means socially for users who have the ability to take their whole music collection with them.

　　The technologies that we use tell us quite significant things about the users and about the cultures in which they live. It's quite a good way of tunneling through to an understanding of the meaning of contemporary culture, to look at how people use some forms of technology.

KM: What drew you to the iPod?

MB: It was a sort of follow-up. I'm writing a new book called *Sound Moves: Technology and Urban Experience*, which examines how we use mobile technologies either to communicate with other people or our own musical identity and pleasure. I had to get up to date—I hadn't predicted the MP3 revolution, so I had to go out and interview MP3 users. The easiest way to do this was to find iPod users.

KM: Who is the average iPod user?

MB: The majority of respondents to my survey are in their late 20s to early 40s. They are middle-class, with a high propensity towards the technology industries. They are the kind of people who work with computers, but who aren't geeky necessarily. Unlike the Walkman, which was much more teenage orientated for a long time, these are older people with more money. That's quite interesting, actually, when you look at how much they start listening to music, but also in terms of their musical taste, which is very eclectic. Apart from one man, who only listens to Glenn Gould playing Bach; I couldn't work out why he wanted an iPod...

KM: Why is the iPod so different from the Walkman and other portable devices?

MB: If you talk to Walkman users, they always describe how difficult it is to decide what music to take with them, and the awful indecision of picking up tapes or CDs and maybe having to change the tape or CD according to their changing mood. They often say that if they don't have the correct music to fit their mood they'd switch it off, because it is better to have no music than the incorrect music.

When you look at iPod users, they can flip from one kind of mood to another with ease. Essentially, they know they've got music for all occasions. Or they can use the shuffle function, if they want, which means that there is constant surprise as to what kind of music comes up, but they do know that it's all their music.

KM: It's interesting that when people use the shuffle function, they are willing to accept a juxtaposition from, say, Lou Reed to Shostakovich to Metallica, which, twenty years ago, they might not have accepted so easily.

MB: This tells us that people's musical tastes and preferences are much more complicated or much less able to be commodified than the industry would like. This kind of destroys the categories, which are very much built up around the music industry. Here you find people constructing, or having constructed for them with the shuffle, this amazing variety of music. A few users have even said how they feel the iPod understands them, because it seems to play things that they want to hear.

KM: What percentage of the iPod's popularity do you think comes from it ease-of-use, and what percentage from the cachet of the object itself?

MB: I think it merges. Nearly all users say what a beautifully designed machine it is, but also refer to its tactile qualities, how lovely it is to touch. Normally, with technology, there is not that sexiness. You have to say that the iPod, and especially the iPod mini, is probably the sexiest small piece of technology you can get your hands on. It's a synergy between, style, esthetics, feel, and function. You can't divorce one from the other.

KM: Many people seem to be infatuated with their iPods...

MB: I think it's the empowerment of having all of your music with you in this small machine. This tells us a lot about the centrality of music in people's sense of their own personal narrative in life. It's like if you could carry around every photograph that meant something to you, and you could look at them with a flick of a switch. The pictures themselves only have meaning to you, because you can place their narrative; if somebody else looks at them they are decontextualized.

I think that music sparks memory in that sense, maybe even more than visuals. These devices are like musical memory palaces, like an emporium of your own identity. There is a strong strand of nostalgia and sentimentality in use, not in the negative sense, but in the sense of this being a narrative of important moments in people's lives.

iPods are extensions of the self, and as such can be seen as love objects or identity objects, and people like to touch the things themselves. A lot of people say that if they lost their iPod that's much worse than losing their mobile phone.

KM: What does the iPod and the way it is used tell us about society and about ourselves?

MB: About ourselves, it tells us how we like to be in control or manage our experience. It also tells us that in a culture where lots of different things prod and push us, we like to reorganize our experience in a more unified way. If you look at how people use iPods you feel a very strong grounding in trying to bring back all the various strands of experience into some kind of unified whole, and in doing so, reclaim a bit of control over that experience. The central theme is this reclaiming of your own time and space in order to make that experience a more pleasurable one—listening to music is, in fact, one of the most pleasurable things that people do. The idea of listening to music wherever you want is intensely pleasurable for people.

What it also tells us is that the physical places that people are in are often relatively discounted. This runs through the whole of Western culture: the gradual erosion of the meanings attached to public space, especially in cities and in suburban spaces. One way in which to make that experience more pleasant is to reconstruct it aurally, to construct your own soundscape; that transforms it for you. That reduces the amount of interaction you have with others; or the interaction you have with others is in your own terms.

Walkmans were the ultimate privatization technology, but iPods have hit the limits of that and are now slightly more social. They allow you both to privatize experience, but also to remake a social experience as well. You can use them at home as a jukeboxes, you can use them at work or in the car. The technology seems to reflect the way in which we construct small bubbles of warmth in a chilly ocean.

iPod users share their musical files with a few people; they'll play music in the car, with their family, and use it as a social thing in the home. But in the street, it is privatized. This tells us something about the way in which we construct or experience our sense of the social in different spaces.

KM: Is it true that you don't own an iPod?

MB: I never used a Walkman whilst I was writing the Walkman book. I borrowed a friend's iPod to see what it can do, but I don't like to use something while I'm studying it because your own use pattern gets confused with other peoples.

KM: Isn't that like going to a foreign country without knowing the language?

MB: Well, I know most of the language, but what it means is that you keep your sense of surprise and you can reflect on it. It gives you a critical distance; you don't prejudice your own results, and it allows you to look a bit more freshly at use.

KM: Are you planning to get an iPod in the near future?

MB: I will, actually, I feel embarrassed now...

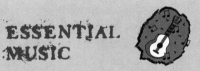

ESSENTIAL MUSIC

Bruckner's 9th Symphony

There is a specific recording of Bruckner's 9th Symphony, conducted by Otto Klemperer in 1972. When I listen to that it's rather like I've just read something like *War and Peace*; the music has a narrative that encompasses the whole world, in around 70 minutes.

The first movement of Bruckner's 9th Symphony is built around three independent but related themes; Klemperer makes these themes flow like a river, and you can hear each stream interweaving around the others. It's like when some people talk about Bach, which is intensely emotional, but also transcendental at the same time—Klemperer plays this piece of music rather like it should be Bach, but with more emotion.

Michael Bull is a professor of sociology at University of Sussex in England.

Index

inform IT